RELIGION IN ANCIENT HISTORY

RELIGION IN ANCIENT HISTORY

Studies in Ideas, Men and Events

S. G. F. BRANDON

LONDON · GEORGE ALLEN & UNWIN LTD
RUSKIN HOUSE   MUSEUM STREET

First published in Great Britain in 1973

ISBN 0 04 200020 3 *hardback*
ISBN 0 04 200021 1 *paperback*

Printed in Great Britain by
Compton Printing Ltd , London & Aylesbury

ACKNOWLEDGMENTS

The author gratefully acknowledges the permission kindly given by the following publishers to quote from the works indicated: Messrs. George Allen and Unwin Limited (S. Radhakrishnan, *The Principal Upanisads*); The Chicago University Press (A. Heidel, *The Epic of Gilgamesh and Old Testament Parallels*); Messrs. J. M. Dent & Sons Limited (F. M. Cornford, *Greek Religious Thought from Homer to the Age of Alexander*); Messrs. J. M. Dent & Sons Limited and Messrs. E. P. Dutton & Company Incorporated (*Chinese Philosophy in Classical Times*, trans. and ed. E. R. Hughes: Everyman Library Edition); The Harvard University Press and Messrs. W. Heinemann Limited (The Loeb Classical Library: Homer, *The Iliad*, vol. i, trans. and ed. A. T. Murray); The Princeton University Press (*Ancient Near Eastern Texts*, Relating to the Old Testament, ed. J. B. Pritchard) Princeton University Press, rev. edn., 1955. Messrs. Routledge & Kegan Paul Limited (E. J. Thomas, *History of Buddhist Thought*, and *Early Buddhist Scriptures*).

PREFACE

The French have a delightful expression which has no apt equivalent in English: it is *haute vulgarisation*. But though it cannot easily be translated, the expression signifies an important aspect of the scholar's vocation, whatever his nationality may be. For if the first charge upon a scholar is to further knowledge in his own particular field, his second duty is to disseminate that knowledge. This he does, primarily, by the publication of books and articles, equipped with all the appropriate apparatus of academic scholarship. But his obligation does not end there. Beyond his academic colleagues and students, there is a larger public of intelligent layfolk whom he should feel privileged and happy to serve, and the more so since they provide the economic foundations upon which academic life is built. They have their own specialist knowledge and skills in industry and commerce; but they are also alert to academic subjects, if clearly presented to them with sympathetic insight. The task of presenting his subject in an interesting and non-technical manner to this wider public is, therefore, the duty of the scholar; but it is also one that he should eagerly undertake, for it is often a healthful exercise for the academic to strive to write lucidly and interestingly for those who do not share his specialist idiom.

The present writer is ever grateful to his Army experience for teaching him how men of all kinds of backgrounds could be interested in history. He recalls the many parties of soldiers whom he took round the ruins of Hippo Regius in North Africa during World War II, and of their evident interest in the ancient struggle of Rome and Carthage for world-empire. In academic life, he has found that the popular magazine *History Today* has provided the opportunity of reaching a public beyond that of university colleagues and students. Being fortunate in professing a subject with a deep human interest, his articles on the history of religions have evidently interested people in different parts of the world; they have, moreover, proved useful to students. Consequently, he has been encouraged to think that it might be worthwhile to present them collected together in a more permanent and easily accessible form. The ready cooperation of Charles Scribner, Jr. has made this possible, and the author is grateful for his interest and help.

Two articles have been included here, because of their related interest, which were not originally published in *History Today* but in the *Bulletin of The John Rylands Library*, Manchester: they are entitled "The Personification of Death in Some Ancient Religions", and "Time as God and Devil". The author is indebted to both the Editors of *History Today* and to the Governors of The John Rylands Library for their kind permission to reprint the various articles concerned. He also wishes to record his thanks to the Editor of *Horizon* for his courtesy in permitting the reprinting of the articles on "The Jesus of History" and "St. Paul". Some of the original *History Today* illustrations are reproduced here, but many other new ones have been added. The annotated bibliographies at the end of the volume are designed to help readers to a fuller study of the subjects dealt with by the articles. Since each article was originally planned as an independent study, their collective arrangement inevitably involves some repetition of related matter. Where this occurs, the passage has been left if it may serve as an *aide-mémoire,* or where its excision would impair the integrality of the article.

Since the Second World War there has been a remarkable growth of interest, in many lands, in the history and comparative study of religion. The interest manifests itself in both academic circles and among the general public. It has, indeed, been aptly called "the new humanism". The hope of the author is that this collection of studies will both stimulate and assist further interest in a subject which is so inherently fascinating and so profoundly important for understanding the nature and destiny of man.

The author wishes to put on record his gratitude to Mrs. Elizabeth Farrow for her most valuable help in preparing the material for publication, and he thanks Miss Susan Wood for assisting with the Index. He is also indebted for the care so courteously given, and so efficiently taken, by Mr. Will Davison and his staff in arranging the presentation of the volume.

S. G. F. Brandon

Department of Comparative Religion,
University of Manchester.

CONTENTS

ILLUSTRATIONS

RELIGION IN ANCIENT HISTORY

CHAPTER 1

The Origin of Religion

IN THEORY AND ARCHAEOLOGY

*The earliest representatives of mankind were concerned
with three fundamental problems—birth, death and the
supply of food—which they attempted to solve by magico-
religious means*

I

Writing in the sixth century B.C., the Greek philosopher Xenophanes
observed: "Mortals think that the gods are begotten, and wear clothes
like their own, and have a voice and a form. If oxen or horses or lions
had hands and could draw with them and make works of art as men
do, horses would draw the shapes of gods like horses, oxen like oxen;
each kind would represent their bodies just like their own forms. The
Ethiopians say their gods are black and flat-nosed; the Thracians, that
theirs are blue-eyed and red-haired."[1] The observation is notable; it
shows that already in ancient Greece there were minds acute to perceive
the essential relativity of religious conceptions.

Whether Xenophanes was the first to look critically at religion is
not known. That men elsewhere had earlier perceived the comparative
aspect of religion is attested in ancient Egyptian literature. The Pharaoh
Akhenaten, that strange genius who tried to change the ancient polytheism
of Egypt into a monotheism, understood that the providence of a single
supreme deity could not be confined to the people of Egypt. Accordingly,

---

[1] *Frags.* 14–16; trans. by F. M. Cornford, *Greek Religious Thought from Homer to
the Age of Alexander* (Dent, 1923), p. 85.

Akhenaten, the strange genius
who tried to change the religion
of ancient Egypt (from a colossal
statue in the Cairo Museum)

in his famous *Hymn to the Aten,*—the sun's disk which manifested the
presence of his god—he proclaimed that this supreme and beneficent deity
had placed a Nile in the sky for other peoples: to his mind the rain that
watered foreign lands was a celestial counterpart of the river Nile which
irrigated Egypt.[2] Egyptian priests also speculated about the beginning of
things. But their purpose was theological, not rationalistic. The priesthoods of various gods each sought to show that their own particular deity
was the original creator, and that all the other gods were descended from
him. In the theological system composed during the Old Kingdom period
(*c.* 2778–2423 B.C.) at Memphis by the priests of Ptah, the origin of
religious worship was actually described. The approach, however, was
essentially mythological: Ptah was represented as arranging for the establishment of the temples and cultus of the other gods. Similar cosmogonies
were composed in ancient Mesopotamia; like the Egyptian systems, they
always assumed the existence of some primordial divine being who was
responsible for the creation of the world and of mankind and its institu-

[2] See Chapter 9.

Ptah, an Egyptian creator-god (from a statue in the Manchester Museum)

tions. According to these Mesopotamian explanations of the origins of things, the human race had been specifically created to build temples for the gods and to feed them with offerings: hence religion was essentially divine service, and constituted the *raison d'être* of mankind.

Such early explanations were theologically-inspired aetiologies, and not rationalistic accounts of the origin of religion. The critical attitude manifest in Xenophanes' statement reveals a very different quality of mind that soon finds further expression in Greek literature. About the year 450 B.C. the philosopher Anaxagoras scandalized the devotees of traditional religion in Athens by declaring that the sun was not divine, but a red-hot mass, and the moon was made of earth, and, therefore, not a goddess; he was condemned for impiety and exiled from the city. About 300 B.C. Euhemerus of Messine propounded a theory concerning the origin of the gods which has perpetuated his memory into modern times as "Euhemerism". In a so-called *Sacred History*, he set forth his ideas in the form of a fictitious account of his travels. He relates how he had visited an island in the Indian Ocean, named Panchaia. There he found a majestic temple of Zeus, who was the supreme deity of the Greek pantheon. In the temple he read. inscribed on a gold stele, a long account of the exploits of Zeus, and of Uranos and Kronos, who, in Greek tradition, were regarded as the divine rulers of the universe before Zeus. This account was designed by Euhemerus to show that these gods had originally been great kings of remote antiquity, who were subsequently deified. His explanation of the origin of the gods was not altogether fantastic; modern research has shown that the deities of many peoples were in origin ancient heroes, whose deeds caused them to be venerated and ultimately divinized.

The extent to which the origin and nature of religion could be rationalized in Graeco-Roman society is seen in the *De rerum natura* of Lucretius. This Roman poet, who lived during the first century B.C., was a follower of the Greek philosopher Epicurus (*c.* 342–270 B.C.), whom he regarded as the true saviour of mankind; for Epicurus, according to him, had been the first to expose the pernicious nature of religion, which enslaved the human mind. Lucretius did not deny the existence of gods; but he held that they had no contact whatever with this world and its inhabitants. He explained the origin of religion in two ways. First, that men dreamed of the gods as beings of surpassing beauty and stature, to whom they attributed omnipotence and immortality. Next:

> "they observed how the array of heaven and the various seasons of the year came round in due order, and could not discover by what causes all that came about. Therefore, their refuge was to leave all in the hands of the gods, and to suppose that by their nod all things were done. They placed the gods' habitation in the sky, because through the sky the night and the moon are seen to revolve, moon and day and night and the solemn stars of night, heaven's night-wandering torches, clouds and sun, rain and snow, winds, lightnings and hail, rapid roarings and threatening throes of thunder. . . . . O unhappy race of mankind, to ascribe such doings to the gods and to add thereto bitter wrath! What groans did they then create for themselves, what wounds for us, what tears for generations to come!" [3]

The free enquiry into the origin and nature of religion, which characterized Graeco-Roman society, was essentially speculative. Although many thinkers were sceptical about traditional religious belief and practice, contemporary scholarship had no effective criteria nor research techniques for a truly scientific investigation of religion. Whether such would

[3] *De rerum natura*, V, 1183ff.; trans. W. H. D. Rouse in the Loeb Classical Library edition of Lucretius.

eventually have been formulated is unknown; the establishment of Christianity as the official religion of the Roman Empire in the fourth century completely changed the religious situation and the ethos of academic thought.

For the scholars of the Church there was only one true religion, namely, their own. Its origin was clear to them. The Bible was the divine record of God's dealings with mankind from the very Creation. In a superb narrative, the purpose of God was vividly presented: the original sin of Adam and Eve had caused God to plan for the redemption of their posterity, which had been achieved by the sacrifice of Christ and the founding of the Church. The early Christians were aware of the existence of other religions; but they easily accounted for their origin. Judaism was due to the culpable obduracy of the Jews in rejecting Jesus as the true Messiah and persisting in the now-superseded Old Covenant, which the coming of Christ had made obsolete. The pagan cults of the Graeco-Roman world were dismissed as the inventions of the Devil and the perversity of man. The pagan gods were seen as demons that had enslaved mankind until humanity was emancipated by Christ. It is interesting to note, however, that, by one of those strange ironies of history, the gods of Greece and Rome did not entirely lose their influence. Through their being identified with the planets, they continued an effective existence in astrology, in which even popes and bishops believed during the Middle Ages.

The emergence of Islam in the seventh century A.D. faced Christians with a new religion that threatened the existence of their own. Although they vigorously opposed it by force of arms, they took no interest in its origin and nature. Generally, Islam was regarded as a form of heresy: Dante, in the *Divina Commedia*, placed Muhammad in the eighth circle of Hell, where he was eternally punished as a schismatic. Of the great religions of Asia, Hinduism and Buddhism, medieval Christendom had but meagre and vague knowledge. Indeed, so great was the ignorance concerning the life and teaching of the Buddha that a garbled version of his deeds was written up by St. John of Damascus (c. 676–756) as the exploits of two saints named Barlaam and Joasaph. Thus the Buddha entered the Calendars both of the Roman and the Greek Church as St. Joasaph, this name being a corruption of the Buddhist title Bodhisatta.

The Renaissance marked the beginning of a change in the traditional Christian attitude to other religions, as it did in so many other ways.

The emerging humanism, with its eager curiosity about the world and human institutions, was soon stimulated by maritime exploration and discovery. The horizon of educated men was no longer limited to Europe: exciting information of new lands and peoples came back with the seamen and other adventurers. Some of these newly discovered peoples were barbarous by European standards; but others, particularly in India and China, possessed civilizations of high achievement. Europeans began to understand that the world was not conterminous with Europe, nor were European ways and institutions the only form of sophisticated living. Then, too, there was the significant fact that all these different peoples, some highly civilized, had their own religions, to which they appeared as devoted as were the peoples of Europe to Christianity.

The chief reaction of the European peoples to this revelation of the existence of vast heathen populations throughout the world was consistent with their Christian profession. These heathen must be won for Christ. Soon missionaries, both Catholic and Protestant, were following the merchants, to the far-off lands, to bring the Gospel to their benighted peoples. But the new knowledge also stimulated some minds to reflect on the significance of both the variety and the similarity of religious belief and practice which were thus revealed. The results of their reflection began to find expression in a series of publications concerned with explaining the origin of such phenomena. Among these early essays in the comparative study of religion was the theory advanced in 1724 by the Jesuit scholar Joseph Lafitau. Noting similarities of idea and ritual in the cults of the aborigines of the New World, in classical paganism, and Catholic Christianity, Lafitau supposed that there must originally have existed a religion of nature-rites that was universal among mankind. In 1760 De Brosses, in a work entitled *Du culte des dieux fétiches, ou parallèle de l'ancienne religion de l'Egypte avec la religion actuelle de Nigritie,* sought to explain the animal-headed deities of Egypt in the light of the religious practices of contemporary savages. Even more revolutionary perhaps was the attempt of Charles-François Dupuis, in 1795, to discern behind the figures of Christ and Osiris, of Bacchus and Mithra, a common tendency of mankind to personify the sun in its annual course through the heavens.

These eighteenth-century attempts to rationalize the complex phenomena of mankind's religious ideas and practices heralded the more scientific work of the next century. The commercial and political domination that the leading European nations achieved in Asia and Africa produced a rich academic harvest. Artistic treasures and manuscripts brought home from the East encouraged the study of oriental languages and cultures, while the new sciences of anthropology and ethnology were stimulated by an abundance of material. Political influence and wealth also enabled archaeologists to search such ancient and hitherto closed lands as Egypt and Mesopotamia. This great mass of new data was eagerly investigated by scholars of Europe and America; and the stupendous task of reconstructing the past of mankind was at last properly begun. It was inevitable that much of this research should have concentrated on the origin of religions. Consequently, during the latter half of the nineteenth century and the early decades of the twentieth, a series of notable interpretations were propounded, some of which are still influential. Space permits only a brief mention of some of the more significant here.

Friedrich Max Müller (1823–1900), who, as a young man, came to Oxford to translate certain ancient religious texts of India for the East-India Company, and who subsequently became Professor of Comparative Philology there and editor of the great series of translations entitled *Sacred Books of the East,* pioneered a new line of research. He maintained that a comparative study of language could reveal common patterns of mythology. Further, that, since language governs thought, the names given originally to celestial phenomena profoundly affected their conception. Thus, by giving the sun a masculine name primitive peoples thought of it as a male person—a sun god.

This use of comparative philology was deemed too doctrinaire by those concerned with anthropological data. They believed that the original form of religion could best be understood by studying the cults of the so-called primitive peoples still existing in the world, such as the aborigines of Australia. A foremost exponent of this anthropological approach was Sir Edward Tylor, who published in 1871 a great work entitled *Primitive Culture,* which was widely influential. In it Tylor advanced a theory known as animism to account for the origin of religion. He proposed, as a "minimum definition", that religion consists in a "belief in spiritual beings". He supposed that primitive man first acquired the idea of "spirit" (*anima*) from his experience of sleep, dreams, shadows, breath and death. Having thus conceived of the spirit as the invisible animating principle in each of his own kind, primitive man attributed the principle to all entities that seemed alive, including the sun and moon and other natural phenomena. Since he was naturally awed by phenomena that appeared powerful, he peopled the universe with mighty spirits and worshipped them.

Of even greater influence than the work of Tylor was that of Sir James G. Frazer (1854–1941). His approach to the study of religion was essentially anthropological. The titles of some of the constitutive volumes of his *magnum opus, The Golden Bough,* indicate its nature and scope: *The Magic Art; Taboo and Perils of the Soul; The Scapegoat; The Dying God; Spirits of the Corn and of the Wild.* Frazer was particularly concerned with the effect of agriculture on religious ideology and practice. In the annual cycle of the death and resurrection of the corn he saw a factor of tremendous import, the influence of which he traced in many religions, including Christianity. Following the suggestion of the German philosopher Hegel, Frazer believed that an "Age of Magic" preceded the "Age of Religion", and that man first sought to coerce the powers behind the natural world by ritual magic, before he sought to win their favour by prayer and sacrifice.

Of the many other attempts to explain the origins of religion we may notice that of Rudolf Otto (1869–1937), because it posited the operation of a non-rational or pre-rational factor. In a book published in 1917 under the title of *Das Heilige,* Otto maintained that man is endowed with a sense of the "numinous".[4] In other words, that man has the faculty of becoming aware, at certain times and places, of the presence of a mysterious force that is wholly different from all else in the world of normal experience. This presence evokes a feeling of the uncanny; and, when experienced, it both terrifies and fascinates. Otto sought, accordingly, to explain religion as stemming from a "unique original feeling response"; which preceded any ratiocination about the source or agent of the experience. The theme of *Das Heilige* was illustrated from Hebrew, Christian and Indian sources. Its inspiration was essentially theological; and it has exercised a considerable influence on modern Christian thought.

The many and diverse theories, advanced during this period by reputable scholars to account for the origin of religion, are generally impressive for their learning and ingenuity. They were mostly patterned on the evolutionary principle, which has dominated Western thinking since the nineteenth century. The majority are characterized also by their

[4] An English translation appeared in 1928 entitled *The Idea of the Holy.*

secular approach and freedom from apologetical motivation. The theological concept of divine revelation, common to most religions, was evaluated only as a datum of religious phenomenology. Despite the professed concern with the history of religions, however, this investigation tended to be based on deductions from the study of primitive societies existent in various parts of the world. As we noted previously, the early anthropologists believed that the ideas and institutions of savage peoples closely reflected the chronologically primitive cultures of mankind. This preoccupation was probably due to the contemporary immaturity of the science of Prehistory. Although archaeological research had greatly extended knowledge of the early civilizations of the Near East, similar advance had not been made in the study of Palaeolithic culture. This defect was serious; for, if the beginnings or earliest forms of religion were to be found anywhere, it would surely be in the remains of the most ancient human communities that archaeological research and excavation could reveal.

II

The earliest skeletal remains of true man (*Homo sapiens*) date from about 30,000 B.C. With the remains, or related to them, relics have been found of the culture of these earliest representatives of our race. Although this is the earliest evidence in the archaeological record, these people, often referred to as the Crô-magnons from the place where their remains were first discovered, were obviously the descendants of unknown generations of *Homo sapiens*. Their immediate precursors, according to archaeological evidence, were a sub-human type usually designated Neanderthal Man. The remains of this species date back to about 100,000 B.C. Even this remote Neanderthal Man had a culture that included a practice of great significance for our subject.

The evidence concerned here is provided by the burial customs of these peoples of the Old Stone Age. But first we must appreciate the significance of the burial of the dead. No other animals so dispose of their dead: generally they just abandon them where they die. Palaeolithic man, however, did not just bury his dead as a practical measure to get rid of them; he buried them ritually. This means that he did things that were not practically necessary to inhumation. Thus stone implements, ornaments of shell or bone, and food were placed in the grave; and often the corpse was covered with a red pigment. Although there are no

A Palaeolithic burial, with funerary equipment: traces of red pigment were found in this grave (Les Eyzies, Dordogne, France)

inscriptions to inform us—writing was not invented until the fourth millennium B.C.—we can make some legitimate inferences from this funerary equipment. The placing of food and tools or weapons in the grave must surely indicate that it was believed that the dead would still need such things. In other words, this evidence suggests that the Palaeolithic peoples believed that death was not the end, and that the dead survived in some way. The covering of the corpse with a red pigment clearly had some purpose. Prehistorians generally agree that the purpose was magical. In primitive thought red is associated with vitality, since it is the colour of blood, the life-substance. To cover a dead body with a red pigment suggests, therefore, some magical practice to restore or maintain its vitality, thus to ensure its continued existence for the afterlife of the deceased.

The posture of the corpse in these Palaeolithic burials is also significant. The dead were rarely buried in the extended position normal to us. Generally they were laid on their side, with the legs tightly flexed and the hands covering the face. The meaning of this posture has been much discussed. Some prehistorians have seen it as merely a more economical form of burial—a flexed body would fit into a smaller hole. Others have suggested that these crouched burials stimulate the prenatal position of the infant in the womb. If this interpretation could be proved, a very significant fact would be known about Palaeolithic man's belief. To lay a dead person designedly in a prenatal posture in the grave might well signify some idea that the dead were laid in the womb of Mother Earth to be reborn. That such a positioning of the corpse was purposeful is certain; but we have no evidence to show what that purpose was. It is also necessary to note that sometimes the body was so tightly flexed that it must have been bound in that position before *rigor mortis* set in. Such instances could indicate a fear of the dead: savage peoples of modern times have been known to bind corpses before burial, to prevent the dead from returning to harm the living.

Palaeolithic archaeology provides other evidence of religious significance. On many sites there have been found figurines, carved out of stone or bone, of women. They are remarkable for two features: the sexual or maternal attributes are grossly exaggerated, but the faces are blank. These figurines, known quaintly as "Venuses", are small and portable. From Laussel, however, in the Dordogne, comes a much larger figure, carved into a block of hard limestone. This "Venus" of Laussel is not only a remarkable piece of sculpture; it provides a clue to the meaning

The "Venus" of Laussel: probably the oldest representation of deity, in the form of the Mother Goddess

of these "Venus" figures. Like the figurines, the Laussel "Venus" is faceless and has the sexual features accentuated; in addition it holds in one hand the horn of a bison. It was discovered together with other sculptured figures, and it appeared to have formed the chief object of a rock-sanctuary, where fertility rites were probably performed.

The emphasis upon the sexual or maternal features in these figures, together with the fact of their blank faces, suggest that they were not portraits of individual women but represented "woman" as the "mother", the source of fertility or continuing life. That these Palaeolithic peoples were urgently concerned with fertility is confirmed by their cave-art, as we shall see; for the animals which they hunted for food are often depicted as pregnant. To these primitive communities, just managing to maintain themselves against the perils of their environment, the need to ensure that they should have children was a major preoccupation. It is possible also that their interest in maternity extended beyond this: the figure of the pregnant female held the promise of the renewal of life to offset the grim negation of death.

These "Venus" figures, therefore, embodying such hopes and aspirations, may justly be regarded as religious objects. With the "Venus" of Laussel we may legitimately go further in our surmise. Since this figure seems to have been the chief cult object of a sanctuary, we may indeed have here the earliest representation of deity. In other words, the Laussel "Venus" may well represent the deification of the maternal principle, and, as such, be the first depiction of the Great Goddess. In the archaeological record the "Venus" of Laussel does, in fact, constitute the first of a long series of such figures that have been found on many ancient sites of Asia and Europe. They can be traced, through the Neolithic period, into the early civilizations of the Near East. They doubtless represent a tradition of deifying the maternal principle that eventually found expression in the Great Goddess conceptions of ancient Egypt, Mesopotamia, Anatolia and the Aegean area.

It seems, therefore, that the concept of deity had already emerged early in the Upper Palaeolithic era. That it found expression in terms of a divine mother naturally leads us on to ask whether the male principle was also deified. The evidence is far more problematic than that concerning the conception of a goddess. First, we may note there is no evidence of a similar preoccupation with the generative aspect of the male; indeed, it has been questioned whether these early peoples understood the male factor in procreation. However that may be, what constitutes the most likely evidence of the idea of a god seems to have a quite different significance from that of the "mother goddess".

This evidence, if such it be, is provided by a very strange creation of Palaeolithic art. It exists, engraved and partly painted, on the wall of one of the innermost recesses of the cave of the Trois Frères in the *département* of Ariège, France. It has the form of a being who combines human and animal features. Its general shape is anthropoid, but the head is surmounted by the antlers of a stag and has the furry ears of an animal. The face resembles that of an owl; and it has a long tongue or beard. The body is covered with the hairy pelt of an animal; and it also has the genital organs of a male beast. Its feet appear to be human. Its posture suggests the action of dancing.

This fantastic figure is generally known as the "Dancing Sorcerer". This designation derives from the interpretation that many prehistorians have given to it. There is some evidence that, in these Palaeolithic communities, sorcerers or shamans may have disguised themselves as animals and mimed their actions in a magical dance. Their acting would have been part of a hunting ritual, intended either to gain control of the animals before a hunt or to propitiate their spirits when killed. This interpretation is reasonable; and modern ethnological parallels can be cited

The "Dancing Sorcerer": possibly a Palaeolithic depiction of the "Lord of Beasts"

in its support. Moreover, it is generally agreed that Palaeolithic cave-art, such as the superb examples at Lascaux show, was magical in intent. The depiction of animals wounded by lances and darts, or as pregnant, was part of a hunting magic, designed to achieve a successful hunt and ensure the supply of further animals.

The so-called "Dancing Sorcerer" could thus represent such a masked dancer. But, if this interpretation be accepted, another problem has to be faced. Why should the depiction of such a dance be made, when the actual dance could have been staged at any time? It is possible to think up answers to the question; a different interpretation, however, merits consideration. The figure is so placed in the cave that it seems to dominate the representations of other animals. The cave gives the impression of having been a sanctuary, of which the figure was the most significant object. Such considerations have led some eminent French prehistorians to regard it as a representation of a kind of divine "Lord of the Beasts", conceived by the Palaeolithic hunters as the owner of the animals they hunted. Since these animals constituted the main source of their food, such a being would be of supreme significance, and worshipped as such. If, then, the so-called "Dancing Sorcerer" represents a kind of embryonic deity, we may conclude that Palaeolithic man's urgent concern about his food-supply induced him to imagine a supernatural being, combining human and animal attributes, whose favour must be won, if game was to be plentiful and easy to catch.

III

We have now surveyed what seems to be the most likely evidence of Palaeolithic man's religion. The conclusions drawn must necessarily be treated with the greatest caution, considering the nature of the data available. But, since this is the earliest evidence we have of human culture, it is legitimate to examine it in this way; and the conclusions reached are significant. They indicate that the earliest representatives of our race were concerned about three fundamental issues: birth, death and the food-supply. Their approach to each of these problems was essentially practical, though it was based upon intuitions of a supernatural or religious character. Death demanded action that involved economic loss; that they so responded attests the strength of their conviction about the reality of *post-mortem* survival. The mystery of birth evoked a response that produced the conception of a Divine Mother, the source of life. The necessity of providing their food resulted not only in the development of weapons and hunting techniques. The Palaeolithic hunters also believed that they could reinforce their own strength and skill by magical means. Their cave-art, which supplied this, may also have served to express their belief in a supernatural being who owned and controlled the animals, and, as such, had to be propitiated.

Such, then, are the earliest forms of religion as revealed by archaeo-logical research. That they were compounded with magic is not surprising; for magical elements are to be found even in the great religions of today. These findings may not be so spectacular as some of the theories about the origin of religion, based on other considerations. And they do not reveal the actual beginnings of religion. They have the virtue, however, of being drawn from the earliest evidence available. Obviously a long period of development lies behind the culture of man in the Upper Palaeolithic period; and somewhere back in that remoter past the first manifestations of religious thought and practice lie. It is possible that future archaeological discoveries will provide information of these begin-nings. For the present we must be content with knowing something of the nature of religion as soon as *Homo sapiens* appears in the archaeological record. That something is very significant for our understanding of human ideas and institutions.

CHAPTER 2

"In the Beginning"

THE HEBREW STORY OF THE CREATION
IN ITS CONTEMPORARY SETTING

From the religious conceptions of the ancient Hebrew people sprang the traditional idea of how mankind originated.

I

Michelangelo has adorned the walls of the Sistine Chapel with the most majestic presentation in linear art of the Hebrew story of the Creation; and his paintings manifest the mighty influence that this ancient legend had come to exercise on Christian thought. The continuance of that influence and its profundity were again singularly demonstrated, in the very different setting of Victorian England, some three centuries after the great Italian artist had finished his masterpiece. The fierce and prolonged public controversy occasioned by the publication of Darwin's *Origin of Species* in 1859 was the natural, if unfortunate, reaction of Christian believers to the shock they received when the truth of the Biblical account of the Creation seemed to be impiously challenged by the new science.

But, while conflict raged between the representatives of the traditional theology and the new evolutionary thesis, other scholars were quietly at work on the fresh material that the archaeological exploration of the ancient lands of the Near East was providing for a more accurate understanding of the Bible; and their researches supplemented and confirmed the conclusions that were being reached by the critical literary

"The most notable presentation in linear art of the Hebrew story of the Creation": Michelangelo's frescoes in the Sistine Chapel of the Temptation and the Fall, which show the mighty influence that this legend has exerted upon Christian ways of thought

investigation of the Old Testament documents that had been inaugurated by Jean Astruc, a French physician, in 1753.[1]

This scientifically conducted study of the Bible has persisted. Today we possess an understanding of its origins and contents that has rendered obsolete the earlier dispute; and not only has the controversy been shown as arising from a false estimate of the Biblical narrative, but a new appreciation of that narrative has been made possible, which has greatly enriched our knowledge of ancient Hebrew thought. Furthermore, through the development of the comparative study of religion, we can now evaluate what is unique in this Hebrew cosmogony, when it is seen in relation to the attempts of other peoples of the ancient Near East to account for the origin of the world and of mankind.

II

Turning first to Egypt, we find in the *Pyramid Texts* (c. 2400 B.C.) that the priests of Heliopolis,[2] the ancient centre of Egyptian sun-worship, explained the origin of things in terms of the Egyptian environment, and also in the interests of their own sanctuary. No doubt it was

[1] Concerning his work, published in that year under the title of *Conjectures sur les mémoires originaux dont il paroit que Moyse s'est servi pour composer le livre de la Genèse*, Astruc, as a devout Catholic, had some fear lest it should be exploited by free-thinkers.
[2] This is the Greek name for the Egyptian city of *Iunu*, which is called On in the Bible.

19

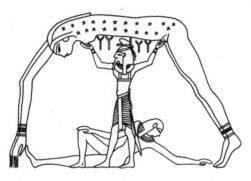

Egyptian Cosmology: Shu, the air-god, raises the sky-goddess Nut from the embrace of the earth-god Geb. The stars on the body of Nut indicate her celestial nature; the Y-shaped symbols depict the four supports of heaven (New Kingdom period)

the annual inundation of the Nile, when the swollen river obliterates all land-marks in the low-lying valley, together with the spectacle of the boundless horizon of the sea to the north, that caused the Egyptians to picture the primaeval state as a featureless waste of water, which they called *Nun:* and the subsidence of the flood-waters and the gradual emergence of the land also suggested the manner of the beginning of life. In the beginning, taught the Heliopolitan priests, from the watery chaos of *Nun* a hillock of earth had appeared, providing a foothold for the self-created sun-god, Atum-Kheprer. This hillock, of course, was the site of the Heliopolitan temple; which fact, according to the calculations of the Heliopolitan clergy, should have made it the most revered sanctuary in Egypt; for here, too, the sun-god began his work of creation. In the neighbouring city of Memphis, a rival cosmogony was propagated. The Memphite god was Ptah, and the priests who served his shrine undertook to exalt him above his rival at Heliopolis by designating him the creator of Atum-Kheprer. Their teaching has come down to us in a rather strange form. Inscribed on a large basalt stone, now in the British Museum, is a hieroglyphic text that tells in its preface how the Pharaoh Shabaka (716–701 B.C.) had caused a very ancient writing concerning Ptah to be preserved by carving its text on this slab. The text, which the consensus of Egyptological opinion attributes to about the same period as the *Pyramid Texts,* is a remarkable document. Whereas the Heliopolitan teaching had depicted the sun-god as performing his acts of creation in a somewhat crude physical manner, this Memphite cosmogony represents Ptah as creating by means of his heart (i.e. his mind) and his tongue, or word. Atum acts as his agent—"There came into being as the heart and there came into being as the tongue (something) in the form of Atum."

In these Egyptian creation-myths, there is a curious lack of concern about the creation of mankind. They seem mainly intent on accounting for the beginning of the process of creation and, in particular, on relating the gods to each other in order of appearance. This limitation of interest was undoubtedly due to the rivalry of the priesthoods who composed these cosmogonies. It is especially remarkable, nevertheless, that in the Memphite system, where mankind is mentioned, no clear reason is given for its creation.[3] Indeed, the only clear indication that we have of the Egyptian conception of the creation of man occurs in a monument of Amenhotep III (1405–1370 B.C.), purporting to record the divine birth of the king. In one of the scenes, the god Chnum is represented as making the infant king and his *ka* (i.e. his double) on a potter's wheel, while the goddess Hathor animates them with the *ankh*, the symbol of life.

The apparent failure of Egyptian thought to account for the origin of mankind contrasts notably with the cosmogonies of the contemporary cultures of Mesopotamia, the other great centre of civilized life in the ancient Near East. For, even in the period of Sumerian hegemony—before 2000 B.C.—the question of the origin and purpose of the human race had already been asked, and an answer had been given. A broken clay tablet, recovered from the site of the ancient Sumerian city of Nippur, tells how mankind had been created by the wise god Enki (Ea), to act as servants to the gods in building temples for them and supplying them with offerings of food.

[3] There is just a faint suggestion in the Memphite Theology that mankind was created to provide temples and offerings for the gods.

Egyptian conception of creation of man. Chnum fashions the figures on his potter's wheel, while Hathor animates them (from a bas-relief depicting birth of Amenhotep III at Luxor)

The most complete and impressive of the Mesopotamian cosmogonies
is the great *Enuma Elish*,[4] or Babylonian Creation Epic. The text of this
Epic was solemnly recited every year in Babylon, at the *akitu* or New
Year Festival, when it was believed that Marduk, the patron god of
Babylon, decreed the destiny of the state for the ensuing year. The Epic,
in fact, was designed to relate how Marduk came to possess the "tablets
of destiny"; and it takes the form of a narrative describing the creation
of both the universe and mankind. It begins by envisaging the primordial
state, in terms of the Mesopotamian environment, as a watery chaos, made
up of Apsu and Tiamat, the personifications respectively of the sweet
river waters and the sea:

> When on high the heaven had not been named,
> Firm ground below had not been called by name,
> Nought but primordial Apsu, their begetter,
> (And) Mummu-Tiamat, she who bore them all,
> Their waters commingling as a single body,
> No reed hut had been matted, no marsh land had appeared, . . .[5]

[4] So called from the first two words of the opening line: "When on high . . ." The Epic
probably dates from the early part of the 2nd millennium B.C.
[5] Translated by E. A. Speiser in *Ancient Near Eastern Texts*, ed. J. B. Pritchard (Princeton
University Press, 1955), pp. 60–1. "Mummu-Tiamat" probably means Mother-Tiamat.

Scene, from a Babylonian cylinder-seal, of two deities fighting a seven-
headed dragon. The depiction is reminiscent of Marduk's slaying of Tiamat,
the monster of Chaos

Regarding water as the source of all life, the Epic goes on to explain how the first gods were generated from the commingling of Apsu and Tiamat. These gods and their progeny in time abuse their begetters, and Tiamat determines to destroy them. In the Epic the personification of the sea now assumes the guise of a great monster, which produces other monsters to aid her in her struggle against the gods, who represent the new order as opposed to the former chaos. The gods choose Marduk as their champion—thus the Babylonian version; in its original form their champion was undoubtedly Ea, who appears in the *Enuma Elish* as the father of Marduk. Marduk engages with Tiamat in a titanic struggle, and defeats and kills her. Then from her body, which he is depicted as splitting into two parts "like a shellfish", he proceeds to form the heaven and the earth.

After his creation of the world, the Epic describes how Marduk made the first of human kind. The god is shown meditating on his plan:

> Blood will I mass, and cause bones to be.
> I will establish a savage, "man" shall be his name.
> Verily savage-man will I create.
> He shall be charged with the service of the gods
> That they might be at ease![6]

To obtain the material for his design, Kingu, one of the monsters of Tiamat, is killed; and from its blood Marduk fashions his new creature, man. This detail of the myth has caused considerable discussion among scholars. Some have interpreted it as an indication of the Babylonians' concern to explain the origin of evil in mankind, in that the substance of man was derived from an evil being. But it seems improbable that such a motive can have operated here since, in this form, the idea does not recur in ancient Mesopotamian literature.

In their cosmogonic thinking, therefore, the inhabitants of Mesopotamia held quite definite views on the *raison d'être* of mankind—namely, that it was to serve the gods. They were equally certain about human destiny. Man, we learn from the great *Epic of Gilgamesh*, has no hope of a happy lot after this life; for, "When the gods created mankind, Death for mankind they set aside, Life in their own hands retaining."[7] In other words, men are mortal because their divine masters have made them such; and with that fate they must be content.

[6] Tablet VI, 5-9, trans. E. A. Speiser in *op. cit.*, p. 68.
[7] See Chapter 10.

III

It is against the background of such ideas of the creation of the world and the origin of man that we have to set the Hebrew story of the Creation in the first two chapters of the book called *Genesis*. But first we must notice that, in these chapters, there are really two accounts of the Creation. The first runs from the beginning of chapter i to ii. 4a, and the second starts at chapter ii. 4b and continues to ii. 25. Now, it has long been recognized that these accounts come from different sources of literary tradition. That with which *Genesis* actually begins is not, however, the older account; it derives from what is known as the Priestly source, and critical scholarship dates it at about 450 B.C. The other account is a conflation of two literary traditions, known as the Yahwist and the Elohist; of these the Yahwist is the slightly earlier of the two and is generally dated for about 950 to 850 B.C.[8]

The Yahwist account is the more interesting and, in view of its subsequent influence, the more significant for the history of Western thought. Since it requires extended study, we must first briefly examine the chief characteristics of the Priestly version. The opening verses of this account strongly recall the primordial state as conceived in the Babylonian *Enuma Elish*. "In the beginning," we are told "the earth was waste and void; and darkness was upon the face of the deep: and the spirit of God moved upon the face of the waters." This idea of "the deep" is of considerable interest, because the Hebrew word for it, *tehōm,* is probably a corruption of the Babylonian name Tiamat, which designated, as we have seen, the personification of the chaos of the primaeval waters. In the Priestly account, this *tehōm* also appears as existent before the divine work of creation. But, although the ancient Mesopotamian idea of a primaeval monster of chaos may ultimately underlie the Hebrew story, there is no trace of the primitive mythology concerning the construction of the world from the body of the monster by a victorious god. In the Priestly version, God creates by means of his word alone—"Let there be light: and there was light"—thus reminding us of the creative acts of the Egyptian god Ptah in the Memphite Theology. With the creation of man, the work of creation culminates on "the seventh day", according to the Priestly writer. Nothing is said of the purpose of man, except that he

[8] See Chapter 11.

is made in the image of God and is ordered by his Creator to "be fruitful, and multiply, and replenish the earth, and subdue it". On man's nature there is also silence, and the account ends by emphasizing the divine benevolence: "And God saw everything that he had made, and, behold, it was very good."

The older Yahwist-Elohist version is considerably different; but, while its imagery is more naïve, its insight into the problem of human nature and destiny is the more profound. This difference of outlook is apparent at once. Little time is spent on describing the creation of the world, and, in contradistinction to the Priestly account, man is made before the animals—indeed, the *raison d'être* of the latter appears to be that of providing companionship for man, in which they prove inadequate (ii. 18–20).

In his creation of man, Yahweh[9] is depicted as forming his creature from earth, in a manner reminiscent of that of the Egyptian creator-god Chnum. The parallelism with the Egyptian conception is further strengthened by the fact that, after moulding man out of earth, Yahweh animates him by breathing into his nostrils "the breath of life"—the goddess Hathor had endowed Chnum's creatures with life by touching them with the *ankh*. The Yahwist author, however, in depicting man as being created out of the earth, probably did not merely avail himself of a convenient image: he seems to have been preparing for the tragic fate of man that he was soon to describe. Thus there is a significant play on the word for man, *ādām,* and that for the earth, *adāmāh,* from which he is made (ii. 7).

In this Yahwist-Elohist legend of creation, no reason is given for the creation of man. A kind of golden age of primaeval innocence seems to be envisaged. Yahweh places Adam (to give the Primal Man his customary designation) in a beautiful garden, where all his material wants are provided and which he has to tend, apparently, without toil. This garden is located "eastward" (undoubtedly from Palestine); and its name "Eden" is probably derived from the Babylonian word *edinu,* meaning "plain" or "steppe ",thus suggesting some Mesopotamian derivation. Here Adam dwells, at first with the animals which are also formed from the earth. An aetiological motive seems to have inspired this account of the creation of the animals—they are made as companions for Adam, and from

---

[9] In the Hebrew text "Yahweh Elohim," which is translated as the "Lord God." "Yahweh" was the personal name of the God of Israel; see Chapter 11, note 1.

An early Christian representation of the creation of Eve from the recumbent figure of Adam, and the Serpent of Eden (top left). From a sarcophagus now in the Lateran Museum, Rome

him they receive their names (ii. 18–20). Aetiological interest also seems to underlie the quaint account that follows of the creation of Eve, the First Woman. Her formation from a rib (the Hebrew means "side") of Adam is held to explain the origin of the word *Ishshah* ("woman") which derives from *ish* ("man" or "husband").

The account of Yahweh's placing of Adam in Eden was clearly designed to lead on to the fatal events that were to decide the destiny of mankind. For the Yahwist-Elohist story was not intended only to describe the creation of the world and of mankind; its purpose was to account for the human situation as seen in terms of the Yahwist *Weltanschauung*. This purpose is adumbrated by Yahweh's warning to Adam: "Of every tree of the garden thou mayest freely eat: but of the tree of the knowledge of good and evil, thou shalt not eat of it: for in the day that thou eatest thereof thou shalt surely die" (ii. 16–17).

This warning is of fundamental significance for the proper understanding of the sequel. Its logic is clear: the Yahwist author clearly envisaged Adam as created originally immortal, and, therefore, differed notably from the Mesopotamian view that the gods had withheld immortality from their human servants. But the straightforward theme of the Yahwist narrative—namely, that in the primordial age of innocence mankind was deathless—is somewhat obscured by the brief mention of "the tree of life also in the midst of the garden" (ii. 9). As we shall see presently, however, there is good reason for thinking that the reference here to the "tree of life" is an interpolation made to anticipate the introduction of a different motif later in the legend. What the writer meant by "the tree of the knowledge of good and evil" is not explained; but, as we shall also see, some indication of its meaning may be inferred from the sequel.

The profoundly moving account of the Temptation and Fall of Man that follows in the third chapter constitutes a scene unsurpassed in its drama in the sacred literature of mankind; and its influence has been immense. The primary motive of the Yahwist writer therein was to show that mankind became subject to death through the disobedience of its first parents to the command of their Creator. But this intention was closely linked with the desire to interpret the hard toil of the agriculturist's life as part of the divine curse that fell upon the human race because of its progenitors' fatal sin. This is all made dramatically manifest in the awful doom that Yahweh pronounces upon the fallen Adam, who attempts to excuse himself by blaming his wife: "Because thou hast hearkened unto the voice of thy wife, and hast eaten of the tree, of which I commanded thee, saying, Thou shalt not eat of it: cursed is the ground for thy sake; in toil shalt thou eat of it all the days of thy life; thorns also and thistles shall it bring forth to thee; and thou shalt eat of the herb of the field; in the sweat of thy face shalt thou eat bread, till thou return again unto the ground; for out of it wast thou taken: for dust thou art, and unto dust shalt thou return" (iii. 17–20). And so the man (*ādām*) is fated to be resolved back into the earth (*adāmāh*) from which his Creator had moulded him.

This interpretation of the agriculturist's life, as a consequence of the original sin of mankind, is significant of the Yahwist tradition. The settlement of the nomadic Hebrew tribes in Canaan had resulted not only in a change of economy, but also in a disturbance of social custom and religious belief. By becoming agriculturists, the Israelites tended to acquire both the arts and the vices of the settled agrarian communities of Canaan, among which were the worship of fertility gods and the practice of their licentious rites. Consequently, the Yahwist prophets, who condemned such conduct as disloyalty to Yahweh, were disposed to look with disfavour upon agriculture and to exalt the pastoralist's life as the better way—a view that recurs in the Yahwist story of Cain and Abel (*Genesis* iv. 2–12). Such a denigration of agriculture is notably absent from Egyptian and Mesopotamian mythology; a reminiscence of it does appear in the Greek poet Hesiod (*c.* eighth century B.C.), who traces the hard toil of agriculture to some divine hostility towards mankind; but here the attitude had a different source of inspiration.

In his account of the consequences of the Fall of Man, the Yahwist writer was able also to explain the origin of a number of other things. Thus, in the divine punishment decreed for the Woman for her part in the fall of Man, the origin of child-bearing and its attendant pain is found: "I will multiply thy sorrow and thy conception; in sorrow thou shalt bring forth children; and thy desire shall be to thy husband, and he shall rule over thee" (iii. 16). How the wearing of clothes started is similarly explained. After eating of the forbidden fruit, Adam and his wife become aware of their primaeval state of nudity. To hide their shame, they had themselves at first resorted to a covering of leaves; later, Yahweh clothed them in garments of skins (iii. 7, 10, 21). An interesting parallel to this attempt to explain the origin of clothes occurs in the Mesopotamian *Epic of Gilgamesh*. There the wild man Enkidu represents mankind in its primitive form; when he is civilized, he learns to wear clothes and eat bread.[10]

The part played by the serpent in the drama of the Temptation and Fall of Man requires discussion. Owing to the fact that Christian theology has identified the serpent in *Genesis* with Satan, the personification of evil, the action of the serpent has become invested with a profound religious significance. In the original story, however, the character and action of the serpent have no such significance. The serpent is presented essentially as an animal, although endowed with the power of speech and logical argument. The doom that Yahweh pronounces upon it is clearly designed to explain the serpent's peculiar method of locomotion; and it also expresses the instinctive fear that men feel for this insidious creature: "Because thou hast done this, cursed art thou above all cattle, and above every beast of the field; upon thy belly shalt thou go, and dust shalt thou eat all the days of thy life: and I will put enmity between thee and the woman, and between thy seed and her seed: it shall bruise thy head, and thou shalt bruise his heel" (iii. 14–15). But the introduction of the serpent into the drama of mankind's loss of immortality has a further significance for the comparative study of mythology. The snake's ability to slough off its old skin has fascinated mankind throughout the world, especially since it has often been believed that the snake thereby possessed

[10] See Chapter 10.

the secret of self-renewal that man so greatly covets. This concern finds significant expression in the *Epic of Gilgamesh,* where the hero is robbed of the magical plant that makes "the old man as the young man" by a serpent which perpetuates its own youth by devouring it.[11] It is possible that the Yahwist author had this Mesopotamian legend in mind when he related the tragedy of Adam; if he had, he must have adjusted it, so that the serpent became an agent in man's loss of immortality and not the immediate cause of it, as in the Gilgamesh story.

Undoubtedly the most difficult part of the Yahwist legend to explain is the meaning of the tree of "the knowledge of good and evil". The penalty for eating of this tree was death; yet in the narrative the immediate consequence of Adam and Eve's eating of it is the consciousness that they are naked. Now, since the Yahwist writer clearly regarded nudity as shameful (ii. 25; iii. 7, 10, 21), it follows from his account that man only acquired a proper sense of decency by eating of the forbidden fruit. But it is obviously impossible that he could have meant that man acquired moral sensibility by disobeying his Creator. Accordingly, it would seem necessary to conclude that the fruit of the "tree of the knowledge of good and evil" meant knowledge of sex and its dangerous potentialities. Confirmation of this comes from the fact that only after the Fall does Eve conceive and bear children. Moreover, the part that the serpent plays in tempting Eve may be significant, since the serpent was also a symbol of fertility in the worship of the Canaanite deities Baal and Astarte. Herein we may have a further clue to the main purpose of the Yahwist writer. The agrarian rituals of the Canaanites were centred on the principle and process of fertility, which in turn were personified in the relationships of a goddess and her young male lover. The rites, in which these deities were worshipped, were designed to promote fertility and often involved temple prostitution. The tendency of the Israelites, after their settlement in Canaan, to adopt such cults, or to worship Yahweh by such rites, was a danger against which the Yahwist prophets continually inveighed. Hence, it is possible that, in representing sexual consciousness as the immediate result of the eating of the forbidden fruit, the Yahwist author believed that the dangerous knowledge of the means of the procreation of life came through man's primordial disobedience to the command of his Creator.

[11] See Chapter 10.

The problem of "the tree of life also in the midst of the garden" remains to be discussed. As we have now seen, the theme of the Yahwist myth of the creation and fall of Adam is that mankind became mortal through the sin of its first parents. The idea of a "tree of life", which thus logically contradicts that theme, after being briefly mentioned in ii. 9, only appears again in the narrative in iii. 22–4. In this short passage, Yahweh is depicted as expelling Adam and Eve from Eden, saying: "Behold, the man is become as one of us, to know good and evil; and now, lest he put forth his hand, and take also of the tree of life, and eat, and live for ever . . ." The obvious disruption of theme that this passage causes, together with the improbability of there being two trees of unique virtue in the original form of the myth, has led many scholars to conclude that the passage concerning the tree of life was a later interpolation. The motif of a plant that will confer eternal youth, or that **of the food of immortality, was well known in Mesopotamian folklore.** We have already noticed the magical plant of which Gilgamesh was robbed in his quest for immortality; and in another legend, that of Adapa, the hero unwittingly rejects the food that would have made him immortal. It would seem likely, therefore, that, as the story of the Flood was worked into the Yahwist narrative because of its prestige in contemporary Semitic tradition, so the idea of a "tree of life" was incorporated here, despite the obvious disruption of theme that resulted.

The Yahwist story of the creation and fall of Man formed part of the Yahwist philosophy of history that is dealt with in Chapter 11. Accordingly, it will suffice to say that the story was designed, in that context, to present the Yahwist view of human nature and destiny. In that sense, too, it forms part of the Yahwist polemic against the contemporary mortuary cultus of the Israelites. The tensions that it consequently caused in the development of Hebrew religion is the subject of Chapter 12.

≽ CHAPTER 3

The Personification of Death
in Some Ancient Religions

How mankind has conceived of the "Last Enemy"

I

Man has been variously defined as a fire-user, a tool-maker, and a political animal. Such definitions are, of course, designed to pick out and to underline some essential human activity which is thought to mark off man as distinct from all other beings. For the same reason man could also be characterized as a "burier of his dead"—although in this remarkable practice *homo sapiens* was, perhaps significantly, anticipated by his hominian precursor, the so-called Neanderthal Man, who carefully buried his dead, probably with some funerary equipment.

The ritual burial of the dead, which thus occurs from the Upper Palaeolithic era, may intelligibly be interpreted either as originating from some instinctive inability on the part of man to accept the ocular evidence of physical disintegration as marking the end of the individual person, or as due to an equally instinctive hope for some of *post-mortem* survival. But, whatever its origin may be thought to have been, it is obvious that even the most primitive mortuary practice must presuppose some reflection about death, which would surely in turn have involved some speculation about the cause of death. Where death was due to an act of violence, as for example when the Palaeolithic hunter was killed by the bison that he hunted, there would have been little problem about his end—the man

31

had obviously died because his body had been torn or broken in some
fatal way.[1] But death by disease, which must surely have happened too
in the Palaeolithic communities, would have been more difficult to explain.
Why had the individual concerned suddenly drooped and then died? Here
it would seem that the imagination would have been called upon to
provide an answer. What kind of answer was provided by the Palaeolithic
mind we have no means of knowing. We can only surmise that, from
what they knew of the cause of death by violence, these Palaeolithic
peoples were likely to have inferred that death by disease must be due
to the attack of some agent whom they could not see, but of whose activity
they had such doleful proof. It is tempting to go on to speculate what
such a conclusion might have meant to the mind of Palaeolithic man:
whether it would have led him to conceive of some awful mysterious being
who would suddenly strike at the individual person and cause him or
her to die.

From such speculation about Palaeolithic man's reactions it will be
safer and more profitable to turn and interrogate the literatures of certain
of the ancient peoples of the Near East, in an attempt to understand how
man first sought to explain the most disturbing fact of his experience as
he observed it happening in the persons of his fellows.

We shall start with the evidence provided by ancient Egypt because,
not only is ancient Egyptian culture one of the earliest of which we have
information, but it is the best documented from our present point of view.
Moreover, the chief reason for this rich documentation is the fact of the
exceeding preoccupation of the Egyptians with the problem of death,
which led to their developing the most elaborate mortuary cultus known
to the history of religions.

When we come to examine the immense corpus of Egyptian funerary
literature, we find, however, that, despite their deep concern about death
and the great efforts which they made to prevent or circumvent its dread
effects, the Egyptians never seem to have formulated either any clear
conception of the nature of death or of its cause. Generally it would appear
that they refused to accept death as a natural and inevitable event that
every living being must experience. In the earliest mortuary texts, namely,

[1] The famous Lascaux picture of a bison killing a bird-headed man constitutes an
interesting instance of Palaeolithic preoccupation with the question of death by violence; cf.
H. Breuil, *Quatre Cents Siècles d'Art pariétal* (Montignac, 1954), pp. 131, 134–5, 148, 150–1
(fig.); F. Windels, *The Lascaux Cave Paintings* (Faber, 1949), pp. 27, 63; A. Laming,
Lascaux (Pelican Books, 1959), pp. 93–6.

the *Pyramid Texts,* which date from about the second half of the third millennium B.C., the idea is expressed that there was once a time when there was no death;[2] but nothing is said of how death subsequently came to enter into the world. The various terms used by the Egyptians for death also give no certain clue as to the intrinsic nature of the concept that they were designed to express. The usual word for "to die ", *mwt,* had as its determinative sign the figure of a man falling on his knees, with blood streaming from his head.[3] The substantive *mwt* ("death") also had this determinative. Two alternative expressions, namely, *mni* (meaning literally, and probably euphemistically, "to land") and *ḥpt* have as their determinative signs the figure of a recumbent mummy or embalmed body.[4]

It is possible, however, that the determinative sign of *mwt,* i.e. the figure of the falling man with blood streaming from his head, could afford some indication of the original nature of the concept, since the same sign serves as the determinative of the word for "enemy" (*ḥfty*).[5] In other words, the use of this determinative may mean that in the Egyptian mind death was regarded essentially as an enemy, and the process of dying as the consequence of a hostile attack. There is indeed certain evidence that would seem to confirm this inference. Most notably there is the legend of Osiris, which formed the rationale of the mortuary cultus. According to this well-known legend, the divine hero had been slain by the assault of an evil being called Set.[6] Now, since the Osirian mortuary ritual was based upon the ritual identification of the deceased person with Osiris in the belief that, by such means, that person would share in the divine hero's resurrection to a new life, Osiris became in a very real sense a kind of Egyptian "Everyman".[7] Accordingly, the Osirian legend provided, as it were, the pattern of every man's destiny, which meant in turn that it undoubtedly supplied the imagery in terms of which the process of death was conceived—in other words, as Osiris died by being struck down by an evil enemy, so death came to each individual person.

[2] *Pyr.* 1466 d. (K. Sethe, *Die altaegyptischen Pyramidentexten,* ii. 303): n ḥprt mt (mwt). The verb ḥpr means "to become, to come into existence."
[3] Cf. A. H. Gardiner, *Egyptian Grammar* (Oxford, 1927), p. 436 (A 14), cf. p. 521 (Z6); Erman-Grapow, *Wörterbuch der aegyptischen Sprache,* ii. 55, 166–7, see also under ḥpj, *op. cit.* iii. pp. 258–9. Cf. A. H. Gardiner in *Encyclopaedia of Religion and Ethics* (ed. J. Hastings), viii. 21.
[4] Cf. Gardiner, *Grammar,* p. 440 (A.54, 55); Erman-Grapow, *op. cit.* ii. 73, iii, 258–9.
[5] Cf. Gardiner, *Grammar,* p. 436 (A.14); Erman-Grapow, *op. cit.* iii. 276.
[6] For the earliest references to the legend see *Pyramid Texts,* 972, 1256, 1500.
[7] See Chapter 8.

Set, the slayer of Osiris

Egyptian literature does indeed contain many instances of death being envisaged thus as the attack of some demonic being. But we encounter a curious problem when we naturally go on to enquire how the Egyptians conceived of such a demonic being or beings. It would be reasonable to suppose that the evil Set, the slayer of Osiris, would have become the Egyptian death-god, for he seems so obviously cast for the part. But, although he does indeed tend to assume the rôle of the Devil in Egyptian theology, Set is never actually represented as the god of death. This fact may be due to a curious reticence that manifests itself in Egyptian iconography about the depiction of the act of dying. Thus, although Osiris is frequently represented as lying dead and being mourned over by the goddesses Isis and Nephthys, he is never shown as being struck down by Set—possibly the current belief in the magical efficacy of pictures and statues prevented the actual representation of such a baleful event. In turn, such a taboo was probably responsible for the fact that in the illustrated versions of the *Book of the Dead,* although so many scenes of incidents in the *post-mortem* career of the deceased are realistically shown, the actual death of the person concerned is never depicted.

If the Egyptians, however, were disposed to imagine death as due to the attack of some evil demon, it would surely seem necessary that they should have had some concrete image in their mind of this awful being—in other words, that they should in some measure have personified

34

their conception of death. That an effective measure of personification did take place the following selection of passages vividly testifies. From the *Coffin Texts* of the Middle Kingdom (*c.* 2160–1580 B.C.): "Save me from the claws of him who takes for himself what he sees: may the glowing breath of his mouth not take me away."[8] Then, a New Kingdom (*c.* 1580–1090 B.C.) document known as the *Wisdom of Anii*: "Death cometh and leadeth away the babe that is still in the bosom of its mother, even as the man when he hath become old."[5] Lastly, a text from the Graeco-Roman period: "Death, his name is 'Come'; every one to whom he calleth comes to him straightway, their hearts being affrighted through fear of him. There is none can see him, either of gods or of men; the great and the small alike rest in him, nor can he stay his finger. He loveth ·all, and robbeth the son from his mother. The old man moves to meet him, and all fear and make petition before him. Yet he turns not his face towards them, he comes not to him who implores him, he hearkens not when he is worshipped; he shows himself not, even though any manner of bribe be given to him."[10]

It would seem evident, then, that the Egyptians, when they thought of death, had in their mind's eye a personified being of horrific form. But what exactly was that form we have no certain information, since, as we have seen, the actual death-event seems never to have been depicted in Egyptian art. In the funerary papyri we certainly have a great abundance of demonic figures represented, but these demons are denizens of the underworld and occupied in tormenting the unrighteous there. If, however, the Egyptians did tend to think of death in terms of Set, the slayer of Osiris, as we have suggested, then it is likely that the image under which they would have personified death, at least mentally, would have been that of the strange Set-animal well known in Egyptian iconography—a creature with sharp pointed ears or horns, a long muzzle or snout, and a tail splayed at its end.

At this point we will leave for the moment further consideration of the ancient Egyptian conception of death; we shall have need to return to it again when we come to consider the evidence of Coptic literature in connection with the personification of death in Early Christianity.

[8] CT VII, Spell 1106; BIL. 527; Cairo 28085, Lacau I. 215. 13; cf. J. Zandee, *Death as an Enemy according to Ancient Egyptian Conceptions* (Leiden, 1960), pp. 23, 185 (B. 9b).
[9] A. Erman, *The Literature of the Ancient Egyptians* (London, 1927), p. 237.
[10] Translated by A. H. Gardiner in *Encycl. of Religion and Ethics*, viii, 22a.

II

Turning from the Egyptian conception, it is instructive to consider briefly the idea of death which was current in the sister civilization of Mesopotamia. For here we meet with a completely different interpretation of human life and destiny, yet one which apparently induced a tendency to personify death such as we have found in Egypt.

According to what we might fairly call Mesopotamian theological thought, the gods had created mankind in order that they might have servants to build temples for them and provide them with sacrifices. But such service was the only *raison d'être* of these human creatures whom the gods had made, so that, when these creatures ceased to be capable of performing it, there was no other purpose for their continued existence. This view of the human situation receives its classic expression in Meso-potamian literature in the speech of Siduri in the celebrated *Epic of Gilgamesh.*[11] Gilgamesh, the hero of the *Epic,* shocked by the revelation .of human mortality that comes to him through the death of his friend Enkidu, seeks to escape his fate by visiting Utanapishtim, the Babylonian Noah, in his remote abode, in order to learn the secret of his fabled deathlessness. In the course of his long and arduous journey thither, Gilgamesh is represented as meeting the mysterious Siduri, who is made the mouthpiece of the *carpe diem* philosophy of life that the traditional Mesopotamian eschatology alone sanctioned. Siduri tells Gilgamesh that his quest for immortality is hopeless, for, as she significantly explains:

> The life which thou seekest thou wilt not find;
> (for) when the gods created mankind,
> They allotted death to mankind,
> (But) life they retained in their keeping.[12]

However, although death is accordingly represented as natural to man, it being an attribute of the nature with which his divine creators endowed him, we find, even in the very poem in which this belief is thus stated, that the process of dying was instinctively envisaged as the seizure of the doomed individual by a demon, a kind of death-god. Thus

[11] See Chapter 10.
[12] Tab. X, col. iii, 1-14; translated by A. Heidel, *The Gilgamesh Epic and Old Testament Parallels* (Chicago University Press, 1949), p. 70.

Enkidu, the unfortunate friend of Gilgamesh, has a presentiment of his coming death and dreams that he is seized by some awful being:

> . . . he transformed me,
> That mine arms were covered with feathers like a bird.
> He looks at me (and) leads me to the house of darkness, to the dwelling of Irkalla;
> To the house from which he who enters never goes forth;
> On the road whose path does not lead back;
> To the house whose inhabitants are bereft of light;
> Where dust is their food and clay their sustenance;
> (Where) they are clad like birds.[13]

In the Babylonian Creation Epic the death-god is actually named Uggae, when the rebel Kingu is accounted to him at his execution for his association with Tiamat in her primordial struggle against the gods.[14] An Assyrian text of about the middle of the seventh century B.C. is even more explicit in the course of its account of the underworld, for it describes "Death (*il-mu-ú* [*tu?*]), with a *mušhuššu*-head, his two hands (were the hands of) men, his two feet (of) serpents."[15]

It must, accordingly, be deemed significant that in two cultures, so very different in their eschatologies as those of Egypt and Mesopotamia, death was personified as a horrific demon that seized its victims and so brought their earthly careers to a dread end.

III

When we turn to consider Hebrew religion in this connection, we are confronted with a richness and a diversity of imagery that forbids any attempt at precise definition. The long struggle of Yahwism against ancient and deeply-rooted mortuary cults has necessarily left its mark in the extant literature in the form of conflicting views of the nature and destiny of man, which in turn involves a certain contradiction in the conception of death.[16] The clearest and most impressive exposition of the origin of death is, of course, that contained in the well-known Yahwist story of

---

13 Tab. VII, col. iv, 31–41; translated by Heidel, *op. cit.* p. 36.

14 IV, 120. Uggae plays no important part in Mesopotamian religious literature and had no place in the main hierarchy of gods.

15 Cf. E. Ebeling, *Tod und Leben nach den Vorstellungen des Babylonier* (Berlin and Leipzig, 1931), i. 5(3). Cf. Heidel, *op. cit.* p. 133.

16 See Chapter 12.

the Temptation and Fall of Adam (*Gen.* ii. 4—iii. 19). Here, in a superb narrative, we have death presented as the penalty imposed by God on mankind in consequence of the sin of its first parents. By implication, therefore, the progenitors of the human race were created to be immortal; but it is uncertain whether we can rightly infer from this that the Yahwist writer intended to suggest that the descendants of Adam would also have been immortal but for the Fall,[17] since, according to the logic of the narrative, the procreation of offspring was one of the consequences of the Fall (*Gen.* iii. 14–16). However that may be, the Yahwist story clearly represents death as originating from man's primordial disobedience to his Maker. This account of the origin of death, however, only applies to mankind; nothing is said by way of explanation of the obvious fact that animals also die. No doubt Yahwist aetiology in this passage is designed to meet a specific situation—possibly the belief in some form of *post-mortem* survival implied in the indigenous mortuary cultus.

The traditional Hebrew anthropology regarded the individual person as a psycho-physical organism, a compound of body and *nephesh*, which was the animating principle. Death was seen as the fatal shattering of this organism, so that what survived was in no sense the real person but some shadowy, and possibly horrific, entity that departed to a grim existence in Sheol.[18] How death, being thus the fatal shattering of the psycho-physical organism that constituted the person, was achieved is not clear. Generally God was regarded as ultimately responsible for the individual's death, since Hebrew monotheism could not allow of the existence of an evil principle or a death-god that operated among men, contrary to the will of God. Consequently, although a few passages can be cited where death itself seems to be hypostatized (e.g. *Hos.* xiii. 14; *Isa.* xxv. 8a), the dominant view is that death was due to the action of God. However, a tendency in Hebrew thought to separate Yahweh from direct contact with human affairs seems to have produced the idea of "the angel of Yahweh" as the agent of death (E.g. 2 *Sam.* xxiv. 15–16). The mysterious *mashith* of *Exodus* xii. 13 and 23, the "destroyer" who slew the first born of Egypt, may, however, have been originally some baleful monster of ancient Semitic folklore before becoming the minister

---

[17] The notion clearly inheres in Yahweh's warning about the consequences of eating of the forbidden tree in Gen. ii. 17, and it is re-echoed in the woman's reply to the serpent's question in Gen. iii. 4.

[18] Cf. A. R. Johnson, *The vitality of the Individual in the thought of Ancient Israel* (University of Wales Press, 1949), pp. 88–90.

of Yahweh or Yahweh himself.[19] In later Jewish thought the angel of
death is given the name "Sammael", i.e. "the drug of God", with reference
to the gall on the tip of the sword with which he is armed, and his
presence in a town is betokened by the howling of dogs.[20]

In view of the strong monotheistic character of Hebrew religion, it
is surely significant, therefore, that, despite belief that death was decreed
by God, the imagination strove to see death as an event in which there
was a personified agent. One can only wonder, in the absence of a Jewish
religious icongraphy, in what form the angel of death was conceived, for
the mention of the sword indicates the conception of a concrete figure.

IV

Before passing on in our survey to the evidence of ancient Greece
and early Christianity, it will be useful to glance briefly at the imagery
of death in ancient Iran, for there was the classic home of religious
dualism. From what can be gathered of Zarathustra's teaching, as it has
been preserved in the *Gathas*, the prophet seems to have taught nothing
significant about either the origin or nature of death. Death appears
essentially as the inevitable prelude to the supreme test of passing over
the fearsome *Cinvato paratu*, i.e. "the Bridge of the Separator", which
will achieve the fateful division between the good and the bad.[21] But
Zarathustra was the reformer of a more ancient faith, which had its roots
far back in the Aryan past of the Iranians. Professor G. Widengren of
Uppsala has made out a strong case for thinking that the characteristic
dualism of Iranian religion also lay back beyond Zarathustra and originates
in the concept of a high-god, who embodied within himself a duality
of attributes—life and death, light and darkness, creativity and destruction.[22] Such a conception of deity would not be strange to the Aryan
mind, since it finds expression in Hinduism and is not entirely absent
from the Homeric protrait of Zeus. However that may be as to origins,

[19] Cf. A. Jeremias, *Das Alte Testament in Lichte des alten Orients* (Leipzig, 1930), p.
411. If the identification of Mot as the Canaanite god of death could be definitely established,
the fact would be of considerable significance in this connection: cf. C. Virolleaud, *Légendes
de Babylone et de Canaan* (Paris, 1949), p. 87; G. R. Driver, *Canaanite Myths and Legends*
(Edinburgh, 1956), p. 161a; R. Dussaud, *Les Religions des Hittites, et des Hourrites, des
Phéniciens et des Syriens* (Paris, 1945), p. 371.
[20] Cf. M. Joseph in *Encycl. of Religion and Ethics*, viii, 41b.
[21] Yasna xlvi, 10–11, li. 12–13. Cf. J. H. Moulton, *Early Zoroastrianism* (London,
1913), pp. 374, 386; L. H. Mills, *Sacred Books of the East*, xxxi. 183. Cf. N. Söderblom, *La
Vie future d'après le Mazdéisme* (Paris, 1901), p. 90.
[22] *Hochgottglaube im alten Iran* (Lund, 1938), pp. 94–145.

it is important to notice that in later Persian religion the concept of
Zurvān, which may perhaps have derived from the ancient high-god of
Iran, contained some remarkably profound and realistic thinking about
the nature of death.[23] For in Zurvān it appears that the Persians deified
Time; but in so doing they recognized a twofold aspect of Time which
finds expression in two forms of the god Zurvān, namely, Zurvān *akarana*,
which meant "infinite Time" and Zurvān *darēgho-chvadhāta*, which was
"Time of Long Dominion", i.e. "finite Time". Now, it was Time under
this second aspect that was regarded as the source of decay and death
in this present world. Its character and activity are vividly presented in
the following passages from relevant Pahlavī texts translated by Professor
R. C. Zaehner, who has concentrated upon the problem of Zurvān.[24]
First, a clear acknowledgement of the essential connection between death
and the time-process: "For Zurvān there is no remedy. From death there
is no escape." Then, of the destructive nature of Time: "As to him whose
eye Time has sewn up, his back is seized upon and will never rise again;
pain comes upon his heart so that it beats no more; his hand is broken
so that it grows no more, and his foot is broken so that it walks no more.
The stars came upon him, and he goes not out another time: fate came upon
him and he cannot drive it forth." So graphic a picture of the operation of
Zurvān naturally prompts the enquiry whether Time could have been so
conceived without the forming of some personalized image of it. The problem involved here is too complicated for present discussion; but it may be
noticed that a reasonable case has been made out for thinking that the
statues of a lion-headed monster adorned with various symbols of Time and
usually identified with Aiōn, which have been found in many Mithraic
sanctuaries, may represent Zurvān *darēgho-chvadhāta* i.e. "Time of Long
Dominion", in other words, the god of death.[25]

V

The rich treasury of the Greek imagination provided a variety of
figures under which death was conceived. But, since their innate propensity to face facts seems to have led them to accept mortality as an essential
attribute of human nature, the Greeks were never really concerned to

[23] Cf. R. C. Zaehner, *Zurvān: a Zoroastrian Dilemma* (Oxford, 1955), pp. 20, 88–90,
203–4, 208, 231–2, 239–242, 275, 382; Widengren, *op. cit.* pp. 266–310; J. Duchesne-
Guillemin, *Ormazd et Ahriman* (Paris, 1953), pp. 118–22.
[24] *Zurvān*, pp. 240–1, see also pp. 397–9.
[25] See Chapter 4.

Thanatos, the Greek personification of Death (from a sculptured column of the temple of Artemis at Ephesus, now in the British Museum)

explain the origin of death, nor did their theology find death a problem relative to man's position *vis-à-vis* the gods. Where, as in their mystery-cults, the individual was encouraged to believe that he could obtain a blessed lot after death, the very logic to the doctrine implied that such a destiny was not normal for men. The reply which Homer puts into the mouth of the dead Anticleia, when her son, Odysseus, tries vainly to embrace her insubstantial form when they meet in Hades, succinctly expresses the accepted eschatology: ". . . this is the appointed way with mortals when one dies. For the sinews no longer hold the flesh and the bones together, but the strong might of the blazing fire destroys these, as soon as the life (*thymos*) leaves the white bones, and the spirit (*psychē*), like a dream, flits away, and hovers to and fro." [26]

Nurtured on such realism, it is not surprising that the Greeks developed no mythology of death. Homer may have preserved some memory of a primitive personification of death in his use of the expression *kēr thanatoio* (the *kēr* of death), and the well-known figure of the winged harpy certainly indicates an early tendency to imagine death as a monster that snatches away his victims. But neither of these images succeeded in establishing itself as a traditional concept. Neither did the more sophis-

[26] *Odyssey* XI. 204–22, trans. A. T. Murray, Loeb. edn. of *Odyssey*, i. 401–3.

The Parting of Alcestis and Admetos: Charun is about to strike the death-
blow (from an Etruscan vase)

ticated picture of Thanatos ("Death") as a winged youth, armed with
a sword and of gentle mien, as he is depicted in the illustration of
the Alcestis legend that adorned one of the columns of the temple of
Artemis of Ephesus.[27] This failure of Greek artistic genius to create an
image of death that could be accepted as expressive of the general attitude
to this most disturbing of human experiences is certainly remarkable, when
we consider its success in providing acceptable representations of so many
other conceptions that stemmed from experience and the inspirations of
hope and fear. We can only hazard the suggestion that the cause of this
deficiency might reside in the fact that the Greeks envisaged death essentially as a natural process or event, and such a conception precluded
any convincing personalized representation of it.

It is instructive to note briefly, for the sake of comparison, the horrific

[27] It would be interesting to know how Thanatos was actually portrayed in performances
of Euripides' *Alcestis* in the Greek theatre. According to references in the play itself, Thanatos
is visibly seen (*ēdē de tonde thanaton eisorō pelas, hierē thanontōn, . . .* ll. 24–25), he is black-
robed (843), winged (261), and armed with a sword (74). Herakles also reports how in a realistic manner he forced Thanatos to surrender Alkestis: *tumbon par'auton ek lochou marpsas
cheroin* (1142). Although thus clearly personified and depicted as a grim being, Euripides'
portrait of Thanatos here differs notably from the Etruscan Charun (see below). The binding of
Death, which implies an effective degree of personification, also occurs in the Sisyphos legend:
cf. H. J. Rose, *Handbook of Greek Mythology* (London, 1928), p. 294.

Etruscan personification of death in the figure of Charun. This monster differs from both the Greek Charon and the Euripidean Thanatos in being represented with a most hideous countenance and armed with a hammer, with which he gives the death-blow. He is often depicted accompanied by an equally repulsive monster, Tuchulcha, who may incorporate some memory of the harpy.

VI

Our survey now enables us to evaluate the mythology of death in Early Christianity, although constriction of space here necessitates that we notice only the more significant aspects.

Since Christianity in its primitive form derived from Judaism, it was natural that Jewish conceptions of death should find expression in the earliest Christian documents. Of these documents the writings of Paul are especially notable for the range and variety of the imagery that could be employed. The conceptions generally lack precision in formulation, and they are often used with that ambiguity of meaning that characterizes so much of Paul's seminal thinking. Thus sin is generally represented to be the cause of death, and explicit reference is made to the Fall of Adam as the occasion of the entry of death into the world (*Rom.* v. 12–13); however, it is often uncertain whether Paul has in mind physical death or some form of spiritual death. In several places Paul appears to hypostatize death (*Thanatos*). Thus he declares that "Thanatos reigned from Adam to Moses" (*Rom.* v. 14). He apostrophizes death, undoubtedly with the words of Hosea in mind: "O Thanatos, where is thy sting (*kentron*)? O Hades, where is thy victory?" (1 *Cor.* xv. 55; cf. *Hosea* xiii. 14), and he proclaims that "the last enemy (*eschatos echros*) that shall be destroyed is Thanatos" (1 *Cor.* xv. 26). This last reference is particularly interesting, because it would seem that Paul must have been drawing here upon some idea of current Messianic eschatology. It presupposes the existence of a hierarchy of demonic beings, evidently hostile to God, that the Messiah would ultimately subjugate. Of this hierarchy, and presumably its strongest member, is Thanatos, whose fate is destruction.[28] We may well ask whether Paul really did thus think of death as a personified being, apparently self-existent and opposed to God. Such a being would indeed be tantamount to the Devil, and his existence would

---

[28] The earliest occurrence of the idea is in *Isa.* xxv. 8a.

surely imply what would virtually have been a dualistic *Weltanschauung*. Doubtlessly it would be unwise to follow out the logic of such implications; nevertheless, we should bear in mind Paul's many references to the *archontes*, the *stoicheia*, and to the *plērōma*, all of which indicate his easy familiarity with the esoteric concepts of a Gnostic hierarchy of supernatural powers.[29]

In the *Apocalypse of John* the same idea, namely, that in the *Endzeit* death will be destroyed, finds expression. In one of the two places where the idea occurs, death is clearly hypostatized, together with Hades, and the two are described as being cast into a lake of fire.[30] In another passage Thanatos is personified, being depicted as riding one of the four baleful horses that John sees in his vision of the tribulation of mankind (*Apoc.* vi. 8). We also meet in this work an interesting reminiscence of Egyptian thought, when we read that, in the extremity of their distress, men will seek Thanatos, but he will flee from them.[31]

It would appear that the essentially Jewish idea, which we meet here in Paul and the *Apocalypse*, that death, conceived as a hypostatized being, would be destroyed by divine action in the *Endzeit*, caught the imagination of Hellenistic Christians and led, curiously, to a development of Christian eschatology that actually contradicted Paul's view, as expressed in 1 *Corinthians* xv. 26, that the destruction of Thanatos would be the penultimate act of the *Endzeit*. Thus, by the time of the composition of 2 *Timothy*, it was apparently believed that Christ had already destroyed Thanatos, i.e. before his *Parousia* and the events that were to mark the *Endzeit* (2 *Tim.* i. 10). According to the second century *Epistle of Barnabas* and Justin Martyr,[32] Christ had achieved this destruction of Thanatos by his own dying and resurrection. This idea quickly becomes elaborated in the myth of Christ's triumphant descent into Hades, where he is vividly pictured as assaulting and overthrowing a thoroughly personified Thanatos.[33] In this so-called *Descensuskampf*-myth another significant development may also be noted, namely, that often Thanatos becomes identified with Satan, which causes him to be invested with all

---

[29] See Chapters 21 and 22.
[30] Apoc. xx. 14, xxi. 4. Cf. R. H. Charles, *The Revelation of St. John* (Edinburgh, 1920), ii. 199–200.
[31] Apoc. ix. 6. Cf. Charles, *op. cit.* 243–4, and above p. 35.
[32] Barn. v. 6; Justin, *Apol.* i. 64.
[33] Cf. Eusebius, *Dem. Evang.* 4, 12, 3f, in J. Kroll, *Gott und Hölle* (Leipzig and. Berlin, 1932), p. 9.

those strongly personalized attributes which it had become customary to ascribe to the personification of the principle of evil.[34] What influences or considerations induced this personification of death in Greek Christianity, seeing that in the pagan tradition the personification of Thanatos had been so singularly weak, are not apparent. Undoubtedly there was the tendency of the pious imagination thus to enhance the drama of salvation; but there is another interesting possibility that should be noted. There exists a certain amount of evidence that the early Christian apologists felt the need of presenting Christ as one greater than Hercules, because in the early Empire there was a revival of the cult of this ancient hero in a philosophized form. Hence, to the pagans' boast that Hercules had once contended with Thanatos and compelled him to relinquish his prey, it would have been helpful to the Christian cause to claim that Christ had done far more, in that through his own death and resurrection he had actually destroyed the dread enemy of men.[35]

However that may be, it is significant that it is in Egypt that we find the most thorough-going personification of death produced by Early Christianity. It occurs in a Coptic document known as the *History of Joseph the Carpenter*, the extant Coptic text of which appears to be a translation of a Greek original dating from about the end of the fourth century.[36] Like many pseudepigraphical works of this kind, it takes the form of a narrative in which Jesus is the principal speaker. Thus he is represented here as telling his disciples about the death of his foster-father, Joseph; it was an early tradition that Joseph had predeceased Jesus. The part of the story that specially concerns us tells how, just before the end, Jesus sees Death (in Coptic, *Mū*) enter the house, together with Amente (the personification of the ancient Osirian underworld), the Devil and other demons, who are come to torment the dying Joseph.[37] At the rebuke of Jesus these monsters are terrified and flee, and Death in particular is actually depicted as hiding himself behind the door.[38] When Joseph's

---

[34] *Acts of Pilate*, vii (xiii) in M. R. James, *The Apocryphal New Testament* (Oxford, 1926), p. 137; Pseudo-Melito, vii, in James, *op. cit.* pp. 212–13. Even if Charles (*op. cit.* i. 169–71) is right in concluding that Apoc. vi. 8b is an interpolation, the manuscript evidence shows it to have been an early one, and it has accordingly its significance for the association of Thanatos with Hades.

[35] Cf. M. Simon, *Hercule et le Christianisme* (Paris, 1955), pp. 112–15.

[36] Cf. S. Morenz, *Die Geschichte vom Joseph dem Zimmermann (Texte u. Untersuchungen*, 56, Berlin, 1951), pp. 23–34, 96, 101, 112.

[37] Sahidic text XIV, 1.

[38] Sahidic text, XXI, 8.

Transformation into Osiris. The deceased is the central figure, who is being directed by the jackal-headed Anubis to his *post-mortem* state of the mummiform Osiris, with whom he is ritually assimilated (from a mummy-shroud of Roman Egypt, Staatliche Museen, Berlin)

last moment comes, Death fears to enter the house again to fulfil his office of separating the dying man's soul from his body, and Jesus is obliged to go out and call him to do his necessary part, though warning him to act gently.[39]

Death could scarcely be more thoroughly personified than it is here, or represented in a more humiliating position. One is naturally curious as to what influences may have operated to have produced so remarkable a portrait. Professor S. Morenz, who has edited the text, has shown convincingly that the scene draws on both Jewish and Egyptian ideas.[40] In view of the inclusion of Amente in the company of the demons who visit the dying Joseph, it would seem reasonable to suppose that the Egyptian Christian responsible for the extant form of the work would

[39] Sahidic text XXIII, 6–8. *Mū* derives from the ancient Egyptian *mwt* (death); cf. W. Spiegelberg, *Koptisches Handworterbuch* (Heidelberg, 1921), p. 57.
[40] E. g. the Jewish parallels cited by Morenz, *op. cit.* pp. 65–6, 71, 80, to Death's hesitation to perform his office. Cf. M. Joseph in *Encycl. of Religion and Ethics*, viii. 41b.

have been more likely to have envisaged death, which he designates by the Coptic word *Mū*, in terms of his native tradition than in terms of Jewish thought, which in any case had no iconography. If this be a reasonable assumption, then we are faced with an interesting question. In describing death thus almost anthropomorphically, the Coptic author must have had some concrete image in his mind's eye—what form would it have taken? Two suggestions might be offered by way of an answer. It is possible that the author, familiar from childhood with the ideas and iconography of his people's ancient faith, would have conceived of Death in the form of Set, the ancient enemy beyond compare of Egyptian tradition. This possibility would, moreover, be greatly strengthened, if Morenz is right in his thesis that the purpose of the writing concerned here was to replace Osiris by Joseph as the pattern of holy dying at the time of the official suppression of paganism in Egypt;[41] for Set was the notorious slayer of Osiris and by a natural association of ideas he could easily have become the demon who came to torment and to slay the dying Joseph. The other possibility is that the Coptic author envisaged Death in the form of the jackal-headed god Anubis. Anubis was a very ancient Egyptian mortuary-god who had been absorbed into the complex of the Osirian myth and ritual. As such he was regarded as a benevolent deity who cared for the dead, as he had originally cared for the dead Osiris. However, by the Graeco-Roman period Anubis seems to have become essentially the *psychopompos*.[42] He frequently appears on mummy-wrappings in a significant scene in which three figures are represented. The figure on the left is in the Osirian mummiform, and evidently represents the deceased person as identified with Osiris. The central figure shows the deceased in his ordinary attire; to his left Anubis is depicted, with his arm around the shoulder of the dead man directing him towards the Osirian figure. The group has been convincingly interpreted as signifying the ritual transformation of the dead man into Osiris, with Anubis acting as the *psychopompos*.[43] Seen in such a context, Anubis seems to assume a more sinister guise than that which he had in the earlier tradition. He is now intimately associated with the event of death, and is virtually the one who leads men from life into death. His appearance in such scenes

---

[41] *Op. cit.* p. 34.

[42] Cf. Bonnet, *op. cit.*, sub "Anubis"; H. Herter in *Reallexikon für Antike und Christentum*, I, sub "Anubis."

[43] See S. Morenz, "Das Werden zu Osiris," in *Staatliche Museen zu Berlin, Forschungen und Berichte*, Band I (1957), 52–70.

"Time and Death", Gaetana Guili Zumbo (1656–1701). An interesting Baroque attempt to relate Time and Death as the ultimate arbiters of human destiny (Victoria and Albert Museum, London)

is also horrific, since he is coloured a dark blue or black, thus accentuating the fearsome aspect of his jackal's or dog's head. It is, accordingly, understandable that a Coptic Christian, familiar with such representations, might also have pictured Death in the awful shape of Anubis.

Here we may leave our enquiry. As a comparative study, it would seem to lead to one conclusion. That, whatever the nature of the eschatology concerned, among these ancient cultures a common tendency manifested itself to envisage death as the assault or the snatching away from life affected by some supernatural being. But the attempt to relate such a being to the theology of each culture concerned was never successful; in fact, with the possible exception of Iran, it was not seriously attempted and so constitutes the weakest point in the logic of each of the systems involved.[44]

44Attention may also be drawn to the Coptic document entitled the "Discourse on Abbatôn by Timothy, Archbishop of Alexandria" (in *Coptic Martyrdoms*, ed. E. A. Wallis Budge, British Museum, 1914), in which the origin of the angel of death is explained in terms of the *Genesis* creation story. The angel at first has the curious name of *Mŭriël*, which probably represents an attempt to present the Coptic word *Mŭ* ("death") with the customary ending of the names of angelic beings in Hebrew. On acquiring his grisly office, *Mŭriël* has his name changed by God to the Hebrew name of *Abbatōn*: cf. *op. cit.* fol. 22a. p. 241. This legend appears in Muslim tradition, accounting for Azra'il as the Angel of Death: cf. H. Schwarzbaum, "The Overcrowded Earth," in *Numen*, iv. 64–6.

CHAPTER 4

Time as God and Devil

Man's interpretation of the most enigmatic factor of his experience

I

Time is one of the most familiar, and yet one of the most mysterious, of the basic concepts of the human mind. St. Augustine perceived this long ago, and he defined the enigma in memorable words: "What then is time? If no one asks me, I know: if I wish to explain it to one that asketh, I know not: yet I say boldly, that I know, that if nothing passed away, time past were not; and if nothing were coming, a time to come were not; and if nothing were, time present were not. Those two times then, past and to come, how are they, seeing the past is not, and that to come is not yet? But the present, should it always be the present, and never pass into time past, verily it should not be time, but eternity." [1]

The enigma, which Augustine here describes in terms of its curious paradoxes, is but one of the aspects of Time as experienced by man. There is another aspect of it that is not enigmatical; indeed it makes its meaning clear with a ruthless unmistakable logic. It is the fact that Time manifests itself in change, decay and death. The dawning mind of the child soon grasps the fact he is living in a world where all things do not continue the same, and that change in his circumstances will often affect him personally, for good or ill. But this is not all: the child soon learns that people grow old and die. And he quickly perceives the

[1] *Confessions*, xi. 17 (trans. E. B. Pusey).

Heh: Egyptian figure symbolising millions of years or unending Time (from a chair found in the tomb of Tutankhamen)

significance of this knowledge for himself. His consciousness of Time causes him to envisage a future in which, he knows, his own death will inevitably occur. Hence, for him, as he grows older, the passage of Time appears increasingly menacing; for it threatens his sense of security and well-being in the most absolute manner, namely, by bringing ever nearer the extinction of his very self.

The experience of the child, which we have briefly sketched here, represents the experience of us all. Since the experience is common, we might, therefore, expect that reaction to it will show a common pattern. This it does; but the forms in which that reaction has most naturally found expression, namely, in religion have varied considerably. The pattern, that underlies this variety, reveals itself in a seeking for security from the effacing flux of Time, in an endeavour to find a safe refuge from Time's menace of decay and death. Thus, to give three examples for illustration: the ancient Egyptians believed that they would be eternally safe after death if they could join the sun-god, Rē, in his unceasing journey through the heavens;[2] in Buddhism security from Time has been sought by identifying it as the inexorable law to which all become subject who mistake this phenomenal world for reality; Christianity, through its doctrine of baptism, promises a new transcendental life through incorporation in Christ, its *summum bonum* being the eternal Vision of God.

This common quest for security from Time's menace, which has found such various expression in the religions of the world, naturally

[2] *Pyramid Texts*, 167, 775, 1453, 1477, 1466d. Cf. Brandon in *The Saviour God* (Manchester University Press, 1963), p. 19.

suggests that Time must be imagined in correspondingly different forms, and that these forms will indicate the estimate of Time's origin and nature held in each of the religions concerned. To examine and evaluate some of these conceptions of Time will be the object of this chapter.

II

It will be most convenient to begin our task by considering the interpretation of Time that finds expression in the *Bhagavad-Gītā*, the great religious epic of Hinduism. By so doing we shall at once become acquainted not only with a most impressive image of Time, seen in one of the great world-religions, but we shall be afforded insight into one of the most significant traditions concerning the nature and status of Time.

The *Bhagavad-Gītā*, which was probably composed in the third or second century B.C., is concerned to present the god Vishnu, in his form of Vāsudeva, as the supreme deity.[3] The poem takes the form of a dialogue between a prince Arjuna and his charioteer, who is Vishnu in disguise. The occasion is the eve of a battle, when Arjuna hesitates to commence the action, being appalled by the prospect of the slaughter that must result from so doing. In the course of the long dialogue which follows, the subject of human duty is discussed in terms of the doctrine of "samsāra", or the transmigration of souls. As the dialogue proceeds, Arjuna becomes aware of the identity of his companion, and he beseeches him to reveal his true self. Vishnu consents, and Arjuna sees a vision of deity as the beneficent Creator of the universe. Arjuna is profoundly impressed by this revelation of the immensity and multiplicity of the divine creative power. But he feels that he has not seen all; that there is yet another side to the supreme deity. He asks that this might also be shown to him. He is warned not to ask for this; but he persists and the revelation is given, and it is terrible. In profound terror, Arjuna beholds all forms of being passing swiftly to their destruction in the awful mouths of Vishnu. Horrified, he cries out: "Thy mouths with many dreadful fangs beholding, Like to Time's universal conflagration, I know the quarters not, I find no shelter. Be gracious, Lord of gods, the world's protector." Then Vishnu

<hr/>

[3] On the significance of the *Bhagavad-Gītā* see R. Garbe in *Encyclopaedia of Religion and Ethics* (ed. J. Hastings), ii. 535b–538b; J. Gonda, *Die Religionen Indiens* (Stuttgart, 1960), i. 267; R. C. Zaehner, *Hinduism* (Oxford, 1962), pp. 13–14; S. Radhakrishnan, *La Bhagavad-Gītā* (Paris, 1954), pp. 15–18; S. Dasgupta, *History of Indian Philosophy* (Cambridge, 1932), ii. 549–52.

answers: "Know I am Time, that makes the worlds to perish, when ripe, and brings on them destruction."[4]

Thus, in the culminating vision of this great spiritual epic of India, the supreme deity is revealed as being of ambivalent nature, manifesting himself as both the Creator and Destroyer of all that exists. To those of us who are nurtured in the Christian tradition of deity as being wholly the beneficent Creator, this Indian theophany appears strange and disturbing. Yet, on reflection, we have to recognize that it connotes a realistic evaluation of our experience of the universe; for we see therein the unceasing operation of two contrary processes, namely, of creation and destruction, of life and death. But the intuition that inspires this Hindu conception of supreme deity goes deeper; for it equates this deity with Time.

This deification of Time in the *Bhagavad-Gītā* is not unique when seen in the tradition of Indian thought, and to appreciate its full significance we must look at it in this wider context. The earliest traces of it are to be discerned in the liturgical hymns, known as the *Rig-Veda*, of those Aryan tribes who invaded northern India about the middle of the second millennium B.C. Many of these hymns are addressed to a god called Varuna, whose name suggests that he was originally connected with the heavens and regarded as the universal lord.[5] This deity was of an ambivalent nature. He was associated with Yama (death), and he was the guardian of "ṛta", the fundamental law or order of the universe. By virtue of his control of the basic pattern of things, Varuna was regarded as comprehending Time and so determining the destinies of men.[6] This early instinct to deify Time, or to associate it closely with the supreme deity, finds further expression in later Indian literature.

Thus, in the *Śvetāśvatara Upanishad*, the god Rudra, who personifies the destructive powers of nature, is exalted as the supreme deity, and is significantly associated with the process of cosmic creation and destruction which all existence in Time entails. For example, he is described

---

[4] *Bhagavad-Gītā*, xi. 25, 32; trans. E. J. Thomas, *The Song of the Lord* (Murray, 1948), pp. 85, 86. Cf. Radhakrishnan, *op. cit.* pp. 289–90, 292; Dasgupta, *op. cit.* ii. 528; F. Edgerton, *The Bhagavad Gītā* (Harvard University Press, 1952), ii. 51.

[5] Cf. C. Eliot, *Hinduism and Buddhism* (London, 1954), i. 60–62; Zaehner, *Hinduism*, pp. 35–42.

[6] On the ambivalent nature of Varuna see G. Dumézil, *Mitra-Varuna* (Paris, 1948), pp. 83–85; Gonda, I. 73–79, 227; R. C. Zaehner, *The Dawn and Twilight of Zoroastrianism* (London, 1961), pp. 66–68, 133, *Hinduism*, pp. 34–42; M. Eliade, *Images and Symbols* (London, 1961), pp. 92–103.

as the power that, "after creating the worlds, withdraws them at the end of Time."[7] He turns the "Brahma-wheel" of the cosmic process, for he is "kālakāra ", "the author of Time", although he also transcends (empirical) Time.[8] In the later *Maitrī Upanishad*, this last distinction is given a more philosophical presentation by invoking the concept of Brahman, the impersonal principle of reality. Thus it is stated: "There are, verily, two forms of Brahman, time and the timeless. That which is prior to the sun is timeless, without parts. For the year, verily, are these creatures produced. By the year, verily, after having been produced, they grow. In the year they disappear. Therefore, the year, verily, is Prajā-pati, is time, is food, is the abode of Brahman, is self. For thus it has been said: 'Time cooks (or ripens) all things, indeed is the great self. He who knows in what time is cooked, he is the knower of the Veda.'"[9]

It is interesting to note that, in subsequent speculation about the nature of reality, Indian thinkers sought to reconcile or harmonize its various aspects in terms of the concept of Tri-murti (the "Triple Form"), according to which the gods Brahma, Siva, and Vishnu severally represented the principles of creation, destruction, and preservation. The attempt, however, appears to have been something of an intellectual *tour de force* that never succeeded in catching the imagination of the peoples of India; it would seem that their experience of the teeming but destructive power of nature demanded a more vivid imagery.[10] Scope for such imagery they found particularly in the various manifestations of Śiva, as Rudra came later to be more commonly known as he gradually acquired, together with Vishnu, the chief place in the pantheon of Hinduism.

It is in Śiva that the ambivalence of deity, according to Indian notions, is seen in its most impressive form. Thus, in the omnipresent symbol of the "lingam", the mighty generative organ of the deity, Śiva is seen as the embodiment of the dynamic persistence of life, in all its teeming abundance and complexity of form. The other side of Śiva finds

[7] *Svetāśvatara Upanisad*, iii. 2, in *The Principal Upanisads*, trans. and ed. S. Radhakrishnan (Allen & Unwin, 1953), p. 725. On Rudra see S. Konow in *Lehrbuch der Religionsgeschichte*, A. Bertholet and Edv. Lehman (Tübingen, 4 Aufl., 1925), ii. 29–30.
[8] *Svet. Upan.*, vi. 1.
[9] *Maitrī Upan.*, vi. 15 (trans. Radhakrishnan, *op. cit.* p. 828). Cf. P. Deussen, *The Philosophy of the Upanishads* (E. T., Edinburgh, 1906), pp. 153–4; Zaehner, *Hinduism*, pp. 72, 96.
[10] Cf. Eliot, ii. 164–5; S. Konow in *op. cit.* ii. 66; Gonda, i. 354; A. L. Basham, *The Wonder that was India* (Sidgwick & Jackson, 1954), pp. 310–11.

expression when he is represented as Bhairava, "the terrible destroyer",
the ghoulish being that haunts cemeteries and places of cremation, and
appears wearing serpents about his head and a necklace of skulls.[11]
Significant also are some of his titles, e.g. Mahā-Kāla ("Great Time"),
and Kāla-Rudra ("all-devouring Time"). In the famous caves of Elephanta
he is portrayed with a terrible symbolism. Having many arms, according
to the sacred iconography of India, in one hand he holds a human figure;
in another a sword or sacrificial axe; in a third, a basin of blood; in a
fourth, a sacrificial bell; with two other hands he extinguishes the sun.
Significant, too, is the manner in which he is represented in a series of
South Indian bronzes, which date from the tenth and twelfth centuries
A.D. In these Siva appears in his rôle of Natarāja ("King of Dancers").
In this guise he performs the cosmic dance, symbolizing the energy of
the universe in its unceasing process of creating, sustaining, and destroying
every form of being in which it manifests itself.

From this deification of Time in the person of Śiva there stemmed
an even stranger imagery which is shocking to the Western mind, but
which it is necessary to seek to understand, if we are to grasp something
of the religious significance of Time. This imagery took its rise from
speculation about the name of Śiva. By a curious process of thought the
god's activating energy, his "śakti", was hypostatized as a goddess.[12] In
the consequent conception an ambivalence of the creative and the destructive, similar to that manifest in the character of Śiva, shows itself. However, interest has been concentrated on the grimmer aspect, with the result
that a being has been conceived that is truly demonic, although venerated
as divine. It takes the form of the goddess Kālī, who personifies Time,
"kālī" being the feminine form of the Sanscrit word "kāla" ("Time").
The appearance of this goddess is horrific: she is black, and wears a
chaplet of severed heads; in her many hands she holds the symbols of
her nature—the exterminating sword, scissors for cutting short the thread
of life, and the lotus-flower of eternal generation. She is often depicted
trampling on the corpse-like body of Śiva, from whom she has emanated.
The late Professor Zimmer graphically describes her: "She is black with
death and her tongue is out to lick up the world; her teeth are hideous
fangs. Her body is lithe and beautiful, her breasts are big with milk.

[11] Cf. Gonda, i. 256; Eliot, ii. 145; J. Dowson, *A Classical Dictionary of Hindu Mythology*
(London, 1950), pp. 45, 298.
[12] Cf. Zaehner, *Hinduism*, pp. 112–15; Gonda, i. 182, 258–9.

Kālī, the Hindu deification of Time. The goddess tramples upon the body of Siva; she is invested with symbols of her destructive powers (India Museum, London)

Paradoxical and gruesome, she is today the most cherished and widespread of the personalizations of Indian cult."[13]

In such a hideous and repulsive figure those nurtured in the Christian tradition must surely see a demon, a thing of pure evil. But Kālī, as we have just noted, is a goddess, the object of a popular devotion. The fact has a profound significance; for the cult of Kālī is clearly not an isolated phenomenon in the long tradition of Indian culture, but reflects a deeply rooted evaluation of existence. From the Vedic period the universe has been seen as the product of a force of ambivalent character, according to human estimate, but as such by an intrinsic logic that links creation with destruction, life with death. In India the creation of life, in all its diversity of forms, has been regarded instinctively as involving a corresponding destruction of these living forms, so that the rhythm of existence might be maintained. This process, viewed in terms of unceasing birth, growth, decay and death, is the "dharma" of the empirical world, and every living being is implicated in it.[14] The process is essentially counterbalancing: creation against destruction, life against death. However, since the destructive aspect is the more emotionally disturbing, it has been that

[13] H. Zimmer, *Myths and Symbols in Indian Art and Civilization* (New York, 1962), p. 215.
[14] On the concept of "dharma" in this connection see Zaehner, *Hinduism*, pp. 3, 134–63; E. Conze, *Buddhist Thought in India* (Allen & Unwin, 1962), pp. 92–106.

side, conceived in terms of Time, that has tended to predominate in the religious imagination. Hence Time has been equated with supreme deity or separately hypostatized in the form of Kālī, and in such forms it commands a widespread popular devotion.

This deification of Time in India, inspired as it has been by a realistic evaluation of experience, and expressive as it is of a fatalistic acceptance of the necessity of decay and death, has not, however, resulted in a religion of hopelessness and despair. A way of salvation has been elaborated through a metaphysic which distinguishes this empirical world as the product of a primordial "avidyā" or ignorance. By mistaking this world for reality, the soul becomes enmeshed in its processes, of which the most fundamental and comprehensive is that of Time. Consequently, it suffers old age, decay and death; and, since Time is cyclic in its movement, the unenlightened soul is doomed to a never-ending series of births and deaths, with all their attendant pain and suffering. Thus, so long as the soul continues to regard this world as real, it remains subject to Time and its grim logic. However, enlightenment can be achieved by a rigorous discipline of mind and body. Then the soul, knowing at last its true nature and destiny, frees itself from the desire for existence here, and, thereby, passes beyond the power of Time.

III

We have noted that the Aryan invaders of northern India worshipped a deity called Varuṇa, who was a high-god of ambivalent nature: he was closely associated with "ṛta", the basic order of the universe and with death. Now, there is reason for thinking that this Varuṇa was the Vedic version of an ancient high-god of the Aryan, or Indo-European peoples, because there are traces of such a deity in the religion of the ancient Iranians, who were also of the Aryan race. The detection or identification of the Iranian counterpart of such a deity is a task for highly specialized scholarship, and, although considerable research and discussion have been devoted to it, there is still much conflict of opinion among the authorities concerned. Since, however, the issue is highly relevant to our subject here, it is necessary that we should try to understand something of its nature.

In 1938 a Swedish specialist in Iranian studies, Professor Geo Widengren, set forth a case for believing that the ancient Iranians had

[15] G. Widengren, *Hochgottglauben im alten Iran* (Lund, 1938), pp. 266–310, in *Numen*, i (1954), 21–22, 40–41, ii (1955), 91; *Mani und der Manichaismus* (Stuttgart, 1961), p. 28.

a high-god in a deity called Zurvān.[15] The name Zurvān means Time, and its use can be traced back to the twelfth century B.C. Unfortunately, however, all the information that exists about the conception and cult of Zurvān comes from later Iranian sources, and some of it relates to a kind of Zurvanite heresy during the Sassanian period, and is, in consequence, suspect as evidence for the earlier form of the belief.[16]

The earliest certain evidence of the Iranian deification of Time comes, curiously, from a Greek writer, Eudemus of Rhodes, who was a disciple of Aristotle. Referring to the beliefs of the Iranians, he states: "Both the Magi and the whole Aryan race . . . call by the name "Space" (*topon*) or "Time" (*chronon*) that which forms an intelligible and integrated whole, and from which a good god (*theon agathon*) and an evil demon (*daimona kakon*) were separated out (*diakrithēnai*), or, as some say, light and darkness before these. Both parties, however, postulate, after the differentiation of undifferentiated nature, a duality of superior elements, the one governed by Oromasdes and the other by Areimanios."[17]

According to the witness of this statement, it would appear that by the fourth century B.C. information had reached the Greek world to the effect that the well-known deities of Iranian dualism, Ohrmazd (Oromasdes) and Ahriman (Areimanios) had been derived from what is termed an "intelligible and integrated whole" (*to noēton hapan kai to hēnōmenon*), which was equated with Time or Space. In the light of what is said about Zurvān or Time in the native Iranian sources, as we shall see, this statement of Eudemus could equally relate to a personification of Time as the progenitor of Ohrmazd and Ahriman or to metaphysical speculation about the primordial nature of Time.

The earliest indication in Iranian sources of a personification of Zurvān seems to be a passage in the *Vidēvdāt*, which, though part of the later *Avesta*, certainly incorporates much earlier traditions. The passage reads: "(The soul) of the wicked and the righteous alike proceeds along the paths created by Zurvān (Time) to the Cinvat bridge created by Mazdāh (Ohrmazd)."[18] Such a brief reference, without any explanation, to Zurvān in this eschatological context must surely imply that the deity

---

[16] Cf. R. C. Zaehner, *Zurvān, a Zoroastrian Dilemma* (Oxford, 1955), pp. 20, 88; U. Bianchi, *Zamān i Ohrmazd* (Turin, 1958), pp. 15–16.

[17] Cited by Damascius (*Dubitationes et solutiones de Principiis*, c. 125 bis), in J. Bidez and Fr. Cumont, *Les Mages hellénisés* (Paris, 1938), ii. 69 (15) 70.

[18] *Vidēvdāt*, 19, 29, in Zaehner, *Zurvān*, p. 275 (A.1), cf. pp. 87, 203–4. Cf. Biancho, pp. 101–2, 245.

and his significance were well known to those who would read the book. It suggests also that Zurvān was closely associated with both the death and the destiny of men.

That the primordial nature of Time was an inference from metaphysical reflection is attested by a late Persian writing entitled *Rivāyat;* whether it relates to a tradition of philosophical speculation reaching back as far as the fourth century B.C. cannot, however, be determined. The passage concerned, nevertheless, merits quotation, since it shows a considerable preoccupation with the nature of Time. Thus, it is argued, "it is obvious that, with the exception of Time, all other things have been created. For Time no limit is apparent, and no height can be seen nor deep perceived, and it (Time) has always existed and will always exist. No one with intelligence says: 'Time, whence comes it?' or 'This power, when was it not?' And there was none who could (originally) have named it creator, in the sense that is, that it (Time) had not yet brought forth the creation. Then it created fire and water, and, when these had intermixed, came forth Ohrmazd. Time is both Creator and the Lord of the creation which it created." [19]

The derivation of Ohrmazd and Ahriman from Zurvān, which Eudemus relates, would seem to indicate the existence of some ancient myth in which the derivation was set forth in an anthropomorphic imagery of creation or generation. Such a myth does indeed exist, but the evidence of it is very late and it is chiefly recorded by Christian and Islamic writers. According to these sources, Zurvān was conceived as the original god. Desiring to have a son who might create the universe, he offered sacrifice to this end for a thousand years. However, before the period was completed, Zurvān was assailed by doubt as to the efficacy of these sacrifices. The doubt was momentary, but it had fateful consequences. From it was generated another son, who partook of its dark nature. Eventually two sons were born to Zurvān. The one, who was Ohrmazd, was good and beautiful, and all that he created reflected his character. The other, Ahriman, was evil and ugly, and his creation was of the same nature.[20]

According to this myth, therefore, Time, deified as Zurvān, was the progenitor of the two opposing cosmic principles: good and evil, light and darkness, creation and destruction. Zurvān, thus, although not himself

---

[19] See Widengren, *Hochgottglaube,* p. 274. Cf. Zaehner, *Zurvān,* p. 410(8), see also p. 409.

[20] See the texts relating to the Zurvanite myth given by Zaehner, *Zurvān,* pp. 419–37.

ambivalent, was the source of that basic dualism, so clearly apparent in the cosmic process and so disturbingly evident in the experience of men. Just how ancient is this myth is unknown. There is no sign of it in the teaching of Zarathustra, the founder of Zoroastrianism, as that teaching has been preserved in the *Gathas*. However, it is significant that Zarathustra represented the two opposing cosmic principles, personified respectively as the Spenta Mainyu and the Angra Mainyu, as the creation of Ahura Mazdāh, the "Wise Lord", as he described the supreme deity. There is also some evidence for thinking that the conception of Ahura Mazdāh may have derived ultimately from an original Indo-European sky-god, of whom the memory survived in Vedic literature in the form of Varuṇa, as we have seen. Such a derivation would explain Zarathustra's presentation of Ahura Mazdāh as the creator of the two principles that unceasingly oppose each other in the universe. It would also help to explain the statement of Eudemus, writing in the fourth century B.C., that the Persians regarded Time as the ultimate source of cosmic dualism personified in Oromasdes (Ohrmazd) and Areimanios (Ahriman).

In view of the nature of the evidence, at this point we must content ourselves with leaving the problem of the origin of the Iranian deification of Time. However, we have further evidence of how the Iranians did conceive the nature of Time, and it is of the highest significance. They distinguished two forms or aspects of Time. The one they named Zurvān "akarana", i.e. Infinite Time; the other they designated Zurvān "dareghō-chvadhāta", which meant the Zurvān "who for a long time follows his own law", or "Time of the long Dominion".[21] In other words, they conceived of a Time that is boundless, without beginning or end, and a Time, which, though of long duration, was definitively limited. These two forms of Time were subjects of much speculation, the most notable results of which, from our point of view was that Zurvān "dareghō-chvadhāta" was derived from Zurvān "akarana", and its dominion was set at twelve thousand years. This form of Time, i.e. Finite Time, was regarded as that under which mankind lives in this world. Thus it is described in the *Bundahishn:* "through Time must the decision be made. By Time are houses overturned—doom is through Time—and things graven shattered. From it no single mortal man escapes, not though he fly above, nor though he dig a pit below and dwell therein, not though

---

[21] Cf. Zaehner, *Zurvān*, pp. 57, 87, *Dawn and Twilight*, pp. 236-7.

he hide beneath a well of cold waters."[22] It is this form of Time that brings old age, decay and death to all men, as another Pahlavī text graphically depicts its activity: "As to him whose eyes Time has sewn up, his back is seized upon and will never rise again; pain comes upon his heart so that it beats no more; his hand is broken so that it grows no more, and his foot is broken so that it walks no more. The 'stars came upon him, and he goes not out another time: fate came upon him, and he cannot drive it off." [23]

In this division of Time into two separate personifications, namely, Zurvān "akarana" and Zurvān "dareghō-chvadāta", we may perhaps discern an originally ambivalent conception of deity such as we have noted in Hinduism in the gods Vishnu and Śiva. However, it would appear that in later Iranian thought, Ohrmazd, i.e. the Ahura Mazdāh of Zara-thustra, came to be identified with Zurvān "akarana" ("Infinite Time"), while Ahriman, the evil principle, was equated with Finite Time, i.e. Zurvān "dareghō-chvadhāta".[24] These equations were destined to have a significance far outside the land of their origin, for they were carried into the world of Graeco-Roman culture by the cult of Mithra.

Evidence of this transportation of so essentially an Iranian concept of Time to the West is found in a most impressive form. In many Mithraic sanctuaries there have been discovered statues of a monstrous being, having a lion's head upon a human body.[25] Most of these images are horrific, for the hideous appearance of the lion's head is accentuated by a huge serpent that coils about the monster's body. The figure is winged, and holds in its hands a long staff and keys; sometimes the emblem of a thunderbolt is shown on its breast, and the signs of the zodiac upon its body. Such symbols evidently denote that this fantastic being had some astrological significance, particularly in connection with fate or destiny. The identity of this monster is not indicated by any inscription on the statues concerned; but their symbolism had already led the Danish anti-

---

[22] In i. 25 trans. Zaehner, *Zurvān*, pp. 239, 315; cf. pp. 57, 95, 96–100, 106.

[23] In Zaehner, *Zurvān*, pp. 240–1, 398–9; see also in *Bulletin of the School of Oriental and African Studies*, XVII/2 (1955), 233. Cf. Biancho, pp. 99–100.

[24] Cf. Zaehner, *Dawn and Twilight of Zoroastrianism* (1961), pp. 175–84.

[25] Cf. Fr. Cumont, *Textes et Monuments figurés relatifs aux Mystères de Mithra*, i. 74, nn. 2 and 3; M. J. Vermaseren, *Corpus Inscriptionum et Monumentorum Religionis Mithriacae* (The Hague, 1956), Fig. 29a, b, 35, 36, 86, 89, 90, 109, 116(?), 125, 144, 152, 153, 156, 157, 188, 197, 210, 211, 227, 230; R. Pettazzoni, *Essays on the History of Religions* (Leiden, 1954), pls. VI–IX, XII. The statues appear to have stood outside the adyton, cf. Duchesne-Guillemin in *Numen*, ii. 191.

Zurvān-Ahriman: Mithraic conception of "Time of the Long Dominion" (Vatican Museum). The lion's head symbolizes the all-devouring nature of Time; the entwined snake denotes the tortuous course of the sun's ecliptic, while the signs of the zodiac on the monster's body indicate Time's association with fate

quary Zoëga, in the eighteenth century, to suggest that they were representations of the Greek concept of Aiōn. A more accurate interpretation was made later by Franz Cumont, the great Belgian authority on Mithraism. Seeing in the symbolism evident reference to Time, he identified the figure with Zurvān "akarana", since this was the Iranian personification of Time and Mithraism was of Iranian origin.[26] Cumont was certainly correct in thinking that the monster represented Zurvān; but it would seem that he was mistaken in identifying it with Infinite Time, with Zurvān "akarana"; for the lion's mask surely indicates "Time that devours all", in other words, Zurvān "dareghō-chvadhāta".[27]

That this form of Zurvān should figure in the iconography of Mithraism may, at first sight, seem surprising, especially since it has no

[26] *Textes et Monuments*, i. 78, cf. p. 301. Cf. Cumont, *Les religions orientales dans le paganisme romain* (Paris, 1939), pp. 140, 277, n. 46.
[27] Cf. Zaehner, *Zurvān*, pp. viii–ix, *Dawn and Twilight*, pp. 129–30; Duchesne-Guillemin, *Ormazd et Ahriman* (Paris, 1953), pp. 126–8, in *Numen*, ii (1955), 190–5.

The Orphic deity Phanes, invested with much of the symbolism of the Mithraic Time-god (bas-relief from Modena, c. 2nd cent. A.D.)

apparent connection with Mithra in his characteristic act of slaying the Cosmic Bull. A clue to the mystery may, however, be provided by what Plutarch tells us of Persian dualism. According to his account, Mithra was connected in a mediating rôle with Ohrmazd and Ahriman, and votive offerings and thank-offerings were made to Ohrmazd and "averting and mourning offerings (*apotropaia kai skuthrōpa*) to Ahriman".[28] This means that Ahriman was venerated or, at least, propitiated in rites in which Mithra was recognized as the "Mediator" (*ho mesitēs*). If Ahriman was thus recognized, and images of Zurvān "dareghō-chvadhāta", with whom Ahriman was associated or identified, were placed in Mithraic sanctuaries, it would be reasonable, also, to suppose that Mithraism took account of

[28] *De Iside et Osiride,* 46. Cf. Bidez-Cumont, ii. 70–74.

this aspect of Time. What this signified seems reasonably clear: the dominion of Zurvān "daregho-chvadhāta" extended over all who lived in this world, and they were subject to his inexorable law of old age, decay and death. If Mithra was the Mediator, as Plutarch says, between Ohrmazd and Ahriman, he, therefore, mediated in some manner between the two forms of Time which these two deities severally personified. In what manner he did this is not known; but his slaying of the Cosmic Bull was undoubtedly regarded as providing new life or immortality for those who were initiated into his mysteries. And such provision would surely have been tantamount to salvation from the dominion of "Time the Destroyer"; in turn, the endowment of immortality would mean that the initiates were brought into communion with Ohrmazd, who was Zurvān "akarana" or Infinite Time.[29]

IV

Evidence of the deification of Time in ancient Greek religion is problematical except where Orphism is concerned, and here signs of Iranian influence seem to be very evident. The most notable instance occurs in a bas-relief, now at Modena, depicting Phanes, a key figure of Orphic mythology. The deity is shown as a nude male figure, standing on an inverted cone from which flames shoot forth, with a similar object above his head—these cones undoubtedly represent two sections of the cosmic egg from which Phanes, the personification of light emerged at the beginning, according to Orphic cosmogony. The figure of Phanes, however, is entwined about by a serpent, and is winged; the feet, moreover, are not human but bestial in form. On the breast the heads of a ram, a lion and a goat are depicted, while the emblem of a thunderbolt is held in the right hand and a long regal staff in the left. Thus, except that the head is human and not that of a lion, the figure is strikingly reminiscent of the Mithraic images of Zurvān "daregho-chvadhāta". The similarity of the iconography is reinforced by an obvious emphasis upon the symbolism of Time; for, in an oval band about the figure of Phanes, the signs of the zodiac are represented in high relief, while the proportions of the cosmos are indicated in the corners by images of the four winds.

The syncretism, which thus finds expression in this Modena sculpture, is not unique; it is in effect a particularly eloquent example of that

---

[29] Cf. Duchesne-Guillemin in *Numen*, ii. 194; Zaehner, *Dawn and Twilight*, pp. 127–30, *Zurvān*, p. 312, cf. pp. 231–2, 234.

complex fusion of ideas and imagery, current in the world of Graeco-Roman culture, which became embodied in the various esoteric cults or pseudo-philosophies known as Gnosticism. The nature of Time constituted an important aspect of the basic problem with which the Gnostics were concerned, namely, to account for the involvement of spirit with matter. The general line along which they formulated their solution was that of the primordial descent or fall of some spiritual entity from its transcendental status and its imprisonment in the physical world. But this solution necessarily required that some explanation should be given of the origin and nature of this lower physical world. This was provided by representing the world, in which mankind finds itself living, as the creation of a power, a Demiurge, of lower status than God, and generally regarded as hostile to the Supreme Deity. Since this demonic creator was lord of the world which he had made, men were subject to him and his laws determined their destiny, until by initiation into the true "gnosis", or knowledge of their situation, they acquired the means of escape from his dominion. Thus a dualistic *Weltanschauung* was propounded, comprising a higher and a lower world, each with its own lord, which is very reminiscent of Iranian dualism. In fact so close is the parallelism that it is not surprising to find in some Gnostic documents that the "prince of this world" is clearly identified with Zurvān "dareghō-chvadhāta", i.e. "Time of the long Dominion", as in Mithraism, as we have just seen. Thus, in the recently discovered Coptic writing entitled the *Apocryphon of John*, it is related that Sophia (i.e. Wisdom) gave birth to a monstrous being which had the form of a serpent and a lion; its name was Jaldabaôth.[30] In turn this Jaldabaôth created a number of beings, including the seven planets to rule the heavens. He is also described as proclaiming that he was the sole lord of the universe: this claim strikingly recalls that made by the Devil in the Gospel account of the Temptation of Jesus.[31] It is also related that Jaldabaôth took counsel with his demonic assistants, and "they caused 'Heimarmenē' (Destiny) to come into being, and they bound the gods of the heavens, the angels, demons, and men by means of measure, epochs and times, so that all came within 'Heimarmenē's' fetter, who is lord over all."[32] In other words, this

---

[30] Cf. W. C. van Unnik, *Evangelien aus dem Nilsand* (Frankfurt-am-Main, 1960), p. 195, cf. p. 86. Cf. J. Doresse, *The Secret Books of the Egyptian Gnostics* (London, 1960), pp. 174–5.

[31] *Apocryphon of John*, 44.14–15. Cf. Luke, iv. 5–6.

[32] *Apocryphon of John*, 72.3–10, in van Unnik, *op. cit.* p. 198, cf. pp. 88–89.

Jaldabaôth is represented as controlling the universe, including mankind, by the time-process. This identification, or association, of the evil Demiurge with Time found expression also in the doctrine of a Gnostic sect called the Marcosians. According to the account of their teaching given by Irenaeus: "In addition to these things, they declare that the Demiurge, desiring to imitate the infinitude, and eternity, and immensity, and freedom from all measurement by time of the Ogdoad above, but, as he was the fruit of defect, being unable to express its permanence and eternity, had recourse to the expedient of spreading out its eternity into times, and seasons, and vast numbers of years, imagining that by a multitude of such times he might imitate immensity. They declare further, that the truth having escaped him, he followed that which was false, and that, for this reason, when the times are fulfilled, his work shall perish." [33]

The references which we have met to the planets and signs of the **zodiac in the course of our brief survey of the relevant aspects of** Mithraism, Orphism, and Gnostic beliefs, reflect the immense influence which astrology had on Graeco-Roman society. The subject, however, is too vast even to attempt to outline here; but we may note that the **stars, or the demonic powers associated with them, were believed to**

[33] Irenaeus, *Adv. Haer.*, i. 17.2; trans. A. Roberts and W. H. Rambaut.

Jaldabaôth. A Gnostic conception of the cosmic Creator, who was associated with Time. The conception possibly derives from the Mithraic Zurvān-Ahriman (engraved Gnostic amulet)

control the destinies of men, while their movements through the heavens determined times and seasons. It is significant, therefore, that in the Christian forms of Gnosticism it was taught that the advent of the Saviour disrupted the courses of the stars, thereby breaking the pattern of their control over the lives of men.[34]

The career of the Iranian concept of Infinite Time, Zurvān "akarana", in the Graeco-Roman world also affords a fascinating subject of study. Here we must content ourselves with noting some of its more remarkable features. At Alexandria the concept appears in early Ptolemaic times under the name of Aiōn, and, in a personified form, it was associated with the state-gods, Sarapis-Helios and Agathos-Daimon.[35] This associa- tion of Aiōn with Sarapis is particularly interesting, since Sarapis was a chthonian deity, connected with or derived from Osiris, the ancient Egyptian mortuary god. Sarapis was also associated with the Greek god Kronos, who was often identified with "Chronos", i.e. Time. It is sig- nificant, therefore, to learn, on the authority of Macrobius, that the statue of Sarapis at Alexandria was accompanied by the image of a three-headed monster. Each of these heads had, according to Macrobius, a temporal significance. The central head, that of a lion, represented "Time present" ("praesens tempus"), because, situated between the past and the future, by its immediacy it constituted reality. The head to the left was that of a wolf; it signified "Time past" ("praeteritum tempus"), since the memory of past events is swallowed up and destroyed. The head on the right side was that of a fawning dog, and it represented "future Time" ("futurum tempus"), which lures men forward with vain hopes.[36]

How far such esoteric imagery was understood, and reflected a widespread preoccupation with the significance of Time, may be doubted. This estimate seems also to be necessary in connection with the concept of Aiōn, when it found its way to Rome, where it was easily assimilated with the old Roman idea of Time as the double-faced deity Janus.[37] The best known representation of this form of Infinite Time is that on the base of the column of Antoninus Pius in Rome. Aeternitas, to give the

---

[34] Cf. H.-C. Puech in *Man and Time* (*Papers from the Eranos Yearbooks*) (ed. J. Campbell, Routledge, 1958), pp. 60–61, n. 28.

[35] Cf. Sasse in *Reallexikon für Antike und Christentum*, i. 195–6; Pettazzoni, pp. 171–3.

[36] Macrobius, *Sat.*, i. 20, 13. Cf. Pettazzoni, pp. 164–70; *Bilderatlas zur Religions- geschichte* (9–11 Lieferung, hrg. J. Leipoldt), Abb. 13, pp. iv–v.

[37] Cf. Sasse in *op. cit.*, i. 197; K. Latte, *Römische Religionsgeschichte* (Munich, 1960), p. 136, n. 2.

The Dance of Death (after Holbein). These scenes illustrate the ubiquity of Death, the victims here being a queen and a soldier. Death is portrayed, according to medieval tradition, as a skeleton with a dart; but the hour-glass shows that it is now associated with Time

concept its Roman name, is here visualized as a heroic male figure, nude, with the majestic wings of an eagle, and holding in its left hand a globe encircled by serpents.[38] However, it may well be questioned whether such an allegorical figure really conveyed more than a rather artificially constructed interpretation of Time.

V

Christianity, true to its Hebraic heritage, could not deify Time, but only regard it as an aspect of divine activity. Consequently, in the iconography of early and medieval Christianity, Time acquired no recognized form of representation. By the sixteenth century, however, as some of the scenes in the Holbein version of the "Dance of Death" attest, Time was identified with Death by representing this grim figure with an hour-glass. In Renaissance art the figure of Father Time appears, conceived as Time the Destroyer, being an aged man, winged, and bearing the baleful scythe and hour-glass. This conception seems to have derived from the classical representation of Saturn or Kronos. However, although the figure of Father Time has established itself in Western tradition, it remains essentially an allegorical creation, lacking the emotive power of the Iranian

[38] See G. Bendinelli, *Compendio di Storia dell'Arte etrusca e romana* (Milan, 1931), p. 324, Fig. 249.

The triumph of Time, attributed to Jacopo del Sellaio. A Renaissance conception of Father Time (Fiesole, Oratorio di S. Ansano)

figure of Zurvān "daregho-chvadhāta", or that of Śiva in Hinduism, or that of the medieval personification of Death.

We may perhaps fittingly bring to a close this survey of the manner in which Time has been conceived as both God and Devil by quoting a passage from the medieval Persian poet, Firdausi. It is a description in which is clearly intermingled the imagery of many traditions: "Concerning the desert and that man with the sharp scythe, and the hearts of moist and dry are in terror of him; moist and dry alike he mows down, and if thou make supplication, he hears thee not. This is the wood-cutter Time, and we are like the grass. Alike to him is the grandson, alike to him the grandsire; he takes account of neither old nor young; whatever prey comes before him, he pursues. Such is the nature and composition of the world that save for death no mother bore a son. He enters at one door and passes out through another: Time counts his every breath."[39]

[39] *Šahnameh*, trans. J. Mohl, in Zaehner, *Zurvān*, pp. 445–6.

CHAPTER 5

The Idea of the Soul

THE HISTORY OF MAN'S MOST FUNDAMENTAL CONCEPT

Part I: In the West

According to the ancient religions of the Near East,
every man possessed a double nature, compounded of physical
and psychical elements, each an essential adjunct of his life.

In 1871 Sir Edward Burnett Tylor, often called the "father of modern anthropology", published a work entitled *Primitive Culture*. It proved to be epoch-making; for he set forth therein belief in "Spiritual Beings" as a "minimum definition of Religion". This theory, which he named "animism", has had a wide currency since as a convenient explanation of primitive forms of human culture.

Tylor naturally derived his term "animism" from the Latin word *anima*, meaning "spirit" or "soul". He argued that men, at an early stage of cultural development, would have wondered about what makes a living body different from a dead one. Also that they would have been puzzled about their experience of dreams: that in sleep they seemed to be able to leave their bodies and go on journeys and sometimes see those who were dead. Reflecting on such things, primitive peoples would naturally have concluded that a kind of inner self or soul dwelt in the body during life, departing from it temporarily in sleep and permanently at death. This soul would have been conceived as a shadowy intangible replica of the

69

living person, being closely connected with the animating breath and
departing with the last breath at death. According to Tylor, from this
conception of the soul as the animating principle in the human person,
early man was led on to attribute a soul to various forms of natural
phenomena that seemed to be alive: hence arose, in due course, the idea
of a sun-god, a moon-goddess, or a god of fire.

II

Since Tylor wrote, much more has been learned of the beliefs of
early man through archaeological and anthropological research, and
through increasing knowledge of ancient languages and the discovery of
more ancient texts. Today we are in a better position to trace out the
early forms and development of this most fundamental concept of mankind: the idea of the soul.

From the *Pyramid Texts* of Egypt we obtain our earliest insight,
through the medium of writing, into man's ideas about the constitution
of his nature: some traditions preserved there go back to the fourth
millennium B.C. As we read these *Texts*, designed to secure the safe passage
of the dead Pharaohs to the next world, it is evident that we have to
do with a tangle of primitive speculation about various aspects of human
personality.

The Egyptians already, at this remote period, conceived of man as
something more than a physical body. The body was indeed regarded
as an essential constituent of life; but there were other entities that were
equally vital. The two most emphasized were the *ka* and the *ba;* their
exact meanings are difficult to comprehend, and we may well wonder
whether the Egyptians themselves could have given a clear explanation
of them. Generally it would seem that the *ka* was·regarded as a kind
of double of the living person and acted as a protective genius: it was
represented by a hieroglyphic sign of two arms upstretching in a gesture
of protection. According to the later evidence of a bas-relief depicting
the divine birth of the Pharaoh Amenhotep III (1405–1370 B.C.), the
ka was envisaged as an exact replica of the individual, being created
together with him and reproducing in its form each stage of growth from
infancy to maturity. Provision had to be made for it at death, and the
tomb was called the *het ka,* "house of the *ka*". Of what substance it
was thought to be compounded is unknown; and it is difficult to be sure
whether the Egyptians believed that it could be seen or touched. The

The soul (*ba*) of Ani visits his mummified body (from the *Book of the Dead*)

ba, which is usually described as the "soul" in modern works on ancient Egyptian culture, was represented in art as a human-headed bird: the head being featured as male or female to correspond to the sex of the person concerned. Its representation as a bird was probably meant to suggest that it was a free-moving entity, untrammelled by the physical limitations of the body. In the vignettes that illustrate the so-called *Book of the Dead*, dating from about 1450 B.C., the *ba* is often depicted perched on the portal of the tomb, or watching the fateful *post-mortem* weighing of its heart, or flying down the tombshaft to visit the embalmed body in its sepulchre below. As with the *ka*, it is uncertain whether the Egyptians thought of the *ba* as a wholly spiritual entity, invisible and intangible. Some texts speak of the *ba* separating from the body at death; but it does not appear to have been conceived as the essential self or the animating principle.

When the ancient Egyptian view of human nature and destiny is considered as a whole, it is very evident that the individual person was regarded as a psycho-physical organism, no constituent part being more essential than another. The elaborate mortuary ritual, that was practised in Egypt for some three thousand years, envisaged a reconstitution of the

person after death. Hence the long process of embalmment to prevent
the decomposition of the corpse, and the subsequent ceremony of the
"Opening of the Mouth", whereby it was magically revivified and given
back its ability to take nourishment, so that it could live on in its tomb,
with its *ba* and *ka*, receiving mortuary offerings of food and drink. The
after-life was never etherealized in the Egyptian imagination, as it has
been in those cultures where the soul alone was regarded as the essential
self, able to exist happily apart from the body. This Egyptian evidence,
however, witnesses to a significant fact: as soon as we have insight into
the human mind through the medium of writing, we find that concepts
have already been elaborated to account for man's intuition that he is
more than a body of flesh and blood.

Turning to the other centre of civilization in the ancient Near East,
Mesopotamia, we meet a very different situation. Here it was believed
that mankind had been made to serve the gods by building temples and
providing them with offerings. But the gods had been careful to withhold
immortality from their human servants. The belief finds succinct expression in one of the most moving passages of the great *Epic of Gilgamesh:*

> (for) when the gods created mankind,
> They allotted death to mankind,
> (But) life they retained in their keeping.[1]

The Mesopotamians, nevertheless, were not complete materialists.
Like the Egyptians, they regarded man as a psycho-physical organism;
but, unlike them, they conceived of the psychical part as a single entity.
This, in the Akkadian tongue, was called the *napištu,* which, originally
meaning "throat", was extended to denote "breath", "life", and "soul".
This *napištu,* however, was not thought of as the inner essential self; rather
was it the animating or life principle. What became of the *napištu* at
death is obscure. Although they did not believe in human immortality,
the ancient Mesopotamians did believe in a kind of *post-mortem* survival.
This may, at first sight, seem a curious contradiction in terms. Actually,
it attests the strength of man's primitive inability to conceive of death
as personal extinction. From the very emergence of *homo sapiens* in the
Upper Palaeolithic period (*c.* 30,000 B.C.), his burial practices prove that
he did not accept death as final, but assumed that the dead would in
some way live on in the grave. Indeed, the history of religions shows

[1] Tab. X, col. ii, 3–5. See Chapter 10.

that the idea of complete personal extinction in death can only be conceived by a sophisticated mind, as, for example, by the philosopher Epicurus (341–270 B.C.). The ancient Mesopotamians had no such sophistication; accordingly they believed that at death some part of the personality did survive the dissolution of the body. But this was not the *napištu*, as might seem natural. Instead, it was believed that death wrought a terrible change in the living person; for he was transformed into an *etimmu*. The word *etimmu* is usually translated "ghost"; but it was not a ghost in the traditional sense, that is to say, an insubstantial wraith of the departed. The *etimmu* needed to be nourished by mortuary offerings, and it had the power to torment the living, if it were neglected; indeed, among the most feared beings of Mesopotamian demonology were the *etimmu*'s of those who had died unknown and received no proper burial rites. But, even when well provided with mortuary offerings, the fate of the dead was grim. They dwelt in *kur-nu-gi-a*, "the land of no-return", "where dust is their food and clay their substance . . . where they see no light and dwell in darkness".[2] It would truly seem that the ancient Mesopotamians might have spared themselves much mental anguish, if they could have conceived of death as complete personal annihilation. That they could not reveals the strength of the primitive conviction that there is something in man's constitution that survives the death of his body.

III

The evolution of the idea of the soul in ancient Greece is especially instructive; it has the additional significance that certain of its aspects profoundly influenced the Christian view.

In pre-Hellenic times, throughout the Aegean area, the evidence of burial customs points to a belief that the dead lived on in a subterranean world, where they were in the care of the Earth Mother, the Great Goddess. There is also some evidence of a Cretan island-paradise, to which the dead needed to be ferried—the idea may be reflected in the later Greek conception of the Isles of the Blessed and the Garden of the Hesperides.[3]

Hellenic thought, however, as it first finds expression in the Homeric poems, envisages a very different situation. In these writings, which

[2] *Epic of Gilgamesh*, Tab. VII, col. iv. 37, 39.
[3] Representations of butterflies found on various Aegean objects have been interpreted as symbols of the soul.

exercised so profound an influence on Greek thought, human nature was regarded as compounded of three entities: the body, the *psychē*, and the *thymos*. The *psychē* was identified with the life-principle, and it was located in the head. The *thymos* was essentially "mind" or "consciousness"; it seems to have been located in the *phrenes*, a term that probably designated the lungs. During the lifetime of the individual, the *thymos* was clearly the more important of these two constituents and represented what, in common parlance, we would call the personality. But at death it was the *psychē*, not the *thymos*, that survived. The *psychē* was then transformed into the *eidōlon*, the insubstantial image or shade of the former living person. In Homer's *Odyssey* the dissolution caused by death and the fate of the *thymos* and *psychē* are graphically described in a passage that tells of the tragic meeting of Odysseus and his dead mother, Anticleia. The hero had endeavoured in vain to embrace her shadowy form; then he cries out: "Is this but a phantom (*eidōlon*) that Queen Persephone (mistress of the underworld) has sent me, that I may lament and groan the more?" The shade of his mother sadly replies: "O me, my child, ill-fated beyond all other men, Persephone, daughter of Zeus, doth not deceive thee, but this is the way with mortals when they die: the sinews no more hold together the flesh and bones, but they are over-mastered by the force of the strong burning fire, as soon as the life (*thymos*) has left the white bones, and the shade (*psychē*) hovers like a dream and flits away."[4]

This rather remarkable view of the constitution of human nature means that the conscious self was not thought to survive death—an inference confirmed by what Homer tells of the state of the dead in Hades. Odysseus, on his visit there, found that the shades, though recognizable by their form, were bereft of consciousness of their past selves; they could gain a momentary recollection only by partaking of the blood of the sacrificed animal—a primitive notion based on belief that blood is the life-substance.

This Homeric view of human nature and destiny underwent a significant change by the sixth century B.C. The distinction between the *thymos* and *psychē* was not maintained, and the *psychē* came to be regarded as the inner essential self, being both the seat of consciousness and the life-principle. The Ionian philosopher Anaximenes (*c.* 500 B.C.), who held that air was the principle of all existence, spoke of the *psychē* as

---

[4] *Odyssey*, XI. 204–22; trans. (with slight changes) by F. M. Cornford, *Greek Religious Thought* (Dent, 1924), pp. 17–18.

"being air, (it) holds us together and controls us.". The poet Pindar (518–438 B.C.) had an even more exalted view of the *psyché:* he maintained that it was of divine origin, and, thereby, immortal.

This higher evaluation of the soul or *psyché* was gradually elaborated in certain circles until it reached its distinctive, and profoundly influential, form in the philosophy of Plato (428–347 B.C.). The intervening stages of development are obscure; but most significant are the conceptions ascribed to Pythagoras (*c.* 531 B.C.), Empedocles (*c.* 493–433 B.C.), and to the initiates of Orphism. An anecdote, satirizing the teaching of Pythagoras, tells how once, on seeing a puppy being whipped, moved with pity, Pythagoras had exclaimed: "Stop, don't beat it; for it is the soul (*psyché*) of a friend that I recognize when I hear its yelping." The story gibes at the implied doctrine of metempsychosis or the transmigration of souls. Further aspects of this doctrine are revealed in an account of the teaching of Empedocles: "Empedocles held that the soul enters the forms of every sort of animal and plant. He says: 'For I have been ere now a boy and a girl, a bush, a bird, and a dumb fish of the sea.' "[5]

The idea of metempsychosis is based on a view of the soul as the inner essential self, independent of the body it inhabits and able to survive its death. Having this innate indestructibility, the soul is thought to pass through many incarnated forms, which may not necessarily all be human. As the quotations concerning Pythagoras and Empedocles show, it was believed that the soul might dwell in plant and animal forms, and yet retain its identity, and, according to Empedocles, recollect its past states. There has been much discussion among scholars as to the origin of this idea in ancient Greece. Since the doctrine of the transmigration of souls is a fundamental tenet of Indian thought, much attention has been given to the possibility that the Greek thinkers derived the idea from India, by way of Persia, with which there was much contact.[6] But such a connection has never been established; and the fact that Zoroastrianism taught no such view would seem to be against it. The idea that souls migrate from one type of body to another might well have stemmed from early forms of Greek speculation about the primary material of the cosmos: we have seen that Anaximenes thought of the soul as being composed of air, which for him was the cosmic principle.

In the mystical philosophy known as Orphism, which profoundly

[5] Diogenes Laertius, viii. 77; trans. Cornford, *op. cit.*, p. 72.
[6] The Indian view of the soul is to be dealt with in Chapter 6.

affected many aspects of Greek thought, the soul's incarnation in various bodies was seen as a penalty incurred for some original sin. The soul, being by nature spiritual and of divine origin, was incarcerated in the physical body and in danger of being polluted by it. The soul's plight is vividly described by Plato in a passage about Orphic belief, with which he clearly had great sympathy:

> "Some say that the body (*sōma*) is the tomb (*sēma*) of the soul (*psychē*), as if the soul in this present life were buried. . . . I think it most likely that the name (i.e. *sēma*) was given by the followers of Orpheus, with the idea that the soul is undergoing whatever penalty it has incurred, and is enclosed in the body, as in a sort of prisonhouse, for safe-keeping. So the body is the place of safe-keeping (*sōma*) of the soul until the penalty is discharged, and not even a letter of the name it bears needs be changed." [7]

The play on words here is important, since the words *sōma-sēma* ("the body, a tomb") was a well-established formula, expressive of this distinctive view of life.

The idea of the pre-existence of the soul, its divine origin and immortal nature, finds its classic expression in the teaching of Socrates and Plato—their particular views on the subject cannot be distinguished since Plato made his master the mouthpiece of his own views. A dualistic estimate of human nature tends to be adopted in Platonic philosophy. The soul is regarded as infinitely more precious than the body, and Socrates is represented as urging his fellow-citizens "to take care of the soul" as their primary task and duty in life. The nature of the soul is a constant theme of the famous *Dialogues;* the *Phaedo* is devoted to proving its immortality. In the *Phaedrus* a complete history of the soul's origin and destiny is outlined, in which the influence of Orphism is evident. In its primordial state the soul is elevated, ethereal by nature, and pure. But some souls, for reasons unstated, cannot maintain their original elevation; they sink down until they find a solid resting-place—a body. Thus begins a process of incarnations in various forms, human and animal. From this contact with matter the soul becomes contaminated and suffers. It is the task of the philosopher, who realizes his true situation by his superior knowledge, so to free himself from the bondage of the body that his soul recovers its original state of bliss.

[7] Plato, *Cratylus,* 400b; trans. Cornford, *op. cit.,* p. 74.

This Orpheo-Platonic conception of the soul, by virtue of its esoteric character, could only have been appreciated by a minority of those disposed to such metaphysical speculation. But it did establish a tradition of thought and aspiration with which some of the leading thinkers of the Graeco-Roman world, such as Philo, Plutarch, and Plotinus, were associated. As we shall see, it exercised a profound influence upon nascent Christianity and undoubtedly inspired the various forms of Gnosticism.

A note on this latter movement is appropriate here, since it will serve to illustrate a profoundly important aspect of the belief in the soul's essential superiority to the body. The Gnostic sects, which existed in the Roman Empire, often closely connected with Christianity, were basically concerned to account for the soul's involvement in a world of material things. Holding that the soul was divine in origin and ethereal by nature, and regarding matter as intrinsically evil, their problem was: how came the soul to inhabit a corruptible body of flesh and blood? The various theories advanced to explain the situation had a common pattern: the soul had fallen, through error, from its original high estate and become entangled with material things. And the methods proposed for the soul's salvation had also a common element. As the word "Gnosticism" indicates, the initiates of each Gnostic sect believed that they possessed a secret *gnosis*, or knowledge, that revealed the soul's true state, and the way whereby it could be delivered from this lower world and return to its proper home and abode with God.[8]

The conception of the soul as a divine, pre-existent and immortal entity, did not, however, represent the main tradition of Greek thought. That tradition, stemming from Homer, was generally pessimistic; and it combined diverse intuitions about human destiny. A primitive fear inspired the Athenian spring festival of the Anthesteria. On that day, it was believed, the souls of the dead left their tombs to revisit their former homes but these souls were not called *psychai*, but *kēres*. The difference is significant: *kēres* had a grisly meaning, and its application to the dead was doubtless inspired by fear of the hostile ghosts, depicted on Greek vases as small black winged figures.

A more negative attitude about the immortality of the soul shows itself in an inscription on a memorial to the Athenian soldiers who fell in battle at Potidaea in 432 B.C.: "The air has received their souls, the

---

[8] See Chapter 22.

Heracles attacks one of the *kēres,* or
hostile ghosts (Greek vase-painting
in the Berlin Museum)

earth their bodies." The stark realism of this statement is matched by
that of the majority of epitaphs on private graves: only the name and
family of the deceased are given, with the word "farewell" sometimes
added. The leading philosophies of Graeco-Roman society also gave no
sanction for any other view. Lucretius, the disciple of Epicurus, in his
De Rerum Natura, provides twenty-eight arguments against the idea of
the soul's immortality; while the *Meditations* of the Emperor Marcus
Aurelius significantly attests the fundamental doubt of Stoicism. Perhaps
most eloquent of the common feeling are the lines said to have been
written by the Emperor Hadrian on his death-bed:

> O little soul, fickle, yet so pleasing,
> My body's guest and constant companion,
> Whither now departest thou,
> Pallid, stiff, and naked,
> Forgetful, too, of thine accustomed humour.

IV

The history of the idea of the soul in ancient Israel is that of the
gradual adaptation of a primitive anthropology to the demands of an
evolving conception of deity. The account of the creation of Adam, the
Primal Man, in the second chapter of *Genesis,* dating probably from about

800 B.C., is significant. Yahweh, the god of Israel, forms Adam from the *'adāmāh*, the clay; then he breathes into him "the breath of life ", so that Adam becomes a "living soul" (*nephesh*). But this divine act of animation does not confer a distinctive status on Adam; for animals are also described as "living souls". The word *nephesh*, which was akin to the Akkadian "*napištu* ",denoted the "vital breath"; it was closely associated with blood, the life-substance, and was thought to be drained away from the body at death. The Hebrews also had the word *ruach*, usually translated "spirit.", to describe the outstanding mental and physical energy that characterized such men as Elijah; but the term never meant "soul" or "spirit" in the sense of the essential inner self.

In Hebrew thought, the living person was consistently regarded as a composite entity, compounded of body and *nephesh*. At death this

Prometheus creating men. The goddess Minerva places the soul, symbolized as a butterfly, in the newly fashioned mannikins (from a sarcophagus of the 3rd cent. A.D., in the Museo Capitolino, Rome)

psycho-physical compound was shattered. That which survived the dissolution, living on under ground, had some continuity of identity with
the living person; but it was regarded with awe and dread. As the
Mesopotamians had a special designation for the dead, so did the
Hebrews, referring to them by the obscure terms *elohim* and *rephaim*.

The increasing emphasis by the Yahwist prophets on Yahweh's being
a just God inevitably affected the traditional view of the individual's
destiny. At first it was taught that Yahweh rewarded the righteous with
long life and prosperity, while misfortune and a speedy end was the lot
of the wicked. But experience proved that things were not so conveniently
arranged; and, the more the justice of Yahweh was emphasized, the greater
became the problem of the innocent sufferer. The *Book of Job* is a
memorial to the poignancy of this problem, at a period when no solution
was possible through hope of redress in an after-life.[9] By the second century B.C., however, the tension was eased by the emergence of a belief that
Yahweh would raise the dead to life again, rewarding the righteous and
punishing the wicked. But this resurrection was essentially a revivification
of the physical body; and it attests the strength of the Hebrew conviction
that the living person was a psycho-physical organism, not an immortal
soul inhabiting a mortal body.

The strength of this belief is the more significant, since it continued
to be maintained even after the Jews had assimilated a measure of Greek
thought, as they did from the second century B.C. onwards. The *Wisdom
of Solomon*, and the writings of Philo and Josephus, show that many Jews
were familiar with, and accepted, the view of the soul as the essential
self, pre-existing the body and surviving its destruction. Yet, despite this
appreciation of the Orpheo-Platonic conception, the old Semitic tradition
prevailed. The immortality of the soul alone was never deemed sufficient,
and Jewish eschatology could only envisage a satisfactory after-life as
the restoration of the whole person, thus necessitating a resurrection of
the body.

V

Because Christianity arose in Judaea, Jewish ideas and terminology
naturally provided the framework of the earliest forms of Christian teaching. This is particularly evident in the view taken of the constitution of

[9] See Chapter 10.

Medieval representation of the resurrection of three souls from their graves (Lat. MS. 145, The John Rylands Library, Manchester)

human nature. In the Synoptic Gospels, the Greek word *psyché* ("soul") is invariably employed in the sense of the Hebrew *nephesh*, to denote physical life or the subject of emotional experience. In the one passage (*Matthew* x. 28), where a distinction is drawn between the soul (*psyché*) and the body, the immediate sequel shows that a *post-mortem* reunion of soul and body is envisaged: "And be not afraid of them which kill the body, but are not able to kill the soul; but rather fear him which is able to destroy both soul and body in hell."

The accounts of the resurrection of Jesus graphically illustrate how completely it was believed that the physical body would be restored. According to the Lukan Gospel (xxiv. 36–43), on seeing the risen Jesus the disciples were terrified, supposing that they beheld a spirit (*pneuma*).[10]

---

[10] The root-meaning of *pneuma* was "wind" or "air"; it was used in the Septuagint to translate the Hebrew *ruach*. In the Gospels *pneuma* is used both for the Holy "Spirit" and evil "spirits," i.e. demons.

Jesus reassures them: "See my hands and my feet, that it is I myself; handle me, and see; for a spirit has not flesh and bones as ye see me have." To prove his material reality still further, Jesus is then represented as asking, 'Have you anything to eat?' They gave him a piece of broiled fish, and he took it and ate before them."

This Hebraic view of man as a psycho-physical organism, with its logical corollary of a physical resurrection for an after-life, soon came into conflict with the Orpheo-Platonic view of the soul, when Christianity was carried into Greek society; and that conflict is dramatically expressed in the account of the Apostle Paul's preaching at Athens. The account in the *Acts of the Apostles* (xvii. 16–34) tells how the Athenians listened quietly to Paul until he spoke of the resurrection of the dead; then they mocked him and turned away. The reason was obvious. The "resurrection of the dead" (*anastasis nekrōn*) in Greek meant literally a "standing-up of corpses". Such an idea was shocking to those nurtured in the philosophy of Plato. To them the body was the prison of the soul, from which it was freed by death. The thought of resurrecting the body was, accordingly, outrageous.

Paul, who laid the foundations of Christian theology, conceived of human nature as compounded of three elements: body, *psychē*, and *pneuma*. For him the *psychē* was the life-principle, akin to the *nephesh*. The *pneuma* he evidently regarded as the inner, essential self. It would appear, however, from his Epistles to the Christians at Corinth, that Paul was keenly aware of the difficulty the Greeks found in the idea of a physical resurrection; and he seems also to have appreciated the Orpheo-Platonic concept of the soul. Faced with the question: "How are the dead raised? With what kind of body do they come?" (1 *Cor.* xv. 35), he endeavours to compromise between the Hebrew and the Greek views. He draws a distinction between the "natural body" (*sōma psychikon*), which dies and is buried, and a "spiritual body" (*sōma pneumatikon*), which is resurrected. In his Second Epistle, Paul seems to have moved closer to the Greek concept of the soul. He writes: "For we know that if the earthly tent we live in is destroyed, we have a building from God, a house not made with hands, eternal in the heavens. Here indeed we groan, and long to put on our heavenly dwelling, so that by putting it on we may not be found naked" (2 *Cor.* v. 1–2). These verses contain a curious mixture of Hebraic and Greek thought. What is specially significant is the idea of an inner self, burdened by the physical body, and looking

Abraham's Bosom: medieval conception of heaven, according to St. Luke's Gospel, xvi: 22ff. Angels carry redeemed souls to Abraham (Cathedral of Reims, 13th cent.)

forward to being clothed by a spiritual body, already pre-existent in heaven. Such a view is not far removed from that expressed in the Orphic saying *sōma-sēma*, "the body, a tomb". But Paul was still influenced by Hebrew tradition in being unable to envisage a *post-mortem* existence without some bodily form, even though it is non-material.

The conception of human nature that Paul and the other New Testament writers bequeathed to the Church was thus basically inconsistent. The soul was regarded as the essential self and immortal; yet a **reconstituted body was deemed necessary for a proper after-life.**

The future of Christianity lay in the Graeco-Roman world, not in Palestine. This meant that Christian theology was thought out by men trained in Greek metaphysic; and the Orpheo-Platonic conception of the soul tended to prevail. Three views of the origin of the soul were set forth in the Early Church, each attesting its essential nature and independence of the body. Tertullian (*c.* 160–220) defined the soul (*anima*) as "sprung from the breath of God, immortal"; the body was its instrument, but both were begotten through the sexual intercourse of the parents. According to the great Alexandrian scholar, Origen (*c.* 185–254), God originally created a definite number of spirits; these received bodies and status as **angels, men, and demons,** as merited by their former conduct. The body contaminates the soul; the soul, however, has the freedom to work out its salvation until the final restoration of all. Despite the great prestige of Origen, his doctrine of the pre-existence of the soul was condemned as **heretical at the First Council of Constantinople in 543.** The third view was first expressed in the late third century by Lactantius, who maintained that, whereas a body can be produced from a body, a soul cannot be the offspring of other souls. This argument was formulated into the generally accepted doctrine of Creationism by Jerome (*c.* 342–420), who taught that "God is daily making souls" for the bodies produced by acts of human generation. Orthodox opinion has continued to take this view.

Belief in the soul's superiority to the body, by virtue of its divine origin and intrinsic immortality, thus became a fundamental tenet of Christianity. It was basic to the whole scheme of salvation; and it inspired the abiding Christian disposition to asceticism, whereby the soul is exalted and the body despised. It finds graphic expression in medieval art, where the soul at death is represented as a little nude human figure issuing forth with the last breath, to be received by angels or demons according to its character.

Notwithstanding this exaltation of the soul, the ancient Hebrew view **of man as a psycho-physical organism was never abandoned. Consequently,** although the soul was regarded as inherently immortal, belief in a resurrection of the physical body has continued an effective part of Christian belief. Christian art and hymnody abundantly attest the realistic manner in which this final revivification has been visualized. Its acceptance by Christians down the ages has been required by the authority of the Scriptures; but, viewed in the context of the history of religions, it is consistent also with that traditional evaluation of man in the ancient Near East: namely, as a being compounded of physical and psychical elements, each essential to life.

The damned, in their resurrected forms, suffering in hell (detail from the Torcello "Last Judgment": see ill. on page 109)

CHAPTER 6

The Idea of the Soul

THE HISTORY OF MAN'S MOST FUNDAMENTAL CONCEPT

Part II: In the East

"The differences that divide the Eastern and Western views of man's nature and destiny have an urgent significance today, as mankind becomes more closely interrelated and interdependent."

I

A subject intrinsically fascinating, and of basic concern for international understanding, is the difference between the Eastern and Western views of human nature and destiny. During the first two millennia B.C., while the ideas of the soul and body that characterize the Western outlook were evolving in the Levant, a very different evaluation was being made in India. The preceding chapter traced out the development of the Hebrew and Greek conceptions of human nature up to their fusion into the Christian doctrine of Man. The purpose of this article is to describe the beginnings of the Indian concept, and its diffusion throughout the East, with some account of the views concerning man's nature and destiny in the religions of Iran and China and in Islam.

II

What the earliest peoples of India thought of themselves and their place in the scheme of things is not known. Excavation of ancient sites in the Indus Valley area has revealed a flourishing urban civilization dating

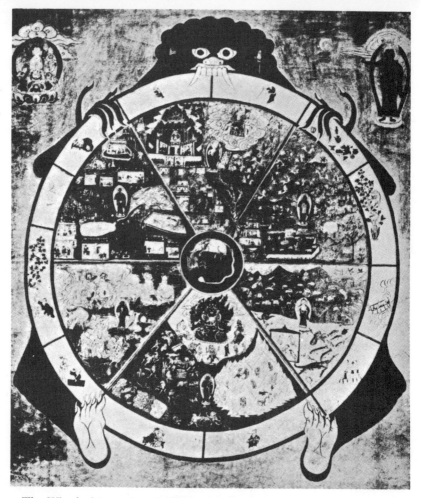

The Wheel of Becoming. A Tibetan Buddhist attempt to depict the cause and nature of human existence. The scenes in the six sectors depict six destinies. The black monster of Impermanence embraces the Wheel, since it devours all forms of existence

back to the third millennium B.C. The inhabitants generally buried their dead, placing in the graves articles of toilet and personal adornment, as well as food—a mortuary practice, well known among primitive peoples, implying belief in some kind of *post-mortem* survival. What part of the person was thought to survive, and in what condition, is unknown. The fact that some cultural affinity existed between these Indus Valley peoples and the Sumerians of Mesopotamia might mean that they shared a common eschatology; but no evidence that they actually did so exists. On the other hand, the many female figurines found on the Indus Valley sites and those of the related Zhob culture of Baluchistan have caused Professor S. Piggott to suggest that there existed a belief in an earth-goddess, "concerned alike with the corpse and the seed-corn".[1] If this suggestion could be substantiated, it would help to explain the sudden appearance of the idea of reincarnation in Hindu literature at a much later date: the analogy of the burial of the corpse and the seed-corn would be pregnant with meaning, and possible parallels in Minoan and Greek religion could be cited.

The Indus Valley civilization was probably destroyed by the Aryan peoples who invaded north-western India about 1500 B.C. These peoples are known to us through their Sanskrit hymns, used on ritual occasions, of which the oldest collection is the *Rig-Veda* (c. 1400 B.C.). These hymns give the impression of a people greatly absorbed in living their lives in this world to the full—a long life, good health, the pleasures of eating and drinking, riches and children represent their obvious values. Nevertheless, although the subject is never formally treated, distinctive ideas about the constitution of human nature were held. Like the Homeric Greeks, these Aryans regarded the individual as compounded of three entities: the body, the *asu*, and the *manas*. The *asu*, frequently referred to as "the living *asu*", was the life-principle; it was akin to the Homeric *psychē* also in being unconnected with the rational, emotional, and volitional activities of the individual. The *manas* corresponded to the Homeric *thymos* in being the seat of the mind, the will, and the emotions.[2] Important though the *asu* and the *manas* were, they were not identified with the essential self: in the mortuary texts invocations are addressed to the person, not to either of these entities as representative of him. What was the nature of this person or self, that survived death, is not clear. Possibly it was conceived as a tiny mannikin, residing in the region of the heart: later Hindu texts, doubtlessly reflecting a primitive tradition, refer to "the person (*parusa*) of the size of a thumb", that is in the midst of the body.

What was the fate of the body, according to Vedic thought, is obscure. At an early stage, when inhumation was the custom, the dead were imagined as living, apparently with their bodies, in a subterranean land, presided over by Yama, the death-god. For some unknown reason, however, a change to cremation had been effected by the time of the

---

[1] *Prehistoric India* (Harmsworth, 1950), p. 127.
[2] See the preceding chapter.

Ṛig-Veda. This change in the body's disposal raised, significantly, problems about its ultimate fate. Although Agni, the fire-god, was imagined as refining a dead man for his *post-mortem* state, it is evident that the dead person was also thought of as a psycho-physical organism that had to be preserved intact. This is vividly attested in a prayer in *Atharvaveda* (XVIII, 2.24): "May nothing of thy *manas*, nothing of the *asu*, nothing of the limbs, nothing of thy vital fluid, nothing of thy body here by any means be lost."

In view of the great revolution that was later to take place in Indian thought about man's nature and destiny, it is important to appreciate the characteristics of this Vedic evaluation, current during the period 1500–900 B.C. Man's life was seen as having two phases. The first, here and now, was clearly the more desirable; and it was to be enjoyed to capacity, both physically and emotionally. The *post-mortem* phase was crudely envisaged as a kind of prolongation of existence here, although its nature might be determined by the quality of one's piety and moral conduct. This two-phase pattern was definitive: there was no hint of the soul's returning to live again in this world. Why this view came to be supplanted, as we shall see, by another that was very different, is a question much discussed by scholars.

The task of tracing out the development of early Indian thought is beset by a basic difficulty: how far did the ideas of the original non-Aryan inhabitants affect what became the Hindu view of life? The caste system was probably elaborated by the Aryan invaders to preserve the purity of their race and cultural heritage; but, in the course of centuries, some intermingling of the two cultures was inevitable. It is of interest, therefore, to note traces of ancient traditions other than the Vedic about human destiny. For example, the idea finds expression that, "The eye must enter the sun, the soul the wind: go into the heaven and go into the earth according to destiny; or go into the water, if that be assigned to thee, or dwell with thy limbs in the plants."[3] This incorporation of a person, or his component parts, at death, into other forms of being, is truly primitive in its conception; but, in the light of the sudden appearance, as we shall see, of belief in the transmigration of souls in Indian thought about 600 B.C., it has significance. Significant also is the idea, preserved in the *Chāndogya Upanishad,* that, after cremation, the dead

[3] *Ās'valāyana-Grkyasūtra,* 4, 5.3.

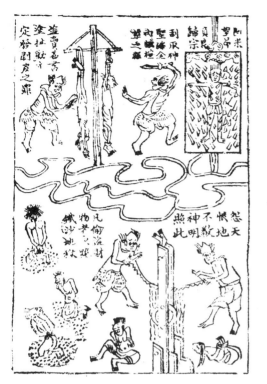

Chinese popular prints representing the torments in the Buddhist hells, through which the dead pass *en route* for their next incarnation

took one of two ways, according to the character of their life on earth. The *devayāna*, the "way of the gods", led ultimately to *Brahman*, the source of all being, passing *en route* through various cosmic phenomena such as the sun and moon. Those who went by this path never returned again. The other way, the *pitryāna*, "the way of the fathers", took the dead, through darkness and gloom, to the abode of the ancestors. After a dismal sojourn there, they returned to earth for a new cycle of incarnate life. Those destined to take the *pitryāna* were, accordingly, faced with the prospect of dying again. The idea occurs also in the *Brāhmanas* (c. 800–600 B.C.), where the impious are threatened with *punarmrtyu*, a "second death".

The new conception of life that was established as the classic expression of Hinduism during the so-called Upanishadic period (c. 600–480 B.C.), stemmed from a movement of asceticism and philosophical reflection that has since characterized Indian culture. It finds expression in a series of writings called *Upanishads,* which attests the concern of Indian thinkers with the basic problems of existence and their genius for metaphysical speculation. In these writings the twin doctrines of *samsāra* and *karma* are propounded. The following passage, from one of the earliest of the *Upanishads,* the *Bṛhadāraṇyaka,* gives a concise account of their operation:

> "The object to which the mind is attached, the subtle self goes together with the deed, being attached to it alone. Exhausting the results of whatever works he did in this world, he comes again from that world, to this world for (fresh) work. But the man who does not desire, whose desire is satisfied, whose desire is the self; his breaths do not depart. Being *Brahman,* he goes to *Brahman.*" [4]

Here the process of *saṃsāra,* or rebirth, is assumed as a fundamental principle of existence. Its cause is *karma,* or "action"; for the individual, by his active participation in life, so implicates himself in this world that, after death, he returns to it again in some other form. *Karma* has a twofold effect: it causes the individual to cling to existence in this world of time and space, and it determines the form of his next incarnation.

The subject of this twin-process of *karma* and *saṃsāra* is the *ātman* or self. The word *ātman* was derived from *an,* "to breathe", and originally it expressed the primitive idea, which we have met elsewhere that the breath is the soul or animating principle. At an early stage in the evolution of Indian thought, this animating breath was undoubtedly conceived as the source of all life, pervading the whole universe. This conception, in turn, led to the idea of a cosmic soul, which was identified with *Brahman,* the divine principle and ground of reality. Accordingly, an essential nexus could be perceived between the individual self (*ātman*) and the Cosmic Soul (*Ātman*) or *Brahman.* Indeed, so essential was the connection that they could easily be identified, as they are in an eloquent passage in the *Chāndogya Upanishad:*

> "This is my self (*ātmāntar*) within the heart, smaller than a grain of rice, than a barley corn, than a mustard seed, than a grain of millet or than a kernel of a grain of millet. This is myself within the heart, greater than the earth, greater than the atmosphere, greater than the sky, greater than these worlds. Containing all works, containing all desires, containing all odours, containing all tastes, encompassing this whole world, without speed, without concern, this is the self of mine within the heart; this is *Brahman.* Into him, I shall enter, on departing hence." [5]

---

[4] *Brh. Up.,* IV, 4, 5; trans. S. Radhakrishnan, *The Principal Upanishads,* pp. 272–3 (Allen & Unwin, 1953).
[5] III, 14. 3–4; trans. S. Radhakrishnan, *op. cit.,* pp. 391–2.

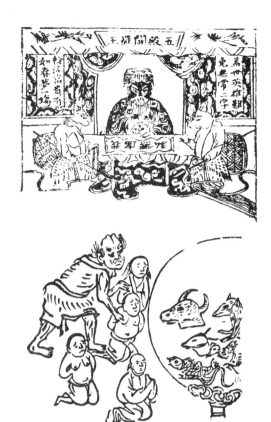

Chinese Buddhist attempt to depict souls, who have completed their *post-mortem* punishment, as seeing in a mirror the forms of their next incarnations, according to their deserts

But, if the *ātman* or self of the individual was essentially one with *Brahman,* the question had to be faced: how came this *ātman* to be subject to the twin process of *karma* and *samsāra?* The answer given by the Indian sages was that the cause was *avidyā*—a profound ignorance that invested the *ātman* as to its true nature. The origin of this *avidyā* is never convincingly explained. The idea seems to have been invented to account for the existential situation. We are reminded of Plato's inability to explain why pre-existent souls cannot maintain their original elevation and sink down into material bodies—it is, indeed, significant that about the same time, 500–350 B.C., in both India and Greece the same problems were being discussed and the same difficulties encountered.[6]

Whatever the origin of this *avidyā*, it led, according to the Indian thinkers, to the universal error of taking the phenomenal world for reality. This *māyā* or illusion resulted in the *ātman*'s regarding itself as a separate, individual entity, attached to life in a world of material things. Conse-

[6] See above p. 76.

quently, its craving for bodily existence, at the end of one incarnation, brought about rebirth in another body. By the law of *karma,* moreover, the condition into which the *ātman* was reborn was determined by the quality of its previous existence: the *ātman* would pass into the body of a beast, if it so deserved.

This unceasing process of *samsāra* was seen as an unending succession of births and deaths, with all their attendant pain and misery. Time was conceived as cyclical in its movement; and, in later Hinduism, a fantastic chronological scheme was elaborated to emphasize the futility of existence in the phenomenal world. This world would last for a *kalpa,* which was made up of one thousand *mahayugas,* each of which comprised twelve thousand years; but these were divine years, and each equalled three hundred and sixty human years. Throughout this frightening span of time, the unenlightened soul was doomed to pursue its weary course of successive births and deaths. At the end of a *kalpa* the world would be destroyed, and the soul would lapse into unconsciousness. Another world would be created by Brahmā, however, and the dreary wheel of existence begin to turn again for another *kalpa,* through which once more the soul would endure countless incarnations, dragging the ever-increasing burden of its *karma.*

The Indian sages taught a way of escape from this dismal fate. It consisted in the *ātman*'s learning to distinguish its own essential self from the empirical self. This empirical self is an illusion, built up from impressions of the phenomenal world, that is mistaken for reality. The idea of a transcendental self or *ātman,* which was contrasted with the self of normal consciousness, undoubtedly arose from the experience of mystical trance, so characteristic of Indian asceticism. It is significant that the practice of Yoga employs various techniques, such as the regulation of breathing, to deaden the time-sense of normal consciousness.

By following a prescribed discipline of mind and body, it was believed that the *ātman* would ultimately achieve *moksa,* that is, final deliverance from the weary cycle of unceasing births and deaths. This deliverance took the form of the *ātman*'s realization of its identity with *Brahman.* As we have seen from a previously quoted passage of the *Bṛhad-āranyaka Upanishad,* "the man who does not desire, whose desire is satisfied, whose desire is the self; his breaths do not depart. Being *Brahman,* he goes to *Brahman.*" But this union with *Brahman* meant the cessation of the *ātman*'s individual existence; for, as the following passage shows, the soul lost its identity: "Just as the flowing rivers disappear in the ocean casting off name and shape, even so the knower, freed from name and shape, attains to the divine person, higher than the high." [7]

This Upanishadic interpretation of human nature and destiny provided the basic pattern of the subsequent Hindu view of life. Variations of it were propounded by later thinkers, of whom the most notable was Śankara. This great thinker, who lived during the ninth century of the present era, formulated the system of the *Vedānta*, which has become the classic expression of the Indian philosophy of life. The system is, in effect, an attempt to accommodate the Upanishadic view of the soul to the needs of those living in a world that, although produced of *māyā*, presents a very urgent impression of its reality. Consequently, while the impersonal *Brahman* remains the principle of reality, it is taught that the phenomenal world is created and ruled by a personal deity Iśvara, who rewards and punishes men according to their deserts. By the traditional rites communion can be had with Iśvara; but it is a temporary state of bliss, for true salvation can only be attained by the soul's identification with *Brahman*.

The popular need for a personal deity, which the system of Śankara tacitly acknowledged, found more congenial expression from the twelfth century A.D. in the movement known as *bhakti-mārga*, the "bhakti-path". The word *bhakti* meant an intense personal devotion to a personal deity, usually Vishnu, who was called the *Bhagavat* or Adorable One. In this *bhakti* cult, however, the Upanishadic doctrine of the soul and its fate was accepted without question. Thus, in the *Bhagavadgītā*, the "Song of the Lord", India's great religious classic, the nature of the soul (*ātman*) is defined: "It is born not, nor does it ever die, nor shall it, after having been brought into being, come not to be hereafter. The unborn, the permanent, the eternal, the ancient, it is slain not when the body is slain." [8] The doctrine of *samsāra* is vividly described: "As a man casting off his worn-out clothes takes other new ones, so the embodied one, casting off its worn-out bodies, enters others that are new." [9] Deliverance from the pain and misery of this process is finally achieved, through personal devotion,

---

[7] *Mundaka Upanishad*, III. 2, 8; trans. Radhakrishnan, *op. cit.*, p. 691.
[8] II. 20; trans. E. J. Thomas, *The Song of the Lord* (Murray, 1948), pp. 33–4.
[9] II. 22; trans. E. J. Thomas.

Buddhist metamorphosis. A Chinese attempt to represent a man (centre figure) emerging from his former self as a snake sloughs off its old skin (from the temple of the Sleeping Buddha, Suchow)

when the soul is united with the *Bhagavat:* "They who have come to me, the great-souled ones, go not to rebirth, the impermanent place of pain; they have gone to the highest state." [10]

III

The Upanishadic view of human nature and destiny found expression not only in various forms of Hindu orthodoxy, such as the *Vedānta* and the *bhakti-cult.* It was also embodied, variously modified, into Buddhism and Jainism, religions that developed outside the fold of Hinduism. Since Buddhism became a world faith, established among many Eastern peoples, it is the Buddhist conception of the soul that must claim our attention here.

Owing to the fact that a considerable period elapsed from the death of the Buddha (*c.* 567–487 B.C.) to the earliest written records of Buddhism, we are not certain of the original content of his teaching. There is reason for believing, however, that the Buddha accepted the doctrines of *karma* and *samsāra.* But he seems to have differed from the Upanishadic sages in his view of the self or soul. Instead of seeing the self as an immortal entity that passed through a series of incarnations, he appears to have denied that there was a real self that survived the death of the

[10] VIII. 15; trans. Thomas, *op. cit.*, p. 69.

body and was reborn in other forms. The following passage from the *Samyutta-nikāya* will show how subtle is Buddhist thought on this funda-mental issue. Buddha is represented as telling his disciple Ananda of his dialogue about the subject with a wandering ascetic Vacchagotta:

> "If, Ananda, when Vacchagotta asked, 'is there an ātman?' I had said, 'there is an ātman,' then I should have been one of those ascetics and brahmins who hold the doctrine of eternalism. But if I had replied, 'there is no ātman,' then I should have been one of those who hold the doctrine of annihilation. And if, when Vacchagotta asked 'is there an ātman?' I had replied, 'there is an ātman,' would it have been in accordance with the knowledge that all things are without ātman? 'No, Lord.' If I had said, 'there is no ātman,' the bewildered Vacchagotta would have become still more bewildered, thinking, 'then did my ātman exist before, and now it does not exist'." [11]

It is possible that this frustrating series of affirmations and negations was designed, in accordance with ancient Indian logic, to indicate that there is an entity that is beyond the ability of language to describe. What is certain, however, is that the early Buddhists held that the human person was a temporary conglomeration of various constituents, physical and psychical. None of these constituents could be isolated as the essential self; neither did the sum of them constitute the self. Nevertheless, since the principle of *samsāra* was accepted, it was natural to ask what caused rebirth, if there was no self that survived death. The answer was given in the so-called Chain of Causation, which is a subtle analysis of what constitutes existence. The final link in this Chain is graphically described in an account of the Buddha's teaching: "Old age and death have rebirth as cause. Then, monks, I thought, 'Now when what exists does rebirth exist, and what is the cause of the rebirth?' And as I duly reflected there came the comprehension of full knowledge: it is when there is becoming (or desire to be) that there is rebirth, rebirth has desire to be as a cause." [12]

This conception of an endless series of reincarnations, caused each time by the persistence of a desire to exist, is difficult to comprehend. Equally difficult is the idea of Nirvāna, which is the goal of the Buddhist

---

[11] Trans. E. J. Thomas, *History of Buddhist Thought* (Routledge, 1953), p. 127.
[12] *Samyutta*, ii. 10; trans. E. J. Thomas, *Early Buddhist Scriptures* (Kegan Paul, Trench, Trubner, 1935), p. 119.

way of life. The word "Nirvāna" means literally "blowing out", as of
a lamp, and so it can be interpreted as "extinction" or "annihilation".
If it does denote merely the final extinction of the desire to exist, then
the achievement of Buddhist endeavour is the complete negation of all
existence. But Buddhist literature tends to speak of Nirvāna in positive
terms, which suggests that some wholly transcendental form of existence
is contemplated. This, in turn, may imply the idea of a transcendental
self, indefinable and known only through mystical trance. This view seems
to be confirmed by the following passage from a Pali writing known as
the *Udāna,* in which the Buddha is represented as saying: "There is an
unborn, an unbecome, an unmade, an uncomprehended; if there were
not, there would be no escape from the born, the become, the made,
the compounded." [13]

The spread of Buddhism throughout Asia has meant a corresponding
diffusion of this, originally Indian, view of human nature and destiny.
During the course of centuries, Buddhism has undergone many great
changes in thought and practice, and many alien ideas and institutions
have been incorporated into it. But the basic ideas described here have
remained generally unchanged. Their acceptance by successive generations
has profoundly affected the outlook of the Asian peoples: it has established
an evaluation of life that differs from the Western view stemming from
Christianity, which in turn drew from the older traditions of Israel and
Greece.

IV

In the history of ideas it is notable that two cultures, each incorporating an original Aryan tradition, and each in frequent contact with the
other, produced very different estimates of human destiny. Vedic India
and ancient Iran drew upon a mythology common to the original Aryan
peoples; but whereas belief in rebirth became basic to Hinduism, it had
no place in Iranian religion.

Our earliest knowledge of religion in Iran comes from the *Gathas.*
But since these writings record the teaching of Zarathustra (from about
570 B.C.), who reformed the traditional faith, we cannot be certain of
what went before.[14] In the *Gathas* two terms are used to denote non-
material constituents of human nature; since these terms are employed

---

[13] Trans. E. J. Thomas, *History of Buddhist Thought,* p. 129.
[14] See Chapter 13.

Japanese Buddhist idea of the judgment of the souls of the dead before Emma-ô, the ruler of the underworld (Musée Guimet, Paris)

without explanation, it is evident that they were already well established and understood. By *urvan* an element of man's constitution was distinguished from the *tanū* (body), surviving the body's death and representing the individual in his *post-mortem* destiny. The other word, *daēnā*, has an obscure etymology; it seems to have described what we mean by "conscience", but in a more personified sense. A word not used in the *Gathas*, doubtless because it concerned an idea uncongenial to Zarathustra, was *fravashi*. Although reference is made in later writings to the holy *fravashi*, who are "under the earth since the time of their decease", it would seem that a primitive idea was involved here, such as is found among other peoples, of the spirits of the dead dwelling below ground, where they help to promote the fertility of the fields, and of man and beast. Whether Zarathustra thought of the after-life as the existence of the disembodied soul is not clear. He speaks of the dead as having

to face a final ordeal of Molten Metal, which some scholars have taken
to imply a resurrection of the body.

In later Zoroastrianism, human nature was regarded as a more
complex thing. Five constituents were distinguished, besides the body:
the vital spirit; the soul that expresses itself through the consciousness;
the consciousness itself; the "image" (an equivalent of the Greek *eidos*
or "form"); the external soul (*fravahr* = fravashi), which remained with
Ohrmazd, the Supreme Lord. The idea of the *daēnā* was retained; and
the deceased was thought to meet his *daēna* after death either as a beautiful
maiden or an evil hag, according to the nature of his deeds. The physical
body was deemed essential to a proper life; so that, at the end, when
Ohrmazd triumphs over the evil Ahriman, the dead are resurrected.
According to the *Bundahishn* (ninth century A.D.), at this resurrection,
"whoever has been the size of a man, they restore him then with an age
of forty years; they who had been little *when* not dead, they restore them
with an age of fifteen years; and they give every one his wife and show
him his children with the wife . . . but there is no begetting of children." [15]

Turning further east in our survey, we may briefly notice Chinese
ideas of the soul before the establishment there of Buddhism from the
first century A.D. The earliest evidence comes from the so-called Oracle
Bones, excavated at Anyang and dating from the Shang Period
(*c.* 1523–1027 B.C.). In these inscriptions the character *kuei* occurs; it
is denoted by a pictogram representing a man with a large head—the sign
has lived on in the Chinese language as a radical denoting "soul". The
occurrence of the cicada on the so-called ritual bronzes of the Shang
Period has also been thought significant by some authorities, since the
cicada became an accepted symbol in China of immortality or rebirth.

During the Feudal Period (722–481 B.C.), the idea developed that
everything in the universe was the product of two alternating principles
called *yin* and *yang*. This conception led to the belief that within each
person there is a *yin*-soul and a *yang*-soul, the one deriving from the earth
and the other from heaven. The *yin*-soul was identified with the primitive
kuei: during life it was called the *p'o,* and after death the *kuei.* The idea
of the *yang*-soul seems to have arisen from the phenomena of animation—it
came as breath from heaven and announced its presence in the first cry

[15] XXX. 26; trans. E. West, *Sacred Books of the East*, V, p. 126.

of the newborn infant. This soul was known as the *hun* during life, and the *shen* at death; it was associated with the mental qualities, and virtually constituted the personality.

The nature and fate of those two souls is succinctly described in the *Li Chi*, a Confucianist compilation dating from about 200 B.C.: "Tsai Wo said, 'I have heard the names *kuei* and *shen*, but I do not know what they mean.' The Master (i.e. Confucius) said, 'The breath (represents) the abundance of the *shen* (part of a creature), the animal soul represents the *kuei* (part). To be able to make a harmony of (the two concepts), *kuei* and *shen*, is the height of philosophy. All living creatures inevitably come to die. Dying they inevitably go back to the earth. This is what is meant by the *kuei* [? the material soul]. The bones and flesh moulder below, and, hidden there, make the soil of the land. But the breath soars aloft to become light, (and is found in) the fragrance and the feeling of sorrow at the sacrifice'."[16] The similarity of this view with that expressed in the inscription commemorating the Athenian dead at Potidaea, cited in the preceding chapter, deserves note.

In Chinese thought, humanity seems instinctively to have been integrated with the universe: man had no special destiny, his nature being subject to the operation of the cosmic principles of *yin-yang*. Such was the genius of the native tradition; but, in time, certain forms of Taoism and Buddhism came to cater for those who needed a more personally inspiring faith, assuring them of a blissful immortality.

To complete our survey of the major interpretations of man's nature and destiny, we must briefly consider the tradition of Islam. This religion, thought long established in India, Iran and other eastern lands, stemmed from Arabia; and it has continued faithful to its original Semitic heritage. Accordingly, the traditional Semitic estimate of man as a psycho-physical organism, of which the ancient Mesopotamian and Hebrew forms were described in Chapter 5, finds expression in Islam. Thus the creation of Adam, as described in the *Qur'ān*, surely reflects the influence of the Hebrew account: ". . . thy Lord said to the angels: 'See, I am going to create a human being from potter's clay, of mud ground down. So when I have formed him, and breathed my spirit into him, fall in obeisance to him'."[17] The soul (*nafs*) seems to have been regarded by Muhammad

16 Trans. E. R. Hughes, *Chinese Philosophy in Classical Times* (Dent, 1942), p. 153.
17 Surah XV. 28–8; trans. R. Bell, *The Qur'ān* (Edinburgh, 1937), vol. I, p. 244.

Islamic view of the torments of the damned, from a medieval Turkish manuscript (Bibliothèque Nationale, suppl. turc. 190)

as the essential self or personality; but, as many passages of the *Qur'ān* show, he considered the body essential for a *post-mortem* life. Hence a physical resurrection of the dead is proclaimed as immediately preceding the Last Judgment; and the everlasting bliss of the saved and the torments of the damned are described in very materialistic terms.

The meagre references to the constitution of man in the *Qur'ān*, though significant, did not satisfy the more sophisticated minds of later believers; and there was much speculation about the nature of the soul. Belief in the pre-existence of the soul was generally established: it was thought that souls were kept ready by Allāh in his treasure-house until needed for their respective incarnations. Despite the attempts of medieval Islamic scholars to define the soul in a more metaphysical manner and the exalted mysticism of the Ṣūfīs, the original Quranic conception of man's nature was never abandoned. The doctrine of a corporeal resurrection has remained as fundamental to Islam as it has to Christianity.

V

The history of the idea of the soul, that has been outlined in these two chapters, is truly the history of mankind's attempt to understand its place and purpose in the world of its experience. That attempt has been age-long: it begins with the dawn of human culture in the Upper Palaeolithic period; and it has continued to the present day. Our modern sciences of psychology and psychiatry pursue a quest that started with the intuition that caused Palaeolithic man to provide his dead with food and other equipment in the grave. Crude and bizarre as many conceptions of human nature have been, they merit our interest and sympathetic study. Moreover, the differences that divide the Eastern and Western views of man's nature and destiny have an urgent significance today, as mankind becomes more closely interrelated and interdependent. These differences can be properly understood only through the history of the ideas that inspire them.

$\mathbb{R}$ CHAPTER 7

The Judgment of the Dead
THE DAWN OF MAN'S MORAL CONSCIOUSNESS

The idea of a posthumous moral judgment, when the sheep will be divided from the goats, is deeply rooted in our cultural history.

I

"After death, judgment." That this brief minatory statement does not sound strange in our secularist society attests the continuing influence of Christian tradition. Whatever the nature of one's personal convictions, the idea that all men after death have to face divine judgment is generally familiar because it was, and is, an integral part of Christian belief. But the idea is not peculiar to Christianity; it occurs in other religions, some of them far older than Christianity—indeed older than Judaism from which Christianity stemmed. The idea, however, although powerfully affective, is not self-evident. To trace its origins and early evolution is worthwhile, not only for its intrinsic interest, but because it affords valuable insight into the history of ethics and human behaviour.

Ancient Egypt may justifiably claim to reveal the "dawn of conscience": it does so for the significant reason that Egyptian religion from the earliest times was profoundly concerned with the destiny of man after death. This concern finds expression first in the celebrated *Pyramid Texts*. These *Texts* were composed by the priests of Heliopolis about 2400 B.C., and inscribed on the interior walls of the pyramid tombs of certain pharaohs of the Fifth and Sixth Dynasties to secure for them a blessed immortality. It is evident that the Heliopolitan priests utilized much

The Egyptian Judgment of the Heart: the scribe Ani and his wife watch fearfully the weighing of Ani's heart against the feather-symbol of *Maat* (truth). Behind the divine scribe Thoth, the monster Am-mut awaits an adverse verdict (*Papyrus of Ani*, British Museum)

traditional material for their purpose. This material was of diverse character and origin: it comprised myths and legends, hymns and prayers, magical incantations and formulae. It would appear that the priestly scribes were prepared to adapt almost anything sanctified by ritual usage for the royal mortuary service; for they envisaged the monarch's passage to eternal beatitude, after death, as beset by all kinds of fantastic dangers, so that every possible means must be enlisted for his salvation. Among the many perils that the dead pharaoh was thought to face was that of proving his royal nature and power. This he is represented as doing mainly by grandiloquent asseverations of his might and divine descent or by his knowledge of magical formulae. In all this no thought of a *post-mortem* judgment on the king's moral character appears; indeed, in view of the current conception of the pharaonic office, such an idea would have been outrageous. Among the *Pyramid Texts*, however, there are passages that seem to envisage some kind of judicial trial after death. They are actually applied to the dead king; but, since they so obviously conflict with his exalted status, they must derive from the funerary ritual of private persons, which the Heliopolitan priests had carelessly incorporated into the royal mortuary texts. Thus, in one place, it is stated that: "There is not a word among men on earth against (pharaoh) Unas"; in another, the declaration is made: "(pharaoh) Pepi has not injured the Pharaoh"—the misapplication

here of this private asservation of innocence of the crime of *lèse-majesté*
is obvious. Although misapplied, these passages have a great significance:
they surely indicate the existence of the idea of a *post-mortem* judgment
of some kind among ordinary Egyptians of the period.

Another passage from the *Pyramid Texts* deserves quotation, since
it seems to foreshadow an important feature of the later Egyptian conception of the judgment of the dead. It is said of the dead king: "He desires
that he may be *maa kheru* through that which he has done." The words
maa kheru mean "true of voice"; they constituted a technical expression
for "justified" or "vindicated" in a juridical sense. The classic instance
of their application is in the legend of Osiris, which formed the rationale
of the Egyptian mortuary cultus and inspired the Egyptian view of human
life and destiny.[1] According to this legend, Osiris, a good king of long
ago, had been foully done to death by his evil brother Set. After he had
been miraculously restored to life, his case was tried before a tribunal
of the gods, who declared him to be *maa kheru* and condemned Set.
It would appear, therefore, that since in the royal mortuary ritual, as
evidenced by the *Pyramid Texts*, the dead king was magically assimilated
to Osiris so as to partake in his resurrection, he also acquired thereby
the Osirian title *maa kheru*. In the *Pyramid Texts* there is no explicit
statement that the king appeared before a divine tribunal; but, with the
assumption of such a title, the suggestion was there; and it was to become
extremely significant in later times, as the royal mortuary ritual was
gradually democratized.

The *Pyramid Texts* were wholly concerned with the eternal destiny
of the pharaoh; but, as we have noted, they give some indication of the
mortuary beliefs of the private persons, especially concerning a *post-
mortem* judgment. These indications are fortunately confirmed by the
evidence of certain inscriptions on private tombs of about the same, or
a slightly later, period. The most notable of these is on the tomb of
Harkhuf of Elephantine, an Egyptian official famous for his exploration
of the Sudan. It takes the form of an address by the dead man to any
visitor to his tomb. He is represented as saying:

> "I was . . . one (beloved) of his father, praised of his mother, whom
> all his brothers loved. I gave bread to the hungry, clothing to the naked,
> I ferried him who had no boat. O ye living who are upon earth [who shall

[1] See Chapter 8.

pass by this tomb whether] going down-stream or going up-stream, who shall say, 'A thousand loaves, a thousand jars of beer for the owner of this tomb!' I will intercede for their sakes in the Nether World. I am a worthy and equipped Glorious One, a ritual priest whose mouth knows. As for any man who shall enter into (this) tomb as his mortuary possession, I will seize him like a wild fowl; he shall be judged for it by the Great God. I was one saying good things and repeating what was loved. Never did I say aught evil to a powerful one against anybody. I desired that it might be well with me in the Great God's presence. Never did I [judge two brothers] in such a way that a son was deprived of his paternal possession." [2]

This inscription needs a brief commentary to make clear its great significance for the history of ethics. Harkhuf was particularly concerned about two things: to obtain mortuary offerings and to prevent the violation of his tomb. For the first, in accordance with contemporary Egyptian practice, he sought to enlist the sympathy of any who passed his tomb, so that they might recite the magical formulae engraved there to conjure up supplies of bread and beer—it was believed that the dead still needed such nourishment. Now, to win this sympathetic response, Harkhuf does not parade his high social status and political exploits; instead, he records his acts of kindliness—succouring the poor and assisting the traveller. In other words, despite his apparent complacency, Harkhuf's claims bear witness to the fact that charitable action was already appreciated in Egypt during the third millennium B.C. His second intention, namely, to safeguard his tomb, reveals another aspect of his moral sense. Not only does he threaten any would-be violator of his tomb with his own effective action; he also warns him that his crime would be judged by the "Great God". The idea contained in this warning is of immense historical importance; it is our earliest certain evidence of the association of deity with the maintenance of morality. The advance here in human thought is a notable one. The primitive conception of deity was the personification of the power manifest in many various forms in the universe. As such, deity is amoral, its action indifferently assisting or injuring mankind. Harkhuf's words indicate that Egyptian religious thought had already advanced beyond such a primitive conception. The identity of the "Great God" is not revealed in the inscription; but the use of the expression

[2] Translated by J. H. Breasted, *The Dawn of Conscience* (Charles Scribner's Sons, New York, 1935), pp. 125–6.

The "justified" Ani is led by Horus into the presence of Osiris, the lord of the dead (*Papyrus of Ani*, British Museum)

in other contexts suggests that it denotes the Sun God, Rē, the supreme **state** deity of Egypt at this period.

That Harkhuf could imagine that the Sun God would punish anyone who violated his tomb affords a clue to the way in which, at this early stage, deity became associated with morality. In ancient Egyptian theology, the Sun God, Rē, was intimately associated with *maat*, which meant "good order", "right", "truth": *maat* was often personified as a goddess and regarded as the daughter of Rē. In essence, *maat* was the fundamental law or order of the universe, which the Sun God was thought to embody and maintain. Such a cosmic law for an ancient Egyptian would be exemplified not only in natural phenomena, but also in the structure and function of the Egyptian state. For Harkhuf, this principle found practical expression in his security to enjoy the provision he had made for his *post-mortem* life in the tomb. Consequently, anyone who violated this right violated *maat*, the fundamental law of the universe, of which Rē was the guardian; and Rē must accordingly take action to redress the wrong.

It is not certain whether the judgment of the Great God, with which Harkhuf threatened would-be robbers of his tomb, was to occur in their lifetime or after death. But there is no doubt that he conceived of some form of *post-mortem* judgment for himself. This is evident from his comment, after detailing his own good deeds: "I desired that it might be well with me in the Great God's presence." Harkhuf, accordingly, believed that the quality of his conduct in this life would decisively affect his life hereafter; and he seems to imply that it was the "Great God" who would take cognizance of his conduct.

The funerary inscriptions of this period, such as Harkhuf's, that attest expectation of a *post-mortem* judgment, give no information as to its form or manner of operation. The first indications of the imagery in which it was conceived occur in a document known as *The Instruction for King Meri-ka-re* (*c.* 2100 B.C.). It takes the form of advice given by an aged king to his son; and it reflects the troubled conditions in Egypt during the period between the collapse of the Old Kingdom and the establishment of the Middle Kingdom. In the passage that particularly concerns us, the old king admonishes his son:

> "The judges who judge the sinner, thou knowest, that they are not mild in that day, when they judge the miserable one, in the hour when the decision is accomplished. Evil is it where the accuser is the Wise One [probably the god Thoth]. Trust not in length of years: they look on the duration of a life as but an hour. Man remains after death and his deeds will be laid before him. But eternity abides, so that one is there, and he is a fool who (considered?) them (i.e. the judges) insignificant. But he who comes to them, not having sinned, he will be as a god, free-striding as the Lord of Eternity." [3]

Here a tribunal is imagined where several judges preside: whether they act as delegates of the Sun God we are not told. A juridical process is presupposed, in which the deceased is charged with his offences by the god Thoth. Since this deity was the Egyptian god of wisdom and the patron of writing, it seems to be implied that the charges are based upon a divine record that has been kept of the individual's life. It was probably from that record that "his deeds will be laid before him" on this fateful occasion.

During the period of the Middle Kingdom (*c.* 2000–1580 B.C.), two significant developments in the conception of the judgment of the dead are attested by the so-called *Coffin Texts,* which reveal Egyptian eschatological belief at the time. Thus, in the following ritual statement, reference is made to a mode of assessment that does not occur in the earlier texts: "The offence of which thou art accused is removed, thy fault is effaced, by the weighing on the balance, on the day of the evaluation of qualities."

[3] Trans. in A. Erman, *The Literature of the Ancient Egyptians* (Methuen, 1927). Reprinted as *The Ancient Egyptians* (Harper Torchbook, 1966).

Another text refers to "this balance of Rē, in which he weighs *Maat*".
Evidently the Egyptians now pictured the *post-mortem* judgment not so
much in terms of a legal process, but as a kind of impersonal assessment
of the individual's deeds or character. In this assessment *Maat* also played
some part, as a criterion or measure of the individual's moral worth.

The other new feature that now finds expression appears to result
from the democratization of the royal mortuary ritual. The magical assimilation of the dead king to Osiris, which the *Pyramid Texts* describe, was
now being practised on behalf of those who could afford to be buried
according to the Osirian obsequies; which meant that titles and formulae,
originally the prerogative of the king, were now assigned to private
persons. Consequently, the dead, on whose behalf this ritual was performed, were entitled *maa kheru,* in the sense that, like Osiris, they had
been vindicated before a divine tribunal. This extension of the title has
been thought by some Egyptologists to mark a declension, or deflection,
from the remarkable moral sensitivity manifested in the earlier period.
It is argued that the acquisition of such vicarious justification by ritual
must mean that Egyptians had ceased to make the moral effort that the
prospect of an effective *post-mortem* judgment would have encouraged.
It is probable that many Egyptians did tend to stifle their conscience by
relying on magic; but we have reason to believe that the idea of the
judgment after death, in the fully developed form that it attained in the
New Kingdom period (from 1580 B.C.), was powerfully effective, and that
it represents a most notable achievement of ancient Egyptian spiritual
culture.

The manner in which the Egyptians came to visualize the judgment
that awaited them after death has been most vividly preserved for us in
the illustrated copies of the so-called *Book of the Dead.* These documents,
written on rolls of papyrus, were placed in the tombs of the dead, to
assist them on their way to eternal beatitude, just as the *Pyramid Texts*
had done in the Old Kingdom period for the pharaohs. Many of the texts
inscribed in them were derived from the *Pyramid Texts* and the *Coffin
Texts.* The more elaborate editions of the *Book of the Dead* contain
vignettes illustrating the accompanying text; and they afford valuable
evidence of contemporary Egyptian conceptions of the hereafter. Two
chapters, 30 and 125, often illustrated, deal specifically with the *post-
mortem* judgment. The scene depicted is pregnant with meaning; but it
requires some explanation to make its full significance clear. The following

Michael the Archangel repels demons who try to interfere with .the fateful scales (detail from a 12th cent. mosaic depiction of the Last Judgment in the Cathedral of S. Maria Assunta, Torcello)

commentary is based upon the representation of it in the *Papyrus of the Scribe Ani,* now in the British Museum, which dates from about 1320 B.C., and is one of the finest extant copies. Its judgment-scene corresponds, except for certain details, with those in other versions of the *Book.*

The deceased scribe Ani, accompanied by his wife, both in a posture of fearful humility, is seen on the left entering the Hall of the Two Truths (*Maāti*). In the centre of the scene stands a great balance, the focal point of the transaction. The jackal-headed mortuary god Anubis kneels adjusting the index of the balance, in the left scale-pan of which the heart of Ani is set to be weighed against the feather-symbol of *Maat* in the other scale-pan. To the right stands the ibis-headed god Thoth, who records the verdict of the balance on his scribe's tablet. Behind him crouches a hideous hybrid monster named Am-mut, the "eater of the dead". The smaller figures to the left of the balance have each their significance. The male figure is that of Shai (destiny); behind him are Meskenit and Renemit, goddesses who presided respectively over childbirth and the nursing and rearing of the infant. The bird-headed figure represents the *ba* or soul of Ani, perched on the portal of his tomb;[4] while the curious rectangular object with a human head may represent the chest in which the umbilical cord of the child was placed after birth. These subsidiary

[4] See above p. 103; also p. 71.

figures, intimately connected with the life and personality of the dead man, intently watch the balance at this critical moment of his destiny. The seated figures in the upper register depict the gods who witness the judgment.

Once the bizarre imagery is understood, this scene occupies a unique place in the history of human culture; for it vividly attests the belief of the Egyptians, more than three thousand years ago, that after death a man's heart would be weighed against truth. To them, the heart was the seat of conscience. Indeed, so highly did they evaluate the moral quality of the heart, that they virtually hypostatized it, and feared that it might witness against them on this dread occasion. Chapter 30 of the *Book of the Dead* contains a prayer, which the deceased then addressed to his heart to spare him: "Heart of my mother! Heart of my form! Come not against me as a witness; oppose me not in the judgment!"[5]

According to the evidence of the *Book of the Dead,* it would appear that the Egyptians thought of the *post-mortem* judgment as comprising two parts. Chapter 125 is entitled: "Words spoken, when one enters the Hall of the Two Truths, to separate the deceased from his sins, so that he may behold the face of all the gods." Thus, the deceased is imagined as coming before a tribunal, and is provided with formulae that he must recite. They consist of two sets of asseverations of innocence in respect of certain offences: the first set is addressed to Osiris, and the second to the forty-two deities who preside over the *nomes* of Egypt. The offences concerned are of both a moral and ritual nature. The following is a representative selection: "I have not done violence to a poor man"; "I have not blasphemed a god"; "I have not killed"; "I have not had sexual relations with a boy"; "I have not snared the birds of the gods"; "I have not driven away the cattle of the god's property."

How these asseverations of innocence were related to the weighing of the heart is not clear. It is possible that the Egyptians regarded the process of judgment as having two parts, the one consequential on the other. In the first, the deceased solemnly declared his innocence. But that was not enough: the truth of his declaration had then to be tested by weighing his heart against *Maat.* Turning again to the *Papyrus of Ani,* we may notice that, after the balance has given a favourable verdict, Ani is proclaimed *maa kheru* ("justified"). Then, in the next scene, he is

---

[5] In the judgment scene in the *Papyrus of Ani* the hieroglyphic text of this chapter borders the figure of Ani.

The Last Judgment (13th cent.) from the Cathedral of Bourges. St. Michael weighs the souls in the centre of the scene. The damned are driven off to the cauldron of Hell, while angels carry the souls of the blessed to Abraham's Bosom. See detail below

depicted as being led by the god Horus into the august presence of Osiris, the lord of the dead, in whose realm he will enjoy eternal beatitude.[6]

When the judgment of the dead, as set forth in the *Book of the Dead*, is sympathetically studied, it is difficult to believe that the form it there attained represents a declension from earlier conceptions. The solemn symbolism of the judgment scene, the apprehensive attitude of the deceased, the fearfulness shown about the heart's testimony, all point to the reality of this *post-mortem* trial for the Egyptians of this period.

[6] In the judgment scene in some other copies of the *Book of the Dead*, Osiris presides over the weighing.

Moreover, there is continuous evidence to show that it remained an effective belief down to Graeco-Roman times. A priest named Petosiris, who lived about the beginning of the Ptolemaic period (305 B.C.), declares in his tomb inscription: "The West (i.e. the realm of Osiris) is the abode of those without fault. Happy is he who arrives there! But none enters therein whose heart is not right in the deed of *Maat*. There is no distinction there between rich and poor; he only counts who is found to be without fault when the balance and its burdens stand before the Lord of Eternity. None escapes from his verdict, when Thoth as the Ape sits upon the balance to make a reckoning with each according to what he has done on earth." And, in a moral tale, preserved in a second century A.D. papyrus, we find the Osirian judgment still being invoked as a familiar concept—except that, in the weighing it is the man's good deeds that are assessed against his bad deeds, and not, as in the *Book of the Dead*, his heart against the feather of *Maat*.

This continuity of belief in a *post-mortem* judgment is certainly impressive. The belief emerges about the middle of the third millennium B.C.; and it appears to have been still effective when, in A.D. 379, the native cults of Egypt were suppressed in favour of Christianity by the Emperor Theodosius I. There is nothing comparable to it in the other religions of the ancient world. The reason is no doubt to be found in the deep-rooted Egyptian conviction that immortality could be secured by ritual means, and in the Egyptians' equally strong belief that the nature of that after-life would be determined by the quality of their life here.

II

Absence of belief in any significant *post-mortem* life necessarily means that there is no basis for believing in a judgment after death. The logic of this situation is clearly exhibited in the religions of the ancient Mesopotamians[7] and Hebrews. The latter is of special interest, because, in process of time, Hebrew religion experienced a change in this respect, and from that change arose ultimately the Christian belief in the judgment of the dead.

For reasons explained in Chapter 12, the early Hebrews came to believe that the part of the human person that survived death descended to Sheol, conceived as a place deep down beneath the earth, where the

[7] See Chapter 10.

shades of the dead dwelt amid dust and gloom. Existence there was virtual annihilation. As the writer of *Ecclesiastes* puts it: "All go unto one place; all are of the dust, and all turn to dust again" (iii. 19). By the time of the Maccabaean Wars (*c.* 165 B.C.), however, the belief was established that the dead would rise to life again, complete with their bodies. Once the necessary foundation had been provided, the idea of a *post-mortem* judgment soon followed. In the *Book of Daniel*, which dates from the same period, resurrection and judgment are connected: "And many of them that sleep in the dust shall awake, some to everlasting life and some to shame and everlasting contempt" (xii. 2–3). In turn, Sheol ceased to be the abode of the dead, where they all existed in the same apathetic fashion. In the *Book of Enoch*, it is represented as a place of punishment, having various divisions, to which the dead are assigned according to their deserts.

Hebrew religion, nevertheless, was essentially ethnic in character, being primarily concerned with the nation as a whole in its relations with its god Yahweh. Consequently, the Hebrew conception of judgment was

The Ladder of Salvation (early 12th cent.), painted on the wall of the parish church of S. S. Peter and Paul, Chaldon, Surrey. Human life is represented as a ladder up which mankind attempts to climb to salvation. In the top scenes St. Michael weighs souls and Christ conquers Hades; below the torments of the damned are shown

inextricably bound up with the destiny of the nation. With the increasing decline of Israel's political fortunes from the second century B.C., Hebrew hopes became correspondingly centred upon a divine act of national restoration. And, since their sufferings were at the hands of the Gentiles, this restoration meant also a vindication of Yahweh's elect people against their heathen oppressors, with the signal punishment of the latter. These hopes find expression in an apocalyptic literature that proliferated in Israel from the second century B.C. onwards; and therein they take on a steadily increasing supernatural character. The idea of a national vindication becomes associated with the expectation of a catastrophic destruction of this present world, so that the anticipated judgment of the dead is transformed into a veritable Last Judgment of universal proportions. A graphic description of this Judgment, and of the Resurrection of the Dead that precedes it, is given in the apocryphal book known as II *Esdras,* the passage concerned dating from about A.D. 100:

> "And the earth shall restore those that are asleep in her, and so shall the dust those that dwell therein in silence, and the secret places shall deliver up those souls that were committed unto them. And the Most High shall be revealed upon the seat of judgement, and compassion shall pass away, and long-suffering shall be withdrawn: but judgement only shall remain . . . and the reward shall be shewed, and good deeds shall awake, and wicked deeds shall not sleep. And the pit of torment shall appear, and over against it shall be the place of rest: and the furnace of hell shall be shewed, and over against it the paradise of delight. And then shall the Most High say to the nations that are raised from the dead, See ye and understand whom ye have denied, or whom ye have not served, or whose commandments ye have despised. Look on this side and on that: here is delight and rest, and there fire and torments. Thus shall he speak unto them in the day of judgement. This is a day that hath neither sun, nor moon, nor stars . . ." (vii. 32–39).

III

Christianity, in its original form, was permeated by contemporary Jewish eschatology. The first disciples, identifying Jesus with the promised Messiah sent by God to deliver Israel, believed that this deliverance was imminent. Recovering from the shock of the crucifixion of their Master, they fervently awaited his triumphant return, on the clouds of heaven, with power and great glory. And this return, they believed, would mark the end of the present world-order. They believed, moreover, as did many other Jews, that the Messiah would execute God's judgment upon the nations. The *Gospel of Matthew* gives a graphic description of this Final Assize:

> "When the Son of man comes in his glory, and all the angels with him, then he will sit on his glorious throne. Before him will be gathered all the nations, and he will separate them one from another as a shepherd separates the sheep from the goats, and he will place the sheep at his right hand, but the goats at his left" (xxv. 31–3).

Down to this point, the imagery employed is true to contemporary Jewish eschatology; but now a significant change occurs. Instead of describing the judgment of the Gentile nations according to current Jewish notions, the discourse becomes an account of the judgment of individual persons, presumably both Jews and Gentiles. The criterion is the attitude that they had adopted towards Christ through their treatment of his disciples. The righteous are rewarded with places in God's Kingdom, while the doom of the wicked is pronounced: "Depart from me, you cursed, into the eternal fire prepared for the devil and his angels" (xxv. 41).

In other words, we see in this passage that Christianity, inheriting the Jewish idea of a Last Judgment, changed it from its original nationalistic character into one concerned specifically with the destinies of individuals. Since this Judgment was believed to take place at the end of the world, it also meant that it was delivered upon those who were alive at the Second Coming of Christ: it was probably assumed that those who had died before his Coming would be resurrected for judgment according to current Jewish belief. This idea of a general judgment at the end of the world, which was regarded as imminent, represents the established view of primitive Christianity. There is, however, some evidence of belief in a judgment occurring immediately after death. The most notable instance is provided by the Parable of Dives and Lazarus (*Luke* xvi. 19–31). Here the destinies of the two men concerned are decided immediately after their deaths, Lazarus being carried to "Abraham's bosom" (a Jewish metaphor for paradise), while the rich man begins his fiery torment in hell.

So far as the New Testament evidence goes, no problem was felt, during the first age of the Church, about the contradiction implicit in these concepts of an immediate *post-mortem* judgment and of a final judgment at the end of the world. Because of the fervent conviction that Christ would soon return, the latter concept prevailed; and it became invested with an awesome imagery, as the *Book of Revelation* shows:

> "Then I saw a great white throne and him who sat upon it; from his presence earth and sky fled away, and no place was found for them. And I saw the dead, great and small, standing before the throne, and books were opened. Also another book was opened, which is the book of life. And the dead were judged by what was written in the books, by what they had done. And the sea gave up the dead in it, Death and Hades gave up the dead in them, and all were judged by what they had done" (xx. 11–13).

The fading of the hope of Christ's Return within the lifetime of the first generation of believers necessitated adjustment of various aspects of the primitive faith—especially so in eschatology. The question inevitably arose: if the Return of Christ and the Final Judgment were to be postponed to an indefinite future, what was the fate of the dead in the meantime? To meet the problem, the Church gradually elaborated its doctrine of purgatory, until it was integrated into that great medieval synthesis of human destiny which finds classic expression in Dante's *Divina Com-media*. Two forms of judgment were envisaged: a particular and a final. The Particular Judgment followed immediately on the individual's death. According to the bull *Benedictus Deus*, in 1336, of Pope Benedict XII, by the verdict given at this judgment on the quality of its earthly life the soul would be admitted either to the Beatific Vision, or sent to purgatory, or consigned to hell. For the great majority of mankind, whose sins were venial rather than mortal, their destination was purgatory, where they would expiate their guilt until the Final Judgment.

The Final Judgment was a subject that the Church sought ever to keep before the minds of the faithful. It was depicted in a terrible imagery, replete with graphic details, on the sculptured tympana of cathedrals, or painted above the chancel arches of parish churches, for all to behold. Preceded by the resurrection of the dead, Christ, as the Awful Judge, dominates the centre of the scene. The archangel Michael weighs the souls of men and women, determining their fates, as once Anubis had attended the fateful balance in ancient Egyptian eschatology. As the verdicts are given, angels lead the saved to eternal bliss, and demons begin to torment the damned, as they drive them into the mouth of hell. Something of the fear of the medieval Christian, as he contemplated the awful doom

The "Doom" in the parish church of St. Thomas, Salisbury: dating *c.* 1500. This most elaborate of English medieval versions of the Last Judgment is painted on the chancel arch; it shows Christ enthroned on a rainbow, with the Heavenly Jerusalem about him. To his right, in the foreground, the dead rise from their graves; to his left, the damned go to Hell

awaiting him, can still be sensed in the words, even in translation, of the Latin hymn, *Dies irae,* dating from the thirteenth century, used in the Mass for the Dead:

> Day of wrath and doom impending,
> David's word with Sibyl's blending!
> Heaven and earth in ashes ending!
> . . .
> Ah! that day of tears and mourning!
> From the dust of earth returning,
> Man for judgement must prepare him.

IV

Despite the tacit abandonment of much of the original imagery, Christianity, both Catholic and Protestant, still teaches that man must face judgment after death. The idea, as we have seen, is very ancient. First appearing in Egypt in the third millennium B.C., it has, since that time, found expression in many religions. Space does not permit comment here on the form the belief has taken in Hinduism and Buddhism, in the cults of China and Japan, in ancient Greek religion, in Zoroastrianism and Islam. An idea so ancient, so enduring, and so widespread is surely of the highest significance for the cultural history of mankind, whatever may be thought of its rational justification. Its influence is to be found in the view of life, and in the literature and art, of many peoples.

❧ CHAPTER 8

Osiris

THE ROYAL MORTUARY GOD OF EGYPT

Early in the history of Egyptian religion, Osiris, the slain king, "emerged as the classic prototype of the saviour-god", whose death and resurrection assure to his worshippers a new life.

I

The oldest written documents, so far known, of the human race are the hieroglyphic texts inscribed on the interior walls of the pyramids of certain pharaohs of the fifth and sixth dynasties. When the first of these *Pyramid Texts* were engraved about 2400 B.C., Egypt already had some six hundred years of history as a unified state with a strong central government, and during that long period great progress had been made in the arts of civilized living. But the *Pyramid Texts* record nothing of this mighty past. Instead, the long lines of hieroglyphs that cover the walls of the sepulchral chambers and corridors of these pyramids are wholly concerned with the eternal destiny of the kings who were buried within them. The achievement of this destiny was evidently regarded as imperilled by all kinds of obstacles that would confront the dead pharaoh as he took his way from this world to the next. It was to help him to overcome them and facilitate his journey that the *Texts* were provided, and they comprise spells and incantations, hymns and prayers regarded as magically effective against various contingencies, natural and super-natural. It seems likely that the *Texts* had actually been recited by the officiating priests during the ritual of burial.

119

The golden coffin of the pharaoh
Tutankhamen, in the form of
Osiris

Throughout the amorphous mass of these *Pyramid Texts* reference
is made to many deities, for Egyptian religion was then, as it continued
to remain, essentially polytheistic. Great prominence is given to the
sun-god, under his name Rē or Atum, which is understandable since the
Texts were redacted by the priesthood of Heliopolis, the centre *par
excellence* of sun-worship, and to which the monarchs of these dynasties
were devoted. But almost of equal prominence is another god of a strangely
different character; for, whereas a god is usually imagined as powerful
and immortal, this one had apparently suffered and died. His name is
Osiris, and the name is curiously represented in hieroglyphs by the symbol
of an eye over a throne, followed by the determinative sign for deity.[1]
His legend was apparently so well known, that nowhere in the *Pyramid*

[1] Several conflicting explanations of the name have been offered by Egyptologists: e.g.
that it means "the seat of the eye," or "maker, or establisher, of a throne," or that it was derived
from a title of the Babylonian god, Marduk.

Texts was it thought necessary to give a formal account of it. Consequently the modern scholar has to endeavour to reconstruct it from various references and allusions in the *Texts*, some of them of an extremely elusive character. On this evidence, it would seem that at the time of the composition of the *Pyramid Texts* the Egyptians believed that a king named Osiris had once reigned in their land, that he had been killed by his evil-intentioned brother, Set, and that his body had been saved from decomposition and revivified by his wife Isis and her sister Nephthys or by Atum-Rē, assisted by other deities. The resurrected Osiris, however, does not resume his life on earth. His cause is tried before the tribunal of the gods at Heliopolis, and he is vindicated and Set condemned; he is succeeded in his earthly kingdom by his posthumous son Horus, and he becomes himself the ruler of the next world.

This curious legend evidently provided the rationale of a series of mortuary rites performed on behalf of the dead king. In other words, it was believed that what had happened once to Osiris could be ritually re-enacted for the eternal benefit of each deceased pharaoh. Thus in the ceremony of embalmment the Osirian precedent was invoked with the words: "Isis brings a libation to thee, Nephthys cleanses thee; thy two great sisters restore thy flesh, they reunite thy members, they cause thy two eyes to appear in thy face" (*Pyr.* 1981). Even more crucial was this text in which the sun-god Atum is invoked to reanimate the dead king Unas, as he had once reanimated the dead Osiris: "O Atum, it is thy son Osiris, whom thou has caused to live and has permitted to remain in life. He liveth and this Unas also liveth; he dieth not, and this Unas also dieth not" (*Pyr.* 167). So closely conceived, indeed, was the parallelism between the dead king and Osiris that in many texts they are actually identified, so that the king is himself addressed as "Osiris Unas" or "Osiris Pepi.", according to his personal name.

From the evidence of the *Pyramid Texts*, it is obvious that Osiris and his legend constituted a factor of basic importance in Egyptian thought at this remote period. For on the pharaonic monarchy the social and economic well-being of the state depended, and according to contemporary ideas the king did not cease to be important to his people when he died. Therefore, that the king's *post-mortem* destiny was so essentially connected with Osiris surely indicates that this deity or divine hero had in some way come to embody some fundamental need or pattern of thought in Egypt. Moreover, it is also evident that this position of Osiris had long

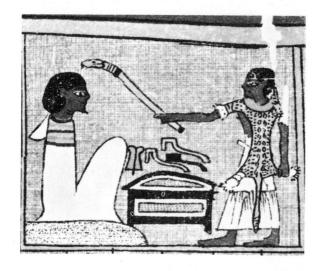

A priest prepares to perform on Ani the ceremony of "the opening of the mouth" (*Papyrus of Ani*)

been established, and there is even some indication in the *Pyramid Texts* that the Heliopolitan priesthood had been forced to recognize the fact, although it ran counter to their policy of exalting the power and prestige of Atum-Rē, their own tutelar deity.

But, as we have already noted, the character of Osiris is strange in terms of the accepted idea of deity. Instead of being the embodiment of power and splendour, as for example was Atum-Rē, Osiris is primarily connected with death and all its grim phenomena; indeed, the significance of his resurrection and ultimate triumph essentially derives from the pathos of his suffering and death. This extraordinary nature of Osiris, and his place in the royal mortuary ritual, have therefore led to many attempts by modern scholars to find some explanation of them. These explanations have taken three main forms, and it is worth while noticing them briefly, because they serve to show how complex is the problem presented by one of the earliest conceptions of deity as well as by that of the origins of Egyptian culture.

Certain passages of the *Pyramid Texts* and of the so-called "Shabaka Stone" [2] connect Osiris with the fructifying waters of the river Nile, upon whose annual inundation the economic well-being of Egypt depended. Now, since the ancient world knew of several gods of vegetation, such as the Dumuzi or Tammuz of Mesopotamia, whose life-cycle symbolized

[2] So-called after the pharaoh Shabaka (716–701 B.C.), who ordered the ancient text to be preserved by engraving it on stone. The Shabaka Stone is now in the British Museum, No. 498. In its original form the text is generally thought to date from the Old Kingdom period (2778–2242 B.C.).

the process of the seasons, the drama of the death and resurrection of Osiris has been interpreted by some authorities as representing the annual death and revival of vegetation in Egypt. What may be regarded as a variation of this line of interpretation is the theory that invokes the analogy of the institution of divine kingship among the Shilluk, a primitive Nilotic people who have survived into modern times. This people worshipped a god called Nyakang, who was regarded as a former king, and with whom all their successive kings were identified; moreover, since a Shilluk king was never allowed to grow old, lest his loss of virility should endanger the prosperity of the land, but was slain before this could happen and replaced by a younger successor, Nyakang was held never to have died. On this analogy it is, accordingly, argued that Osiris embodied the primitive Egyptian concept of kingship as the source of the vitality and prosperity of the land. Originally, it is assumed, the Egyptian king was ritually slain on the approach of old age and succeeded by his son: thus is to be explained the identification of the dead king with Osiris, and the living king with Horus, his son and heir. The third attempt at explanation assumes that the Osirian legend preserves the memory of the struggles that took place among the small rival states of predynastic Egypt before the union achieved about 3000 B.C. Osiris is, accordingly, regarded as a historical character, an ancient king who had succeeded in establishing an earlier, but an abortive, unified government, and whose memory was revered for the peace and prosperity that he had thus created. But this happy state of affairs had been rudely shattered by a rival power, identified with Set, and Osiris had been killed. Horus, in turn, represented the avenger and heir of Osiris, being the leader of a long, but ultimately successful, struggle against Set.

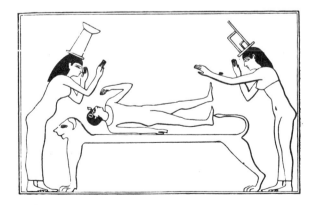

"Thy two great sisters restore thy flesh, they unite thy members. . ." Isis and Nephthys with the dead Osiris (from a bas-relief of the temple of Isis at Philae)

Such, briefly, are the main theories concerning Osiris and his legend. Each provides an ingenious explanation of certain aspects of the problem involved; but none has won general acceptance as affording a completely adequate solution. The position is not surprising, in view of the nature of the evidence at our disposal for reconstructing this remote period of ancient Egyptian life and thought. Yet, although we cannot penetrate to the origins of the Osirian legend, we can be reasonably confident in our assessment of what Osiris meant to Egyptians in historical times. There can be little doubt that, however closely they may have associated him with vegetation or fertility, the Egyptians instinctively envisaged Osiris as a real person who had been struck down by physical violence and had suffered death as all men experience it. Although his resurrection was a supernatural act, the re-assembling and preservation of his dismembered body were imagined with all the realistic detail of the Egyptian practice of embalming the dead. In their iconography, moreover, the Egyptians always depicted Osiris in human form—in fact, with his body swathed as the traditional mummy, but with the head free of the mummy-wrappings and crowned with the tall white crown of Upper Egypt and the hands holding the emblems of pharaonic sovereignty. This invariable anthropomorphic presentation of Osiris is the more remarkable, since the other Egyptian deities are generally shown with animal heads or bodies.[3] It is also significant that, throughout their land, the Egyptians venerated certain places as depositories of various parts of the dismembered body of Osiris, and at one of the most famous, Abydos, where it was believed that his head had been buried, a play was periodically enacted, commemorating his passion and triumphant resurrection.

For the history of religions, and indeed for the history of Egypt itself, the importance of Osiris, however, does not reside primarily in his rôle of the royal mortuary god as attested by the *Pyramid Texts*. He did, indeed, continue in this rôle during the whole dynastic period, even into Ptolemaic times; but gradually his cult became democratized until all who could afford the requisite minimum of the Osirian obsequies, could look to him for the assurance of a happy lot in the after-life. The process of transformation was a long and complex one, and certain of its stages are now by no means clear; but it had a decisive effect on the development

[3] There are some exceptions; e.g. Ptah and Amen are usually depicted in human form. It should be noted that sometimes the *dd* column, a symbol of Osiris, was given a human face and arms.

of some of the basic ideas of religion and morals. As a result of this transformation, Osiris emerged as the classic prototype of the saviour-god, who by his own death and resurrection can assure to his devotees a new life after death. But this is not all: besides his soteriological character, Osiris also acquired that of the judge of the dead or, alternatively, that of the god before whom the dead were to be judged. It is, accordingly, worth our while to trace out the main lines of this evolution—not an easy task; for besides the fragmentary nature of the evidence and its intrinsic difficulty, the conservative temperament of the Egyptians caused the ancient kingly formulae still to be used when the ritual was being employed, or a dedication made, on behalf of some ordinary person, man or woman.

II

As we have noted, the *Pyramid Texts* are wholly concerned with the *post-mortem* well-being of the pharaoh; nothing is said in them about the fate of other folk, even of the members of the royal house or of the aristocracy. On grounds of internal evidence, however, it would seem likely that the *Pyramid Texts* embody material derived from popular conceptions of death and the hereafter; and the fact that the tombs of nobles are often grouped about that of the pyramid of the monarch suggests that it was believed that the court would attend its ruler in death. But, as far as our evidence goes, during the Old Kingdom period (2778-2242 B.C.) Osiris was essentially the royal mortuary god, through ritual identification with whom the king was believed to live again after death. It is rarely that the name of Osiris appears during this period in the inscriptions of private tombs.

What is termed the Old Kingdom marked the first vigorous blooming of Egyptian culture after the establishment of the strong central government of the pharaonic monarchy. But by the sixth dynasty, for a variety of reasons, the royal authority began to weaken, and a period of political and social unrest ensued during which local magnates increased their power, arrogating to themselves many of the royal prerogatives. This revolution of privilege is reflected in the mortuary cultus. Even when a central government was re-established in what is known as the Middle Kingdom period (2160-1580 B.C.), it is found that the nobles are being buried in large wooden coffins on which are painted series of texts, some of them derived from the *Pyramid Texts*, in which the earlier mortuary

Isis nursing Horus: representations of Isis as the divine mother were venerated by the Egyptians both in their temples and in their homes. A bronze statuette, probably Ptolemaic

privilege of the pharaohs is tacitly assumed. In particular, the deceased is identified with Osiris, his name being coupled with that of the god. Two extracts from these so-called *Coffin Texts* may be cited in illustration of this practice, and also of the way in which the Osirian legend dominated belief: "O Osiris (*name of the deceased*) raise thyself to life; thou diest not. Whoever abuses the offering that I bring this day to Osiris N, he abuses the gift that (the goddess) Hathor brings. It is a kingly offering that Geb (the earth-god) gives for his son Osiris N; take it to thyself. It is pure in the presence of the king. I am thy son, thy heir" (*C.T.*I. 48). "Behold, I have found thee lying there. Weary is the great one. . . . Then speaks Isis to Nephthys: 'This is our brother! Come, let us raise up his head; let us gather his bones—for the protection of his limbs! Come, let us protect him! In our presence let him be weary no more! . . . O Osiris, live, stand up thou unfortunate one that liest there! I am Isis. I am Nephthys' " (C. T. 74).

These are typical examples of this funerary literature. Bizarre though it may seem to us in its compound of magical spell and mythological reference, even through the medium of translation something of its original power can be still felt—the power of the implied belief that, through ritual identification with Osiris in his death, the dead man might share in his resurrection to a new life. And in such texts, too, something of the attraction of Osiris may be glimpsed. Although the powerful priest-hood of Heliopolis had sought to make Rē, the sun-god, the supreme protector of the dead, their attempt, despite the immense prestige of this great state deity, had failed against the influence of Osiris. And the cause of this failure is significant for the history of religions. It is undoubtedly to be found in the greater human appeal of Osiris. For, whereas Rē, by virtue of his transcendental nature, was far removed from human affairs, Osiris was presented as one deeply acquainted with the common experi-ence of suffering and death. While the Egyptian would have visualized Rē in his traditional form of a falcon-headed man, crowned with the disc of the sun, in Osiris he was taught to see one who had triumphantly emerged from the fate that he must himself ultimately undergo. And, besides this ability to evoke a sympathetic response at the deepest level of human experience, the Osirian legend also endorsed other human values. The story of Isis' devotion to her dead husband and her solicitude for their infant son, menaced by the murderous Set, made her the pattern of womanly virtue. Many are the representations of her as the holy mother, nursing her divine son, which the Egyptians venerated in their temples and their homes. And in Horus, grown to manhood, they had the ideal of the pious son who avenged his father's death and served his *post-mortem* needs—indeed, it was in the rôle of Horus that a man's son performed the essential mortuary offices for his dead father.

This process of the democratization of the royal mortuary ritual, to which the *Coffin Texts* of the Middle Kingdom bear witness, is com-pleted in the New Kingdom (1580–1090 B.C.). From now on even the poor man could hope that by ritual assimilation to Osiris he might rise to a new life. Now began the custom of placing in the tomb, for the benefit of the dead, a selection of prayers, hymns and incantations, written on a roll of papyrus, instead of being painted on the large coffins as in the earlier period. The selection of these mortuary texts could be varied in extent to suit all purses. The poor man could buy for his *post-mortem* use a cheap edition of merely the essential texts, with spaces left before the title "Osiris" for the insertion of his own personal name.

These New Kingdom collections of mortuary texts have become known as the *Book of the Dead*, from the descriptive title used by the early Egyptologists of the last century. The texts concerned are of diverse origin, and some derive ultimately from the *Pyramid Texts*. Certain of the more elaborate editions are finely illustrated with vignettes depicting incidents in the experience of a deceased person on his way from this world to the next and in his life there. Such editions, of which the British Museum possesses one of the finest in the *Papyrus of Ani*, provide a most valuable insight into the mind of an Egyptian as he sought to express the fears and aspirations that the prospect of death stirred within him, coloured by the ancient tradition in which he had been nurtured.

A representation of Osiris, who wears the white crown of Upper Egypt, and holds the crook and flail, traditional emblems of Egyptian royalty. Behind Osiris is the *Ded-* column, a symbol closely connected with his cult

III

Among the illustrations of the *Book of the Dead*, there is one that surely affords the most dramatic portrayal of religious belief that has come down to us from the ancient world. It illustrates a situation with which Chapters 30 and 125 of the composition are concerned: that in the *Papyrus of Ani*, just mentioned, is perhaps the best example, and the following description is based upon it. The first scene shows the scribe Ani, for whom this copy of the *Book of the Dead* was made, entering, after death, into what is known as the "Hall of the Two Goddesses of Truth". He is shown in an attitude of humility and apprehension, and is followed by his wife in a like posture. In the centre of the picture stands a large pair of scales, in one pan of which is depicted the heart of Ani and in the other a feather, the symbol of *maat*, the goddess of truth. The jackal-headed mortuary god Anubis adjusts the index of the balance, while the ibis-headed Thoth, the divine scribe and god of wisdom, records the verdict on his scribe's tablet. In the upper register of the picture, intended to represent the side of the Judgment Hall, is shown a company of the chief gods of Egypt. Behind Thoth crouches a strange monster, made up of crocodile, lion and hippopotamus; it is designated *am-mut*, "the devourer of the dead". The meaning of the scene is plain. The heart, which represents the conscience, of the dead Ani is being weighed against the symbol of truth and justice. The hieroglyphic text of Chapter 125 of the *Book of the Dead* gives two lists of offences for the dead to abjure on this solemn occasion: the offences detailed there provide a valuable commentary upon contemporary Egyptian ethics, for ritual, social and private misdeeds are equally included.

In the Judgment Scene, as depicted in many other papyri, the weighing of the heart takes place in the presence of Osiris. In the *Papyrus of Ani* Osiris is not actually shown as then present; but he appears in the next scene, which obviously forms the sequel to the action of the actual judgment. Having emerged successfully from the awful test—failure would have entailed deliverance to *am-mut*—Ani is proclaimed *maa kheru* ("true of voice") and led by Horus into the august presence of Osiris. The last episode of the drama shows the justified (Osiris) Ani worshipping the Lord of the dead, who is solemnly depicted in his traditional mummiform, enthroned and vested with the symbols of pharaonic royalty, and attended by the faithful Isis and Nephthys.[4]

[4] See illustration on p. 106 above.

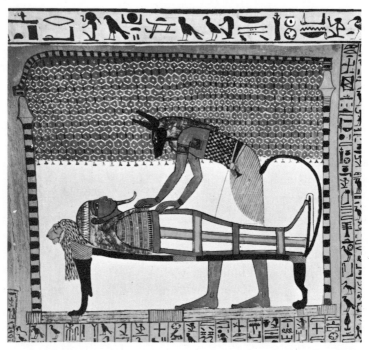

The jackal-headed mortuary god Anubis, who also assisted at the
weighing of the heart, here ministers to the dead man's mummy

This Judgment Scene of the *Book of the Dead,* despite all its bizarre
imagery, provides the most impressive witness to the moral achievement
of ancient Egypt. That individual men and women should have to answer
in the next world for their conduct in this was a belief that the Egyptians
held many centuries before the idea emerged in Iran, or Greece, or Israel.
In the *Book of the Dead* the belief had attained its most complete and
dramatic form; but it had had a long ancestry in Egypt. Already in the
Pyramid Texts reference is made to a *post-mortem* judgment in a context
(*Pyr.* 892a) that suggests that the idea was current among ordinary folk.
Then, in another passage (*Pyr.* 316d), it is said of the dead king: "He
desires that he be *maa kheru* through that which he has done." This
statement is highly significant, because the expression *maa kheru,* as was
noted above in connection with the scribe Ani, meant "true of voice."
In the Osirian legend, after his vindication against Set before the tribunal
of the gods, Osiris had been declared *maa kheru;* and this became the
accepted title of each deceased person who had successfully passed the
ordeal of the weighing of his heart. Accordingly, it seems possible that

the dead king desired to be declared "true of voice" following the Osirian precedent. Next, it may be noted that expectation of a *post-mortem* judgment, in which a man's deeds are set in contrasting heaps, appears in a writing known as the *Instruction for King Merikerē,* dating from about 2100 B.C.; and the idea of a judgment before the "Great God" seems implied in an inscription of a private tomb of about the end of the Old Kingdom period; but in neither instance is this judgment explicitly connected with Osiris. In the *Coffin Texts* of the Middle Kingdom, however, the ascription of the title *maa kheru* to the deceased becomes the normal practice, and definite reference is made to Osiris as the judge of the dead.

Several Egyptologists have maintained that, despite its dramatic solemnity, the Osirian judgment scene actually constitutes a perversion of the developing moral consciousness of the Egyptians. It is argued that, by the New Kingdom period, the Osirian devotee was trusting essentially in magic to avoid the consequences of his misdeeds in the after-life, and that, by the ascription of the title *maa kheru,* he gained a vicarious justification through Osiris and not by his own moral efforts. There is undoubtedly some truth in this charge; and probably many were content to trust to such means to supplement their own shortcomings. But one has only to study the relevant texts carefully to see that the *post-mortem* judgment was a stern reality to the Egyptian. In Chapter 30 of the *Book of the Dead,* there is a prayer in which the dead man significantly beseeches his heart not to witness against him at the dread moment. And then, we have evidence that the idea of the Osirian judgment continued, as an effective moral factor in Egyptian life, long after the end of the New Kingdom. This evidence can only be briefly referred to here, though it merits fuller study. At the beginning of the Ptolemaic period (c. 323 B.C.), a priest named Petosiris states in his tomb inscription that in the next world there is no distinction between rich and poor; for "he only counts who is found to be without fault when the balance and its burdens stand before the Lord of Eternity". And the Osirian judgment forms the dramatic turning-point of a popular story contained in a document apparently written in the second century A.D., thus implying its contemporary relevance even at this late period.

Space does not permit of the further tracing out of the history of the Osirian cult. But we must note that it has had a longer history than

The three pyramids of Gizeh, monuments to the belief in their own immortality cherished by Egyptian sovereigns, whose mortuary cult, as time went on, was taken over by their subjects

that of any other religious faith. For the cult of Osiris had its roots somewhere in the fourth millennium B.C.; and it continued as an effective force down to the official suppression of paganism by the Roman emperor Theodosius (A.D. 379-395).[5] Throughout that immense period, even when Ptolemy I (305-282 B.C.) undertook to make of Osiris, under the name of Sarapis, a universal state god whom both his Greek and Egyptian subjects could worship, the cult still preserved its essential form. Indeed, as striking evidence of this continuity is the fact that we owe our most complete account of the Osirian legend to the Greek writer Plutarch, who, probably early in the second century A.D., set it forth in the form of a religio-philosophical tractate. And it is perhaps not surprising that, when the cult of Osiris finally disappeared from the world, it was succeeded by the religion of Christ, the new saviour-god, who also died and rose to life again.

[5] As an interesting example of the continuing influence of the Osirian faith in Roman times see the illustration of the mummy case of Antemidoras in Chapter 22.

CHAPTER 9

Akhenaten

THE HERETIC KING OF EGYPT

*Inspired by his own vision of God, one of Egypt's
strangest rulers "sought, virtually single-handed,
to impose it upon the profoundly conservative
polytheistic tradition of his people".*

I

The visitor who moves through the Egyptian galleries of some great
museum sees in serried ranks the sculptured or painted representations
of the great gods and pharaohs of that ancient land. In stiff hieratic poses,
they seem to embody a strange and remote way of life that continued
unchanged for nearly three millennia. The forms and insignia of the kings
who built the great pyramids in the third century B.C., and of the gods
whom they worshipped, appear to be essentially the same as those in which
the Roman rulers of Egypt of the first century A.D. are represented in
association with the Egyptian gods. The perceptive visitor may notice,
however, as he passes through the chronologically arranged exhibits, that
this impressive continuity of tradition is briefly broken about 1360 B.C.
He finds that the stiff hieratic poses suddenly disappear, and a more
flowing and natural form of representation has replaced them—and, more
surprising still, the pharaoh is depicted in intimate scenes of domestic
life, instead of the formal ritual or martial acts that were traditional, and
obviously *de rigueur*. Moreover, this pharaoh is not, as were his predecessors and successors, associated with the traditional gods—instead, he and
his queen appear worshipping the disc of the sun, whose descending

"A man with a misshapen body, a strangely elongated head and drooping jaw. . ." Sandstone effigy of the heretic sovereign from his Sun Temple at Karnak (Cairo Museum)

rays end in hands that bless the royal pair or hold to their nostrils the *ankh,* the symbol of life.

This strange and very brief interlude in the tradition of ancient Egyptian art is linked with one of the most remarkable figures not only of Egyptian history but of the history of mankind—the pharaoh Amenhotep IV, or, as he chose to call himself, Akhenaten. To appreciate something of the significance of his achievement, and of his extraordinary personality, we must make a brief appraisal of the nature and trends of Egyptian civilization until his time.

II

Throughout their long history the Egyptians remained ever conscious of the unique significance of one event—the union of Upper and Lower Egypt under the first pharaoh, Menes, which occurred about 3000 B.C. Modern scholars find it difficult to identify this king from the sparse records of the period that have survived. But, without doubt, the final elimination of a number of small warring states and their replacement by a strong centralized monarchical government marked a decisive stage in the development of Egyptian civilization. Since the economy of Egypt depends on the annual inundation of the Nile, the construction and maintenance of irrigation works to control and utilize the life-giving water are of primary importance and, in turn, necessitate an efficient control of the labour potential. The office of overseer of canals is significantly one of the earliest mentioned in inscriptions. Hence, from the beginning in Egypt, the kingship, which provided such control, was not merely a convenient form of political government, but was invested with a sacred character as being the source of national prosperity and well-being. The pharaoh[1] was accordingly regarded as being himself divine, in fact the incarnated son of Rē, the sun-god, the supreme deity of the Egyptian state. As such, he was treated as a god, whose command was law and whose person was the centre of the daily ritual of service and adoration.

As well as being himself a god, the pharaoh was the supreme pontiff and minister of the gods of Egypt. It was he, at least theoretically, who built their temples and provided them with their offerings. But above all this was his relationship to the sun-god, Rē, who was essentially the "Great God". The Egyptians worshipped many gods; but their religion really centred around two deities. One was the personification of the sun, of whose presence, splendour and power all who live in Egypt are urgently and unceasingly aware. During the first great epoch of Egyptian history, the so-called Old Kingdom period (c. 2700–2185 B.C.), the cult of the sun-god became the state religion *par excellence*, and was intimately associated with the person and office of the king. Its centre was at Ōn, which the Greeks later called Heliopolis, the "sun-city". The priesthood there, in the mortuary texts that they placed in the pyramids of some of the pharaohs of the fifth and sixth dynasties to secure their safe passage to the next world, exalted their god by representing him as the creator of the world, who at first appeared self-existent out of the primaeval watery chaos of Nun.[2] To these Heliopolitan theologians the sun-god was known by a variety of names or titles, some of which derived from his identification with other ancient gods who had solar or royal connections. Thus, under his name of Rē, which meant the "sun", he was associated with the local god of Heliopolis, Atum, whose name possibly denoted "complete" or "universal" being. Another title was that of Kheper, which was derived from a word meaning "to exist" or "to come into being"; and under this form the sun-god was curiously represented by a scarab-beetle. Again, the sun-god was identified as

[1] The title "pharaoh" derives from the Egyptian words *per aa*, meaning the "Great House": cf. the Turkish title, the Sublime Porte.
[2] See Chapter 2.

"Horus of the two horizons", and depicted as a falcon-headed man, crowned with the sun's disc.

Once the position was achieved, the sun-god remained ever after the supreme god of the Egyptian state, and one of the royal titles, held in turn by each king, was that of "son of Rē". The achievement of this status, however, did not mean that Heliopolis continued to enjoy the privilege of being the centre of the state cult, and that the priesthood there retained the power and prestige that was certainly theirs in the Old Kingdom era. The revival of pharaonic power about 2000 B.C., after a period of decline, marked a new epoch of Egyptian culture known as the Middle Kingdom. The change led to a shift of the centre of royal power from the area in which Heliopolis lay, near the junction of Upper and Lower Egypt, to Thebes in Upper Egypt. This move of the seat of government survived the subjugation of Egypt by the Hyksos (1730–1570 B.C.); and, when these hated foreigners were expelled by the Theban prince Amosis, and Egypt entered upon a career of imperial expansion, the power and prestige of Thebes became immense. This meant, in terms of Egyptian thought, the exaltation of the local god of Thebes and the patron deity of the Theban dynasty.

This Theban god was in many ways a mysterious being. His name "Amun"[3] seems to have signified "that which is hidden", and he was generally represented in human form, wearing a cap surmounted by two tall plumes. With his exaltation as the state god, tradition demanded that he should be identified with the sun-god: hence he became known as Amun-Rē. In turn, it would appear that his priesthood undertook to provide a theological basis for his newly acquired precedence; and, according to the accepted tradition, this took the form of a cosmogony which presented Amun as the creator of the world and Thebes itself as the first land to emerge from the primaeval deep of Nun. Some of the Theban kings proved to be mighty warriors; and Egyptian power was extended southwards into the Sudan and northwards far into Syria. These conquests they piously attributed to their god; and they loaded the magnificent temples, which they built for him, with the spoils of their wars. The following extract from a hymn of victory, set up in the temple of Karnak by Thutmose III (1490–1436 B.C.), affords eloquent testimony

---

[3] The ancient Egyptian language contained signs representing only consonants and semi-vowels. Consequently, in transliteration vowels have to be supplied and may be given variously, e.g. "Amun" can be written "Amen," and "Amon."

of this royal devotion. The hymn takes the form of an address by
Amun-Rē to the king:

"Words spoken by Amun-Rē, Lord of the Thrones of the Two Lands:
Welcome to me, as thou exultest at the sight of my beauty, my son and
my avenger, Men-kheper-Rē,[4] living for ever! I shine forth for love of thee,
and my heart is glad at thy good comings into my temple, while my hands
endow thy body with protection and life. How sweet is thy graciousness
toward my breast! I establish thee in my dwelling place . . . I give thee
valor and victory over all foreign countries; I set the glory of thee and
the fear of thee in all lands, the terror of thee as far as the four supports
of heaven. I magnify awe of thee in all bodies. I set the battle-cry of thy
majesty throughout the Nine Bows."[5]

The cult of Amun thus became linked with the fortunes of Egypt
at the time of its greatest power and prosperity. Amun, it seemed, had
not only assisted his royal protégés in freeing Egypt from a foreign yoke,
but he had also extended his providence to endowing them with an
empire, the like of which had not been known. Egypt now dominated
the world of the Fertile Crescent, and its riches poured into her, making
many wealthy and inflating the native sense of superiority towards all
outside the sacred land of the Nile. The priesthood of Amun in particular
grew rich and powerful on the reputation of their god and on the
endowments of the grateful pharaohs.

It must not be thought that the cult of Amun was without any
genuine spiritual inspiration. There is evidence that it was capable of
leading on men's minds to the concept of a beneficent Creator, who was
as much concerned with the smaller beings of his creation as with the
imperial destiny of Egypt. The following extract, which is taken from
a hymn to Amun-Rē, is especially significant for our subsequent study
of Akhenaten's thought since it is of an earlier date:

"He (i.e. Amun) who made the herbage [for] the cattle,
And the fruit tree for mankind,
Who made that (on which) the fish of the river may live,
And the birds *soaring in* the sky.
He who gives breath to that which is in the egg,
Gives life to the son of the slug,

[4] A title of Thutmose III, meaning "the form of Rē abides."
[5] A traditional title of the enemies of Egypt. The passage is translated by J. A. Wilson
in *Ancient Near Eastern Texts*, ed. J. B. Pritchard (Princeton University Press, 1955), pp. 373-4.

And makes that on which the gnats may live,
And worms and flies in like manner;
Who supplies the needs of the mice in their holes
And gives life to flying things in every tree.
Hail to Thee, who did all this!
Solitary sole one, with many hands,
Who spends the night wakeful, while all men are asleep,
Seeking benefit for his creatures." [6]

We must now turn to consider the second of the two deities, in whom, as was mentioned above, the religion of the Egyptians was essentially centred. This was the god Osiris, who they believed had been a good king who reigned in their land long ago, and who, after being murdered by an evil being called Set, had been raised to life again and become the lord of the dead.[7] Osiris appears in the earliest Egyptian records, namely, the *Pyramid Texts* (*c.* 2400 B.C.), as the god of the royal mortuary ritual. It was believed that, by ritual assimilation to Osiris, the dead pharaoh, like Osiris, would again be raised to life. Through a process of democratization, this royal mortuary privilege was gradually extended; so that by the time of the New Kingdom (1575–1087 B.C.), everyone who could afford the prescribed Osirian obsequies could look forward to a similar resurrection. Since the Egyptians were profoundly preoccupied with the prospect of death and the hereafter, the Osirian faith conditioned their entire attitude towards life and destiny. It inspired the whole elaborate process of embalming the bodies of the dead and their ritual burial in carefully constructed tombs, equipped with costly furniture and mortuary offerings. Indeed, each Egyptian believed that his eternal well-being essentially depended upon the proper performance of this service for him when he died.

III

Such, then, was the main structure of Egyptian religion, when the pharaoh Amenhotep III died about the year 1367 B.C. and was succeeded by his son, who had the same name, meaning "Amun is content". In view of the strange events that were to follow, it is natural to ask whether they were in any way adumbrated during the previous period. There is some evidence, though not much, that the actual disc of the sun itself,

[6] Translated by J. A. Wilson in *Ancient Near Eastern Texts*, p. 366.
[7] See Chapter 8.

Tutankhamen, the heretic's successor, who himself submitted to the god of Thebes, and his wife: the back of a throne overlaid with gold leaf, found in the pharaoh's tomb. The Queen sprinkles her husband with scented water (Cairo Museum)

called in Egyptian the *aten*, was beginning to receive special attention. The sun's disc had from the Old Kingdom period been used as a symbol of Rē, the sun-god, being depicted as surmounting his head in the various forms in which he was represented. But now reference is made to the disc as an independent entity. Thus we hear that Queen Tiye, the wife of Amenhotep III and the mother of the new king, possessed a ceremonial barge which was called "The Aten gleams"; while a Theban inscription dating from this time refers to the "Steward of the Mansion of the Aten"—surely an indication that a cult of the Aten was already being practised in Thebes.

This evidence has prompted some scholars to suppose that the priesthood of Heliopolis, the ancient seat of the sun cult, were seeking to re-establish the primacy of their god. The fact that the upstart Theban deity, Amun, was identified with Rē afforded the priests of Heliopolis little consolation. They had lost their former influence, and possibly some of their revenues, to those who served Amun in his mighty temple at Thebes. Accordingly, it is suggested, the Heliopolitan clergy sought to withdraw their god from the unprofitable identification with Amun by stressing the essential solar aspect. Hence they began to present the sun's disc, the *aten,* alone, without any anthropomorphic associations, as the image of the sun-god. The suggestion is a reasonable one; but, on the meagre evidence that exists, it cannot be proved. What is certain is that some cult of the *Aten* was already known; the fact, however, is of little significance for understanding the remarkable revolution of religious faith and practice that was now put in hand in Egypt by its new king.

Amenhotep IV, to give him the title with which he began his reign, was to prove by his achievements that mentally he was not as other men are, but was urged on by a strange genius for religious experience and its expression. Physically, too, he was not as other men. The new art, which now begins to show itself, was evidently inspired by a desire for realistic representation, and the king was depicted with such a degree of bodily abnormality that we must conclude that his known desire for the truth caused the artists he employed to depict him as he actually was. And so, in his sculptured portraits, we see a man with a misshapen body, a strangely elongated head and drooping jaw, yet with a face that commands attention by the deep pensive gaze of the eyes. The brooding genius of the portraits surely portrays the man who now sought to overthrow the religious tradition of his kingdom and substitute for it his own conception of God.

It is tantalizing that what was clearly one of the most interesting episodes in the long history of Egypt, and indeed of the Ancient World, should be known to us only through a few inscriptions, many of them in a fragmentary condition. Only by the most ingenious detective work have scholars succeeded in piecing together something of the story of this remarkable man and his equally remarkable undertaking. No narrative account of his reign can be given; and we must be content to trace its developments only at those points illuminated by some piece of the extant evidence. Thus, we note that, at the commencement of his reign, he was, like his royal predecessors, presumably a devotee of Amun, commemorating his devotion in his name Amenhotep; in a carving in the sandstone quarry at Gebel Silsila, he is actually represented as worship-

Akhenaten liked to be represented among his family in intimate domestic scenes. Here, beneath the rays of the solar disc, he nurses one of the princesses (chalkstone relief in the Berlin Museum)

ping Amun-Rē. But, in the accompanying inscription, the young king is described as the "first prophet of Rē-Harachte, Rejoicing-in-the-Horizon in his name Shu ('sunlight') which is Aten". This titulary is especially significant when seen in the context of later developments. For it reveals a concentration on the cosmic aspects of the sun; and it is notable for its absence of reference to any of the usual identifications with local gods, particularly in the form of Amun-Rē. It would seem that the king did not remain content with this description of the sun-god, upon whom his devotion was surely concentrating. The names "Rē-Harachte" conjured up the traditional representation of the sun as either a falcon or a falcon-headed man; and such a conception of his god was now becoming distasteful. By the sixth year of his reign a significant change of imagery has been made. The sun-god now appears only in the form of the solar disc (*aten*), with its rays streaming downwards and terminating in hands that bless or caress his royal devotees.

About the same time, even more decisive changes occur. The king's own name, as we have seen, commemorated an attachment to Amun, as did the names of many of his predecessors. Clearly, it could no longer be tolerated; and so it disappears from the royal inscriptions and is replaced by Akhenaten, meaning "It-is-pleasing-to-the Aten" or "He-who-is-serviceable-to-the Aten".[8] But the king obviously felt that some more drastic break with the past was necessary, if he were to succeed in establishing his new faith. Early in his reign, he had built a sanctuary for the Aten near the great temple of Amun at Thebes; but he must have understood that the cult of Amun was too powerfully entrenched there to be affected by such measures. Consequently he decided that he must himself cut free from Thebes and its associations, and establish his god in a new and unpolluted capital.

In this decision he believed that he was guided by the Aten; and he selected a place some three hundred miles to the north of Thebes, known today as Tell el-Amarna, for the site of the new city. It is fortunate that some inscriptions on boundary stones that marked the area have survived to tell us something of Akhenaten's mind at this time. The following extracts describe the king's speech at the foundation ceremonies. Akhenaten is addressing the assembled company of high officials, nobles and captains of his court, as "they lay on their bellies before his Majesty, kissing the ground before his mighty will". "Behold ye Akhetaten,[9] which the Aten has desired to be made for him, with memorials to his name for eternity without end. For it was my Father, the Aten, who led me to this Akhetaten. There was no official who brought me to it; no person whatever in the whole land directed me to it, so that he (can) say that he created Akhetaten in this place. Verily it was the Aten, my Father, who directed me to it, that I might make it for him . . . Behold, the Pharaoh discovered it. It (the site) belonged to no god, it was owned by no goddess, it had no lord, it had no mistress, who as its owner could operate here."

The courtiers are then represented as making appropriate reply to the king: "It is thou who leadest unto him (the Aten) every land, and puttest every city under tribute for him. [Thou causest all men to be

---

[8] C. Aldred (*Akhenaten: Pharaoh of Egypt*, Thames & Hudson, 1968, p. 185) translates the title as "The Effective Spirit (= incarnation) of the Aten." The word *akh* could mean "glorified spirit" and denoted the "blessed dead."

[9] The name of the new city means "The Horizon of Aten."

subject to him], who has made them for himself. All lands and alien places, and the Ha-nebu (the Aegean peoples) come laden with their gifts for the god who has given them life. For he it is, through whose rays men live and whose breath fills their nostrils . . ." Then Akhenaten solemnly declares: "I create Akhetaten for the Aten, my Father, in this place. I will not make Akhetaten for him to the south, or to the north, or the west or the east of this place. Nor will I pass beyond the southern boundary stone of Akhetaten southwards; nor will I pass beyond the northern boundary stone of Akhetaten [northwards] to make Akhetaten for him there . . . I will make the temple of the Aten for the Aten, my Father, in Akhetaten at this place . . . I will make (the shrine) of 'the shadow of Re' of the great Wife of the King, (Nefertiti) for the Aten, my Father, in Akhetaten at this place . . . I will make for myself the Palace of the King . . . I will make the Palace of the Royal Spouse in Akhetaten at this place. A tomb shall be made for me in the mountain of the sun-rise [of Akhetaten]. A sarcophagus shall be made therein, with the million of jubilees which the Aten, my Father, has decreed for me. A sarcophagus shall be made therein for the great Wife of the King (Nefertiti) with this [million of years . . .]. (A sarcophagus shall be made) therein for the King's daughter, Merit-aten, with this million of years."

Queen Nefertiti, Akhenaten's consort, from whom finally he seems to have become estranged (sandstone head, now in the Staatlichen Museen, Berlin)

The inscription, from which these extracts are taken, contains a passage that refers ominously to the reaction of the priesthood of Amun to the religious policy of Akhenaten: "[My Majesty has heard of the priests of the temple of Amun in Thebes, that in word and deed they proceed against the Aton]. But so truly as my Father lives . . . it is worse than that which I heard in the Fourth Year. It is [worse] than that which I heard in the [Third?] Year; it is worse than that which I heard in the [Second Year?]. [It is worse than that which Neb-Maat-Re (i.e. king Amenhotep III) heard]. It is worse than that which Men-Kheperu-Re (i.e. king Thutmose IV) heard . . ." [10]

It is unfortunate that the last passage does not describe more precisely these activities of the priesthood of Amun. That its members should have reacted strongly against the reformation of Egyptian religion that Akhenaten was intent on pursuing is understandable; for it was surely aimed at overthrowing the power and wealth that they had acquired through the prestige of their god. The references to some trouble from the same source in the reigns of Akhenaten's father and grandfather are interesting. They could be interpreted as indicating that the royal house had already clashed in some way with the priesthood of Amun. If this were so, a likely cause may have been that the growing pretensions of these clergy, controlling as they did the state cult, were beginning to threaten the royal prerogative; and Akhenaten's policy may have been motivated by a desire to meet this danger as well as by devotion to his chosen god.

In what form the final rupture came between Akhenaten and the traditional cults of his people is not known. What is known is that he resorted to active measures to suppress the worship of the hated Amun: agents were sent throughout the land to chisel out the name of Amun wherever it appeared on monuments or in inscriptions. A drive, though not so thoroughly pursued, was also made against the other gods. So far as the evidence goes of tombs found at Tell el-Amarna, it would seem that the Osirian funerary ritual was also abandoned; although the layout of the tombs remained the same, prayers to the Aten took the place of the customary mortuary texts inscribed on the walls and on the funerary equipment.

The nature of Akhenaten's faith in his god is eloquently revealed

---

10 Translated from *Die aegyptische Religion in Text und Bild* (ed. G. Roeder), Band IV (Zürich and Stuttgart, 1961), pp. 38–45.

in a hymn of praise to the Aten, which, although inscribed in the tomb
of a noble, was surely the composition of the king himself. The following
extracts show something of the various facets of this faith:

Thou appearest beautifully on the horizon of heaven,
Thou living Aton, the beginning of life!
When thou art risen on the eastern horizon,
Thou hast filled every land with thy beauty.
Thou art gracious, great, glistening, and high over every land;
Thy rays encompass the lands to the limit of all that thou hast made;
As thou art Re, thou reachest to the end of them;
(Thou) subduest them (for) thy beloved son.
. . . .
When thou settest in the western horizon,
The land is in darkness, in the manner of death.
They sleep in a room, with heads wrapped up,
Nor one eye sees the other.
. . . .
At daybreak, when thou arisest on the horizon,
When thou shinest as the Aton by day,
Thou drivest away the darkness and givest thy rays.
. . . .
Washing their bodies, taking (their) clothing,
Their arms are (raised) in praise at thy appearance.
All the world, they do their work.
. . . .
Creator of seed in women,
Thou who makest fluid into man,
Who maintainest the son in the womb of his mother,
. . . .
On the day when he is born,
Thou openest his mouth completely,
Thou suppliest his necessities.
When the chick speaks within the shell,
Thou givest him breath within it to maintain him.
When thou hast made him his fulfilment within the egg, to break it,
He comes forth from the egg to speak at his completed (time);
He walks upon his legs when he comes forth from it.
. . . .
The countries of Syria and Nubia, the *land* of Egypt,
Thou settest every man in his place,
Thou suppliest their necessities:
. . . .

Thou makes a Nile in the underworld,
Thou bringest it forth as thou desirest
To maintain the people (of Egypt)

. . . .

All distant foreign countries, thou makest their life (also),
For thou hast set a Nile in heaven,
That it may descend for them and make waves upon the mountains,
Like the great green sea,
To water their fields in their towns.

. . . .

Thou art in my heart,
And there is no other that knows thee
Save thy son Nefer-kheperu-Re Wa-en-Re,[11]
For thou hast made him well-versed in thy plans and in thy strength.[12]

The hymn clearly breathes a spirit of deep joy and of devotion for the deity whom Akhenaten conceived as embodied in the sun's disc. It is truly lyrical in its description of the reaction of the earth and its inhabitants to the rising and setting of the sun; and it shows a vivid appreciation of the various manifestations of the divine providence. It is notable also for its universalism: the care of the Aten is not limited to the people of Egypt but extends throughout the known world of that day—the references to the two Niles are significant of the terms in which an Egyptian instinctively thought. But, the last lines quoted here reveal Akhenaten's estimate of his own status *vis-à-vis* this god, whom he proclaims as the creator, the sovereign lord and sustainer of the universe. It is he who is the sole mediator between the Aten and mankind; it is he alone who knows and understands the divine wisdom. In this Akhenaten remains essentially in the tradition of the pharaohs: he is the unique son and representative on earth of the sun-god, and to him only can men directly approach—a fact that is made evident in much of the Amarna sculpture.

IV

Despite the egoism of his religion, Akhenaten certainly infused into Egyptian art that spirit of naturalism which has made Amarna art so distinctive and attractive an interlude in a long conservative tradition

[11] Another title of Akhenaten meaning "Beautiful are the forms of Rē, the Sole One of Rē."

[12] Translated by J. A. Wilson in *Ancient Near Eastern Texts*, pp. 370-1.

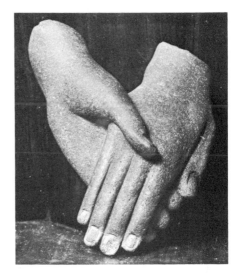

Hands, probably from a group representing Akhenaten and his Queen (now
in Berlin)

of artistic representation. It has given us also a number of intimate scenes
of the king's domestic life, besides that superb series of sculptured heads,
of which the portrait of the beautiful Nefertiti is now world-famous. In
the domestic scenes, we behold the king in intimate converse with his
wife, fondling and kissing his little daughters, and even gnawing a
bone—and there is one tragic sketch of Akhenaten and Nefertiti lamenting
over the dead body of one of their daughters. Never before, and never
again, would such revelations of the pharaoh's private life be made.

But how did this strange adventure end? Once again, unfortunately,
detailed evidence is lacking. It would appear that such was the sanctity
and prestige of the kingship that no violent revolution overthrew
Akhenaten; he seems to have reigned for at least seventeen years. Yet,
clearly he did not win the support of the mass of his subjects for his
reformation; in Akhetaten it would seem that his following was composed
mainly of time-serving courtiers. Arrayed against him must surely have
been the dispossessed priesthood of Amun, as well as indignant priests
of other deities. And to their opposition was undoubtedly added that
of the army, which had to watch, inactive, the break-up and loss of
Egypt's empire in Syria. Akhenaten has indeed been claimed as history's
first pacifist. But this is to presume principles for which we have no
evidence; it is more likely that Akhenaten was so absorbed in establishing
his new faith that he neglected the reports of garrison commanders and
of allied princes, urgently requesting military aid in the steadily worsening

situation in which they found themselves. Those who were proud of
their country's empire, and had grown rich from it, must have longed
for a new king who would take the field again, as did the great warrior
pharaohs of the past.

How the end came we cannot tell. It would seem that the idyllic
atmosphere conveyed by the *Hymn to the Aten,* and apparent in the
Amarna art, did not continue. Sometime after the twelfth year of his
reign, there is some indication that Nefertiti was, in some way, estranged
from Akhenaten; there is even evidence that he had taken another queen.
Akhenaten had no son; and it would seem that, towards the end of his
rule, he associated his son-in-law, Smenkhkare, with himself on the
throne. The intention that he had recorded on the boundary stone of
Akhetaten years before—that he should be buried within the environs
of his sacred city—seems never to have been fulfilled. A mummy, found
in a ravaged tomb in the Biban-el-Moluk in 1907, has been identified
by certain eminent Egyptologists, through the patched-up coffin in which
it was contained and other relics, as that of Akhenaten. The identification
has not yet been established; but the mystery that invests these pathetic
remains would be consonant with the obscurity that surrounds the final
passing of Akhenaten and his work.

His ephemeral successor seems to have made his peace with Amun,
as did the other son-in-law who followed him—Tutankhamen, whose
name, changed from Tutankhaten, commemorates his submission to the
mighty god of Thebes. Vengeance on the heretic king was duly taken
by the devotees of Amun. As Akhenaten had erased the name of Amun,
so his own monuments were smashed, his name was obliterated, and he
himself was condemned to ignominy as "the enemy of Akhetaten".
Attempts have been made to trace the influence of Akhenaten's concept
of his god in Hebrew monotheism. The case must necessarily remain
"non-proven". Akhenaten's true significance, however, does not lie in
that direction. It lies in the strange genius of the man himself, who,
inspired by his own vision of God, sought, virtually single-handed, to
impose it upon the profoundly conservative polytheistic tradition of his
people.

CHAPTER 10

The Epic of Gilgamesh

A MESOPOTAMIAN PHILOSOPHY OF LIFE

"Possibly some innate realism prevented the Mesopotamians from seeing death other than objectively. But the Epic of Gilgamesh *remains an eloquent witness to the poignancy of their interrogation of the meaning of human life and destiny."*

I

To move from the rooms devoted to ancient Egyptian civilization in one of our great museums to those in which the relics of ancient Mesopotamian life are displayed is to experience a sudden change of ethos. Although these two earliest civilizations of the Near East were contemporaneous and in their material achievement equal, each was characterized by a distinctive spirit that can still be clearly felt, even through the media of the broken monuments that modern archaeology has recovered. To the museum visitor this difference is perhaps most manifest as he passes from viewing the specimens of Egyptian linear and plastic art to those of Mesopotamia. Although in the Egyptian scenes strange and repellent deities often appear in solemn ritual acts, there are numerous representations of the ordinary events of social life that clearly reveal a real *joie de vivre* and appreciation of both the beautiful and the homely. Where scenes of violence are depicted, as in the many monuments of royal victories, the representation usually has a kind of symbolic character, so that the grim physical realities are not intruded on the viewer. Very different is the impression given by the remains of Meso-

Assyrian hero holding a lion; a large relief from Khorsabad in north-eastern Iraq, a city founded by King Sargon in the eighth century B.C. It may represent Gilgamesh

potamian art, whether of Sumerian, Babylonian or Assyrian origin. There is a notable absence of representation of the events of everyday life; warfare and its consequences form the subject of the bulk of the surviving monuments, and in its depiction a grim satisfaction seems to show itself by rendering with the utmost realism the grisly details of the fate of those who were conquered. Even when the Assyrian monarchs chose to alternate such monuments of their triumphs with accounts of their prowess in hunting, the artists not only gloried in their great ability to represent in stone the lithesome strength of the lions that were hunted, but they were equally concerned to portray the reality of the beasts' dying agony when transfixed with arrows and lances.

The grim spirit that pervades Mesopotamian art is the more remarkable when it is recalled that, to continue the comparison, so much of our evidence of Egyptian art comes from the tombs and might consequently be expected to have been sombre in both subject and spirit.

That Egyptian art is not so, despite its mortuary connexions, has its explanation in a fact that affords a clue to the difference of ethos between Egyptian and Mesopotamian culture. The intense preoccupation of the Egyptians with death, which is so strikingly attested by their mummies, tombs, mortuary equipment and funerary papyri, was fundamentally inspired by optimism. As a preceding chapter showed, the ancient Egyptian believed that, through ritual assimilation to the resurrected god Osiris, he could attain to a new and blessed life after death. Hence, although he naturally feared the awful experience of death, he could view his destiny optimistically, believing that by divine grace and his own effort he could continue his personal existence into the next world and in a happy condition. The inhabitant of ancient Mesopotamia, be he Sumerian, Babylonian or Assyrian, had no such hope. His religion taught a dismal eschatology. He was instructed to believe that the gods had created mankind to serve them by building temples and offering regular sacrifices. But that was mankind's only *raison d'être;* beyond that there was nothing for which its members could strive or hope. To their human servants the gods were generally thought to be benevolent and to prosper their undertakings, provided that men in their turn were loyal and diligent in their service. Disobedience would result in the withdrawal of divine providence, and the disobedient would thereby be exposed to the assault of maleficent demons who brought disease and other misfortunes. But divine providence extended only to this life; for the gods had withheld immortality from their creatures. Thus, even a life of pious service to the gods was of no avail; man's destiny, as an individual, was limited to the years of his life in this world.

But the ancient Mesopotamian did not believe that death brought annihilation. Indeed, he might have been happier if he could have believed so. The concept of personal annihilation required a greater degree of sophistication than Mesopotamian thought was then capable of, and it would seem that the primitive instinct to envisage the continuance of personal identity led to a belief in a form of *post-mortem* survival. Death was thought to effect an awful change in the individual, who became an *edim* or *edimmu*. It is not certain how this change was envisaged. Some texts seem to imply that there was a transformation of being into something hideous and repulsive; other evidence appears to indicate that the dead preserved consciousness of their personal identity and could be affected by the provision or the lack of mortuary offerings.

But, whatever the form of their existence, their condition was most wretched. At death they departed to the realm of the infernal god Nergal, which was grimly named *kur-nu-gi-a,* "the land of no-return". It was thought to lie deep beneath the earth on which mankind dwelt. It is graphically described in a curious text known as the *Descent of Ishtar into the Underworld* as "the house in which there is no light, and those who dwell therein have earth for their sustenance and clay for their food, and are in profound darkness; they are clothed like birds with wings; dust is both door and bolt of that place". The Hebrew conception of *Sheol,* as it is found in *Job* x. 21–2, derives from the same eschatological tradition. Moreover, in *kur-nu-gi-a* there was no distinction between the dead, high or low, good or bad—all were in the same condition of hopeless misery. Hence this life had not that moral significance for the Mesopotamian that it had for the Egyptian, who believed that his condition in the next world would be determined by his conduct in this, for after death his heart would be weighed against the symbol of truth in the presence of Osiris.

Taught to see his destiny in terms of this grim eschatology, it was inevitable that the inhabitant of ancient Mesopotamia should adopt a pessimistic view of life. This did not mean that life in Mesopotamia was more unhappy than it was elsewhere in the ancient world. There is, indeed, an abundance of evidence that the good things of life were sought after and enjoyed as much as they ever were in Egypt. And, strangely perhaps to our thinking, there is evidence too of genuine devotion to the gods and apparent joy in their service, although it was by their decree that men were mortal. Despite this testimony to the general tenor of social life, the logic of the traditional eschatology was, however, inescapable, and, beneath the surface of ordinary life, it is evident that many were deeply concerned with the inevitable problem of coming to terms with their dismal end. Of this quest the literature of ancient Mesopotamia has left us a supreme memorial in the *Epic of Gilgamesh,* which is not only our earliest example of epic composition, but also the first attempt to discuss the problem of man's destiny.

II

The *Epic of Gilgamesh* in its most complete form survives on twelve large clay tablets, which were recovered from the remains of the library in the temple of Nabu and from the palace library of King Assurbanipal

Fragments of the *Epic of Gilgamesh* date back to Akkadian times in Mesopotamia; bronze head of an Akkadian ruler of the third millennium B.C.

at Nineveh. These versions of the *Epic* date from the seventh century B.C.; but it is evident that the work in some form is far older, for fragments of it have been found in Sumerian and early Akkadian. From the fact that some of these older pieces contain variants from the Assyrian version, there is reason for thinking that the *Epic* in its most complete form is a composition made up of a number of earlier independent legends. One particularly interesting indication of this, to which attention will be more closely drawn below, is the interpolation into the narrative of the story of the Flood, which was evidently of quite independent origin and purpose and wholly unconnected with the Gilgamesh theme. It has been suggested by some scholars that the *Epic* in its more complete form is the product of philosophical reflection that manifested itself at Babylon about 2000 B.C. Certainly, in the form in which we have it from the Assyrian libraries, it is a carefully conceived literary composition, intended to present a definite philosophy of life through the recitation of the tragic career of a hero well known to contemporary folklore.

Gilgamesh was clearly one of the great figures of Mesopotamian tradition. He is represented on early Sumerian seal-stones engaged in heroic labours, his name appears in the Sumerian king-list inscribed on the Weld-Blundell prism, now in the Ashmolean Museum at Oxford, and it is frequently found in the formulae of omens and oaths. Gilgamesh thus appears to have been a kind of semi-divine hero in Mesopotamian folklore; but, although he is described as partly human and partly divine, the pathos of his tragedy as it is presented in the *Epic* resides in the fact that he knows himself to be mortal as other men are.

A recent editor of the *Epic* has said, "The Gilgamesh Epic is a meditation on death, in the form of a tragedy." [1] It is truly such; but it is also much more. Its author—if indeed one man alone was responsible for its completed form—has made his narrative the vehicle for the only viable philosophy of life that the accepted eschatology allowed, and he has, moreover, taken the opportunity therein to give expression to current thought on a number of minor issues. An interesting instance of this occurs in what might fairly be called the first act of the drama.

When the curtain rises on the first scene, we are given a vivid picture of what tyrannical rule meant in an ancient Sumerian city-state. Gilgamesh is the prince of Uruk; he is a man of dynamic character, handsome in appearance, and mighty in his strength. To him Uruk owes its great walls and temple; but from his lust and rapacity its citizens suffered—no boy or maiden was safe from him. To save the people of Uruk from their ordeal the gods take a hand, and a mighty wild man named Enkidu is created to contend with Gilgamesh and control his demonic energy. The presentation of Enkidu, who is one of the key characters of the *Epic*, is skilfully managed and utilized to show what were believed to be the effects of civilized living on mankind. When we first see Enkidu he is a wild hairy creature, who lives with the animals, and eats grass and drinks water as they do. To tame Enkidu a courtesan, who probably served in the temple of Ishtar, the tutelary goddess of the city, is sent out to him. She teaches him to eat bread, to drink wine and to wear clothes, and she seduces him with her sophisticated arts. And so Enkidu is civilized. The consequences of his change of life are described with subtle insight. The former savage finds that the bond of sympathy that had

[1] A. Heidel,*The Gilgamesh Epic and Old Testament Parallels* (Univ. Chicago Press, 1949), p. 10.

The *Epic of Gilgamesh* was preserved on clay tablets in the palace library of the Assyrian Kings at Nineveh; a relief of King Ashurnasirpal II, hunting lions

existed between himself and the animals is broken, and they now flee from his sight and he has lost his former swiftness of foot and cannot follow them.

A civilized man, mighty in stature and strength, Enkidu now enters into Uruk and meets Gilgamesh. A tremendous struggle ensues between them. Gilgamesh finally conquers, but he respects the strength and spirit of his adversary, and the two become fast friends. Together they then set out on some heroic exploits, which includes the slaying of a terrible ogre. With considerable dramatic skill, in view of the sequel, the occasion is used to depict Gilgamesh as making light of the danger of death in his thirst for glory.

On their victorious return to Uruk the heroes are led to insult the great goddess Ishtar and to kill a sacred bull. The gods decide that one of them must be punished by death, and Enkidu is chosen.

His fate is made known to Enkidu in a dream, and, as in the legend of the *Descent of Ishtar into the Underworld,* the process of death and the "land of no-return" are described with that grim realism that must be regarded as typical of the ancient Mesopotamian mind. Enkidu dreams that he is seized by the death-god and carried off:

. . . to the House of Darkness, the dwelling of Irkalla,[2]
To the House, from which there is no return for those who enter,
By the way, whose course turns not back,
To the House, whose dwellers are bereft of light,
Where dust is their sustenance, clay their food,
Clothed are they as a bird with garment of wings,
The light they see not, in darkness dwelling.
In the House of Dust which I entered,
The sceptres were abased, the crowns deposited:
There dwelt the mighty ones, who had borne rule in early time . . .
In the House of Dust which I entered,
There dwelt the high-priest and he who led the lamentation,
There dwelt the master of incarnations and the ecstatic,
There dwelt the chief ministers of the great gods . . .

(Tablet VII, 33-42, 45-48).

Enkidu falls sick, and as his end approaches he bitterly laments
his fate, and he curses the courtesan who had lured him from his rustic
life to live in the sophisticated city. He dies, and Gilgamesh mourns
his loss with a poignancy of expression that can still be felt, even through
the medium of translation into a modern language:

"He who with me underwent all hard[ships]—
Enkidu, whom I loved dearly,
Who with me underwent all hardships—
Has now gone to the fate of mankind!
Day and night I have wept over him.
I would not give him up for burial—
In case my friend should rise at my plaint—
Seven days and seven nights,
Until a worm fell out of his nose.
Since his passing I have found not life,
I have roamed like a hunter in the midst of the steppe."[3]

But Enkidu's death robs Gilgamesh not only of the presence of
his friend; it comes to him as an awful revelation of the common fate
of man. Although he shrugged off its threat in the days of their high-
hearted companionship, now that he had seen death at close range in

[2] The name of the queen of the underworld.
[3] Old Babylonian version translated by E. A. Speiser in *Ancient Near Eastern Texts* (ed.
J. B. Pritchard), Princeton University Press, 1955, pp. 89-90.

his friend, he was terrified. For in Enkidu's death he saw the presage of his own:

> "I also shall die: will it not be with me as it is with Enkidu?
> Woe has entered my heart,
> The fear of death has seized me."

Confronted now with the chill fact of his own mortality, Gilgamesh's instinct is to flee. But where can he go to escape the common lot of man? In his agony of mind, he recalls that two human beings alone had escaped that fate. Away beyond the world's end dwelt the legendary Utanapishtim and his wife, the sole survivors of an earlier race of men whom the gods had destroyed in a mighty flood. To Utanapishtim, therefore, Gilgamesh determines to go to learn the secret of his immortality.

The way to the dwelling place of Utanapishtim is long and difficult and beset by many dangers. But Gilgamesh struggles on, and in the course of his journey he meets Siduri, whose title has been variously translated as the "winemaiden", the "divine barmaid", and the "alewife". Whatever the original meaning of the epithet, Siduri is meant to play an important rôle in the *Epic*. She inquires of the weary, travel-stained Gilgamesh the purpose of his journey. When she learns of his quest, she replies:

> "Gilgamesh, whither runnest thou?
> The life which thou seekest thou wilt not find;
> (For) when the gods created mankind,
> They allotted death to mankind,
> (But) life they retained in their keeping.
> Thou, O Gilgamesh, let thy belly be full;
> Day and night be thou merry;
> Make every day (a day of) rejoicing.
> Day and night do thou dance and play.
> Let thy raiment be clean,
> Thy head be washed, (and) thyself bathed in water.
> Cherish the little one holding thy hand,
> (And) let the wife rejoice in thy bosom.
> This is the lot of [mankind]." [4]

---

[4] Tablet X, col. iii (Old Babylonian version), translated by A. Heidel, *The Gilgamesh Epic and Old Testament Parallels* (University of Chicago Press, 1949), p. 70.

In these words is set forth the quintessence of the Mesopotamian philosophy of life—a practical guide to living that was necessitated and coloured by the accepted eschatology. And the fact that the author of the *Epic* has put its statement in the mouth of Siduri is surely significant. In the ancient legend that the Yahwist writer utilized in the story of Noah in the Hebrew book of *Genesis* (v. 28–9, ix. 20), Noah is represented as mitigating the hard lot, to which mankind had been condemned, by the discovery of the use of wine "that maketh glad the heart of man". In the *Epic of Gilgamesh,* which also draws on the common treasury of Semitic folklore, Siduri, the personification of wine, counsels the labouring Gilgamesh to solace himself to the fullest with those joys that are available to man and not to waste himself in the pursuit of a hopeless quest.

But Gilgamesh will not heed this *carpe diem* philosophy, and he presses on against the terrors and miseries that continue to beset his path. At length his patience and fortitude are rewarded, and he wins his way to the remote abode of Utanapishtim and his wife. But this achievement avails him nothing, but rather serves to emphasize the hopelessness of his quest. For, when he enquires of Utanapishtim the secret of his immortality, the latter in reply tells him the story of the great Flood that had destroyed all mankind, and from which he and his wife alone of humans beings had escaped in a great ship that they had built. It was in consequence of their marvellous escape that the god Enlil had decreed that they should never die and had placed them in their remote abode far beyond the habitations of other men. Their case, then, was unique, and the explanation of it served but to emphasize to Gilgamesh the hopelessness of his quest, for he could not win immortality in that way.

The interpolation of the legend of the Flood at this point of the *Epic* shows great literary skill. Although it does in fact interrupt the theme of the narrative by introducing a different topic of great intrinsic interest, the Flood story is cleverly made to reinforce the argument that mortality is the natural state of man. We may rejoice that the author of the *Epic* in its completed form did thus interpolate the Flood story, because it has preserved to us a celebrated legend of ancient Mesopotamia, of which only fragments have survived in other contexts. It is, indeed, exciting still to read the account of George Smith who first identified the story, when sorting and arranging the broken tablets of the Ninevite libraries:

"Commencing a steady search among these fragments, I soon found half of a curious tablet which had evidently contained originally six columns. . . . On looking down the third column, my eye caught the statement that the ship rested on the mountains of Nizir, followed by the account of the sending forth of the dove, and its finding no resting-place and returning. I saw at once that I had here discovered a portion at least of the Chaldean account of the Deluge." When Smith announced his discovery to the Society of Biblical Archaeology on December 3rd, 1872, a great sensation was caused. The importance of the discovery for the study of the Old Testament was at once understood, and the *Daily Telegraph* of London reflected the public interest by providing £1,000 to send Smith to Nineveh to search for further fragments of the precious tablets.

That the author of the *Gilgamesh Epic* chose thus to incorporate the legend of the Flood into his narrative affords an instructive parallel, and possibly the precedent, to the action of the Yahwist writer whose work is preserved in our present version of the book of *Genesis*. As the Mesopotamian seems to have felt that he must incorporate this wondrous

"The grim realism typical of the ancient Mesopotamian mind"; an effigy of King Ashurnasirpal II, a ninth-century B.C. ruler

A terra-cotta relief of Lilith,
a death-bringing demon of
Babylonian tradition

story of the ancient past into his composition and did so with commendable skill, the Hebrew in his generation appears also to have been similarly
desirous of working it into his narrative; but his literary ability was not
so great and its introduction badly interrupts his theme of Noah as the
Heilbringer of mankind by his invention of viniculture (*Genesis* v. 28–9,
vi. 9–ix. 17, ix. 20).

But to return to the main theme of the *Gilgamesh Epic:* what follows
after Utanapishtim tells his story seems, perhaps, to the modern mind
a kind of anti-climax. The logic of Utanapishtim's story would appear
a fitting *dénouement* to the account of Gilgamesh's quest, and the discon-
solate hero's return to his native city the proper ending to his tragedy.
But the ancient author thought otherwise. He goes on to tell how
Utanapishtim's wife took pity on the forlorn Gilgamesh and persuaded
her husband to reveal to him the secret location of a marvellous plant
that has the properties of an elixir of eternal youth: it is appropriately

called "The old man becomes young as the man (in his prime)". The plant grows in the depths of the sea, and Gilgamesh dives for it by attaching heavy stones to his feet as the modern pearl-divers of Bahrein used to do. Having obtained the means of prolonging his life, Gilgamesh is now presented in another guise. Instead of availing himself at once of its wondrous virtue, he determines to take the plant back to Uruk, apparently to share the boon with his people. But fate prevents him. As he bathes at a water-hole, the plant is seized by a serpent which appropriates its virtue. The episode is of considerable interest for the comparative study of folklore. The snake's ability to slough its skin has obviously fascinated many primitive peoples. They have concluded that the snake has the secret of renewing its youth, a secret that mankind covets. Possibly the ancient Mesopotamian writer thought that his theme required that he should explain the serpent's apparent possession of the secret that man so dearly sought. Again it is instructive to compare Hebrew traditional lore on this point. In the *Genesis* story of the Temptation and Fall of Adam (iii. 1–19), the serpent is the agent whereby man loses his original immortality, although the serpent does not, as in the *Gilgamesh Epic*, obtain immortality for itself.

With empty hands, his quest in vain, Gilgamesh finally returns to Uruk. The moral of his failure needs no underlining. Man is by nature mortal and he must learn to accept his fate and adjust his view of life accordingly. The *Epic* ends rather strangely with Gilgamesh exulting in

Disobedience to the gods exposed mankind to the assault of maleficent demons; the wind-demon, Pazuzu

the excellence of the construction of his city. Perhaps here lies its final point—a man should find contentment in the work that he can do for the community of which he is a member.

The Assyrian recension of the *Epic* contains a twelfth tablet that records an incident that has no place in the narrative of Gilgamesh's quest, but which undoubtedly has been added because of a certain similarity of subject matter. It depicts Gilgamesh desiring to see Enkidu, who is held in the underworld, owing to his violation of certain taboos. Nergal, the lord of the underworld, permits the shade of Enkidu to ascend to the world above. The two heroes meet and embrace each other. Then Gilgamesh asks his dead friend to tell him about the underworld. At first Enkidu refuses to tell him, because the truth is too horrible to hear. Gradually, however, he reveals the conditions there, beginning with a grim account of the decomposition of the physical body. This description of the underworld seems designed for some special purpose, for it becomes an account of the differing conditions in which various categories of the dead dwell. Although the general state of all is grim, those whose heirs are diligent in their mortuary service and those who have fallen in battle have a better lot than certain others, especially those who have died in remote places and whose bodies lie unburied. Clearly the text of this tablet has no part in the impressive theme of the *Epic* contained on the other tablets. Its purpose probably was to promote the regular performance of the prescribed mortuary service.

III

Man's attempt at different ages and in various cultural environments to make sense of his experience of life and to understand his own nature and destiny is a subject of deep and abiding interest, and one of basic concern to the historian. Thus the *Epic of Gilgamesh* is a document of unrivalled value for the insight that it affords into the *Weltanschauung* of the ancient Mesopotamians. For the comparative study of religions its value is also immense. We have already touched upon the differences of the Egyptian and Mesopotamian views of life; interesting comparisons can also be made with other contemporary cultures of the ancient world. Although the subject is too vast and too complicated to be entered upon at this juncture, it is worth noting that in ancient Israel the cult of Yahweh also had an eschatology as dismal as that of Mesopotamia. The inadequacy of this eschatology to a faith aspiring to a conception of deity as the

embodiment of both supreme power and absolute justice is the cause
of Job's agony as he questions his fate in the noble book that bears
his name. To more mundane spirits among the Jews, who were prepared
to see life in terms of the traditional faith, the logic of the old eschatology
induced a philosophy of life remarkably reminiscent of the hedonism of
Siduri in her counsel to Gilgamesh: "Go thy way, eat thy bread with
joy, and drink thy wine with a merry heart. . . . Let thy garments be
always white; and let not thy head lack ointment. Live joyfully with the
wife whom thou lovest all the days of thy vanity: for that is thy portion
in life, and in thy labour wherein thou labourest under the sun . . .
for there is no work, nor device, nor knowledge, nor wisdom in the grave
(Hebrew, 'Sheol'), whither thou goest" (*Ecclesiastes* ix. 7–10).[5] The
history of Hebrew religion, in a very true sense, is the record of the
struggle of the individual for the assurance of ultimate personal significance against the eschatology of an ethnic faith that accorded him
only a temporary significance.

The basic importance of eschatology in the evaluation of the individual and his destiny, thus so eloquently attested in the literatures of

[5] *Ecclesiastes* probably dates from about 250 to 150 B.C.

Top of a stele, now in the Louvre,
inscribed with the law code of
King Hammurabi of Babylonia who
flourished about 2100 B.C.

Mesopotamia and Israel, receives abundant confirmation in the writings of ancient Greece, where the traditional Homeric eschatology was equally pessimistic. It will suffice here to cite one most notable instance. It occurs in the celebrated account of the living Odysseus' descent into Hades to learn the cause of his misfortunes (*Odyssey*, XI, 487–491). Odysseus meets there the shade of the great Achilles, who had been the champion *par excellence* of the Greek military aristocracy, fighting before the walls of Troy until his death in the battle. Odysseus salutes him and dilates on the great reputation that his prowess had won, ending with the trite assurance: "Wherefore grieve not at all that thou art dead, Achilles." The reply of Achilles is devastating in its exposure of the hollowness of fame among the living when seen from the other side of the grave. "Nay, seek not to speak soothingly to me of death, glorious Odysseus. I should choose, so I might live on earth, to serve as the hireling of another, of some portionless man whose livelihood was but small, rather than be lord over all the dead that have perished." [6]

In ancient Greece, the inadequacy of the Homeric eschatology to meet the individual's need for the assurance of some tolerable destiny was partly met by the mystery cults of Eleusis and of Orphism. But Mesopotamian religion was never able to provide the comfort of some *post-mortem* hope. Significantly the dying-rising god of vegetation, Tammuz, though having certain traits in common with Osiris, never became the supreme saviour-god and judge of the dead that Osiris was in Egypt. Possibly some innate realism prevented the Mesopotamians from seeing death other than objectively. But the *Epic of Gilgamesh* remains an eloquent witness to the poignancy of their interrogation of the meaning of human life and destiny.

[6] Translated by A. T. Murray in the Loeb Classical Library edn. of the *Odyssey*.

⚸ CHAPTER 11

The Jewish Philosophy of History

The majestic narrative of the fortunes of the Jewish people,
as unfolded in the Pentateuch, incorporates four different
strains of literary tradition. Once fused together, they
produced a philosophy of history that has influenced not only
Israel itself but the whole of Christian Europe.

I

Each year for countless generations on the fourteenth day of the month Nisan the Jews, wherever they may be throughout the world, keep the Passover. On the evening of that day they gather in their homes to eat bitter herbs, together with unleavened bread. They do this to commemorate what they believe to have been one of the greatest crises in the history of their people, namely, the Exodus from Egypt.

This Passover festival does in fact enshrine and typify the essential spirit of Judaism, and it provides the key to that peculiar attitude to the past that has moulded the strange destiny of the Jewish people, and, through Christianity, has profoundly affected the *Weltanschauung* of the Western nations. For the Passover festival itself witnesses to the propensity of the Hebrew mind to explain all its institutions and customs in terms of the sacred history of Yahweh's[1] dealings with Israel.

There is much reason for thinking that the sacrificial eating of a young lamb and the use of unleavened bread were originally separate and

---

[1] It may be helpful to explain this name. In Hebrew the name of Israel's god was written by the consonants YHWH; but, to avoid pronouncing the sacred name, that of *adonay* ("my lordship") was substituted. Consequently the original vowel sounds have been lost, and Yahweh represents the form of the name generally accepted by modern scholars.

165

'The Passover Meal.' For countless generations the Jews have
annually commemorated the
'Exodus' of their ancestors from
Egypt

independent ritual customs, of which the ancient Hebrews had forgotten
the original meaning, and which consequently were given a historicized
explanation.[2] The annual sacrifice of the first-born of the flocks to a
menacing deity, and the apotropaic marking of the doors of their tents
with the blood of the victim, appear to be the rites of a primitive pastoral
people such as, undoubtedly, were the early ancestors of the Hebrews.
On the other hand, the ritual eating of unleavened bread is the custom
of an agricultural community, observed at the time of harvest when for
a while bread is made from the new corn without using the leaven that
remained from the old corn. The purpose of such a custom is to effect
a break with the past and its misfortunes. But in Hebrew literature these
two ancient rites, with their different cultural settings, are given a common
origin in the events of the Exodus. Thus it is related that on the night
of their departure from Egypt the Israelites were divinely instructed, in
order to escape the destruction that was to fall upon the Egyptians, to
mark their doors with the blood of a lamb, whose body they were to
roast and eat before dawn, with bitter herbs (*Exodus* xii. 1–14, 21–28).

[2] After the destruction of the Temple in A.D. 70 the eating of the paschal lamb ceased.

The use of unleavened bread is explained as originating from the fact that the Israelites fled from Egypt in such haste that they took their dough before it was leavened and consequently were obliged to eat unleavened bread for a while (*Exodus* xii. 15–20, 34, 39). Further, the fact that the *Exodus* narrative at this point was definitely intended to establish the commemorative aspect of these rites is clearly shown by the following passage: "And it shall come to pass when your children shall say unto you, What mean ye by this service? That ye shall say, It is the sacrifice of the Lord's (i.e. Yahweh's) passover, who passed over the children of Israel in Egypt, when he smote the Egyptians, and delivered our houses" (xii. 26–27).

The intention thus to connect the origin of these ancient rites with the Exodus from Egypt is indicative of the key position that the Exodus held in the memory of the Hebrew people; and it eloquently attests the way in which appeal has constantly been made to the event as the supreme authenticating episode of the nation's past.

II

The dramatic story of Israel's escape, under the inspired leadership of Moses, from the Egyptian bondage appears as an episode, howbeit a crucial one, in a long narrative that traces out the fortunes of the nation from the time of its great ancestor, Abraham, to its settlement in the land of Canaan. The theme of this narrative is that the god Yahweh had promised Abraham that he would make his descendants a mighty nation and settle them in Canaan (*Genesis* xii. 1–7), a land to which they were obviously not indigenous and that was actually occupied by another people. In the Pentateuch, i.e. the five so-called books of Moses and the book of Joshua, the eventual fulfilment of this divine promise is skilfully presented in a series of consequent episodes, namely: the making and renewing of the divine promise to the nation's ancestors, Abraham, Isaac and Jacob; the settlement of Jacob's sons in Egypt through the good offices of Joseph; the growth of Jacob's descendants into a populous nation in Egypt and their later oppression by the Egyptians; Yahweh's commission to Moses to rescue his people and Pharaoh's opposition; the punishment of the Egyptians and Israel's exodus from "the house of bondage"; the covenant between Yahweh and Israel at Mount Sinai and the delivery of the Law; the final triumphal settlement in Canaan, the land of the divine promise, after forty years' sojourn in the wilderness.

But this majestic narrative of the gradual achievement of Yahweh's promise has been shown by the critical research of modern scholarship to be an artificial composition of many diverse traditions, to which many writers contributed over a long period of time. Indeed, in its completed form, such as we now have it, the story dates only from about 400 B.C. However, the motive behind its formation was constant, namely, to demonstrate Yahweh's unfailing providence for Israel, by appeal to the evidence of the past. This evidence of the past was, of course, a tendentious presentation of ancient traditions. But the very fact that such a presentation was undertaken is of the greatest significance, because this is the earliest known attempt at a philosophy of history, in so far as it seeks to interpret the past teleologically in terms of the operation of a divine purpose. Before we can, however, appreciate the full proportions of this undertaking, we must briefly consider a very complex literary problem.

The investigations of several generations of Old Testament scholars have revealed that the Pentateuch incorporates four main sources of literary tradition (or, perhaps more correctly, politico-religious tradition, since it is distinction of this character that renders the literary traditions significantly different from each other). Three of these traditions are particularly important for our subject. They are technically designated the Yahwist (J), the Elohist (E), and the Priestly (P) sources, for the following reasons. The Yahwist source is characterized by its consistent use of the name Yahweh for the god of Israel;[3] it appears to be the oldest tradition of the three, and the general consensus of expert opinion dates it somewhere between 950 and 850 B.C., i.e. during the period from the reign of Solomon to that of Jehoshaphat. The Elohist source is so called, because until a distinctive point in the narrative, as we shall see presently, it employs the Hebrew word *Elohim* for God, and not the name "Yahweh"; this E source appears to be slightly later in date than J. The Priestly tradition is distinguished by its special interest in priestly legislation, and it seems to be a kind of editorial commentary binding together an earlier form of the narrative, probably constituted by a fusion of J and E; this P source is generally regarded as dating from about 450 B.C.

This brief description of the three main strands of tradition that underlie the narrative portions of the Pentateuch has been necessary here,

---

[3] The name is rendered into English as "the Lord" or "Jehovah"—hence the use of the letter J to denote the source.

Captive Semite, with arms bound behind his back; relief on the pedestal of a statue of Rameses II

since it will enable us to appreciate the significance of the following remarkable fact.

In the third chapter of *Exodus*, which tells how Moses received his divine call to rescue Israel from the bondage of Egypt, Moses is represented in verses 13 to 15, which derive from E, as not knowing the name of the deity who was then commissioning him, and he has to be informed that it was Yahweh, and that Yahweh was the god whom the patriarchs of Israel had worshipped. In *Exodus* vi. 2–3, in another context, P is even more explicit in stating that the name Yahweh had hitherto been unknown and that the patriarchs had not worshipped their god under this name: "And God spake unto Moses, and said unto him, I am Jehovah (i.e. Yahweh): and I appeared unto Abraham, unto Isaac and unto Jacob as God Almighty,[4] but by my name Jehovah (Yahweh) I was not known

---

[4] In Hebrew *El Shaddai*: an epithet probably meaning "the mountain-god."

unto them." On the other hand, as we have already noted, J consistently uses the name Yahweh for the god of the patriarchs of the nation, thus clearly implying that there had been a continuity of Yahweh-worship from the earliest times.

Now, it is evident that this agreement of E and P, despite the contrary view of J, must indicate the existence of a well-established tradition that the worship of Yahweh by the Israelite people as a whole commenced somewhere about the time of the Exodus and apparently in connection with that event. This indication is, moreover, confirmed by the memory that persists throughout the whole corpus of Hebrew literature that the nation's relationship to Yahweh had begun at a definite time in the past by the establishment of a covenant between them. The occasion is graphically described as happening at Mount Sinai, where the Ten Commandments and other ordinances of Yahweh were delivered to the people by the hand of Moses (*Exodus* xix. 1 ff.).

It is here that we encounter one of the most difficult, but also one of the most fascinating, problems of ancient Hebrew history. It would appear that a group of Hebrew tribes, which came to know themselves collectively as Israel, at some period adopted the worship of a deity named Yahweh and that under the leadership of this deity, or his human representative Moses, escaped from a position of servitude in Egypt and successfully established themselves in Canaan. There has naturally been much speculation among scholars about the origins of this deity. A good case has been made out for thinking that Yahweh had been the god of a Midianite clan called the Kenites, with whom Moses had been associated; in the present state of our knowledge, however, certainty cannot be reached. Similarly, there has been much searching of the records of Egypt and other contemporary peoples for independent information about the series of strange events that attended the Israelites' escape from Egypt as related in the Hebrew book called *Exodus*. Again, the evidence that exists is very puzzling. In brief, it might fairly be said that those scholars who have specially occupied themselves with the question accept the historical reality of the Exodus, though not the historical accuracy of the Hebrew record of it, and they would date its event about 1230 B.C., during the reign of the pharaoh Merneptah.

There can be no doubt that the series of events that constituted the Exodus and the settlement in Canaan impressed themselves so indelibly upon the Hebrew mind that ever after they were regarded as

Semitic prisoners of war begging for mercy: bas-relief from the Tomb of Horemheb, built by the future pharaoh at Memphis while he was still leading the Egyptian armies against the peoples of the Near East

definitive for the whole life and destiny of the nation. Indeed, to such a degree does this appear to be so, that there is much reason for believing that it was out of the experience of those events that the nation of Israel itself emerged.

Valuable work in this connection—work that has generally been well received by other authorities—has been done by the eminent German scholar, Martin Noth. The constitution of twelve, apparently distinct, Hebrew tribes into a unified body under the name of Israel, which the Hebrew records attest, reminded Professor Noth of certain analogous organizations in the ancient world. Thus in Greece and southern Italy, during the classical period, certain neighbouring states would form a union, called an amphictyony, for the purpose of mutual defence or to facilitate trade. These amphictyonies were centred each on some temple, whose god became the divine patron of the association, and where periodic festivals were held to commemorate and renew the union. Another significant feature of these leagues was that allegiance to the amphictyonic god did not preclude the participating states from continuing to worship their own particular local deities.

The analogy provided by these early Greek and Italian amphictyonies has indeed thrown valuable light on the organization of the Twelve Tribes of Israel and enabled many puzzling features to be understood. It would accordingly appear that certain Hebrew tribes, possibly those who regarded Joseph as their eponymous ancestor, succeeded in escaping from Egypt in some signal manner under the leadership of Moses. These Joseph-tribes, who worshipped Yahweh, then formed a kind of amphictyonic union with other kindred tribes for the purpose of installing themselves in Canaan. Yahweh thus became the divine patron of this military union of Hebrew tribes, and the organization acquired the name of the Twelve Tribes of Israel.[5] Some memory of the founding of this union seems to be preserved in *Joshua* xxiv, where Joshua, the successor of Moses, is represented as addressing the elders of Israel at Shechem after their first successful incursion into Canaan. Joshua calls upon them to confirm their allegiance to Yahweh, and in doing so he makes significant reference to the fact that many of the tribes were still serving the gods that their ancestors had worshipped: "Now therefore fear Yahweh, and serve him in sincerity and in truth: and put away the gods which your fathers served beyond the River,[6] and in Egypt; and serve Yahweh. And if it seem evil unto you to serve Yahweh, choose you this day whom ye will serve; whether the gods which your fathers served that were beyond the River, or the gods of the Amorites, in whose land ye dwell: but as for me and my house, we will serve Yahweh" (verses 13–14).

It would appear probable, both in the light of the Hebrew tradition preserved in the Old Testament and on the analogy of the Greek and Italian amphictyonies, that the union of the Twelve Tribes was periodically commemorated at a festival held at some sanctuary of Yahweh, possibly at Shechem and later at Shiloh, where the Ark of Yahweh was kept. Now, it is reasonable to suppose that at such festivals the *raison d'être* of the union was celebrated by a liturgical recitation of the mighty acts of Yahweh in delivering the people from Egypt and settling them triumphantly in Canaan. A relic of this liturgical recitation may be preserved to us in the remarkable formula that appears five times in the J narrative in connection with the Exodus and the settlement in Canaan. It runs, with slight variations: "I will bring you up out of the affliction of Egypt unto the land of the Canaanite, and the Hittite, and the Amorite, and the

---

[5] The name Israel is first given to Jacob in *Gen.* xxxii. 28. It means "God strives," and may possibly have been an ancient war-cry; it appears as an ethnic name on a monument of the pharaoh Merneptah (*c.* 1230 B.C.).

[6] The Euphrates.

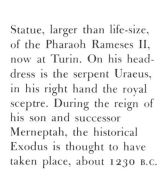

Statue, larger than life-size, of the Pharaoh Rameses II, now at Turin. On his head-dress is the serpent Uraeus, in his right hand the royal sceptre. During the reign of his son and successor Merneptah, the historical Exodus is thought to have taken place, about 1230 B.C.

Perizzite, and the Hivite, and the Jebusite, unto a land flowing with milk and honey."[7] This detailed list of the inhabitants of Canaan and the quaint metaphor describing the economic richness of the land could very reasonably have been part of such a commemorative liturgy. Its continued use in some liturgical form would well explain its frequent quotation by the Yahwist and other writers.

It is undoubtedly in some such liturgical commemoration of Yahweh's providence for Israel during the critical events of the Exodus and the invasion of Canaan that the origin of that appeal to the past, which came to characterize Hebrew thought, is to be found. But its early development, until it was elaborated into a definite philosophy of history, requires some explanation.

Critical examination of the Hebrew records reveals that the original Israelite invasion of Canaan was an incomplete affair. Certain territories only were seized, and in many places the Canaanites succeeded in main-

[7] *Exodus* iii. 8b, 17, xiii. 5, xxxiii. 2, xxxiv. 11. It is also found elsewhere.

Sinai, the Mountain of Moses, scene of the great law-giver's instruction by the God of Israel

taining themselves. Jerusalem, for example, did not pass into Israelite possession until the time of David. Now, it appears that, after the first successful incursion into Canaan, the union of Israelite tribes tended to break up as its individual members became occupied with their own particular problems of settlement. This tendency to political disengagement and independence involved a corresponding dissolution of the common allegiance to Yahweh and a return to the ancestral gods or to the adoption of Canaanite gods. Naturally the devotees of Yahweh strove to stop this process of disintegration, which meant a disastrous decline of the power and prestige of their god. Soon the logic of events came to reinforce their denunciations of such disloyalty to Yahweh. The break-up of the Israelite amphictyony inevitably resulted in a decline of military strength. And this movement coincided with an increasingly successful reaction on the part of the original inhabitants of the land, who were probably joined about this time by the Philistines who installed themselves along the coastal plain. Consequently the various Israelite tribes began to suffer a reversal of fortune. The sequel can be followed in the *Book of Judges*. When a group of Israelite tribes, under the inspiration of some Yahwist leader, rallied to their former allegiance to Yahweh, their united front secured victory. The situation was lost again when their loyalty and their union lapsed, and it so remained until a new prophet recalled them to the source of their strength.

Hence, the classic pattern of Israel's historic experience took form. Loyalty to Yahweh meant unity and success; disloyalty meant national disintegration and defeat. And the logic of this process confirmed the old Yahwist appeal to the past. In summoning the Israelite tribes to return to their allegiance, the Yahwist prophets instinctively cited the mighty deeds that Yahweh had accomplished for his people in the past.

III

Such *ad hoc* appeals to the past as evidence of the efficacy of Yahweh's providence for Israel eventually inspired the formation of that Yahwist philosophy of history which scholars have traced through the Pentateuch, and possibly other books, and have designated J as we have seen. Whether its formation was the work of one writer or of a school of writers cannot now be known. But what is certain is that its achievement set the definitive pattern of the Jewish interpretation of history.

The attractive suggestion has been made that J was composed about the time of David's reign (*c.* 1000 B.C.), since the idealized list of Joshua's conquests in *Judges* i. coincides with the boundaries of David's kingdom. However that may be, there is much reason for thinking that J was produced at some time when there was need to stress the essential unity of Israel. This was done, as we have seen above, most notably by J's categorical presentation of Yahweh as the god whom Israel's ancestors had consistently worshipped. Despite the established tradition, so clearly attested by E and P and by *Joshua* xxiv. 13–14 as we have noticed, that the ancestors of the tribes that constituted Israel had originally served other gods, J paints a picture of the past that was calculated to foster a sense of national unity around one national god, namely, Yahweh. Thus the Twelve Tribes are represented as descended from the sons of Jacob, who in turn descends through Isaac from Abraham. Accordingly, the tribes are given a series of common ancestors who piously serve Yahweh, and are rewarded for their unswerving loyalty by the promise that their descendants should grow into a great people and possess the land of Canaan, in which they were only sojourners.

Next in J's narrative, through the skilful use of the Joseph-saga, Israel as a nation is located in Egypt, and the stage is set for the mighty drama of the Exodus and of the Settlement in Canaan, that marks the fulfilment of Yahweh's ancient promise. And so, in a carefully articulated narrative, made vivid by the strong characterization of persons and events, J presents

King Jehu offers tribute to the Assyrian monarch Shalmaneser III in his palace. Jehu, wearing a pointed cap, bows low at the Assyrian's feet

his people with a majestic demonstration of Yahweh's unceasing providence for them, from the remote days of their eponymous ancestors to their ultimate establishment in the land that they now called their own.

But that was not the whole of J's achievement. To the majestic story of Yahweh's guidance of the destinies of Israel from the days of Abraham there was added, as a dramatic prelude, an account of Yahweh's creation of the world and of the first human pair, Adam and Eve, and of their subsequent Fall and its consequences for the human race. This primaeval history is traced on through the drama of the Flood to the story of the building of the Tower of Babel. Having by this event explained the origin of languages and the cause of mankind's dispersal throughout the world, J skilfully effects the transition from the narrative of Yahweh's dealings with mankind as a whole to that of the call of Abraham which introduces the theme of Israel's destiny.[8]

J's great conspectus of the past, as the field of the operation of Yahweh's purpose, provided the inspiration and pattern for subsequent writers who gradually fashioned the Hebrew interpretation of history until it reached the form in which we now have it. But, before its final stages

[8] This section of J's narrative, which is known as the "Primaeval History," runs from *Genesis* ii. 4–xi. 9.

were achieved, other events gave a new perspective to the Hebrews' attitude to the passage of time.

IV

Yahweh's ancient promise to the patriarchs of Israel was for the first time accomplished during the reigns of David and Solomon. In the course of those years, Israel's control of Palestine extended to the traditional limits of Dan to Beersheba. The period of Israel's sovereignty proved, however, to be very fleeting. Viewed in the general context of Near Eastern affairs at this time, Israel's hour of triumph coincided with a brief interlude of quiescence in the powerful states of Egypt and Mesopotamia. But Israel's position was essentially precarious. A small and comparatively poor people, Israel had settled itself in an area through which ran the main lines of communication between Egypt and Mesopotamia. Inevitably, therefore, it was destined to become the victim of the power-politics of the great empires that in turn strove for the hegemony of the Near East.

Consequently, as soon almost as Yahweh's promise had been fulfilled by the completion of the conquest of Palestine, the Jews began to find themselves threatened and then subjugated by their more powerful neighbours, notably by the Assyrians and Babylonians. In the year 722 B.C. the northern kingdom of Israel was overthrown and two years later the Assyrian King Sargon II transported the flower of its people to Mesopotamia. For another century the southern kingdom of Judah managed to survive; but at length it, too, was overwhelmed. In 586 B.C. the Babylonians, under Nebuchadrezzar, destroyed Jerusalem and sent the majority of the inhabitants of Judah into captivity in Babylonia.

The reaction of the devotees of Yahweh to this grim change of fortune was profound; and it took a form pregnant with consequences for the future—and not only for Israel, but for a large part of mankind. At first, such prophets as Amos, Hosea and Isaiah seem almost to have welcomed the Assyrian menace, and Assyria was proclaimed Yahweh's rod to punish his people for their iniquities. But the increasing disasters that befell Israel, especially after Josiah's reforms, were soon felt to be a challenge to Yahweh's ability to protect his people and keep them secure in the land of his promise. Accordingly, while the prophetic message continued the traditional pattern of Yahwist admonition, it acquired a new and significant elaboration. Appeal is still made to the past as evidence of the efficacy of Yahweh's providence; present misfortune is explained as divine punish-

The inhabitants of a conquered city are deported by Assyrian soldiers with their flocks and herds: bas-relief from the palace of Tiglath-pileser

ment for past unfaithfulness; and hope of future deliverance is promised, if the nation will repent and return more zealously to the service of its god. But this promise of future deliverance begins to take the form of the Messianic hope. The belief is propagated that, when Israel's fortunes reach their nadir, Yahweh will then send his special representative, his Messiah, who with supernatural power would overthrow the triumphant heathen and restore Israel in glory to their own land. In some of its forms, the belief envisaged this divine intervention as entailing the catastrophic end of the present world order.

Thus the ancient Yahwist appeal to the past was elaborated into a philosophy of history that embraced the entire time-process from its creation to its final *dénouement*. History was interpreted teleologically as the gradual revelation of the purpose of Yahweh; and so the passage of time was invested with decisive significance. Instead of the cyclic view of time that underlay the thought of other ancient peoples, and which found classic expression in the Stoic doctrine of the Great Year that periodically returns to its beginning, the Jews came to see time as the awful, but inspiring, revelation of the purpose of God.

Viewed in the light of the subsequent fortunes of Israel, this Yahwist interpretation of history has been the cause both of the sufferings and of the preservation of an amazing people. It was the belief that Yahweh would redeem his ancient promise that led the Jews in A.D. 66 into their fatal challenge of Roman power, which had as its inevitable consequence the catastrophic overthrow of their nation four years later. But it was the same belief that gave Israel the spirit to survive all their subsequent tribulation down the centuries, and that finally achieved the restoration of the national state in its ancient land in 1948 and its re-possession of Jerusalem, its holy city, in 1967.

But the influence of the Yahwist philosophy of history was not limited to Israel. Through Christianity, it came to mould that teleological evaluation of history that characterizes European thought. And, if space permitted, it could be shown to be the ultimate inspiration of the Western belief, despite all disillusionment, that there is purpose in living and that the future holds promise of better things.[9]

[9] See Chapter 25.

CHAPTER 12

The Book of Job

ITS SIGNIFICANCE FOR THE HISTORY OF RELIGIONS

The Book of Job *illustrates mankind's earliest attempt to discuss the problem of innocent suffering in relation to the idea of a just and omnipotent deity.*

I

The visit of Saul to the witch of Endor, on the eve of the battle of Gilboa, is one of the most dramatic scenes of ancient Hebrew literature (1 *Samuel* xxviii. 3–25). Filled with foreboding about the issue of the battle and forsaken by the god of his people, the King of Israel sought to know his fate by evoking the spirit of the dead prophet Samuel. That, in his desperation, he should thus have resorted to necromancy is indicative not only of Saul's dark nature; it exemplifies also a situation of profound importance for the understanding of ancient Hebrew religion. According to the narrative, Saul had himself officially proscribed such necromantic practices; yet, at a moment of great crisis, he instinctively turns to them; and, what is equally significant, he readily finds a skilful practitioner who is able to satisfy his needs. Moreover, the graphic detail with which the raising of Samuel is described, and, notably, the unexplained use of the technical term *'ōbh* (translated as "familiar spirit"), suggest that the writer of the account was well acquainted with necromancy and expected his readers to be so.

The whole curious episode constitutes a peculiarly vivid illustration of the cultural tension abundantly attested elsewhere in the Hebrew scriptures. It grew out of the policy adopted by the party within the state of Israel that was concerned to ensure that the god Yahweh should be established as the sole god of the nation. As the previous chapter explained, it was a confederation of Hebrew tribes under the patronage of Yahweh that had achieved the conquest of Canaan. But the confederacy was a loose one; and, after the settlement in Canaan, the tribes showed a constant inclination to revert to the service of their ancestral gods, or to adopt the Canaanite deities. Consequently, the devotees of Yahweh condemned all such worship as disloyalty to Yahweh, deserving of his wrath. Among the rites thus condemned were ancient mortuary rituals that presupposed that the dead lived on in their tombs and needed the tendance of the living. Archaeological research in Palestine has provided abundant evidence from various periods that offerings were made to the dead at their tombs. Both the archaeological data and many references in the ancient Hebrew scriptures show that the mortuary cult was based upon the belief that the dead, or at least some of them, became very potent beings: for example, in the account of the raising of the spirit of the dead Samuel, when Saul asks the woman what she sees as the result of her incantation, she replies, "I see a god (*elohim*) coming up out of the earth."

The Yahwist prophets, however, not only condemned this mortuary cult: they taught a view of human destiny that precluded any belief that the dead had an effective *post-mortem* existence. The dead, they main-

Ezekiel's Vision of the Valley of Dry Bones, in which the dead arise to life; fresco of the third century A.D. Herbert J. Gute, Copy of a Dura Europos Synagogue Mural *The Vision of Ezekiel,* Yale University Art Gallery

tained, departed to Sheol, which was located far beneath the ground—
probably even beneath the waters of the great deep upon which the whole
world was thought to rest. This land of the dead was conceived as an
immense pit, surrounded by walls with gates. It is graphically described
in the *Book of Job* (x. 21–2), when that unfortunate contemplates his
approaching end:

> Before I go whence I shall not return,
> Even to the land of darkness and of the shadow of death;
> A land of thick darkness, as darkness itself,
> A land of the shadow of death without any order,
> And where the light is as darkness.

This Hebrew conception of Sheol evidently derived from ancient Mesopotamian eschatology. There the subterranean realm of the dead was
grimly named *kur-nu-gi-a* ("the land of no return"); and it was imagined
as a great city of seven walls and gates where the shades of the dead
dwelt miserably in dust and gloom.[1]

With this view of the fate of the dead went the Yahwist teaching
about human nature, as it is set forth in the story of the Creation and
Fall of Adam.[2] Yahweh had made the first Man from the dust of the
earth, and, in consequence of his sin, had decreed that he should return
to it again when he died—"for dust thou art, and unto dust shalt thou
return"; and in that decree all Adam's descendants were involved.

Accordingly, the Yahwist theologians denied all hope of immortality
or of a tolerable *post-mortem* existence. They were, however, too un-
sophisticated in their thinking to be able to conceive of the complete
annihilation of the individual personality at death. Instead, they held a
primitive belief in a form of *post-mortem* survival; but they insisted that
such survival had no religious significance, since, even if Yahweh's power
could extend to Sheol, it was of no avail; for "the dead praise not thee,
Yahweh; neither they that go down into silence" (*Psalm* cxv. 17).

This surprising denial of ultimate significance to the individual
person stemmed from the fact that Yahwism was, in origin and essence,
an ethnic religion. Despite the many vividly conceived portraits of individuals such as Moses, David and Jeremiah that appear in the ancient
Hebrew writings, the abiding focus of concern is the relations between
Israel, the nation, and Yahweh, its god. Even when attention seems to

[1] See Chapter 10.   [2] See Chapter 5.

be concentrated on the career of some individual, the interest in him is essentially inspired by the manner in which his actions, for good or ill, affected the chosen people in its service of its divine patron.

With this fundamental and primary concern of Yahwism—that the nation as a whole should continue unswervingly loyal to Yahweh—went an appropriate view of the individual's part in preserving this relationship. It was simply taught that Yahweh rewards the pious with a long and prosperous life and many sons to preserve his name in Israel, while he punishes the impious with misfortune and an early death.

II

Experience, however, too often proved that this convenient arrangement of fortune did not, in fact, prevail—too often it was the wicked who flourished like the proverbial green bay-tree, while the just were afflicted with misfortune and suddenly cut off. And, this problem, which the logic of experience created, was steadily made more acute by the development of the conception of Yahweh. For the prophets progressively emphasized his moral character, while at the same time exalting him as the only true god and ruler of the universe. But, if Yahweh was the god of justice as well as omnipotent, how were the obvious misfortunes of the godly to be explained?

That this question in time tormented certain of the more sensitive-minded of the Jews, the *Book of Job* serves as an eloquent reminder. In the corpus of Hebrew writing it holds a unique place, as it does in the history of religions; for it illustrates the earliest attempt to discuss the problem of innocent suffering *vis-à-vis* the conception of a just and omnipotent deity. 'And the problem, as it is presented here, was made the more acute, as we shall see, through the Yahwist denial of an effective after-life to the individual human being.

The *Book of Job* raises many complicated literary questions concerning its original form and authorship; and expert opinion puts its composition at various dates between 700 and 200 B.C. But uncertainty about such matters does not detract from its immense significance; for the book as a whole became an accepted part of the Hebrew inheritance and, as such, is representative of Hebrew thought.

In its present form, the book has a prose prologue (chapters i–ii) and epilogue (chapter xlii), the intervening portion being in verse. The prologue is used to outline the tragedy of Job's situation, and to introduce

The theme of innocent suffering is eloquently debated; Job and his "Comforters" depicted in an engraving by William Blake, about 1825

the dialogue in which the theme of innocent suffering is so eloquently debated. In the prologue, the integrity of Job, who seems to have been a well-known figure of Semitic folklore, and the completely undeserved nature of the misfortunes that befall him, are depicted in the strongest colours, so that there can be no doubt that this is the test case for the vindication of divine justice. Further, although Satan is represented as the immediate agent in Job's sufferings, the ultimate responsibility is clearly ascribed to God: hence, no solution is possible in terms of a cosmic dualism of good and evil forces, such as was being taught by Zarathustra about the same time in Iran. Between the two poles, therefore—Job's innocent suffering and the absolutism of God—the drama of Job's agony, in seeking to reconcile the evidence of his experience with the doctrine of divine justice, is designedly played out. The poignancy of the drama is infinitely increased, since it is presented in terms of the orthodox Yahwist creed that, for man, death is the end. That belief is tragically attested by Job:

> For there is hope of a tree, if it be cut down, that it will sprout again . . .
> But man dieth, and wasteth away:

> Yea, man giveth up the ghost, and where is he?
> As the waters fail from the sea,
> As the river decayeth and drieth up;
> So man lieth down and riseth not:
> Till the heavens be no more, they shall not awake,
> Nor be roused out of their sleep.   (xiv. 7–12)

The poetical part of the work takes the form of a series of dialogues between the unfortunate Job and his three so-called "comforters". Eliphaz, Bildad and Zophar.[3] These friends, who ostensibly come to commiserate with him, are made the mouthpieces through which the Yahwist philosophy of life is presented, and its inadequacy to meet Job's case is demonstrated. Thus, in his first speech, Eliphaz states the traditional view, of which his subsequent speeches, and those of his companions, are but variations on the same theme. Its quintessence is given in the admonition that Eliphaz addresses to his unfortunate friend:

> Remember, I pray thee, who ever perished, being innocent?
> Or where were the upright cut off?
> Accordingly as I have seen, they that plough iniquity,
> And sow trouble, reap the same:
> By the breath of God they perish,
> And by the blast of his anger are they consumed.   (iv. 7–9)

To Job's questioning of the justice of the fate that had befallen him, orthodox disapproval is significantly expressed in the account that Eliphaz goes on to give of a revelation that had come to him by night:

> There was a silence, and I heard a voice saying,
> Shall mortal man be more just than God?
> Shall a man be more pure than his Maker?
> Behold, he putteth no trust in his servants;
> And his angels he charges with folly:
> How much more them that dwell in the houses of clay,
> Whose foundation is in the dust,
> Which are crushed before the moth!   (iv. 17–19)

And Eliphaz concludes, after observing that trouble is native to man, by setting forth the official estimate of the good life, in which Job may yet participate, if he will but trust in the divine ordering of things:

[3] The general consensus of expert opinion holds that the speech of Elihu is a later interpolation.

Thou shalt know also that thy seed shall be great,
And thine offspring as the grass of the earth.
Thou shalt come to thy grave in full age,
Like as a shock of corn in its season.
Lo this, we have searched it out, so it is;
Hear it, and know it for thy good.   (v. 25-27)

But Job will not accept this interpretation of life—he knows its speciousness from his own experience. In his subsequent speeches he becomes less and less concerned with answering the charges of his friends, namely, that his refusal to admit his presumed guilt proves him an obdurate and secret sinner. Instead, he grows ever more immersed in the agonizing problem of the seeming conflict between the certainty of God's omnipotence and the supposition of His justice:

I will say unto God,
Do not condemn me;
Show me wherefore thou contendest with me.
Is it good unto thee that thou should oppress,
That thou shouldest despise the work of thine hands . . .
And searchest after my sin,
Although thou provest that I am not wicked;
And there is none that can deliver out of thine hand?
Thine hands have framed me and fashioned me,
Together round about; yet thou dost destroy me.
Remember, I beseech thee, that thou hast fashioned me as clay;
And wilt thou bring me into dust again?   (x. 2-9)

An offering for the deceased, in the manner practised by Israel; a stele from Zinjirli, Southern Turkey

In the depth of his despair, Job can only supplicate the Almighty to cease from tormenting him for the little space of life that remains before he departs to the dark oblivion of Sheol. It is this acceptance of the doctrine of Sheol that underlines the terrible futility of his sufferings and of his life; and it challenges to the uttermost his belief in the justice of God. If only he could have hoped that vindication might come after death, Job's whole problem would have assumed a different aspect. But Yahwist doctrine precluded any such hope. There could be no *post-mortem* judgment such as the Egyptians envisaged;[4] for down in Sheol there was no distinction between the just and the unjust—all dwelt there in the dust and darkness. Once, as he struggles between faith and despair, it seems that Job, in the very agony of his mind, has won through to the conviction that death would not end all. Unfortunately, the celebrated passage (xix. 25–6), although it has been confidently used in Christian liturgy, is invested with obscurity, owing to the confused state of the extant text:

> But I know that my redeemer liveth,
> And that he shall stand up at the last upon the earth:
> And after my skin hath been thus destroyed,
> Yet from (without) my flesh shall I see God:
> Whom I shall see for myself,
> And mine eyes shall behold, and not another.[5]

Whatever may have been the original meaning of these verses, it is quite certain that the author of *Job* did not find the solution of the problem with which he was involved in some belief that God would adjust, in another life, the inequalities of fortune suffered in this. Instead, he seeks a solution by comparing the immensity of the operations of God with the puny affairs of man. Thus, after Job finally challenges the Almighty to justify himself, the work closes with the great theophany in chapters xxxviii–xli, in which the question of the justice of man's lot *vis-à-vis* his Creator is dwarfed into insignificance by a display of divine omnipotence. The prose epilogue that follows offers an even more inadequate solution. It merely constitutes a "happy-ever-after" ending, by relating how God at last rebukes Eliphaz and his companions for the counsel that they had given; while he rewards Job by giving him

---

4 See Chapter 7.
5 For alternative renderings see the notes to the passage in the (English) Revised Version of the Bible, and the (American) Revised Standard Version.

An ancient Jewish rock-tomb, with its stone rolled away from the door

greater material prosperity than he had formerly enjoyed and a numerous progeny and a long life—in other words, all that constituted the good life of the pious according to the Yahwist view.

Although its two endings thus provide no true solution of the problem discussed, the *Book of Job* abides as one of the most notable monuments of Hebrew religious thought. It reveals the tension that had arisen within an essentially nationalistic religion, due to the inadequacy of its teaching concerning the individual's life and destiny. In Israel the individual was emerging to self-consciousness from the primitive sense of communal solidarity; he was now beginning to demand from his religion the assurance of ultimate personal significance. That the *Book of Job* fails in the end to satisfy this demand, and can only offer the traditional answer, reveals the inability of Yahwism then to free itself from a policy that its earlier situation had dictated. In time, another situation, also occasioned—at least in part—by political factors, was to work a change of attitude; but, before we proceed to consider this development, we must briefly notice what has been cited by some scholars as a Babylonian parallel or anticipation of the Hebrew Job.

On some clay tablets, found in the libraries of Assyria but probably incorporating earlier material, there is inscribed a text that has become

known variously as the *Ludlul bel nemeqi*,[6] or *The Righteous Sufferer*.
It takes the form of a complaint, placed in the mouth of an anonymous
person overwhelmed by unmerited misfortune. Taught by his religion
that suffering is divine punishment for neglect of one's proper service
to the gods, he seeks in vain to know how he has offended:

> My affliction increases, right I cannot find.
> I implored the god, but he did not turn his countenance;
> I prayed to my goddess, but she did not raise her head.
> The diviner through divination did not discern the situation.
> Through incense-offering the dream-interpreter did not explain my right.
> I turned to the necromancer, but he did not enlighten me.[7]

Unable to comprehend the cause of his ill fate, the sufferer is led to
exclaim against the apparent injustice of those gods, whom he had served
so well, in making their actions inscrutable to men:

> Oh that I only knew that these things are well pleasing to a god!
> What is good in one's sight is evil for a god.
> What is bad in one's own mind is good for his god.
> Who can understand the counsel of the gods in the midst of heaven?
> The plan of a god is deep waters, who can comprehend it?
> Where has befuddled mankind ever learned what a god's conduct is?
> He who was living yesterday has died today:
> Instantly he is made gloomy, suddenly he is crushed.[8]

The complaint continues: the wretched man graphically describes
his sufferings and the physical degradation that goes with them; and he
appears to be at the point of death—his situation is as hopeless as Job's,
since Mesopotamian eschatology was as grim as the Hebrew. But the
situation abruptly changes, without apparent explanation; and the narrative goes on to tell of the saving intervention of Marduk, the patron
god of Babylon, who restores the sufferer to a state of physical well-being.

Although there are many striking parallels between this anonymous
Babylonian sufferer and the Hebrew Job, it would appear that the purpose
of the Mesopotamian writing was not to discuss the problem of human
suffering and divine providence. Its purpose seems rather to be that of

---

[6] A transliteration of the opening line which may be translated: "I will praise the Lord
of Wisdom."

[7] Translated by P. H. Pfeiffer in *Ancient Near Eastern Texts*, ed. J. B. Pritchard (Princeton
University Press, 1955), p. 434b.

[8] Trans. Pfeiffer, *op. cit.*, p. 435a.

commemorating the grace of Marduk in restoring one so abjectly cast down—indeed, the truer Hebrew parallel to this theme is probably to be found in *Psalm* xxii. The *Book of Job,* despite its failure to find an adequate solution to its own peculiar problem, is the more significant document for the religious history of mankind.

III

When a change did come in the Hebrew evaluation of human destiny, it appears to be significantly linked with the political fortunes of the nation. It is first adumbrated in Ezekiel's strange vision of the Valley of the Dry Bones (*Ezek.* xxxvii. 1–14). The prophet foretells how **Yahweh will restore the wellnigh defunct Israel which now languishes in its Babylonian captivity (*c.* 580 B.C.). The vision is admittedly symboli-**cal in its import; but the vividness of its imagery implies that it was modelled on certain concrete conceptions. The moribund nation is pictured as a mass of dry bones, scattered over a valley. To bring it to life again, the bones have to be re-assembled "bone to his bone", and re-clothed with sinews and flesh. But the process of revivification is not completed until the reconstituted bodies are animated by the specially invoked winds. The whole process, as it is recorded, is clearly conditioned by contemporary notions of the constitution of human nature. According to Hebrew ideas, each human being was a psycho-physical organism, compounded of the material body and a non-corporeal entity called the *nephesh.* The two components were so essentially interrelated that, if restoration from death were to be contemplated, it would inevitably involve a reconstitution of both body and *nephesh.*

Ezekiel's vision concerned the nation only; but it also indicates that the idea of the resurrection of individual persons to life after they had died could now be entertained by a Yahwist prophet; and it shows, too, the terms in which such an idea would be conceived. What was thus anticipated in the sixth century B.C. had become an established belief by the second century B.C. Our first clearly dateable evidence occurs in an account of a notable deed of Judas Maccabaeus (*flor.* 165–161 B.C.). During the heroic struggle of the Jewish patriots against the Hellenising policy of the Seleucid king, Antiochus Epiphanes, there had been found on the persons of some fallen Jewish soldiers evidence of their infringement of the sacred Law. In consequence of this discovery, Judas made a collection of money and sent it to Jerusalem as a sacrifice for sin, thus

An Islamic version of Ezekiel's Vision of the resurrection of the dead Israelites in the Valley of the Dry Bones (16th cent. Turkish MS., in the Türk-Islam Eserleri Museum, Istanbul)

"doing therein right well and honourably, in that he thought of a resurrection. For if he were not expecting that they that had fallen would rise **again, it were superfluous and idle to pray for the dead**" (2 *Macc.* **xii.** 43–4).

This acceptance of belief in a resurrection of the dead eased that tension with which the *Book of Job* vibrates; for now death was no longer to be regarded as the virtual end of the individual person. And the *post-mortem* vindication for which Job had sought also makes its appearance in Jewish belief during this time of heroic crisis. Thus in *Daniel* xii. 2, the old Sheol doctrine is tacitly repudiated in the categorical assurance that the revivified dead would be judged:

"And many of them that sleep in the dust of the earth shall awake,
some to everlasting life, and some to shame and everlasting contempt."

The establishment of these related beliefs in the resurrection and judgment of the dead appears to have been due to popular pressure within the Jewish state; and it was for long resisted by a conservative minority. The books of *Ecclesiastes* and *Ecclesiasticus* (both 2nd century B.C.) still reflect the old Yahwist tradition; and, even in the first century A.D., as Josephus and the Christian documents show, the Sadducees, who constituted the sacerdotal aristocracy of the nation, still maintained that "there is no resurrection" (*Mark* xii. 18). It was, significantly, not until after the overthrow of the national state by the Romans in A.D. 70 that the wheel of change turned full cycle, and what was once Yahwist orthodoxy became proscribed as heresy—thus, in the rabbinic *Tractate Sanhedrin*, the pronouncement is made that, among those who have no share in the world to come is "he that says there is no resurrection of the dead prescribed in the Law".

But this development of Jewish eschatological belief was destined also to have repercussions far beyond the bounds of Israel. Because Christianity stemmed from Judaism, belief in a physical resurrection was naturally accepted into the new faith, as the accounts of the resurrection of Christ so graphically show. The problem, which soon arose, of accommodating this essentially Hebrew conception to Greek notions of the immortality of the soul, has left an indelible impress on subsequent Christian thought and has profoundly affected many aspects of Christian culture.

Zarathustra and the Dualism of Iran

*In the sixth century B.C., which witnessed the lives of
Confucius and Gotama the Buddha, Zarathustra in Iran
was preaching a religion that for many centuries held
his compatriots' allegiance.*

I

It is one of those strange coincidences of history that the sixth century B.C. saw the birth of four great world religions. For Israel, that century marked the soul-shaking experience of the Babylonian Captivity and the subsequent restoration of the nation's life with the rebuilding of the Temple (520–16 B.C.), which virtually inaugurated the religious system we know as Judaism. Far to the east, in China, during the same period, Confucius lived and taught his countrymen the way of life that was preserved down the centuries until its overthrow in recent years by the Communist régime. About the year 567 B.C., in northern India, Gotama was born, who, as the Buddha (the "Enlightened One"), founded a religion that was destined to spread throughout a large part of Asia and become the faith of millions in succeeding generations to the present day. In Iran, about the same time, Zarathustra, or Zoroaster as he came to be known to the Greeks,[1] was preaching a religion that for many centuries held the allegiance of the Iranians and exercised much influence on the religious ideas of the Jews and of the Graeco-Roman world, although it survives today only among the Parsees of India.[2]

---

[1] 628–551 B.C. seem to be the most likely dates for Zarathustra's life.
[2] It is estimated that there are now only about 10,000 followers of Zarathustra left in Iran.

Rock-relief at Naqsh-i-Rustam, showing the investiture of the founder of the Sassanian Empire, Ardashir I, by the god Ohrmazd in A.D. 226

These faiths, in their original forms, had little in common with each other: why they all should have arisen within the same century affords a fertile topic for speculation to those interested in the comparative study of human culture. In effect, each faith represents a distinctive interpretation of man's nature and destiny; but that which stems from Zarathustra is peculiar in constituting a sustained effort to account for the unceasing conflict of good and evil in the world. As such it repays study, especially in view of certain aspects of its subsequent development; it is also significant as the faith of a people who played an important part in the history of the ancient Near East.

In seeking to know the origins of Zoroastrianism, and of him who founded it, we are faced at the outset with wellnigh insurmountable difficulties. These difficulties arise from the fact that the earliest written documents of Iranian culture are the *Gāthās* which comprise the utterances of Zarathustra.[3] But since they are essentially the *ad hoc* pronounce-

[3] The *Gāthās*, i.e. "hymns," form part of the *Yasna*, one of the three principal divisions of the corpus of Persian literature known as the *Avesta*.

ments of an inspired prophet, they contain no direct information about the contemporary situation, or biographical details. Consequently, from them we glean scarcely any facts about Zarathustra himself or the place and time in which he lived. We do indeed learn that he converted a king named Vishtāspa; but the identity of this monarch has been much disputed. It has been argued that this Vishtāspa was the father of the famous Darius, the Persian King of Kings (522–486 B.C.), so that such a connection would have associated Zarathustra with the Persian dynasty of the Achaemenids. The more general opinion, however, is that Vishtāspa was a ruler of ancient Chorasmia—an area that perhaps coincided with the present Iranian Khorasan, Western Afghanistan and the Turkmen Republic of the U.S.S.R. Zarathustra found shelter with Vishtāspa, which suggests that he came from elsewhere: Media was perhaps his native province. The environment that seems implied by the *Gāthās* is that of a peaceful pastoral people, concerned with cattle-breeding, but who are menaced by the attacks of fierce nomadic tribes. Zarathustra himself appears to have been a man of moderate fortune; for he complains "few cattle are mine . . . I have but few folk." His life, moreover, seems to have been lived out in the countryside: the *Gāthās* contain no reference to towns or the institutions of civic life.[4] In one place Zarathustra remarks, incidentally, that he was a priest (*zaotā*), which necessarily implies the existence of some cult, though of what deity nothing is said; that he derived his livelihood from the exercise of his priestly office seems unlikely.

The poverty of biographical information in the *Gāthās* is not the only problem that besets the study of Zoroastrian origins. The texts themselves are written in a very difficult language, which is still imperfectly understood by modern scholars. Their interpretation of many passages is much disputed, and so great has been the divergence of opinion that Zarathustra has been represented as both a primitive shaman, who intoxicated himself with burning hemp, and an astute politician closely related to various ruling houses in the land.

Another problem of even greater seriousness derives from the unique character of the *Gāthās*. Zarathustra was clearly a religious reformer; but we have no direct information of the religion that he reformed. Only by a most involved study of the internal evidence of the *Gāthās* them-

[4] In the *Avesta* Zarathustra is only connected with Raghā, which was close to the modern Tehran.

selves, of early Sanskrit writings, and of later Persian literature, which is permeated by Zoroastrian influence, is it possible to piece together something of earlier Iranian belief, and, thus, to assess the originality of Zarathustra. Perhaps some insight into the issue, as well as something of the flavour of Zarathustra's utterances, can be best given by considering this passage in which the prophet sets forth the fundamental premiss of his teaching:

> "I will speak of the spirits twain at the first beginning of the world, of whom the holier thus spake to the enemy: 'Neither thought nor teachings nor wills nor beliefs nor words nor deeds nor selves nor souls of us twain agree.' I will speak of that which Mazdāh Ahura, the all-knowing, revealed to me first in this (earthly) life. Those of you who put not in practice this word as I think and utter it, to them shall be woe at the end of life. I will speak of what is best for this life. Through Right does Mazdāh know it, who created the same as father of the active Good Thought, and the daughter thereof is Piety of goodly action. Not to be deceived is the far-seeing Ahura. I will speak of that which the Holiest declared to me as the word that is best for mortals to obey: he, Mazdāh Ahura (said), 'they who at my bidding render him obedience, shall attain unto Welfare and Immortality by the action of the good Spirit . . . By his wisdom let him teach me what is best, even he whose two awards, whereof he ordains, men shall attain, whoso are living or have been or shall be. In immortality shall the soul of the righteous be joyful, in perpetuity shall be the torments of the Liars. All this doth Mazdāh Ahura appoint by his Dominion.'" (*Yasna* xlv. 3–7)[5]

This passage, expressed in the typically involved diction of the *Gāthās*, requires some commentary. First, it must be observed that Zarathustra claims, without explanation, that what he is proclaiming has been revealed to him by a supernatural being whom he calls Mazdāh Ahura. The words mean the "Wise Lord", and, since this being is also described as "the all-knowing" and "all-seeing", it is evident that to Zarathustra he was the supreme deity.

It is natural to assume that this Ahura Mazdāh[6] was already known to those whom Zarathustra addressed; for he could scarcely have proclaimed himself the prophet of an unknown god. The identity of Ahura

---

[5] Translated by J. H. Moulton in *Early Zoroastrianism*, pp. 370–1 (Williams & Norgate, London). For a more recent trans. cf. J. Duchesne-Guillemin, *The Hymns of Zarathustra*, pp. 93–5.

[6] In the *Gāthās* the double name is not completely fixed. In the later *Avesta* the order is invariably Ahura Mazdāh.

Mazdāh has been, however, the subject of a long, and so far inconclusive, debate among specialists in Iranian studies. The ancient Iranians were an Indo-European people, and they were closely related culturally and linguistically with those Aryan tribes who invaded north-western India about the middle of the second millennium B.C. Consequently the *Rig-Veda*, the sacred literature of these Aryans, has been used by modern scholars to throw light upon early Iranian culture prior to the rise of Zarathustra. Now, there is much evidence to show that the gods mentioned in the *Rig-Veda* were also originally worshipped by the Iranians under slightly different names. Among these gods was one who could conceivably have provided the prototype of Zarathustra's "Wise Lord". It is Varuṇa, the Vedic god of the heavens. Because of his cosmic supremacy, this deity was essentially associated with the maintenance of *ṛta*, the fundamental principle of law or order in the universe, which was also equated with truth. The equation is significant, since *asha* ("truth") was also one of the essential attributes of Ahura Mazdāh, according to Zarathustra.

But, if the prototype of Zarathustra's "Wise Lord" was Varuṇa, the genius of the prophet mightily transformed the conception of this ancient divinity. For, whereas in the Indo-Iranian pantheon Varuṇa had been one god among many equal in might and majesty, Zarathustra exalted Ahura Mazdāh as the unique god and creator of the universe. The other gods were either classed as *daēvas* (demons), or metamorphosed into the curious company of the *Amesha Spentas* ("Bounteous Immortals"), which are represented as the companions or attributes of Ahura Mazdāh.

In this process of the reformation or transformation of the ancestral religion of his people, Zarathustra seems, however, to have eliminated one deity completely. This was Mithra, a god of great importance in the Indo-Iranian pantheon, and one who was closely associated with Varuṇa. Zarathustra's silence about this deity is puzzling, and it constitutes one of the basic problems to our understanding the origins of Mithraism, which was later a religion so popular with the Roman armies throughout the Empire. It is possible that, in exalting Varuṇa as the Supreme Lord of the universe, Zarathustra found Mithra a peculiar embarrassment by virtue of his high status and connection with Varuṇa. He may have deemed it best to ignore Mithra altogether—unless, as it has recently been suggested, he equated this deity with the *Spenta*

Mainyu, a fundamental concept of his theology to which we must now turn.

In the passage from the *Gāthās,* on which we have been commenting, Zarathustra not only proclaims himself the prophet of Ahura Mazdāh, the supreme god; he also sets forth one of the classic statements of that dualistic conception of the universe for which Zoroastrianism is justly famous. In announcing: "I will speak of the spirits twain at the first beginning . . . ," he appears to be elaborating on an already existent belief among his countrymen concerning two primaeval spirits or forces that are operative in the universe and in their natures are contrary to each other. In the passage quoted, Zarathustra appears to imply that those who serve Ahura Mazdāh will be rewarded by the good or holy Spirit (the *Spenta Mainyu*). The moral issue implied here is made more explicit in another Gāthā:

> "Now the two primal spirits, who revealed themselves in vision as Twins, are the Better and the Bad in thought and word and action. And between these two the wise once chose aright, the foolish not so. And when these twain spirits came together in the beginning, they established Life and Not-life, and that at the last the Worst Existence shall be to the followers of the Lie, but the Best Thought to him that follows Right. Of these twain spirits he that followed the Lie chose the worse things; the holiest spirit chose Right, he that clothes him with the massy heavens as a garment. So likewise they are fain to please Ahura Mazdāh by dutiful actions." [7] (*Yasna* xxx. 3-5)

We have here the very quintessence of Zarathustra's teaching. He envisages the world as the battleground between two conflicting spirits or principles, that are coeval and respectively good and evil, creative and destructive, true and false. Mankind is involved in their conflict, for its members have to choose on which side each will align himself—a fateful choice that has *post-mortem* consequences. For the history of religions, however, the conception raises a particularly interesting problem. As we have noted, in referring as he does to these two opposing cosmic forces, Zarathustra was evidently assuming that his audience was familiar with the idea. Accordingly, this dualistic view must antedate the prophet, having its roots back in the ancestral faith. The issue has been the subject of much specialist discussion in recent years, without, how-

---

[7] Trans. Moulton, *op. cit.,* pp. 349-50. Cf. Duchesne-Guillemin, *op. cit.,* p. 105.

The central figure on this 8th-cent. B.C., silver strip from Luristan may represent Zurvān, the ancient Iranian god of Time (Cincinnati Art Museum).

ever, a definite conclusion being achieved owing to the intractability of the material involved. Several scholars have sought to show that in the tradition of Indo-Iranian religion there was the concept of a high-god, who was ambivalent in character, being both the creator and the destroyer, the source of both light and darkness. Such a concept would represent a primitive Aryan estimate of life which realistically assessed the apparent balance of the forces of life and death, of good and evil in the world. One deity in particular has been suggested for the rôle of this ancient ambivalent deity, namely, Zurvān. The origin of this mysterious god, who seems to have been a deification of Time, has been the subject of much learned controversy. The name can be traced back to the twelfth century B.C.; but whether the deity then had the character that we shall see him having later cannot be proved on the evidence available.[8]

Another aspect of this fascinating problem concerns Ahura Mazdāh. What was the relationship between Zarathustra's "Wise Lord" and the two primaeval spirits in their unceasing struggle? Zarathustra was obviously not a systematic thinker, and his teaching contains many illogicalities. In the passages that have been quoted the two opposing spirits are

[8] See Chapter 4.

represented as co-existent from the beginning of things. Since they are respectively the source of each opposing aspect of phenomena—life and death, good and evil—it would seem to follow that Zarathustra regarded this dualism as an original and abiding feature of existence. But, if Ahura Mazdāh was the supreme god, how could this order of things be? The problem is made more perplexing by certain statements in another *Gāthā*. Here, in a series of questions that presuppose affirmative answers, Zarathustra clearly sets forth Ahura Mazdāh as the creator of the universe. One of the questions has strange implications: "This I ask thee, tell me truly, Ahura. What artist made the light and darkness?" Light and darkness in the dualistic scheme are respectively aspects of the two opposing cosmic forces. It would appear, therefore, that Zarathustra thought of Ahura Mazdāh as in some way the source or originator of these two forces. That he should have done so is not surprising in the light of what we may reasonably infer about the nature of ancient Iranian religion. It could well be that the deity from whom Zarathustra derived his "Wise Lord" was originally a divinity of ambivalent character, embodying within himself the principles of both life and death, light and darkness. Zarathustra had sought to make this god the embodiment only of all that was highest and best, and to account for the dualism of existence in terms of two opposing spirits. He could not, however, solve the problem of the origin of these spirits, and the ancient tradition of divine ambivalence caused him in some of his utterances to represent Ahura Mazdāh as their creator. This probable conclusion is important, because, as we shall see, it helps in explaining a curious interlude later in the religious history of Iran.

The essential significance of Zarathustra's teaching would appear to lie in his passionate assertion that this cosmic struggle between good and evil faced individual men and women with a moral decision. Whatever the illogicality of his metaphysics, Zarathustra identified Ahura Mazdāh only with the good, and he vehemently maintained that both man's duty and eternal destiny required that he put himself, in thought and deed, on the side of good against the evil. Evil, personified in the *Angra Mainyu,* the Destructive or Evil Spirit, he also identifies with the *Druj,* i.e. the "Lie". And the followers of the Lie, the *drvants,* he rather significantly equates with the fierce nomadic tribes that ravage his people.

In his eschatology, Zarathustra employs two concepts whose origins cannot be traced in the earlier tradition of Indo-Iranian religion; his unexplained use of them suggests that they also were already familiar in some form to his hearers. Thus he speaks, with special reference to the unrighteous, of the grim ordeal that awaits all after death:

> "His Soul (?) stripped naked (?) shall be afraid at the Bridge of the Separator,
> Having strayed from the path of Righteousness
> By its deeds and those of his tongue."[9]

The significance of this "Bridge of the Separator", the *Cinvato paratu*, was greatly elaborated in the later Zoroastrianism, and the idea even found its way in time into the eschatology of Islam. It occurs only in this place in the *Gāthās*, and what is said of it there is not enlightening. However, a reference in another *Gāthā* (*Yasna* xlvi. 17) seems to indicate that the "Separator" was *Asha*, the personification of right or truth. Accordingly, Zarathustra appears to have envisaged a *post-mortem* test awaiting mankind, some fateful crossing of a bridge where the criterion would be moral character. But this was not the only ordeal that the dead had to face; they had also to pass through fire and molten metal:

> What reward thou hast appointed to the two parties, O Wise One,
> Through thy bright fire and through molten metal,
> Give a sign of it to the souls of men,
> To bring hurt to the wicked, benefit to the righteous.[10]

Another puzzling feature of Zarathustra's recorded teaching is his emphatic condemnation of the killing of oxen and eating their flesh. This condemnation comes in a passage containing other references that reveal the extent of our ignorance of Zarathustra's environment and the traditions he had inherited. After inveighing against the *daēvas* and their human followers, he exclaims: "In these sins, we know, Yima was involved, Vivahvant's son, who desiring to satisfy men gave our people flesh of the ox to eat. From these shall I be separated by thee, O Mazdāh, at last."[11] Yima appears to have been a famous figure of Indo-Iranian mythology, being a kind of Primal Man, and Vivahvant, whose son he is, was a sun-god. Evidently, therefore, Zarathustra is concerned here with some piece of ancestral mythology, of which we have no other knowledge. Why the killing and eating of an ox should be such a heinous

---

[9] *Yasna* li. 13; trans. Duchesne-Guillemin, *op. cit.*, p. 145.
[10] *Yasna* li. 9; trans. Duchesne-Guillemin, *op. cit.*, p. 143.
[11] *Yasna* xxxii. 8; trans. Moulton, *op. cit.*, p. 356.

Mithras slaying the bull; in this sacrifice the blood was identified with the new corn

offence is not clear. It is natural to recall that the cow has been a Hindu tabu-animal; but the case is different here, since Yima's action would surely have constituted a divine precedent sanctioning the eating of cattle. This, however, is not the whole problem, and there is another aspect of it that continues to perplex scholars in their search for the origins of Mithraism, which became so popular later in the Roman Empire. As we have seen, Zarathustra ignores Mithra; now we find him condemning Yima's primordial slaying of the ox—we are inevitably reminded of Mithra's sacrifice of the Cosmic Bull which was represented in every Mithraic sanctuary. It would, accordingly, seem that in his reformation of the ancestral religion of Iran, Zarathustra was embarrassed both by the existence of Mithra and by some primordial act of sacrifice that was undoubtedly regarded as life-giving or life-renewing. The problem still awaits solution; but we may note that it has recently been suggested that Zarathustra recast an ancient myth of two primal Twins by identifying Mithra with the *Spenta Mainyu* (Good Spirit) and Yima with the *Angra Mainyu* (Destructive Spirit), and that in time Yima's sacrifice was attributed to Mithra.[12]

[12] R. C. Zaehner; *The Twilight and Dawn of Zoroastrianism* (1961), p. 140.

II

Zarathustra's field of operation, as we have seen, was in the eastern provinces of what became the Persian Empire of the Achaemenids. How far he was successful in propagating his ideas during his own lifetime is unknown. The earliest datable evidence of the progress of his movement is contained in the inscriptions of the Achaemenian kings. Although the name of Zarathustra is not mentioned, it is evident that those monarchs were *māzdayasni*, i.e. "worshipper of Mazdāh". Thus Darius proclaims: "Such was Ahura Mazdāh's will; he chose me a man, out of the whole earth and made me king of the whole earth. I worshipped Ahura Mazdāh and he brought me aid. What I was commanded to do, that he made easy for me. Whatever I did, I did in accordance with his will."[13] In his celebrated inscription at Behistun, the King also significantly equates rebellion with the Lie, and elsewhere he maintains that he is a "friend of Truth, not of falsehood". His son, Xerxes (486–465 B.C.), in an inscription announces that he had suppressed the *daēvas* that had previously been worshipped in the Empire, and he concludes the record of his religious policy with the commendation: "The man who has respect for the law which Ahura Mazdāh has established and who worships Ahura Mazdāh in accordance with Truth and using the proper rite, may he be both happy when alive and blessed when dead."

From these inscriptions it would appear that these Achaemenian rulers were familiar with, and had accepted, certain fundamental tenets of Zarathustra's creed. Moreover, about the year 441 B.C. Artaxerxes I introduced a reformed calendar into his Empire, and in it the months were named after the main Zoroastrian divinities. It seems, however, that this royal or official faith was not the pure milk of Zarathustra's doctrine, but was diluted with other beliefs and customs that were probably too deeply rooted to be abandoned—such syncretism is well known in the history of religions. In this process, whereby the Prophet's message was adapted to the requirements of a popular faith, the mysterious **caste of** the Magi seems to have played a decisive part. From them doubtlessly came the ritual veneration of fire[14] and the exposure of the dead to be devoured by vultures, customs so characteristic of later Zoroastrianism. Certain other deities also were worshipped alongside of Ahura

---

[13] Trans. Zaehner, *op. cit.*, p. 155.
[14] According to *Yasna* xliii. 9, Zarathustra was a fire-worshipper.

Mazdāh—most notably Mithra, who thus found his way into Zoroastrianism.

The achievements and the downfall of the Achaemenian Empire are
chiefly known to us through the records of the Greeks and the Jews.
To the Greeks the Persians were the traditional enemy, by whom their
land was twice invaded, and from whom it was gloriously delivered by
the immortal actions at Marathon (490 B.C.), Salamis (480 B.C.) and
Plataea (479 B.C.). It is, accordingly, notable that Herodotus, who relates
the sufferings and the triumph of his people during this war, also records
that with the Persians truth was the greatest virtue and lying the most
heinous of crimes. The statement may witness to the influence of Zara-
thurstra; for he had taught the followers of Ahura Mazdāh to repudiate
the *Druj* (the "lie"). For the Jews it was the liberal policy of Cyrus
(559–530 B.C.) that had enabled their exiles in Babylonia to return home
and rebuild the Temple of Yahweh at Jerusalem. But contact with the
Iranians left its impress also upon their religious thought: in post-Exilic
Jewish literature there are many signs of an incipient dualism—it is
particularly evident in the Dead Sea Scrolls, and it is to be found also
in some books of the New Testament.

Greece took her revenge on Persia when Alexander of Macedon
overthrew the Achaemenian Empire in 330 B.C. With this loss of national
independence, the fortunes of Zoroastrianism become obscure. Throughout the rule of the Greek dynasty of the Seleucids (312–65 B.C.), who
succeeded Alexander, little is known of it, and the establishment of an
Iranian government under the Parthians (250 B.C.–A.D. 226) did not
significantly improve its situation. Restoration eventually came in A.D.
226 with the founding of the Sassanian dynasty, which, like that of the
Achaemenids, stemmed from the province of Pārs and so was equally
entitled to be called Persian as well as Iranian.

In many ways, the Sassanian rule marked a revival of Iranian vigour
comparable to that under the Achaemenids, and it was distinguished in
A.D. 260 by the spectacular defeat of a Roman army and the capture
of the Emperor Valerian. With this revival of national spirit went a revival
of the national religion, i.e. Zoroastrianism.

According to a document known as the *Dēnkart* (ninth century A.D.),
Ardashir, the founder of the new dynasty, was concerned to establish

Zoroastrian legends were influenced by the coming of Islam; here the god Ahriman appears as an elderly figure tempting the Iranian equivalents of Adam and Eve

a religious orthodoxy for his realm. To this end he issued a decree: "The interpretation of all the teachings from the Religion of the worshippers of Mazdāh is our responsibility: for now there is no lack of certain knowledge concerning them." The latter part of the statement was, however, over-optimistic. There certainly seems to have been no lack of religious traditions in the country; but there had grown up such a variety of interpretation concerning them that it became necessary to distinguish heresy from orthodoxy.

The cause of these differences was essentially theological; the fact shows there was then in Iran an intellectual preoccupation with religious issues, thus attesting the continuing vigour of Zoroastrianism. The problem resided in the meaning of Zarathustra's classic statement about the two primal Spirits in *Yasna* xxx. 3–4, quoted above. As we have seen, the Prophet had undoubtedly regarded the two Spirits as the creatures of Ahura Mazdāh; but in process of time the Wise Lord had himself become identified with the *Spenta Mainyu*, the Good Spirit. This identification meant that Ahura Mazdāh, or Ohrmazd as he was now called, was reduced unintentionally to a status equal to that of the Evil Spirit, now named Ahriman.[15] The resultant dualism was accordingly radical, for Ohrmazd and Ahriman were now regarded as coexistent from the beginning. This raised a serious problem for the faithful: if Ohrmazd and Ahriman were coexistent, what ground was there for hope that Good would ultimately triumph over Evil?

To meet this difficulty, it would appear that some time before the Sassanian era an attempt had been made by certain Iranian thinkers to explain the origin of the conflict between Good (Ohrmazd) and Evil (Ahriman) by positing a remoter or transcendental cause. To this end they invoked the concept of the ancient god Zurvān, which, as we have seen, personified Time. Although no Iranian document records the beginning of this undertaking, Greek scholars apparently knew something of it, and a disciple of Aristotle, Eudemus of Rhodes (late fourth century B.C.), noted that, "both the Magi and the whole Aryan race . . . call by the name 'Space' or 'Time' that which forms an intelligible and integrated whole, from which a good god and an evil demon were separated out, or, as some say, light and darkness before these. Both parties, however, postulate, after the differentiation of undifferentiated nature, a duality of the superior elements, the one being by Ohrmazd and the other by Ahriman."

The statement is important, for it attests the fact that Time, together with Space, had been deified in Iran as far back as the fourth century B.C., and that it was regarded as the source of good and evil, or light and darkness. Whether the conception goes back beyond that cannot, as we have already seen, be determined on the extant evidence; but it is likely that it did. Of the attempt to use it to solve the problem of Zoroastrian dualism our existing information unfortunately comes only from the accounts of Christian, Manichaean and Muslim writers, and is consequently likely to be in some way distorted. However that may be, these accounts generally agree in describing a remarkable piece of mythological speculation. Its purport was that Zurvān, desiring a son who would create heaven and earth, offered sacrifice for a thousand years to obtain his birth. Towards the end of this period, however, Zurvān began to doubt the efficacy of the sacrifices, and from this doubt was conceived another son who was to be Ahriman. Finally two sons were born, Ohrmazd

---

[15] Ohrmazd derived from the Pahlavi Auharmazd; Ahriman came *via* the Pahlavi from *Angra Mainyu.*

and Ahriman, the one radiant with light and the other dark and repulsive. Their diverse natures duly found expression in what they created; for Ohrmazd made all that was good and beautiful, while from Ahriman came forth all that was ugly and evil.

This Zurvanite myth effectively explained the origin and relationship of the dual principles of good and evil; but it did so at the cost of making Zarathustra's Ahura Mazdāh (i.e. Ohrmazd) into a derivative being who owed his existence to Zurvān. Zurvanism predominated during the third century A.D., enjoying the patronage of some of the Sassanian monarchs. An orthodox form of Zoroastrianism, however, eventually prevailed. It

An Islamic version: Gushtasp, Zoroaster's royal patron, is entertained by the legendary King Isfandiyar; a Persian miniature

rejected the Zurvanite solution as heresy, and, ignoring the illogicalities involved, proclaimed both the supremacy of Ohrmazd and the unceasing opposition of Ahriman.

This controversy doubtless weakened Zoroastrianism, which, by this time, was also feeling the competition of Christianity and Manichaeism. However, it was not destined to be replaced in the land of its birth by either of these faiths, but by another that had been preached by a prophet of Arabia. In A.D. 652, the Sassanian government was overthrown by Muslim invaders, and Zoroastrianism as the national religion shared in the nation's disaster. Gradually, as a result of various pressures, Islam was accepted by the Iranians, until only an ever-diminishing minority remained faithful to Zarathustra's teaching. Only among those who fled to India in the eighth century, to form the Parsee community, has the ancient faith of Iran continued a vigorous, though circumscribed, life.

Zoroastrianism, unlike Buddhism and Christianity, never sought to become a world religion. But its influence did extend beyond Iran. We have already noted its effect on Judaism and Christianity; its influence may similarly be traced in Hermetic and Gnostic literature and in Manichaeism. Its most notable legacy to the West, however, found expression in a curiously contorted form. In the Mithraic cult, that spread throughout the Roman Empire, images of a lion-headed monster were venerated: recent research has shown that these probably represented a form of Zurvān, known as *Zurvān dareghō-chvadhāta*,[16] with whom Ahriman was identified—Iranian dualism, thus, in its latter years witnessed in the West to the reality of the creative and destructive forces operative in the universe.

---

[16] I.e. "Time of Long Dominion," that brings decay and death.

CHAPTER 14

Herod the Great

JUDAEA'S MOST ABLE BUT MOST HATED KING

Herod won and held the respect of a series of Roman statesmen and, despite the hatred of his subjects, he made them prosperous while he lived.

I

When Caesar fell beneath the daggers of the Republican conspirators on that fatal Ides of March in 44 B.C., the destinies of many people were involved. The civil war that followed between the Republicans and Caesar's friends would lead finally to the principate of Octavian, the so-called "architect of the Roman Empire". But many others, far from Rome, learned of great Caesar's death with deep foreboding for their own fortunes. Among them in distant Palestine was a young Idumaean named Herod, whose father had recently appointed him to govern Galilee.

Herod's position was already precarious before the news of Caesar's death arrived. For he owed his appointment as governor of Galilee to his father Antipater who had risen to be the chief minister of Hyrcanus II, the high priest and ethnarch of the Jewish people. This Hyrcanus was the feeble representative of the Hasmonaean dynasty, which had been established by the valiant Maccabees who successfully led the Jewish national resistance to Seleucid domination in 165–142 B.C. The able and astute Antipater had become the virtual ruler in Judaea, owing to the incompetence of Hyrcanus. But Antipater was hated by the Jewish people, not only for his success in acquiring such power and prestige, but because

Coin of Herod the Great: Herod's coinage is notable for its avoidance of human figures that would have been offensive to his Jewish subjects

of his Idumaean birth. The Idumaeans were an Arab people who inhabited the area south of Judaea, known today as the Negeb. About 129 B.C. they had been forcibly converted to Judaism by the Hasmonaean king John Hyrcanus I; but the Jews had never accepted them as fully members of their own race and religion, and they referred to them derisively as "*hēmijoudaioi*", i.e. "half-Jews". Antipater, who had largely gained his position through his effective support of Julius Caesar in the latter's bid for power in the Roman state, had in 47 B.C. appointed his sons Phasael and Herod tetrarchs respectively of Jerusalem and Galilee. Herod, who was then twenty-five years of age, at once began to show a characteristic energy of action by proceeding vigorously against the bandits who then infested Galilee. He captured and summarily executed a certain Hezekiah and a number of his followers.[1] In so doing he violated the Jewish law, which required that a man should be executed only after trial and a capital sentence by the Sanhedrin. Herod had, accordingly, given his enemies pretext for proceeding against him, and he was obliged to leave Palestine and take service with Sextus Caesar, a relative of the dictator, who was then legate of Syria.

Thus, at the beginning of his career, Herod had already become involved with the two forces that were to shape his destiny. These forces were in Herod's life essentially interrelated: for the hatred that the Jews felt towards him because of his alien origin caused him to depend vitally on Roman support, and so implicated him in the vicissitudes of Roman political life at one of its most dangerous epochs.

[1] The Jewish historian J. Klausner (*Jesus of Nazareth*, London, 1929, pp. 140–1) regarded Hezekiah and his followers as "zealot patriots."

The death of Julius Caesar imperilled Herod, as it did also his father Antipater and Phasael his brother, for they had all identified themselves strongly with Caesar's cause. It seemed that the day of reckoning had come for them; and so it would surely have done, if Antipater's control of Judaea had been less firm and if Cassius, the Republican commander who came to Syria, had been concerned only with punishing the former supporters of Caesar. But Cassius needed to consolidate his own position and that of his party in the East, and for this he urgently wanted money. A heavy sum was demanded from Judaea; it was raised by Antipater, Herod with his usual energy quickly collecting Galilee's allocation. The Roman must have appreciated the qualities shown by the young Idumaean on this occasion, for Herod received again the military command in Coele-Syria which he had formerly been given by Sextus Caesar.

But this unexpected improvement of his prospects was quickly jeopardized by misfortunes at home and by the changing pattern of power in the Roman world. In handling each of these crises, Herod showed that, besides his proved capacity for energetic action, he possessed great courage and tenacity of purpose, together with the ability to recommend himself as useful to those Romans who were striving among themselves for the mastery of the world. The true nature of the trouble in Judaea is difficult to assess from the account of the Jewish historian, Josephus. It appears that a certain Malichus, a man of unknown origin, succeeded in challenging the position of Antipater by worming his way into the confidence of Hyrcanus. In the struggle for power that followed Antipater was murdered at the instigation of his rival. Herod at once resolved to avenge his father and eliminate one who now barred his way to the control of Judaea. But he could not strike immediately; for Malichus had the support of Hyrcanus, who, weak and foolish though he was, was yet the acknowledged ruler of the Jewish nation. The way in which Herod carefully played his enemy, so that finally he contrived his death outside Palestine at the hands of Roman soldiers, is a masterpiece of the relentless prosecution of a purpose cloaked by subtle dissimulation.

But this success brought Herod no rest. Having eliminated one rival for the mastery of Judaea, he soon found himself faced by another with far stronger claims than either he or Malichus could muster. Antigonus, a nephew of Hyrcanus, was the next representative of the Hasmonaean line, and he now appeared in Judaea, supported by the forces of his kinsman Ptolemy, the prince of Ituraea, and Marion, whom Cassius had

Mark Antony, from a gold coin struck at Ephesus in 41 B.C., and Cleopatra, from a tetradrachm struck at Ascalon in 30 B.C.

appointed to rule Tyre. Herod succeeded in repelling their attacks; but scarcely had he recovered from this danger before he found himself once more perilously involved in the changing fortunes of the Roman contestants for world supremacy. In the year 42 B.C. the Republican party was decisively defeated at Philippi, and Herod's patron, Cassius, died there. The Roman world was now ruled by the triumvirate of Mark Antony, Octavian, the nephew of Caesar, and the ineffective Lepidus. Antony soon came to the East, and the Jewish nationalists at once seized the opportunity to complain about Herod to the most powerful of those who had defeated Herod's patron, Cassius. But Herod knew his man, for in his youth they had met when Antony was serving in his first campaign in the Levant. Accordingly, Herod anticipated his enemies' complaint and made his peace with Antony by recalling their former friendship, his father's valuable services to Caesar, and by a judicious gift of money. The Jewish deputation was dismissed, and Antony appointed Herod and his brother Phasael tetrarchs and committed the government of Judaea to them.[2]

The appointment did not mark the end of their troubles. While Antony was in Syria, he was in desperate need of money and the provincials were forced to meet his exorbitant demands. The levying of such imposts by the Idumaeans, in the service of their Roman master, did nothing to reconcile the Jews to their rule. Herod did, however, seek to strengthen his position with them by betrothal to Mariamme, the grand-daughter of Hyrcanus, their high priest and titular ruler. But, before he could properly establish himself in his office, Herod's fortunes were

[2] How the government was divided between them is not known. Relations between Herod and Phasael were always excellent.

once more overthrown by external events and this time reached their very nadir of defeat and despair. In the year 40 B.C., while Antony was dallying in Egypt with Cleopatra, Syria was invaded by the Parthians, the inveterate enemies of Rome in the East. When Antony saw the extent of the disaster, he abandoned the province and withdrew to Asia Minor to recruit forces from the West. In Palestine Herod could not compound with the invaders, because Antigonus had already bribed Pacorus, the Parthian leader, to place him on the throne of Judaea. Many Jews rose in support of Antigonus and his Parthian allies, and Herod and Phasael were besieged in Jerusalem, where their situation soon grew desperate. Phasael, with Hyrcanus, was lured away from the city by promises of negotiations: his unsuspecting nature cost Phasael his life, while the aged high priest, mutilated so that he could no longer hold his sacerdotal office, was carried off to captivity in Mesopotamia.[3] Herod, who had refused to be enticed from his defences, was now obliged himself to seek safety outside Jerusalem. His retreat, encumbered as he was with his family and many other refugees, demanded all his resources as a military commander. After beating off Parthian and Jewish attacks, he succeeded in reaching the friendly territory of Idumaea. Leaving there the bulk of his followers, he took his womenfolk, including Mariamme, his betrothed, for shelter to the great fortress of Masada, on the shores of the Dead Sea.[4] It was now his intention to enlist the help of Malchus, the king of the Nabataean Arabs, whom his father had effectively helped in the past. But, when Malchus forbad him to enter his kingdom for fear of the Parthians, Herod decided to seek Antony in Egypt.

It may be that Herod had then no other alternative than to look for help from Rome, despite all his experience of what dependence on Roman power could mean. There is reason, however, for thinking that for all the confusion of Roman political life and the weakness of the Roman position in the East that the Parthian invasion had signally demonstrated, Herod was convinced that the future lay with Rome. And so when he arrived in Alexandria and found that Antony had already departed, he refused an offer of Cleopatra, the Egyptian queen, to command an expedition that she was planning, and took ship for Rome.

Herod had, presumably, made his way to Rome to enlist Roman

---

[3] According to Josephus, Antigonus actually bit off the ears of Hyrcanus. The Mosaic Law in *Leviticus* xxi. 17–24 forbade the ministrations of priests who were not physically whole.
[4] See the illustrations of Masada in Chapter 19.

help for the restoration of his position in Judaea, that is, to drive out Antigonus and his Parthian allies and to restore him, Herod, as tetrarch—though whether under the nominal rule of Hyrcanus would have been uncertain until the fate of the Hasmonaean high priest was known. The actual outcome of Herod's visit is, therefore, surprising, and it is made more so by the conflicting accounts that Josephus gives of his intentions. In successive paragraphs in the extant Greek text of the Jewish historian it is stated, first, that in Rome Herod bribed Antony to secure his appointment as king: next, that he sought to obtain the kingship for Aristobulus, the younger brother of Mariamme and grandson of Hyrcanus.[5] But, whatever the truth as to his intention on this crucial occasion, the fact is that both Antony and Octavian undertook to have Herod proclaimed king of Judaea by the Senate. Thus by Roman decree the rule of the ancient Jewish dynasty of the Hasmonaeans ended, and in its place was established that of an Idumaean upstart, dignified, moreover, with the title of king.

The award to Herod then of such a position affords most eloquent testimony of the high regard in which he was held by the two leading Romans of the day. There in Rome, driven from his country and at the very nadir of his fortunes, his personal qualities were evidently recognized as plans were made for the restoration of Roman authority in the East. In Herod, the Romans clearly saw a man whom they could trust as a *rex socius* to hold firmly that pivotal position that Judaea naturally had in the strategy of the East, commanding as it did the military high road from Syria to Egypt and the caravan routes of commerce with India.

But Herod's was as yet an empty title. In Judaea, Antigonus was reigning, and his forces were besieging Herod's family and supporters at Masada. Herod was soon back in his country; but, although the Romans were beginning to re-assert themselves against the Parthians, the venality of their local commanders frustrated all his efforts to eject Antigonus from his strong position in Jerusalem. With the small forces at his disposal, Herod relieved Masada and subdued opposition in many districts. But it was not until he was able to appeal personally to Antony, who had taken over the siege of Samosata in 38, that he finally secured the cooperation of a Roman officer who was proof against the bribery of Antigonus. Accordingly, in the following year, supported by the troops

---

[5] Thus according to the *Jewish Antiquities* (xiv. 381–7). In his *Jewish Wars* (i. 282) he says Antony resolved to make Herod king because of his heroic qualities (*aretē*).

Herodian fortifications at Caesarea, the great port which Herod built in honour of the Roman Emperor

of Antony's lieutenant, Sosius, Herod laid seige to Jerusalem. A savage struggle followed and endured for five months. As in 63 B.C. against the attack of Pompey, and as they were to do on that last fatal occasion in A.D. 70, the Jews now fought with fanatical courage in the defence of their holy city. Because Jerusalem was subdivided by walls and contained a number of strong places, it had to be captured piecemeal, a process that added to the toll of slaughter and destruction. The Temple of Yahweh was the last centre of resistance, and it was only by the vigorous intervention of Herod that the holy of holies of Israel's unique shrine was saved from desecration by the furious legionaries. Antigonus begged for his life before Sosius, who scornfully addressed him as "Antigone"; he was sent bound to Antony and finally scourged and beheaded in Antioch.

II

It was in a devastated land that Herod now began to rule as king. Its people had suffered terribly, its wealth had been squandered, and its capital ruined in the effort to wrest it from its last Hasmonaean ruler. Deeper than ever, therefore, must have been the hatred of the Jews for the Idumaean who had now become their king by Roman decree and Roman swords.

Herod's task was, accordingly, no easy one; but it was complicated

and made more perilous by two other factors. The mastery of the Roman
world still remained undecided between Antony and Octavian. Clearly
in the coming struggle one of the two would be eliminated, and in his
fall those who supported him would surely be involved. Antony's attachment to Cleopatra tended also to give the conflict another aspect than
that of a struggle between two Roman commanders. For the ambition
of the Egyptian queen sought, with Antony's help, to oppose to the upstart
power of the West an Eastern empire centred on that ancient land over
which her dynasty ruled. How Herod viewed this issue is not known.
He had shrewdly appraised the might of Rome, and he did not trust
Cleopatra; but of the two Roman rivals he was committed personally to
Antony, and his kingdom was dangerously close to Egypt.

So far, then, as foreign policy was concerned, Herod could only
support Antony, which he did loyally, and hope that his patron would
emerge successfully from the struggle. With the other danger he could
effectively deal, but only at a terrible cost to his own personal peace and
happiness. For his Jewish subjects the highest office in the state was that
of high priest. The Hasmonaeans had associated this office with political
power. Now that Hyrcanus was physically disqualified, and his own alien
origin forbad his assuming it, Herod appointed an obscure priest Ananel
to the high priesthood. In so doing he passed over an obvious
Hasmonaean candidate. It was Aristobulus, the young brother of his wife
Mariamme and grandson of Hyrcanus. The decision was regarded as
an insult by the Hasmonaean family, and Alexandra, the youth's mother,
enlisted the help of Cleopatra to get the appointment changed. Herod
felt obliged to accede, and Ananel was deposed in favour of Aristobulus.
But this concession did not placate Alexandra. Intrigue continued with
Cleopatra, who probably desired to get rid of Herod and so dominate
Judaea. As Herod understood this and saw the popularity of Aristobulus
with the Jews, he concluded that his position could never be secure while
a possible Hasmonaean rival lived. Accordingly, he contrived the young
high priest's death, with characteristic subtlety, as a bathing accident. But
his Hasmonaean relatives were not deceived: he lost whatever love
Mariamme might have had for him, and the hatred of Alexandra immeas-
urably deepened. Through the mediation of Cleopatra he was summoned
by Antony to account for the deed; despite the Egyptian queen, however,
he escaped condemnation—probably Antony felt that he could not afford
to lose so useful an ally.

Herod's relations with Cleopatra form a curious, and an obviously critical, episode in his career. He had been summoned to Laodicaea for his interview by Antony, who was there preparing an expedition into Armenia. The Egyptian queen was there, and, although she failed to secure his condemnation, she prevailed upon her Roman lover to give her one of the most valuable assets of Herod's kingdom, namely, the famous balsam gardens and palm groves at Jericho. Herod was too discreet to resist, though he astutely secured the lease of them from Cleopatra. After inflicting this loss on the Jewish king, Cleopatra chose to return to Egypt by way of Judaea. Herod was obliged to escort her through his kingdom, but, whatever his resentment, he showed her the utmost courtesy. In his account of the episode Josephus adds what appears to be an incredible story. He asserts that the Egyptian queen actually tried to seduce Herod: he admits that he could not understand her motive— whether she was genuinely enamoured of Herod or whether she sought thus to cause him to compromise himself in the eyes of Antony. Josephus inclines to the latter interpretation, which would seem the more feasible if his story be true. He goes on to tell that not only did Herod reject her advances, but he actually meditated killing her, as being a menace to Antony and many others.

Whatever the truth of Josephus' tale, it is certain that Herod was closely involved with Cleopatra; but in the end her hostility proved to be his salvation. The struggle between Antony and Octavian was mount- ing to its climax. When the campaign opened that led to the battle of Actium in 31 B.C., Herod at once placed his forces at Antony's disposal; but Cleopatra, perhaps because she did not want her lover helped to victory by the able Idumaean, persuaded Antony to engage Herod on an expedition against the Nabataean Arabs. When Herod returned victori- ous to Judaea, he learned of the decision at Actium and that his Roman patron had retired in defeat to Egypt with Cleopatra. Herod did not waver in his loyalty. He offered all his resources to Antony, but on one condi- tion—that he killed Cleopatra. The offer was astute, though ruthless. It was his liaison with Cleopatra that had lost Antony the great popularity that he had enjoyed in contrast to the cold Octavian; it was Cleopatra's behaviour at Actium that had caused him to desert his faithful troops. To destroy her now as an enemy of Rome, and, with Herod's help, take over Egypt, might still have given Antony a chance to restore his fortunes or at least make his cautious enemy hesitate in following up his success.[6]

---

[6] War had been declared only on Cleopatra.

A large scale model of Herodian Jerusalem, reconstructed according to the recent archaeological research (in the grounds of the Holy Land Hotel, Jerusalem)

But Antony would not free himself thus of Cleopatra, and Herod felt discharged from his obligation to him. Even thus released, however, the prospect before Herod was daunting. He had been too closely associated with Antony to think that he could hope to escape involvement in his defeat.

Herod went to meet Octavian in Rhodes in the spring of 30 B.C.; but, before leaving for this fateful interview, he took the precaution of executing the old and helpless Hyrcanus lest he should be used in some plot for an Hasmonaean restoration. At Rhodes Herod did not attempt to excuse himself. He told Octavian frankly of the support he had given to Antony, and that he would himself have fought at Antony's side at Actium but for the Arabian campaign. He added also that he only forsook Antony now because he had rejected his advice concerning Cleopatra. Once more Herod's value was appreciated by a Roman statesman: Octavian not only confirmed him in his kingdom, but added to it and restored his Jericho estates.

Octavian's triumph brought much needed peace to the Roman world: it gave also to Herod the opportunity at last for the peaceful development of his land. This opportunity he exploited to the fullest, and Judaea

entered upon a period of unexampled prosperity. The country's main
economic resources were two-fold: agriculture and the revenue derived
from the trade routes that passed through it. In view of the immense wealth
of which Herod disposed, enabling him to finance great building projects
and twice make substantial reductions in taxation, it would seem that
his income from commerce must have been very great. It was undoubtedly
to safeguard the caravan routes and maintain that security upon which
all depended that Herod undertook the building or reconstruction of a
number of great fortresses and organized a considerable army of foreign
mercenaries. To further trade he also provided Judaea with a new port
equipped with harbour installations and a huge mole, naming it Caesarea
in honour of his imperial patron.

III

King of the Jews and a Jew by religion, yet an Idumaean by race,
Herod pursued what appears to be an ambivalent cultural policy. Both
in Judaea and in places beyond he supported Graeco-Roman civilization
by buildings and endowments. At Jerusalem the "Actian Games" were
instituted in honour of Octavian's victory; Samaria was rebuilt as a Greek
city, with a temple dedicated to Augustus as Octavian was now known;

Recent (1968) excavation
of the west wall of the
Jerusalem Temple, reveal-
ing the fine Herodian masonry

other places in Palestine received baths, fountains and colonnades. Rhodes, Antioch, Athens, Nicopolis, and Damascus were among the foreign recipients of his munificence, while Greek scholars were welcomed to his court. Much in this Hellenization was offensive to Herod's Jewish subjects; however, he was careful not to affront their religious feelings too obviousiy—most notably he refrained from placing human images on his coins. But his supreme service to his subjects' religion was his rebuilding of the Temple at Jerusalem. The work was on a most lavish scale, and its beauty and magnificence became proverbial—an eloquent testimony to the wonder which the great edifice evoked is preserved in the disciple's exclamation to Jesus: "Master, see what manner of stones and what buildings are here!" (*Mark* xiii. 1).

The apparent ambivalence of Herod's policy surely attests his deep insight into the problem of Jewish-Gentile relations. He shared Augustus' aim to unify the peoples of the Empire in a common culture. But his own subjects, by their peculiar religious beliefs and customs, so uncompromisingly held, constituted an obstacle of a most disturbing kind. For the Jewish people were not confined to Judaea: Jewish communities were found throughout the Empire, each distinctive by its social and religious habits. This distinction was resented by their Gentile neighbours, and anti-semitism could be a disruptive force. Herod's policy was sagacious and far-sighted. In Palestine, while seeking to placate his Jewish subjects by the magnificent rebuilding of their Temple, he accustomed them to the art and institutions of Graeco-Roman culture. In other lands he showed by his benefactions that a Jewish monarch could appreciate Hellenism, hoping doubtlessly thereby to improve the relations of the Diaspora Jews with their Gentile neighbours.

Herod's statesmanship was appreciated by Augustus and his great friend and minister, Agrippa, and he received many tokens of their high regard. But, whatever his success elsewhere, in Judaea he became both the author and subject of an ever-darkening tragedy. He failed to overcome the Jews' instinctive dislike and distrust—rabbinic literature ignores his part in the construction of the Temple that it so lovingly describes. But it is in the terrible ruin of his domestic life that the essential tragedy lies. Herod never freed himself from the Hasmonaean curse. His marriage alliance to that house, which should have strengthened his position, became the source of all his woe. He was passionately devoted to the beautiful Mariamme; but he remained ever subject to the influence of

Herod directing the Massacre of the Innocents, according to Geralamo Mocetto (1458–1531)

another woman—his sister, Salome, and she proved to be the evil genius of his life. Jealous of Mariamme, she unceasingly intrigued against her and her relations. Owing perhaps to his fundamental sense of insecurity *vis-à-vis* the Hasmonaeans, it was not difficult for Herod to persuade himself or be persuaded of the hostile intentions of various members of that distinguished family. Page after page of Josephus' narrative tells in vivid detail how successively Aristobulus, Hyrcanus, and Mariamme's mother, Alexandra, went to their deaths. Then there is the supreme tragedy of Mariamme herself—executed for infidelity by a husband who nigh well died with grief at her loss. But the awful succession of victims did not end there. Salome's hatred of Mariamme turned to Mariamme's sons, though they were Herod's sons, too. Once more the web of intrigue, suspicion and misunderstanding was spun about Herod until he was led to destroy the young princes, Alexander and Aristobulus, through whom a Herodian-Hasmonaean dynasty might have been established. Herod's heir was now Antipater, his son by a former wife, who had played his part in the destruction of Mariamme's sons. However, he too went to his death for intriguing against his father, thus provoking Augustus to remark on hearing the news that he "would rather be Herod's pig than his son".

That one so shrewd and experienced in human affairs as Herod should have fallen to such intrigues is astounding. The only feasible explanation for the execution of his sons, which occurred in his latter years, is that his reason was deranged by the hideous disease from which he eventually died in 4 B.C. It is during these last awful years of his life that he also became infamously linked with the birth of Jesus in the story of the visit of the Magi and the Massacre of the Innocents. The story, as recorded in *Matthew* ii. 1–18, clearly has the form of a Jewish-Christian *midrash;* but the killing of the children would have been no impossible deed for Herod then to have done.

Josephus but once gives Herod the title of "Great". That he deserved that title might be disputed. Nevertheless, with Herod, whether in his achievements as soldier and statesman or in his crimes and suffering, there was nothing petty. He won and held the respect of a series of Roman statesmen, and, despite the hatred of the Jews, he made them prosperous and preserved them while he lived from direct subjugation to Rome.

The Jesus of History

". . . Theology is essentially theological interpretation
put upon historical fact. Can we . . . reach back
to the fact behind the interpretation?" This problem
confronts every student of primitive Christianity.

I

Each day, for some fifteen centuries, in its liturgical services the
Christian Church has made a formal declaration of its faith. Its creeds,
in which this faith is defined, embody many metaphysical statements such
as those concerning the doctrine of the Trinity; but they make also
reference to a historical event that is basic to the whole structure of
the faith—it is the statement that Jesus Christ "suffered under Pontius
Pilate, was crucified, dead and buried.".[1]

This reference imparts to Christianity its distinctive character among
the religions of mankind. For, whereas the other religions attach no
essential significance to the historical careers of their respective founders,
Christianity owes its very *raison d'être* to certain events in the life of Jesus
of Nazareth. The credal reference to his crucifixion by Pontius Pilate
attests to this essential anchoring of Christianity to a specific historical
situation; for Pontius Pilate was the Roman procurator or praefectus who
governed Judaea between the years A.D. 26 and 36.[2]

In earlier centuries the fact of the historical career of Jesus was taken
for granted, and attention was concentrated upon the transcendental
significance of the events of his life; in other words, emphasis was laid

[1] The practice of reciting the (Nicene) Creed at the Eucharist started in the fifth century.
Before that time various forms of credal statement were used in Baptism.
[2] See Chapter 17.

The Emperor Tiberius (A.D. 14–
37), who appointed Pontius
Pilate as governor of Judaea
(bust in the Capitoline Museum,
Rome)

rather upon the divine Christ, the saviour of mankind, than upon the
historical Jesus of Nazareth who had lived and died in first-century
Palestine. Christian art provides eloquent witness to this attitude. Thus,
the favourite representation of Christ in the catacombs and on the early
sarcophagi (4th cent.) is as the Good Shepherd, in which rôle he is
depicted as a beardless youth in Greek attire.[3] Where incidents of the
Passion are represented at this period, both Christ and the other actors
are shown in contemporary Roman dress, no attempt being made to depict
the original Judaean setting of the drama. This apparent indifference to
the actual historical event manifests itself in turn in Byzantine art; and
its traits are well known in medieval and Renaissance religious painting
in that, for example, the Roman soldiers attendant at the Crucifixion are
presented in the arms and armour contemporary to the time of the artist.[4]

The change that began to show itself early in the nineteenth century
in the appreciation of historical evidence and the ideal of historical
accuracy soon affected the study of Christian origins. If the historian's

[3] It has recently been suggested that the "Shepherd" figure was originally a pagan symbol
of *philanthropia;* painted on the walls of Christian burial places in the catacombs, the figure
represented Christ as the guardian of the departed soul from daemonic attack.

[4] Some later Renaissance painters showed their classical taste by representing the soldiers
in the Passion and Crucifixion scenes in ornate Roman armour.

essential duty in his exploration of the past was to discover and state the relevant facts, "how it actually happened" according to Ranke's famous dictum, then the beginnings of Christianity had to be investigated as objectively as any other historical phenomenon. The task was soon taken in hand. The writings of the New Testament now began to be interrogated as historical documents to evaluate their evidence for the events that they purport to describe, or as witnesses to the situation that produced them—as in the case of St. Paul's Epistles. This new attitude naturally provoked vigorous and sometimes bitter controversy. In particular, since the Gospels were now approached with a critical mind and not in the spirit of the traditional piety, interest was concentrated on the many obvious discrepancies in their record: instead of the former effort to harmonise their witness concerning the life of Jesus, significance was seen in the variations of their traditions. This research has continued to the present day, and it still goes on as vigorously as ever. As has happened in many other fields of scientific investigation, the problems involved here have generally been found more complicated and harder of definitive solution as more has been learned about them. For example, it has come to be recognized that the emergence of Christianity cannot be treated as an isolated phenomenon: it can only be understood in the context of its historical environment. This has meant an increasingly detailed investigation of the political, economic, and cultural situation of both Jewish and Graeco-Roman society during the period 100 B.C. to A.D. 200. And the materials for such investigation have been steadily increased by archaeological research, most notably in recent years by the discovery of the Dead Sea Scrolls, the excavations at Qumrân and Masada, and the Coptic documents found at Nag Hammadi in Egypt. However, despite the increasing complexity of the quest and the many unsolved problems that remain, it is possible to draw certain conclusions about our knowledge of Jesus of Nazareth as a historical person.

II

First, it may be said, as being beyond dispute in all serious scholarship, that Jesus of Nazareth did actually live. It is necessary to say this, since the view was put forward at the beginning of this century, with considerable ingenuity and apparent learning, that Jesus was a creation of mythical thought—a view that is sometimes repeated today in semilearned publications. The historicity of Jesus is clearly attested by the

"Before the cock crows. . ." An early depiction of Peter's denial of Jesus (from a 4th-cent. sarcophagus in the Lateran Museum, Rome)

Roman historian Tacitus, who was a pagan and obviously hostile to Christianity. Writing in the early years of the second century about the persecution of the Christians by Nero (A.D. 64), he says: "Christus, the founder of the name (i.e. Christians), had undergone the death penalty in the reign of Tiberius, by sentence of the procurator Pontius Pilate, and the pernicious superstition was checked for a moment, only to break out once more, not merely in Judaea, the home of the disease, but in the capital itself (i.e. Rome)."[5] The unequivocal, though hostile, nature of this testimony was undoubtedly matched by the record of the first-century Jewish historian, Josephus—unfortunately in the extant Greek text of his *Antiquities of the Jews* the account given there of Jesus has evidently been amended by later Christian censorship.[6] But the most convincing evidence of all to the historicity of Jesus is surely provided unconsciously by the Christian Gospels. It lies in the admission that the founder of the movement had been crucified as a revolutionary by the Roman

[5] *Annales* XV. 44, trans. J. Jackson (Loeb Classical Library edn., vol. iv).
[6] See Chapter 20. The question is discussed at length by the author in his book *Jesus and the Zealots* (Scribners, New York, 1968), pp. 359–368.

governor of Judaea, Pontius Pilate. In view of the incriminating character of this fact, which, as we shall see, was a cause of extreme embarrassment to the first Christians, it is incredible that it could ever have been invented by them.

But, if the fact of the historical existence of Jesus is beyond reasonable doubt, it does not necessarily follow that the records that we have of him can be accepted as reliable historical accounts. It is here that we begin to encounter the complexities of research into the origins of Christianity.

The earliest non-Christian references to Jesus, as we have just seen, attest to the fact of his execution in Judaea at the hands of the Romans; but beyond that they tell us nothing more than the inferential fact that a Roman and a Jewish historian writing some seventy or eighty years after the event viewed Jesus, and the movement that stemmed from him, with cynical hostility. We are, therefore, left with the Christian records, preserved in the New Testament, as our only source of detailed information about the person and career of Jesus. These writings, however, were all composed by men who were profoundly convinced that Jesus of Nazareth was the incarnated Son of God, and that by his death he had saved mankind from eternal perdition; moreover, they believed also that he had risen to a new supernatural form of life and that he would soon return again in power and glory to judge mankind. Accordingly, we have to do in these writings with theology and not with history: however, the

The Church of the Nativity, Bethlehem; originally built in the 4th century over the traditional birthplace of Jesus

issue is not quite as simple as that; for the theology is essentially theological interpretation put upon historical fact. Can we, then, reach back
to the fact behind the interpretation? Here is the peculiar task of the
historian of primitive Christianity.

It is demonstrably a task of the most baffling complexity; but it is
also one that demands the most delicate handling on other grounds. For
the subject of investigation is not just an ancient historical situation of
merely academic interest—it concerns the very origins of one of the world's
great religions that still commands the allegiance of millions of persons.

III

The earliest Christian writings that have been preserved to us are
the letters of the Apostle Paul. They afford us an insight into Christian
thought and activity within some twenty years of the Crucifixion. The
evidence of these writings is very puzzling. They show that Jesus was
already regarded as the divine saviour of mankind; but they exhibit very
little concern with the earthly career of Jesus as a historical person.
Moreover, as is shown in Chapter 21, Paul's letters reveal the existence
of a serious difference between his interpretation of the person and mission
of Jesus and that taught by the original community of Jewish disciples
at Jerusalem.

When we turn to the Gospels, our first impression is that here we
certainly have straightforward narratives about Jesus. The impression,
however, cannot be sustained on closer scrutiny. For not only is the
presentation of Jesus in the *Gospel of John* markedly different from that
in the other three Gospels, but these latter in turn differ among themselves
on some fundamental points. For example, the *Gospel of Matthew* locates
the appearance of the Risen Christ to the disciples in Galilee, whither
they are divinely commanded to go (*Matt.* xxviii. 7, 10, 16–20)—a
tradition that appears to be confirmed by the *Gospel of Mark* (*Mk.* xvi.
7). On the other hand, the *Gospel of Luke* and the *Acts of the Apostles*,
writings having a common authorship, both locate the post-Resurrection
appearances in Jerusalem and its immediate environs (*Lk.* xxiv. 13–52;
Acts i. 1–12), and in *Acts* i. 4 it is expressly stated that the disciples
were forbidden to leave the city. That such a discrepancy, about so
important a matter, could exist surely indicates that the writings concerned
embody traditions that must have grown up among different, and possibly
rival, groups of believers.

An early depiction of the arrest and trial of Jesus (from a late 4th-cent. ivory lipsanotheca in the Museo Civico dell' Età Christiana Brescia)

Discrepancies such as this have long since caused scholars to recognize that each of the Gospels contains its own cycle of tradition about Jesus, which in turn reflects its own peculiar outlook and interests. Moreover, it is also agreed that these traditions, before reaching their present literary form, had been shaped to meet the needs of the various Christian communities, some of them located outside Palestine, to which they severally belonged. This is a factor of great importance in any assessment of the historical significance of these traditions. But it is particularly important in connection with the *Gospel of Mark,* since authoritative opinion is agreed that the Gospels of Matthew and Luke have generally followed the narrative framework of *Mark*—a fact that means that *Mark* is the earliest written account that we have of Jesus.

This priority of the Markan Gospel accordingly invests it with a peculiar significance. As the first narrative record of Jesus, its composition must surely mark a new departure in Christian practice—what event, it may reasonably be asked, had brought about this change? We have no evidence to enable us to give a categorical answer; the present writer has, however, recently set out at length elsewhere a case for believing that the cause was the series of events, beginning in Palestine in A.D. 66, that culminated in the destruction of Jerusalem by the Romans four years later.[7] During that bitter struggle of the Jewish people to throw off the yoke of Rome, leading to its awful *dénouement* in the utter ruin of their holy city and Temple, the original Christian community in Jerusalem disappeared. Since this community, which included the disciples and "eye-witnesses" of Jesus, had hitherto been the source of tradition and authority to the infant Christian movement, the catastrophe of A.D. 70 left Christians elsewhere facing a difficult and a dangerous situation. For, not only had they lost the guidance of the mother church of Jerusalem; they were in danger, through the Jewish origins of their faith, of being suspect to the Roman government as implicated with Jewish nationalism— had not their founder himself been executed as a revolutionary against Rome?

It is generally accepted that the *Gospel of Mark* was written in Rome. Hence it was written for the Christian community dwelling in the very metropolis of the Empire, whose rule had been repudiated by the Jewish rebels—it was a community too that, a few years before, had suffered terribly under the Emperor Nero as convenient scapegoats to be blamed for a fire that had devastated the city. It was in this perplexing and dangerous situation, therefore, that a member of the church in Rome, whom we know as Mark, undertook to provide for his fellow Christians an account of the life of their Master that would give them guidance about recent events and a defence against the charge of subversive sympathies.

Obviously the most embarrassing fact for these Roman Christians was the crucifixion of Jesus by Pontius Pilate on a charge of sedition. The fact was clearly so well known that it could not be denied. Mark was, accordingly, faced with the task of explaining away its implicit offence. He does this by transferring the responsibility for the condemnation of Jesus from the Roman governor to the Jewish authorities. Thus, he represents Pilate as convinced of the innocence of Jesus but forced by the evil machinations of the Jewish leaders to crucify him as a rebel. In handling his case Mark was not very adroit, and the discrepancies in his account of the two trials of Jesus and the episode of Barabbas are so obvious on analysis that his intention can be clearly discerned.[8] The conclusion to be drawn from this attempt of Mark to transfer

---

[7] "The Date of the Markan Gospel," in *New Testament Studies*, vol. 7 (Cambridge, 1961).
[8] *Mk.* xiv. 53–xv. 15. See Chapter 16.

The Dome of the Rock, Jerusalem. The 7th-century mosque erected on the site of the Temple, in which Jesus worshipped

the responsibility for the Crucifixion from the Romans to the Jews is of fundamental importance for our knowledge of the historical Jesus. It puts beyond doubt the fact of the execution of Jesus as a revolutionary by the Romans—a fact so significantly inconvenient to the Christians of Rome at the time of the Jewish war. But was Jesus really guilty of such a charge? According to *Mark*, our earliest Gospel, Jesus was not guilty; and, as we have seen, he tries, not very successfully, to represent the condemnation as due to the false accusations of the Jewish authorities, who sought the death of Jesus for other reasons. However, Mark unwittingly provides evidence that there may have been other grounds for the Roman condemnation. Most notably, in his list of the twelve disciples of Jesus (iii. 14–19), he names one as "Simon, the Cananaean". The word "Cananaean" comes from an Aramaic expression meaning "Zealot". Now, the Zealots were the extreme nationalist party among the Jews and played the leading rôle in the revolt against Rome. If Mark had followed his usual practice of explaining Aramaic terms to his readers, he would have been obliged to have recorded here that one of the disciples of Jesus had been a Zealot. The fact that he leaves the word "Cananaean" unexplained is, accordingly, indicative of his embarrassment about the matter: it may be noted that, when Luke wrote some twenty years later, the Jewish war was a thing

of the past and he could safely describe Simon as "the Zealot" (vi. 15;
cf. Acts i. 13).

This tacit Markan admission of the existence of compromising
evidence relative to Jesus' condemnation by Pilate illuminates and confirms other information. For example, not only do all the Gospels record
that armed resistance was offered by the disciples in Gethsemane when
Jesus was arrested, but *Luke* relates that Jesus actually gave instructions
to the disciples to arm themselves before going there—instructions that
were, significantly, unnecessary since they were already armed (xxii.
36–38). Then, it is also recorded that, when he made his triumphal entry
into Jerusalem, Jesus had been acclaimed in terms of political Messianism
as "Blessed is the King that cometh in the name of the Lord" (*Lk.* xix.
38).

In our quest for the historical Jesus it would seem, therefore, that
behind the apologetic of the Gospel record there lies the memory of certain
facts that provide at least a *prima facie* explanation for the execution of
Jesus by the Romans. There is also the further fact that, as is well known,

Ruins of the late 2nd-century synagogue at Capernaum, erected on the
site of the synagogue in which Jesus taught

at this period the Jews expected that God would save them from their heathen bondage by sending His Anointed One, i.e. the Messiah, to effect their liberation. It is also equally well known, and the fact is attested by the very use of the title "Christ", that from the beginning Christians had identified Jesus with this expected Messiah or Christ. But how this identification arose is obscure, and on its elucidation our understanding of the historical Jesus vitally depends.

Once more we must turn to *Mark* for our earliest information. On analysis it is found that the apologetical theme that runs throughout this Gospel is concerned not only with explaining that Jesus was innocent of sedition against Rome; it seeks also to show that the divine nature of Jesus was not recognized by any Jew during his lifetime—the first person to perceive his divinity was, according to Mark, the Roman centurion at his crucifixion (xv. 39). The theological intention which is operative here has, of course, to take account of the attitude of the original Jewish disciples of Jesus. This is done most notably by Mark in the episode at Caesarea Philippi recorded in viii. 27–33. Here he relates that when Jesus had asked his original disciples who they believed him to be, Peter, as their spokesman, acknowledged him as the Messiah. But that was not enough; and Mark goes on to explain that, when Jesus next told them that he must suffer and die, Peter would not accept this rôle for his Master and was in consequence terribly rebuked. Thus, according to Mark's presentation, Jesus' own disciples could only accept him as the Messiah of Israel; it was left to the Gentiles, guided undoubtedly by Paul, to perceive his true character as the divine saviour of mankind who redeems by his own death—a truth symbolized in the recognition by the Roman centurion of the dying Jesus as the son of God.[9]

It may be reasonably concluded, therefore, that the actions and teachings of Jesus had been such as to cause his original disciples to recognize him as the Messiah. But this conclusion raises the vital question: how far did Jesus conform to the expected rôle of the Messiah? Attempts to answer this question have long been confused by the instinctive Christian belief that the divine saviour of mankind could not have involved himself in contemporary Jewish politics. This conviction, as we have seen, first found expression in Mark's attempt to explain the Roman execution of Jesus as due to Jewish malice. However, not only have we noted

[9] See Chapter 21.

evidence that might suggest that there was a political aspect to the activity of Jesus, we must recognize also that Jesus himself would have been obliged to have made his position clear concerning the Roman rule in Judaea. It would seem that three courses of action would have been open to Jesus in this connection. He could conceivably have refused to commit himself either way on the issue. But it is difficult to believe that any Jew could have abstracted himself so completely from the life and interests of his countrymen at this time; moreover, it would not be credible that one who had adopted such a non-committal attitude could have won so great a measure of popular support as Jesus had evidently done. Alternatively, he could have maintained that it was better to accept the Roman rule as a *fait accompli* than risk the perils of rebellion—a view that was taken by the Sadducean priestly aristocracy. But, if he had thus counselled submission to Rome, how could he have stirred any of his fellow Jews to recognize him as the Messiah?—and would such a pacific attitude have brought him ultimately to death at the hands of the Romans? There remains, therefore, but the third possibility: that, as a patriotic Jew, Jesus acknowledged the Roman rule as contrary to the divine will and identified himself with his people's aspiration for freedom.

But, if it is likely that Jesus accepted the justice of his people's cause against Rome, to what extent did he identify himself with an active policy to secure their political freedom? To this question no certain, or even probable, answer can be assuredly returned. The extant evidence is equivocal. On the one hand, there are indications, which we have noticed, that the Roman condemnation might have had at least some appearance of justification. Against this are a number of points that suggest that Jesus refused to accept fully the rôle of the militant Messiah. The Gospel tradition clearly reflects Jesus' concern with the profounder spiritual issues of man's relationship to God; the Temptation stories seem to preserve a recollection that Jesus had turned from the easier path of worldly success; and the betrayal by Judas Iscariot may have been due to that disciple's disillusionment because of Jesus' pacifism or to an attempt to force his Master's hand to violent action against his enemies. Yet it must also be recognized that all these points are capable of a different interpretation. For it is clearly evident that the pacifist portrait of Jesus was an apologetical necessity for Christians against the deep-rooted suspicion of the Roman authorities that Christianity was a revolutionary movement of Jewish origin.

Christ (beardless) depicted as the Kosmokrator ('ruler of the universe'). Early sixth-century mosaic, S. Vitale, Ravenna.

IV

Whatever may have been Pilate's reasons for condemning Jesus, it is certain that the Crucifixion had demoralized his disciples and over-thrown their faith in his Messiahship. For there was no expectation that the Messiah should be killed: still less that he should die the accursed death of the Law, which was crucifixion. The death on the cross should, therefore, on all human reckoning, have been the dismal end of the movement that Jesus had initiated. There had been before, and there were to be later, other Messianic claimants in Israel, but the influence of none of them long survived their overthrow. Consequently, the fact that from the crucified Jesus stemmed one of the world's great religions is explicable only in terms of the strength of his disciples' subsequent conviction that God had raised him from death and that they had communion with him.

The process of the disciples' mental adjustment after this tremendous experience can still be traced in the Gospel tradition. As Jews, they instinctively sought in their sacred scriptures for some foretelling of the death of the Messiah. They found it in Isaiah's mysterious prophecy of the Suffering Servant of Yahweh (*Isaiah* xlii. 1–4; xlix. 1–6; l. 4–9; lii.

Jesus as the Good Shepherd. This was a favourite representation of Jesus
in early Christian art (from a 4th-cent. mosaic pavement at Aquileia)

13–liii. 12). Their identification of Jesus with this tragic figure is vividly
presented in narrative form in *Luke* xxiv. 13–27 and *Acts* viii. 26–35.

Having thus found a satisfactory explanation for the Crucifixion, the
original disciples naturally continued to think of Jesus as the Messiah,
to whose glorious return in power to "restore the kingdom to Israel" they
now eagerly looked forward. In the meantime, in presenting him as such
to their fellow-countrymen, they used incidents from his life and reminis-
cences of his teaching as proof of his Messianic character and in justification of their own faith. Hence, an oral tradition about Jesus, in anecdotal
form, was formulated which was in time to form the basis of the written
Gospels. But it was a tradition that was essentially shaped by the
catechetical and apologetical needs of these primitive Christian communities in Palestine: there was, of course, among them no intention to preserve

an accurate historical record of Jesus for posterity. The events leading up to the Crucifixion naturally constituted their chief topic of concern and were dealt with at greater length than the rest of the career of Jesus: but, having found scriptural warranty for the death of the Messiah, his execution by the Romans was no problem for the Jewish disciples such as it became later for Gentile believers—indeed, among Jews it would rather have redounded to the credit of Jesus as being a martyr's death for Israel.

Such, then, appears to have been the formation of the tradition about Jesus among the Jewish Christians of Palestine prior to the catastrophe of A.D. 70. It is consistent, too, with the fact that those original followers of Jesus continued to live as zealous orthodox Jews, worshipping regularly in the Temple at Jerusalem—obviously there was nothing in their faith in Jesus that they felt to be incompatible with their continuing allegiance to Judaism. It is, accordingly, difficult to see how Christianity, thus interpreted, could ever have become a world religion but for the genius of Paul. It was Paul's inspired interpretation of the Crucifixion as the essential nexus in a divine plan for mankind's salvation and his exaltation of Jesus as the divine saviour that provided the definitive pattern of subsequent Gentile Christianity.

But the moulding of the tradition of the historical Jesus according to this transcendental pattern was not the work of Paul. It was the supreme achievement of Mark. Faced, as we have seen, with the perilous situation confronting the Christians in Rome about the year 70, Mark fashioned that oral tradition of Jesus as the Messiah of Israel into the superb narrative that unfolded his true character of the divine saviour of mankind.

⤷ CHAPTER 16

The Trial of Jesus

THE ENIGMA OF THE FIRST GOOD FRIDAY

"So far as the historian can evaluate the evidence,
it would seem that Pontius Pilate regarded Jesus as guilty
of sedition. Whether he was right is another matter."

I

By a strange irony of history, the surest thing known about Jesus of Nazareth is that he was executed by the Romans for sedition against their government in Judaea. The circumstances of Jesus' birth, the length of his public ministry, and the exact content of his teaching are all matters of uncertainty, but the cause of his death is beyond doubt. For the fact that Jesus was crucified as a rebel on the orders of Pontius Pilate, the Roman procurator of Judaea,[1] is attested by all four Gospels, and it is briefly mentioned by the Roman historian Tacitus, writing early in the second century. The witness of the Gospels is especially significant, because the fact of the Roman execution of Jesus on such a charge was very embarrassing for the early Christians. They would obviously have never invented it; indeed, they would probably have not recorded it, if the fact had not been so well known.

That the Gospel writers do describe the crucifixion of Jesus, and the events that led up to it, at considerable length, is, in fact, the real cause of the mystery that invests the tragic event. For their accounts are

---

[1] A recently discovered inscription at Caesarea indicates that Pilate's office was known as that of *praefectus*.

Christ before Pilate: painting by Duccio (d. 1319), at Siena

found, on analysis, to be inspired by a strong apologetical motive—indeed, they are attempts to explain the embarrassing fact that Jesus was actually executed as a political offender. Because of this apologetical intent, any attempt to elucidate the problem of the Roman condemnation of Jesus must begin with an evaluation of the Gospel evidence.

The pivotal document is the *Gospel of Mark;* for it is the earliest of the Gospels, and its narrative framework was closely followed by the authors of the Gospels of Matthew and Luke. The *Gospel of John,* which is later in date, generally reproduces the Markan presentation of the Trial and Crucifixion of Jesus, though evidently being more concerned with the theological significance of these events.

The *Gospel of Mark* represents an innovation in Christian thought and practice. No one had hitherto thought of writing a narrative account of the career of Jesus. The reason for this was undoubtedly the fact that the first Christians believed so strongly that Jesus would shortly return from heaven, with supernatural power, to bring the existing world-order

to an end. In other words, in the three or four decades since the Crucifixion no need had been felt to record the earthly life of Jesus for posterity—
because there would be no posterity!

What, then, caused the change that produced the *Gospel of Mark?*
Clearly we must look for some adequate cause; the change implies a truly
profound alteration in the primitive Christian outlook. To answer the
question means knowing the date of the Gospel. Scholars have been
accustomed to date it for the period A.D. 65–75. Now, during this decade
occurred the Jewish revolt against Rome. It had been coming for some
time, owing to Roman maladministration and the Jewish conviction, so
fervently held, that the Elect People of Israel could pay allegiance to no
other lord than Yahweh, the god of Israel. The revolt broke out in the
year 66, and for the next four years the life of the Jewish nation was
convulsed in war, until final catastrophe overwhelmed it in 70, when
Jerusalem was captured and razed, and its famous Temple destroyed by
fire.

The effect of this Jewish War upon the infant Christian Church was
profound. Hitherto the Christian movement had been directed and controlled from Jerusalem, where the original community of apostles and
disciples had been established. This community, the Mother Church of
Christianity, disappeared in the catastrophe of A.D. 70. The consequent
situation was fraught with peril and perplexity for Christians elsewhere.
Not only had they lost the original source of the authority and tradition
of their faith, but they faced the very real danger of being regarded by
the Roman government as "fellow-travellers" with Jewish nationalism. At
no place was this danger greater than in Rome itself, the capital of the
Empire that had been so sorely tried by the Jewish revolt. It was for
the Christian community in Rome that the *Gospel of Mark* was originally
written.

This fact of the Roman origin of the Markan Gospel is of supreme
significance for determining the date of its composition. The question
that now faces us, in the light of the preceding considerations, is: when,
during the period A.D. 65–75, would the need have arisen among the
Christians of Rome for a written record of the career of Jesus, seeing that
this need had never been felt before? The evidence points irresistibly to
one answer only: the need arose out of the situation caused by the Jewish
War against Rome.

The *a priori* probability that this was so finds remarkable confirma-

The Menorah or seven-branched
lampstand of the Jerusalem
Temple (from the Arch of Titus,
Rome)

tion when we examine the *Gospel* itself. But first we must notice another
fact of great importance in this connection. In the year 71, the Emperor
Vespasian, together with his sons Titus and Domitian, celebrated a
splendid triumph in Rome to commemorate their victory over rebel
Judaea.[2] The occasion was one of great significance for both the Roman
people and the new imperial dynasty of the Flavii. Since the death of
Nero in 68, the Roman state had suffered a series of grave disasters. It
had been plunged in civil war shortly after the Jews had revolted. The
Jewish War itself had begun with the crushing defeat of a Roman army
by the rebels.[3] The consequences were likely to have been felt afar; for
Judaea occupied an important place in the Roman strategical position
in the Near East. The country lay athwart the main routes connecting
Egypt with Syria; there was also a large Jewish population in Mesopotamia, likely to make common cause with their Judaean brethren against
Rome, a situation that the Parthians in turn could have exploited for
invading the Roman provinces. The Romans had, accordingly, been badly
frightened by the Jewish War, and they were profoundly grateful to

[2] Domitian had not actually taken part in the Judaean campaign. Titus had commanded
at the siege of Jerusalem.
[3] See Chapter 18.

Vespasian, who had both put an end to the civil war and crushed the Jewish rebels.

The occasion was important to Vespasian and his sons, for they were founding a new imperial dynasty. It would obviously be to their advantage to make the most of their victory by impressing the people of Rome with their achievements. Coins were issued commemorating the conquest of Judaea; but it was the triumph that provided the best opportunity for bringing home to the Roman people the magnitude of their victory. We are fortunate in having a detailed account of it from Josephus, the Jewish historian, who had actually served as a general on the Jewish side.[4] Through the streets of Rome, on the day concerned, the victorious legionaries paraded, with the trophies of their victory and multitudes of Jewish captives. The treasures of the Temple were borne in the triumphal procession, the great *Menorah* or seven-branched candelabra, the altar of shew-bread, the silver trumpets, and the purple curtains that had veiled the Holy of Holies—a sculptured representation of the scene still adorns the Arch of Titus in the Roman Forum. The procession also included tableaux depicting scenes from the War, which, Josephus tells us, impressed the people by their realistic presentation. The triumph culminated with the execution of Simon ben Gioras, one of the chief Jewish leaders, as Vespasian offered a sacrifice of thanksgiving to Jupiter in the great temple on the Capitol.

This triumph must have made the Jewish revolt very real to the people of Rome; for it was designed to render them vividly aware of the gravity of the danger from which the new Emperor and his son had delivered them. Among the spectators that day were doubtless many Christians, who thus beheld the spectacle of Israel's ruin. But the sight would have given them other thoughts than those that moved their pagan neighbours. This evidence of Jewish sedition must have been a disturbing reminder of the fact that Jesus, the founder of their faith, had also been executed for sedition against Rome. They would have been made embarrassingly aware that many of their fellow citizens were likely to view Christianity as Tacitus did when he wrote: "Christus, the founder of the name, had undergone the death penalty in the reign of Tiberius, by sentence of the procurator Pontius Pilate, and the pernicious superstition (*exitiabilis superstitio*) was checked for a moment, only to break out once

---

[4] See Chapter 20. See the Roman coins on p. 280.

more, not merely in Judaea, the home of the disease (*originem eius mali*), but in the capital itself, (i.e. Rome), where all things horrible or shameful in the world collect and find a vogue."[5]

The *Gospel of Mark* reflects the situation of the Roman Christians at this time with an amazing fidelity. Space allows us to select one passage only that, on analysis, unmistakably indicates the time and purpose of the Gospel's composition. In chapter xii. 13–17, Jesus is represented as being questioned about the duty of the Jews to pay tribute to Rome. Since this issue could have had no spiritual significance for the Christians of Rome, we may reasonably ask why the author of the Gospel devoted space to it? The answer can only be that the subject was politically important to the Roman Christians. The conclusion in turn raises the obvious question: when could the Christians in Rome have thus been interested in the attitude of Jesus to the Jewish obligation to pay tribute? The answer is equally obvious: when the issue had been so disturbingly intruded upon the attention of the Roman Christians by the Flavian triumph in A.D. 71, as we have seen.

In this passage about the Tribute Money, the Jewish leaders are depicted as trying to make Jesus compromise himself on a matter that was a burning issue for the Jewish nationalists—the non-payment of tribute was one of the causes of the revolt in 66. The author of the Markan Gospel represents Jesus as endorsing the Jewish obligation to pay tribute to Caesar; but there are grounds for grave doubt that this was really the view of Jesus.[6] The Markan presentation, however, was needed in Rome at this time; for it assured the Christians there, and any others who might read the Gospel, that Jesus was loyal to Rome and opposed to Jewish nationalism.

II

This involved discussion concerning the origins of the *Gospel of Mark* has been necessary, in order to evaluate its account of the Trial of Jesus. On investigation, this Gospel is found to be an account of Jesus, composed by a member of the Christian community in Rome to meet the needs of his fellow Christians, in danger and perplexity owing to the Jewish

---

[5] *Annales*, XV. 44; trans. J. Jackson, Loeb Classical Library, vol. IV (Heinemann, 1951), p. 283.
[6] The reasons are set out at length, with full documentation, in my book, *Jesus and the Zealots* (Manchester University Press, 1967). See also below pp. 275–7.

The Via Dolorosa, Jerusalem: the traditional way taken by Jesus to his crucifixion

War and the publicity given to it by the Flavian triumph in Rome. This apologetical purpose is evident in many ways other than that we have just noted. But the essential point of concern for the author was the Roman execution of Jesus. Even though he represented Jesus as loyal to Rome over the tribute question, there remained the undeniable fact that Pontius Pilate had crucified Jesus as a rebel. How was this awkward and disturbing fact to be explained?

The author of *Mark* endeavours to meet the difficulty by transferring the responsibility for the Crucifixion from the Roman governor to the Jewish leaders. He prepares for this by showing the Jewish leaders, variously described as "the scribes and Pharisees" and the "high priests", as planning to destroy Jesus from the very start of his ministry. Thus we are told that, after Jesus had healed a man with a withered hand on the sabbath, "The Pharisees went out, and immediately held counsel with the Herodians against him, how to destroy him" (iii. 6). This theme of the malicious intent of the Jewish authorities is gradually developed,

The "Dominus Flevit" church on the Mount of Olives, marking the traditional spot where Jesus wept over Jerusalem on his last visit to the city

as the narrative proceeds. How their intent would be implemented is foretold in detail in a prophecy assigned to Jesus himself: "Behold, we are going up to Jerusalem; and the Son of man will be delivered to the chief priests and the scribes, and they will condemn him to death, and deliver him to the Gentiles; and they will mock him, and spit upon him, and scourge him, and kill him; and after three days he will rise" (x. 33–34).

After describing further encounters with Jesus during the last days in Jerusalem, Mark relates how the Jewish leaders finally succeeded in arresting him, owing to the defection of one of his disciples. The fact is significant; for it indicates that Jesus was too strongly supported by the crowd for the Jewish authorities to arrest him publicly. Mark does not tell for what specific reason they then seized Jesus; we have only his earlier, general assertions that they had determined to destroy him from the beginning of his ministry.

Mark admits that the Jewish authorities sent a heavily armed band to arrest Jesus, and that there was some armed resistance to his arrest in Gethsemane. He minimises this resistance as "one of those who stood by drew his sword, and struck the slave of the high priest and cut off his ear" (xiv. 47). He does not disclose, as the later Evangelists do, that the disciples were armed and that it was one of them who struck the blow.

After his arrest, according to Mark, Jesus was taken, it still apparently being night, before the Sanhedrin, the highest Jewish tribunal. The trial that follows is described in a way that raises a whole host of problems, both with regard to procedure and to what really happened. Mark's opening statement reiterates his theme of the evil intent of the Jewish leaders: "Now the chief priests and the whole council sought testimony against Jesus to put him to death; but they found none. For many bore false witness against him, and their witness did not agree" (xiv. 55–6). The impression that Mark's statements are evidently meant to convey is that the Jewish authorities, determined on destroying Jesus, used the trial as a legal pretext for accomplishing their aim. What is said about the "false witnesses", however indicates a rather different situation. For, if they had suborned persons to give false evidence about Jesus, the Jewish leaders were strangely punctilious in rejecting that evidence when it was not mutually corroborated—surely they would have arranged things better, or have been less scrupulous about the rules of evidence, if they had "rigged" the trial.

But Mark was obviously more concerned to establish the responsibility of the Jewish leaders for the Crucifixion than to present a logically coherent narrative. This also seems to be the explanation of his next statement. According to him, the only specific charge made against Jesus was when "some stood up and bore false witness against him, saying, 'We heard him say, I will destroy this temple that is made with hands, and in three days I will build another, not made with hands.' Yet not even so did their testimony agree" (xiv. 57–9). Mark describes this charge as "false witness", thereby suggesting that it was not true; and this suggestion is confirmed by the statement that the evidence of these witnesses did not agree. However, as *John* ii. 19 and the *Acts of the Apostles* vi. 14 indicate, there seems to have been a tradition in the primitive Christian community in Judaea that Jesus had made some utterance against the Temple; and Mark himself seems to imply this in xiii. 1–2.

Certain suggestions can be offered to elucidate the problem here. In the first place, it is unlikely that Jesus had actually threatened that

THE TRIAL OF JESUS

he would destroy the Temple, for we know that his disciples continued to worship there and regarded it as the dwelling-place of God—this devotion would be hard to explain, if Jesus had so spoken against the Temple. Further, the accusation is rejected by Mark as false testimony. What seems the most probable solution is that the charge at the Sanhedrin trial arose out of the attack that Jesus had made a few days before on the Temple trading-system (xi 0 15–18). This system was necessary for the efficient running of the Temple *cultus*. Jews making the prescribed money offerings to the Temple had to change the Roman currency, which was offensive to the sacred Law, into a suitable Temple currency. Those who came to offer sacrifices needed to buy the sacrificial animals there. These facilities were licensed by the high priest. Such transactions, as well as the banking facilities offered by the Temple, provided a lucrative income to the sacerdotal aristocracy who managed the Temple. This sacerdotal aristocracy, moreover, controlled "native affairs", under the Romans: the high priest was appointed by the procurator. This pro-Roman aristocracy was naturally hated by patriotic Jews; and, in attacking their trading organization in the Temple, Jesus was in effect attacking their control over the people and religion of Israel.[7] There can be little doubt that Jesus' action in the Temple was a much more serious affair than it is represented to have been by Mark and the other Evangelists. And there is every reason to believe that it would have constituted one of the chief charges preferred against him. The Jewish authorities undoubtedly were concerned to discover what exactly was Jesus' intention in making this attack. Mark's curious reporting of the charge and of the conflict of evidence suggests that the Jewish authorities were unable to get a clear statement of what Jesus had said about his aims during his action in the Temple.

According to the Markan account of the Sanhedrin trial, after failing to get sufficient evidence about the Temple affair, the high priest then asked Jesus directly whether he claimed to be the Messiah of Israel: "Are you the Christ, (i.e. Messiah), the Son of the Blessed?" That he should have asked such a question, following on the Temple charge, clearly shows that the high priest connected revolutionary action with one who might claim to be the Messiah. In contemporary Jewish belief, the Messiah would bring the existing world-order to an end.

Mark reports Jesus as affirming that he was the Messiah in terms

[7] In A.D. 66 the Zealots seized the Temple and appointed a high priest by the ancient custom of drawing lots.

The Garden of Gethsemane, seen across the Kedron Valley. The traditional Garden lies to the left of the facade of the modern church

of current apocalyptic expectation: "I am; and you will see the Son of man sitting on the right hand of Power, and coming with the clouds of heaven" (xiv. 62). The high priest takes this answer as blasphemy, and, with the concurrence of the Sanhedrin, condemns Jesus to death.

Now we encounter one of the greatest problems of the Markan account. In the first place, although Josephus tells of many Messianic pretenders during the period A.D. 6–70, there is no record of any being condemned to death by the Sanhedrin for making such a claim. Secondly, according to Jewish Law, the penalty for blasphemy was death by stoning— the death of Stephen provides a contemporary instance of this (*Acts* vi. 12ff.). But the Sanhedrin does not proceed to arrange for the execution of this sentence in the case of Jesus. Instead, Mark goes on to relate, without a word of explanation, that, in the morning, the Jewish authorities handed Jesus over to Pontius Pilate. The charge preferred by them is not mentioned, but it was obviously a political one; for Pilate immediately asks Jesus, "Are you the King of the Jews?" (xv. 1–2).

This action of the Jewish leaders, and the alteration of the charge, have caused much debate among scholars. There seems to be evidence that at this time the Sanhedrin could condemn on a capital charge; but the sentence had to be confirmed by the Roman governor. Presumably, if the Sanhedrin had condemned Jesus to death for blasphemy, they would have applied to Pilate for confirmation. If this had been given, Jesus would have been executed by stoning. That this was not so, and that Jesus was delivered to Pilate charged with sedition, indicates that the Jewish authorities were concerned with the political, not the religious, significance of Jesus. This concern is intelligible. The high priest and the Sanhedrin were responsible to the Roman governor for Jewish affairs. Jesus' triumphal entry into Jerusalem and his action in the Temple had clearly disturbed the peace and good order of the Jewish state, besides challenging their own position. That the Romans would hold them responsible for the continuance of the menace that Jesus constituted is attested by *John* **xi. 48, where Caiaphas the high priest is reported as saying to the** Sanhedrin: "What are we to do? For this man performs many signs. If we let him go on thus, every one will believe in him, and the Romans will come and destroy both our holy place and our nation."

Consequently, the action taken by the Jewish leaders was in accordance with their responsibilities, and it anticipated Roman action. Having arrested Jesus, they examined him about his aims and supporters, preparatory to handing him over to Pilate. The charge was essentially a political one, although it must be remembered that politics and religion were inextricably bound up in Judaea at this time. *Luke* gives the most explicit account of the charges preferred against Jesus by the Jewish leaders: "We found this man perverting our nation and forbidding us to give tribute **to Caesar, and saying that he himself is Christ a king" (xxiii. 2).**

We must return to the Markan account, remembering that it is the earliest version. *Mark* represents Pilate as convinced of Jesus' innocence; "for he perceived that it was out of envy that the chief priests had delivered **him up" (xv. 10). Now, if this was indeed the opinion of Pilate, the** course open to him was obvious. He had the authority and power to dismiss the case. We know a great deal about the character of Pilate from Philo of Alexandria and Josephus. These Jewish writers agree in showing Pilate to have been a tough-minded man, ready to use force, and not one to be intimidated by the Jewish leaders and people.[8] Consequently, if he had been convinced that Jesus was innocent, he was unlikely to have hesitated about thwarting the intention of the Jewish leaders. What

[8] See Chapter 17.

Tombs of the Hellenistic period in the Kedron Valley, which Jesus must have seen

Mark tells of his subsequent conduct at the Trial, is, therefore, difficult
to reconcile with his character, as well as with logic, as we shall see.

Instead of dismissing the case, Pilate is depicted as trying to save
Jesus by availing himself of an otherwise unknown custom. According
to *Mark*, it was the custom at the Passover for the Roman governor to
release a prisoner chosen by the crowd. There is no other evidence for
such a custom. This negative witness is important, because Josephus is
careful to record all the privileges granted to the Jews by the Romans.
But that is not all. Such a custom is inherently impossible. Judaea was
seething with revolt; its government would have been annually frustrated
by having to release a notable prisoner—according to *Mark*, on this
occasion a dangerous rebel, probably a Zealot, was freed.

But, even if we pass over the improbability that such a custom
existed, what *Mark* tells of Pilate's use of it passes beyond belief. He
depicts this tough Roman procurator, who was backed by a strong military
force, as resorting to this custom to save a man he adjudged innocent.
In so doing, he invites the Jerusalem mob to choose between Jesus and
a rebel leader, Barabbas, who had killed Romans in a recent insurrection.
To have given the crowd such a choice would have been the height of
folly, if Pilate had sought thus to save Jesus. The mob's decision was
a foregone conclusion. Led by the chief priests, they naturally chose
Barabbas, to them a patriotic hero. Frustrated, Pilate is represented as

weakly asking the mob: "what shall I do with the man whom you call the King of the Jews?" (xv. 12).

The picture of a Roman governor consulting a Jewish mob about what he should do with an innocent man is ludicrous to the extreme. But to this extreme the author of the Markan Gospel was evidently prepared to go, to explain away the problem of the Roman execution of Jesus. Thus he completes his picture of Jewish responsibility for the Crucifixion. The Jewish leaders, who were determined on destroying Jesus from the very beginning of his ministry, finally succeed in their fell design by forcing the reluctant Pilate to do their will. To round off this presentation of Jewish guilt, *Mark* describes the Jewish leaders, on Golgotha, as mocking the dying Jesus, while the Roman centurion recognizes his divinity as he dies: "Truly this man was the Son of God!" The death of Jesus is marked by the rending of the Temple Veil, thus symbolizing the obsolescence of Jewish religion (xv. 37–9).[9]

Mark's account of the career of Jesus and the circumstances of his crucifixion would have been welcomed by the Christians of Rome. The embarrassment of Jesus' execution for sedition against Rome was alleviated by the explanation of Jewish responsibility. Far from condemning Jesus to death, the Roman Christians now knew that Pilate actually recognized his innocence and tried to save him. Jesus had, moreover, given proof of his loyalty to Rome in the matter of the tribute, and the Roman centurion had been the first to perceive his divinity. The Jewish leaders who had plotted his death, and the Jewish people that had demanded it, had brought upon their nation the terrible catastrophe of A.D. 70, which had been so graphically commemorated in the streets of Rome in A.D. 71.

III

Mark's explanation of the Roman execution of Jesus, motivated as it had been by the needs of the Christian community in Rome in A.D. 71, exercised a formative influence on subsequent Christian tradition. The writers of the Matthaean and Lukan Gospels accepted it, elaborating upon it according to the particular requirements of the communities for which they wrote. Their additions were inspired by the need to allay a widespread belief in the Roman Empire that Christianity was in origin and

[9] The Roman Christians would have been familiar with the Temple curtains, for they had been displayed in the triumph in A.D. 71.

nature a revolutionary movement. Thus the *Gospel of Matthew* expands *Mark's* brief and reticent mention of the armed resistance in Gethsemane by representing Jesus as rebuking the disciple who drew the sword: "Put your sword back into its place; for all who take the sword will perish by the sword" (xxvi. 52). The author of this Gospel was writing for a Jewish Christian community, probably in Alexandria, where there was a great need to damp down revolutionary feeling after the fall of Jerusalem in A.D. 70. The words, attributed to Jesus here, had a poignant significance in the light of the disaster that had befallen the Judaean Jews in consequence of their resort to war.

An addition that Matthew also makes to the Markan account of the trial of Jesus was destined to have tragic consequences for the Jewish people. To emphasize the innocence of Jesus, Pilate is represented as publicly repudiating responsibility for the condemnation of Jesus. He washes his hands symbolically before the people, declaring, "I am innocent of this man's blood." The Jewish people are made to answer: "His blood be on us and on our children!" (xxvii. 24–6). The legacy of these words has been terrible; they have been cited to justify centuries of Christian persecution of the Jews. It is significant that only at the recent Vatican Council has a formal declaration been made, exonerating subsequent generations of Jews from responsibility for the murder of Christ.

IV

The historian, who seeks to understand why the Romans executed Jesus for sedition, has first to investigate the *Gospel of Mark,* as we have endeavoured to do here. He has to penetrate behind Mark's apologetical presentation, to discern what really happened on that first Good Friday. So far as a reasonable assessment can be made, it would seem that the Jewish authorities arrested Jesus because they regarded him as a menace to the peace and well-being of the Jewish state, for which they were responsible to the Romans. After interrogating Jesus, they handed him over to Pontius Pilate, accusing him of seditious teaching and action. Pilate, who probably knew something of Jesus' activities, accepted the charge and ordered his crucifixion. He gave orders that the *titulus,* stating the cause of his condemnation, should be placed at the head of the cross: it read: "This is Jesus, the King of the Jews." Pilate also ordered that two *lēstai* should be crucified with Jesus. The fact is significant; for we know that the Romans called the Zealots, the Jewish resistance-fighters,

"The Crucifixion", by Andrea Mantegna (1431–1506), now in the Louvre, Paris

lēstai, i.e. brigands. These men had doubtless taken part in the recent insurrection in Jerusalem (*Mk.* xv. 7). That Jesus was crucified between two rebels surely indicates that Pilate regarded him as such.

Thus, so far as the historian can today evaluate the evidence concerning the Roman execution of Jesus, it would seem that Pontius Pilate regarded Jesus as guilty of sedition. Whether he was right in his assessment is another matter.

Pontius Pilate in History and Legend

About 1938 years ago, a Roman Governor of Judaea
made a decision that has lent his name to posterity.

I

The "irony of fate" is a much-used, and frequently abused, expression for the unpredictable outcome of human action taken with quite different intent. The expression has never been more justified than by the consequences of an order given by the Roman Governor of Judaea at the Passover of the year A.D. 30.[1] By sentencing to death a Galilean Jew accused of sedition, this Governor, Pontius Pilate, unwittingly ensured that his own name should be remembered daily through nineteen subsequent centuries in all parts of the world. For the Jew, whose crucifixion he ordered, became the Saviour God of a new world religion. Each day, at innumerable altars, that crucifixion and he who ordered it are remembered in the words of the Christian creed: "Suffered under Pontius Pilate, was crucified, dead and buried."

What is known of this Roman, whose official act so long ago has so strangely earned him such undying infamy? On one count comparatively little; on another, much that is significantly and intensely interesting. The evidence will be best described in its chronological sequence.

First, there is a partially obliterated Latin inscription on a stone slab, found recently (1961) during excavation of the Roman theatre at

---

[1] The date of the Crucifixion is not known. A.D. 30 is the most probable estimate; but a good case can also be made for A.D. 33.

An inscription of Pontius Pilate, recently found at Caesarea; it proves that his official title was *Praefectus*, not *Procurator*

Caesarea, which was the headquarters of the Roman government of Judaea. This is the only contemporary epigraphic evidence so far known of the existence of Pontius Pilate in Judaea during the reign of the Emperor Tiberius. It corrects a long-standing error by designating Pilate as *Praefectus Iudae*, instead of Procurator, which had hitherto been the title accorded him, probably owing to a reference of Tacitus, which we shall presently note. The difference of title implies no significant difference of status. The Roman governor of Judaea, whether designated "praefectus" or "procurator", was responsible for the peace and good order of the country. He had a military force, normally adequate for this purpose, at his disposal; he also had what is known as the *ius gladii*, that is, authority to inflict the death sentence. His immediate superior was the legate of the province of Syria, who commanded a legionary army and would intervene in Judaea in a situation beyond the procurator's control. The inscription found at Caesarea, besides attesting to Pilate's existence and title, also suggests that he had carried out some building operation at Caesarea, doubtless connected with the theatre there.

The next information, in date, about Pilate is provided by Philo, the Jewish philosopher of Alexandria, who was a contemporary. It is given, incidentally, in the form of a letter, allegedly written by the Jewish prince Agrippa to the Emperor Gaius, known popularly as Caligula. Philo quotes the letter in a work entitled *Legatio ad Gaium,* which records Caligula's project (A.D. 39–40) to erect a colossal image of himself in the Temple at Jerusalem and of Jewish attempts to dissuade him from so outrageous an act of sacrilege. Philo's tractate is essentially a polemical work, designed to demonstrate Jewish piety and peaceable disposition against Roman malignity. How far the document, which Philo purports to quote, is an authentic letter addressed by Agrippa to Gaius is unknown; it is unfortunate also that no indication is given of the date of the affair concerning Pilate, to which it refers.

Agrippa's, or Philo's, account of Pilate's character must first be noted. He is described as "naturally inflexible and stubbornly relentless", and he is accused of "acts of corruption, insults, rapine, outrages on the people, arrogance, repeated murders of innocent victims, and constant and most galling savagery". This portrait of Pilate was apparently intended by Agrippa to explain the affair which he is relating. His purpose in his lengthy account of it was to show Caligula how Tiberius, his imperial predecessor, had respected Jewish religion and rebuked a Roman official who sought to insult it—he presumably hoped that the lesson would persuade Caligula to desist from his own intended violation of the Temple.

Pilate, according to Agrippa, had maliciously planned to offend the Jews on the pretext of honouring Tiberius. To this end, he had set up on the former palace of Herod, now the Roman headquarters, in Jerusalem certain gilded shields. They bore no image or emblem offensive to Jewish religious sensibility; a brief inscription only recorded the Emperor's name and that of the person who dedicated the shields to him—this was doubtless Pilate, but Agrippa evidently preferred not to mention this significant fact. That such a seemingly innocuous form of honouring the Emperor should have upset the Jews, as it did, is amazing. No explanation is given of the nature of the offence. The most likely cause would seem to be that the dedicatory inscription contained some reference to the Emperor's divinity, which the Jews interpreted as an insult to Yahweh, the god of Israel. The implied proclamation of an alien divinity in the holy city of Jerusalem was probably the essence of the offence.

The ruins of the temple of Augustus at Caesarea, to which Tiberius ordered the gilded shields to be transferred

A Jewish delegation, headed by four Herodian princes, petitioned Pilate to remove the shields, which, so they claimed, violated their native customs. On Pilate's harsh refusal, the Jews are represented in Agrippa's letter as being torn between their loyalty to the Roman Emperor and obedience to their religion. They implored Pilate not to provoke them to revolt; they called on him to produce the authority for his action and threatened to appeal to Tiberius. According to Agrippa (or Philo), this threat profoundly disturbed Pilate, who feared that his maladministration would thus become known to his imperial master. That this fear, and not that he had exceeded his authority in the matter of the shields, is represented as causing Pilate such concern excites suspicion, as does also the sequel, as to the real situation. On Pilate's continual refusal to remove the shields, the Jews complained to the Emperor. Tiberius' anger towards Pilate, on hearing the petition, is described in the most extravagant language. Nothing short of the immediate dismissal of the offending Governor from his office and summoning to Rome for exemplary punishment could be expected from such an outburst as the letter describes. Yet the actual outcome is strangely quiet and undramatic. Tiberius merely ordered Pilate to transfer the shields from Jerusalem to the temple of Augustus at Caesarea.

Taking Philo's account as it stands, it looks very much as if it is

an attempt to denigrate Pilate in the interests of Jewish apologetic. The
fact that Pilate continued in office, despite the case that Philo builds
against him, proves that Tiberius regarded him as an efficient governor.
The Emperor's decision about the transference of the offending shields
was doubtless a wise move when faced with Jewish intransigence over
such a minor issue. And his arranging to have them placed in the temple
of his deified predecessor, Augustus, at Caesarea was surely a compliment
to his officer, whose attempt to honour him had met such a bigoted
affront.

The incident, as related to Philo, is difficult to reconcile with what
Josephus records of Pilate's term of office. Josephus, himself a Palestinian
Jew, and a younger contemporary of Philo, was equally well placed to
have learned what had happened in Judaea about ten years before he
was born. Moreover, he professed to be a historian, and what he tells
of Pilate purports to be history, not apologetic, although that factor was
not absent as we shall see.[2]

From the record of Josephus, we can deduce that Pilate held office
in Judaea from A.D. 26–36. Such a considerable term is significant. To
have maintained Roman rule over so difficult a people as the Jews for
ten years, and in the service of a hard and suspicious master such as
Tiberius was, attests the ability and good sense of Pilate, and implies
that he must have become very experienced in Jewish affairs. Another
interesting fact that may be inferred from Josephus is that Pilate must
have worked well with Caiaphas, whom he found as high priest at the
beginning of his governorship, for he retained him in this office until
his own departure from Judaea in 36. The high priest was the recognized
head of the Jewish people, and was appointed by the Roman governor.

Josephus' account of Jewish affairs during Pilate's tenure of office
has curious proportions. For, despite the fact that it covered ten years,
he records only three events which are unrelated to each other. His
selection of these events, and his silence about others, as we shall see,
constitute a problem; its answer is probably to be found in the complex
apologetical motives that underlie his writings.

The first action of Pilate, recorded by Josephus, curiously parallels
Philo's affair of the inscribed shields, which he does not mention. It seems
to have occurred at the beginning of Pilate's governorship: the two

[2] See Chapter 20.

accounts that Josephus gives, in *The Jewish War*, and his *Jewish Antiquities*, are not entirely consistent. He introduces his account in the latter work with the statement that Pilate "led his army from Caesarea and established it for winter-quarters in Jerusalem, for the purpose of destroying the laws of the Jews". From this surprising statement it is not clear whether Pilate was acting on superior orders or his own initiative. The motive ascribed to Pilate is extraordinary, and it calls for explanation which Josephus does not give. It has been suggested that Pilate was acting on instructions from Sejanus, the powerful favourite of Tiberius, who was distinctly anti-Jewish. There is no evidence either way; but, as the following action indicates, Pilate was surely not taking his own line.

Since the troubles that marked the incorporation of Judaea into the Roman Empire in A.D. 6, it had apparently been the custom of the Roman governors to send their troops for garrison duty in Jerusalem without the usual emblems on their standards. This was a concession to Jewish religious scruples. Roman military standards were adorned with images of the Emperor and other symbols, which made them cult-objects and they were venerated as such. The concession was a considerable one, because Roman troops were proud of their standards; but it was probably intended to be only a temporary measure until the Jews grew accustomed to their subject state and understood Roman practice. According to Josephus, Pilate ended the concession. He acted with discretion, carefully calculated. The troops were ordered to bring their standards into the city by night, with the images covered; the intention doubtless being to establish something of a *fait accompli* when they were displayed next day. But, whatever his motive, when the Jews saw the standards with their images, they were outraged. Pilate had apparently returned to Caesarea, and there, according to Josephus, a great multitude of Jews sought him out and demanded the withdrawal of the standards. Seeing that Caesarea is some sixty miles from Jerusalem, we may well wonder how such a mass demonstration was so efficiently organized and well behaved, as Josephus relates. Pilate refused the petition: the reason he gave is significant—to remove the standards would be to insult the Emperor. But the Jews were not to be put off; they continued for six days to demand that the sanctity of their holy city should not be thus violated. On the sixth day Pilate planned an act of intimidation. He arranged to hear the Jewish petition again in the stadium, which he surrounded with soldiers. When threatened with death by these, the Jews remained firm and ready to die for their sacred law. Duly impressed by their resolution, Pilate ordered the offending standards to be removed.

With this edifying conclusion, Josephus ends his account of the episode. But the historian is left asking many questions which that account raises but does not answer. Josephus represents the affair as due to Pilate's malicious intent towards the Jews. But it is more likely that the Prefect was acting under orders from Rome. If the incident took place at the beginning of Pilate's term of office, as Josephus seems to indicate, a change in imperial policy then is intelligible. The appointment of a new governor was deemed a suitable occasion to withdraw what was regarded as a temporary concession. Pilate was probably advised to act with discretion, and not risk a revolt if the Jews proved too intransigent. How the incident is to be related to that described by Philo, and why Josephus makes no reference to that, are topics for debate and speculation.

Equally puzzling is the next episode of Pilate's involvement with the Jews that Josephus records. This second clash arose out of Pilate's decision to improve the water-supply to Jerusalem by building an aqueduct. Josephus unfortunately gives no information about the antecedents of the affair. The project would seem to have been commendable, and the real ground for the ensuing Jewish objection is uncertain. In the

The site of the stadium at Caesarea; this was probably the place where Pilate threatened the Jews who protested about the standards

The Roman theatre at Caesarea, the administrative headquarters of Pontius Pilate

Antiquities, Josephus seems to suggest that the Jews opposed the under-taking because it meant Pilate's interference with the internal affairs of Jerusalem. In the *Jewish War* he appears to connect the resulting disturb-ance with Pilate's use of "the sacred treasure known as *Korbōnas*". This was money of a sacrosanct nature deposited in the Temple, which could not be used for secular purposes, no matter how necessary. In taking it to defray the cost of the aqueduct, Pilate would have committed sacrilege. Doubtless there was an involved background to the whole affair which Josephus did not choose to reveal.

Whatever that background was, Jewish reaction was violent, and extended to personal abuse of the Prefect. Pilate's counter-measures, if Josephus is to be believed, were most odd. Instead of deploying his troops to quell further disturbance or interference with the work, he arranged for them to mingle, disguised and with concealed clubs, among the protesting Jews. At a preconcerted signal, they were ordered to attack. The plan was successful. The Jews suffered heavy casualties, and the unrest ceased.

As historical records these accounts are very unsatisfactory. There is no reason to doubt that they do describe real encounters between Pilate and the Jews. But they are clearly tendentious. Josephus was more

A silver denarius of the
Emperor Tiberius

concerned, in the interests of his apologetic, to denigrate Pilate than to
explain the relevant facts of each occasion. A similar obscurity invests
what he tells of the situation that ended Pilate's career as Prefect of Judaea
in A.D. 36.

The trouble on this occasion was with the Samaritans, not the Jews.
The Samaritans were a people who claimed to be descendants of the
original Israelites. They maintained that their temple on Mount Gerizim,
and not the Temple at Jerusalem, was the covenanted sanctuary of the
God of Israel. There was a deep-rooted hostility between the Jews and
the Samaritans, whose territory lay between Judaea and Galilee. Like the
Jews, the Samaritans also looked for the coming of the Messiah. About
the beginning of the year 36, they were caught up in a Messianic movement. Led by a prophet who promised to reveal sacred vessels hidden
by Moses, they assembled in arms at Mount Gerizim. Pilate acted swiftly
by sending troops to deal with the situation. In the ensuing engagement,
many Samaritans were killed, and those taken prisoner were executed.
The affair, as described by Josephus up to this point, is intelligible; but
not the sequel. According to his account in the *Antiquities* (there is no
mention of it in the *Jewish War*), the Samaritan leaders complained to
Vitellius, legate of Syria, about Pilate's action, maintaining that they had
had no intention to revolt. Vitellius ordered Pilate to Rome, to explain
to the Emperor, not his conduct in the Samaritan affair, but "the accusations of the Jews".[3] In the absence of other information, we are left in
ignorance of the real cause of the termination of Pilate's long tenure of

---

[3] This seems to have been the earliest reading: some MSS. give "Samaritans" instead
of "Jews," which looks like an emendation.

office. Josephus supplies just one further detail: Tiberius had died before Pilate reached Rome. At that point Pilate passes out of history into legend.

II

Our next source of information about Pilate is equally problematical; but the difficulties are of a different order. It is the Christian Gospels that provide the most widely-held impression of this Roman official, because of his involvement with Jesus. But before considering their presentation and its problems, we must notice the significance of an isolated reference to Pilate in Luke's Gospel. Jesus, on a certain occasion, was told of "Galilaeans whose blood Pilate had mingled with their sacrifices" (xiii:1). Its incidental nature stamps this reference as authentic; but to what does it refer? It suggests some serious incident in the Temple at Jerusalem. Josephus does not record it; but neither does he the incident of the gilded shields described by Philo. And who were these Galileans? It could be that they were Zealots, members of the Jewish "resistance" against Rome, who were sometimes called "Galileans", probably after their founder Judas of Galilee.

It is, however, the Gospel presentation of Pilate's dealings with Jesus of Nazareth that commands attention. In the four narratives concerned, that is, the Gospels of Mark, Matthew, Luke and John, it is this Roman governor who was ultimately responsible for sentencing Jesus to death for sedition, and it was his troops who carried out the execution. Yet, all four Gospels, in slightly varying ways, endeavour to show that Pilate was not really responsible for the crucifixion of Jesus, but that he was forced to order it by the Jews. Indeed, on analysis the intention is evident, in each account, to present Pilate as actually a witness to the innocence of Jesus, and the Jews—or their leaders—as determined to destroy him. It could be argued, of course, that this is what really did happen; for the dramatic Gospel narratives of the trial and crucifixion of Jesus present a convincing case on a cursory reading. But, as was shown in the previous chapter, "The Trial of Jesus", this presentation originates from the *Gospel of Mark*. The author of this Gospel, writing in Rome shortly after the suppression of the Jewish revolt in A.D. 70, and faced with the danger of the Roman authorities regarding Christians as "fellow-travellers" with Jewish nationalism, was concerned especially with the embarrassing fact of Jesus' execution by Pilate for sedition. Since the fact could not be

"Ecce Homo" by Titian (1543), in the Kunsthistorisches Museum, Vienna

denied, it had to be explained away. This he did by representing the
Jewish leaders as bent on the destruction of Jesus, and forcing a reluctant
Pilate to do their will. But a critical examination of the Markan account
quickly reveals the impossibilities and absurdities of this interpretation.
Yet it was effective in its time; and it was followed by the other Gospels,
which elaborated its thesis in various ways.

These records of the trial of Jesus, when looked at objectively, have
a distinctly anti-Jewish pattern. They present what is essentially a contest
between the Roman magistrate, who recognizes the innocence of Jesus
and seeks to save him; and the malevolent Jews intent on murdering their
victim. In the *Gospel of John* this contrast assumes the form of a cosmic
dualism. Pilate endeavours to protect the Son of God from the children
of the Devil, for so are the Jews designated (John vii. 44). In the
Matthaean Gospel the contrast was destined to have the most terrible
consequences. The author of this Gospel adds to Mark's account the
episode concerning Pilate's wife and Pilate's public repudiation of responsibility (xxvii. 24–5). The lady's dream attests to the righteousness

of Jesus, and Pilate's act of ablution confirms his pronouncement: "I am innocent of the blood of this just person: see ye to it." The Jews are represented as eagerly accepting responsibility: "His blood be on us, and on our children."

This symbolic attempt to repudiate his responsibility has been taken to characterize Pilate, to his detriment. He has, accordingly, been seen as a man abjectly lacking the courage of his own convictions; who, to avoid a riot or the Jewish innuendo about his loyalty to the Emperor, sent an innocent man to his death and then pretended to dissociate himself from the crime. But the reality was clearly very different. The evidence, on analysis, points to a more credible situation. Pilate ordered the crucifixion of Jesus, because he believed him to be guilty of sedition. Jesus had organized a Messianic entrance into Jerusalem, and had attacked the Sadducean establishment of the Temple, which was pro-Roman. His activity had coincided with what seems to have been a Zealot-led insurrection against the Romans, probably under Barabbas. Owing to the defection of Judas Iscariot, the Jewish leaders succeeded in arresting Jesus. After examining him about his claims and his supporters they handed him over to Pilate as a rebel. Pilate accepted the charge, probably regarding Jesus as the ring-leader of the recent insurrection; for he ordered him to be crucified between two *lēstai* ("brigands"), which was the official designation for Zealots.

The fact that Pilate ordered the crucifixion of Jesus as the rebel, who claimed Messianic kingship, is clearly admitted in the Gospels, even though it is explained away. The fact is also confirmed by the laconic statement of the Roman historian Tacitus, writing early in the second century. Introducing his account of the persecution of the Christians by Nero, he explains: "Christus, the founder of the name, had undergone the death penalty in the reign of Tiberius, by sentence of the procurator Pontius Pilate, and the pernicious superstition was checked for a moment, . . ."[4] In other words, the fact of Pilate's sentence is basic and intelligible as the act of a Roman governor responsible for the maintenance of Roman rule in his province. The Gospel attempt to make Pilate into a witness to Jesus' innocence is the earliest essay in Christian apologetic: its fundamental improbability is matched by its internal contradictions.

---

[4] *Annales* XLIV, trans. J. Jackson (Loeb Classical Library).

The "Tower of David", the lower portions of which belonged to Herod's palace, used by Pilate as his Jerusalem headquarters

III

Pilate's career in legend is almost as interesting as it is in history. The urge to make him a witness to Christian truth steadily grew during the first three centuries of the Church's life. It produced some incredible claims. The apologist Tertullian (c. 160–220), for example, actually asserted that Pilate, "in his secret heart already a Christian", sent such a report to Tiberius as to convince the Emperor that Jesus was divine. Pilate's wife, given the name of Procla, was canonized as a saint in the Eastern Church, and Pilate achieved this distinction himself among the Ethiopian Christians. But Pilate's memory could also be invoked by the pagan opposition. In 311 the Emperor Maximin, as part of his policy against the Church, published "Memoirs of Pilate", and even made them compulsory study for school children. Unfortunately, no specimen has survived, to show whether they were based on official sources. When

Maximin was overthrown by Constantine, the first Christian Emperor, all copies were evidently sought out and destroyed. These anti-Christian "Memoirs" prompted the production of *Acts of Pilate* by Christians, designed to heighten Pilate's testimony, and eventually to present him as dying a martyr for Christ.

But with the Church's triumph over paganism in the fourth century, Pilate's reputation suffered a change. Doubtless because he was no longer useful as an official Roman witness to the innocence, and even to the divinity of Jesus, Christians began to look more critically at him. The Church historian Eusebius (c. 260–340) marks the change, by relating that Pilate committed suicide, "for the penalty of God, as it seems, followed hard after him". More elaborate forms of this legend were soon current, which told of the crowds of demons that beset his corpse. Mount Pilatus in Switzerland still commemorates the Procurator's supposed burial place, in an area replete with legends of diabolical activity.

In the absence of knowledge, speculation has been natural about the fate of the man who sentenced to death one believed by millions to be the incarnate Son of God. But the cynicism of Anatole France warns us of what might have been the prosaic reality. He depicts the aged Pilate in retirement at Baiae, replying to a question about Jesus: "Jesus of Nazareth? I don't remember him."

CHAPTER 18

The Fall of Jerusalem, A.D. 70

*The Roman destruction of the Jewish national state
that year had profound consequences both for the
Jewish people and Christianity.*

I

During the excavations at Khirbet Qumrân, on the site of the
settlement of the Jewish community whose library is now known as the
Dead Sea Scrolls, tragic evidence was found of its disastrous end. Broken
walls, arrow-heads and signs of burning witnessed to the victorious assault
of the troops of the Xth legion, who in June, A.D. 68, under their general
Vespasian, wiped out Jewish rebel resistance in the area east of Jerusalem.
Two years later, on August 10th, the Roman legionaries, under
Vespasian's son Titus, stormed the last defences of the great Temple at
Jerusalem. This action marked the virtual end of the Jewish revolt against
Rome, which began in A.D. 66. For four years the small Jewish nation
had offered a heroic, though fanatical, resistance to the might of Imperial
Rome. They were inspired by their belief that they should serve no other
lord than Yahweh, their god, who had chosen them as his Elect People
and given them the possession of Canaan as their holy land. In terms
of military resources, their bid for national independence was doomed
to failure; but they trusted to Yahweh to save them as he had delivered
their forefathers from the bondage of Egypt, and blessed with success
the struggle of their people, under Maccabaean leadership, against the
domination of the Seleucid rulers in the second century B.C.

From the time of their discovery, the Dead Sea Scrolls have served
to draw popular attention to the stirring events of Jewish history in

Jerusalem, from the Mount of Olives. The Temple area is clearly visible, with the Dome of the Rock marking the site of the great altar of the Temple

Palestine during the first century of our era. And this interest has been greatly increased by the subsequent excavation of the great fortress of Masada, by the Dead Sea, where the last defenders of Israel's freedom preferred death to surrender to the Romans. But it may not be fully appreciated how crucial in human affairs has been the Jewish War of A.D. 66 to 70, which ended with the catastrophic destruction of Jerusalem.[1]

For the Jewish people the catastrophe that then befell their nation was destined to have age-long repercussions. The defeat of their attempt to shake off the suzerainty of Rome meant that they ceased to exist as a nation occupying their own homeland and in possession of their own metropolis. Down the centuries from that time the Jews were fated to be an exiled people, scattered throughout the world and often terribly persecuted, yet making great contributions to the culture, science and commerce of the nations among whom they dwelt. Thus they continued until 1948, when miraculously recovering from the Nazi holocaust designed to exterminate their race, the Jewish immigrants to Palestine succeeded in re-establishing the state of Israel there, to be followed in 1967 by the re-possession of Jerusalem, their holy city which had been lost to them since the year 70. This amazing restoration of Israel in the

[1] See Chapter 19, where an account of the war of A.D. 66–70 and the siege of Jerusalem is given.

land of Yahweh's ancient promise, and the unhappy disturbance of the
Middle East that has resulted from it, thus have both their origin in
that far-off revolt of the Jews against Roman domination and its disastrous
ending. And the long-drawn-out drama has clearly not finished yet; for
the new state of Israel must inevitably effect most profoundly both the
future of the Jewish people as a whole and those Arab nations among
which it has been established.

II

But if the destruction of Jerusalem in A.D. 70 had such profound
consequences for the Jewish people, and in recent years for their Middle
Eastern neighbours, it has effected no less profoundly that religion which
stemmed from first-century Judaea, namely, Christianity. The extent of
that effect is only now being properly appreciated, as new information
about Jewish life in the first century and new evaluation of ancient sources
have gradually necessitated a re-assessment of the traditional view of
Christian Origins.

The traditional view was based mainly upon the evidence of the
New Testament and the writings of two fourth-century bishops, Eusebius
and Epiphanius. According to the New Testament writings, particularly
the *Gospels* and *Acts of the Apostles,* Jesus of Nazareth was the Son of
God, incarnated to be the Messiah of Israel and the Saviour of mankind.
But the Jews rejected him as their Messiah and caused him to be crucified
by the Romans. God, however, raised him from the dead, so that he
was able to revive the faith of his disciples and give them a world-wide
commission to preach his gospel, before ascending to heaven. How the
disciples fulfilled their commission is duly described in the *Acts of the
Apostles,* which purports to show how the infant Church, founded in
Jerusalem, quickly spread throughout Syria, Asia Minor and Greece until
it was established at Rome, the metropolis of the then known world.

In this narration, although Judaea appears as the homeland of the
new faith and the Mother Church is located at Jerusalem, scarcely any
reference is made to contemporary Jewish history. Consequently the
impression is given that Christianity was completely insulated from the
political affairs of the Jewish nation. This impression is further strengthened by the complete absence of any reference in the New Testament
to the Jewish revolt in A.D. 66, to the four years of bitter warfare, or
to the disastrous siege and destruction of Jerusalem in 70, as contem-

porary events. Reference to Jerusalem's ruin only appears as a prophecy made by Jesus some forty years before its event.[2]

This apparent unconcern of Christians with the fatal revolt of the Jews against Rome seemed, in turn, to be adequately explained by what Eusebius and Epiphanius had to tell about the Christians resident at Jerusalem before its destruction in A.D. 70. According to Eusebius, the earlier of these two writers: "when the people of the Church in Jerusalem, having been commanded by an oracle, given by revelation to men approved before the war, to depart from the city and to dwell in a certain city of Peraea, namely, Pella, (and) when those who believed on Christ had migrated thither from Jerusalem, so that the royal city of the Jews, and the whole of the land of Judaea, had been utterly forsaken by holy men, the judgment of God finally overtook those who had abused Christ and his apostles and completely wiped out that generation from among men."[3]

The motif of divine vengeance taken on the Jews for the Crucifixion of Christ is obvious in this passage, and it forms part of Eusebius' interpretation of the overthrow of the Jewish nation. Elsewhere (*op. cit.*, III, vii. 8–9) he explains that because God is patient he did not immediately punish the Jews, but waited forty years until the Apostles ceased to reside in Jerusalem. Epiphanius' account, which is similar, is

[2] E.g. *Lk.* xix. 41–44; xxi. 20–24.
[3] *Ecclesiastical History*, III. v. 3.

Coins of the Jewish insurgents (i) Silver shekel, inscribed "Shekel of Israel" and dated "Year 3" (i.e. A.D. 68–9); (ii) Reverse of shekel, inscribed "Jerusalem the Holy"

briefer and more vague, and it is given in connection with his explanation
of the origins of a later Jewish Christian sect called the Nazoraeans. The
present writer has submitted each of these accounts to a detailed analysis,
and he is convinced thereby of their unhistorical character.[4] They appear,
on examination, to derive from the legendary claims made by certain
Christians from Pella who settled in the Roman city of Aelia Capitolina,
which the Emperor Hadrian built in 130 on the ruined site of Jerusalem.
These Pella Christians pretended that they were the descendants of the
original Christians of Jerusalem. But their claims were not treated seriously
by other Christians at the time; and the later Church of Jerusalem was
never accorded that respect and authority to which it was entitled, if
it had indeed been recognized as descended from the Mother Church
of Christianity.

But though the Pella legend was not treated seriously in the Early
Church, it was accepted until recently by modern scholars as explaining
why the New Testament writings ignore the destruction of Jerusalem,
except in terms of its being foretold by Jesus. Thus they concluded from
this apparent insulation of the original Jewish Christians from the political
life of their nation that the convulsion of Jewish national life in the years
66 to 70 had had no significant effect upon the Church. The original
Christian community of Jerusalem had withdrawn in time from the
doomed city, so that the agony of the Jews could be watched from afar,
with a kind of academic detachment, as the merited punishment of a
people that had rejected their Messiah.

That this conclusion was accepted for so long without critical
interrogation was the result of two factors. First, it was consistent with
the traditional view that Jesus was pacifist in teaching and action, and
that being of divine nature and concerned with the spiritual salvation
of mankind, he would not have involved himself in contemporary Jewish-
Roman politics. The other cause was that the view of the Jewish historian
Josephus was accepted—that the disaster that overwhelmed the Jews in
A.D. 70 was due to a fanatical party of brigands, called Zealots, who
goaded a peaceable people into fatal revolt against their Roman over-
lords.[5] But influential though these causes were, it seems surprising in
retrospect that there was no curiosity about the fact that if the original
Christian community had escaped intact from Jerusalem to Pella, it did

[4] Cf. *Jesus and the Zealots* (New York, 1968), pp. 208-217.
[5] See Chapter 19.

not continue to play in Pella the leading rôle in the new religion that it had hitherto had at Jerusalem. For the evidence both of St. Paul's Epistles and the *Acts of the Apostles* shows that the Mother Church of Jerusalem was the accepted source of faith and authority, to which even an apostle of the standing of Paul had to report. If that Church had indeed migrated to Pella, it would surely have continued to direct and control the Christian movement and the fact would be clearly evident in Christian writings. But the strange truth is that, after A.D. 70, the Mother Church of Jerusalem disappears completely and without trace. The strangeness of that fact should certainly have been seen as an indication that the real situation was not so simple and assured as the traditional view held it to be.

III

Since the Second World War a number of factors have conspired to set the beginnings of Christianity in a new and more intelligible light. The discovery of the Dead Sea Scrolls and the investigations carried out at Qumrân have revealed an aspect of Jewish religious life at the time of Jesus hitherto unknown, and one which has afforded some suggestive parallels to primitive Jewish Christianity. Then there has come a new evaluation of the Zealots. Two factors operated to bring this about. The "resistance" groups that combated the Nazi occupation forces of various European lands stirred a sympathetic interest in nationalist forces that wage guerrilla warfare, and conduct subversive activities, against a powerful foe that has robbed them of their national freedom. This new appreciation of "resistance" action disposed scholars to look more sympathetically at the Zealots, the ancient Jewish "resistance" against the Roman government of Judaea. This disposition was, in turn, powerfully reinforced by the establishment of the new state of Israel in 1948, and by the subsequent excavation of Masada as a national gesture of recognition to the ancient patriots who died there. As the next chapter will show, these excavations have revealed the fundamental religious inspiration of Zealotism. And this new evidence has coincided with a critical assessment of Josephus' presentation of the Zealots in his writings, which has hitherto been so influential. In consequence, it is now realized that Josephus for personal reasons consistently denigrated the Zealots, attributing the character of bandits and imputing to them the blackest of crimes. However, a careful analysis of his reports shows that Josephus unwittingly

The Jewish Wailing Wall (1968). The lower part of the Wall formed the western wall of the Temple

testifies to two of the fundamental principles of Zealotism, namely, their absolute devotion to the sovereignty of Yahweh over Israel and their rejection of the payment of tribute to Rome as being tantamount to apostasy to Yahweh. This rehabilitation of the Zealots has, in turn, confirmed that the Jewish revolt against Rome in A.D. 66 was essentially religious in inspiration and character.

This new understanding of the religio-political situation in Judaea during the period A.D. 6 to 70, which coincided with the lifetime of Jesus and the beginnings of the Christian Church, has led to a fresh scrutiny of the New Testament documents. For it has become, consequently, harder to believe the traditional view that Jesus and his disciples lived untouched by, and unconcerned with, the deep religious patriotism of their people.

As a result of this new look at the Christian writings, certain features that had hitherto been disregarded or otherwise interpreted have assumed a fresh significance. The *Gospel of Mark*, the earliest of the four Gospels, provides two clues that pre-eminently indicate a very different situation from that assumed by the traditional teaching about the beginnings of Christianity.

It is generally agreed that the *Gospel of Mark* was written at Rome somewhere between A.D. 65 and 75, and that it was designed to meet the needs of Gentile Christians resident there for an account of the life and teaching of Jesus. This being so, it is consequently significant that the author of the Gospel was concerned to explain to his readers what had been Jesus' attitude to the question whether the Jews should pay tribute to Rome. Thus, in chapter xii.13–17, Jesus is represented as being questioned by Pharisees and Herodians about the tribute in order "to entrap him in his talk". The incident is, accordingly, so introduced as to rebut an implied charge that Jesus had condemned the payment of tribute to Rome. Thus to what is presented as the Jewish leaders' malicious question: "Is it lawful to pay tribute to Caesar or not? Should we pay, or should we not?", Jesus replies: "Render to Caesar the things that are Caesar's, and to God the things that are God's." As Mark presents this answer, it is clearly intended to be understood as avoiding the trap set for Jesus to incriminate himself with the Roman authorities. In other words, Jesus' reply, in this context, means that he endorsed the Jews' obligation to pay the tribute—they had to "render to Caesar the things that are Caesar's". And this is how the answer has been understood generally by Christians—indeed, it has often been quoted as Christ's command that Christians should obey and support the civil government.

On closer scrutiny, however, both the passage itself and Jesus' recorded answer are found to have a very different significance. In the first place, it is indeed curious that Mark, writing for the Christians of Rome at the time of the Jewish revolt, should have deemed it necessary to make clear what was the attitude of Jesus towards the Jewish payment of tribute to Rome. For the issue had no spiritual significance for the Roman Christians, and it supposedly dealt with an incident that had happened in Judaea some forty years before. The *Gospel of Mark* is not a long book, and there must surely have been many topics of a religious nature concerning the ministry of Jesus that merited recording instead of this which related only to Romano-Jewish politics. In the light of these considerations, the fact that Mark did choose to record it must indicate, therefore, that the subject was then a very pertinent one for the Roman Christians. In other words, in A.D. 70 the Christians in Rome were urgently concerned with what had been the attitude of Jesus towards the Jewish payment of tribute to Rome. And the significance of this fact is enhanced, and surely explained, by the further fact that one of the causes of the Jewish revolt of 66 was the non-payment of the tribute.

But there remains the problem of the answer of Jesus to the tribute question, as recorded by Mark. It is, curiously, an ambiguous answer to what had been a very clearly phrased question: "Is it lawful to pay tribute to Caesar or not? Should we pay or should we not?" As we have seen, Mark so introduces the incident that his readers are led to interpret Jesus' answer as ruling that the Jews were obliged to pay this tribute, thus attesting that Jesus was not guilty of opposing the Roman rule in Judaea. But it might reasonably be asked why he did not make Jesus' answer more explicit by presenting it as a categorical affirmation of the Jewish obligation to pay? That he did not do so can have only one explanation: the saying that he records was too well known to be changed or ignored. In other words, it appears that there was already in circulation, and known to the Roman Christians, a saying of Jesus' about the tribute: "Render to Caesar the things that are Caesar's, and to God the things that are God's", and that, from Mark's point of view, this saying needed explanation. The explanation which he provides, as we have seen, makes the saying into an endorsement of the Jews' duty to pay tribute to Rome. But what did it mean originally when uttered by Jesus? In the light of what we now know of the Zealots, there can be little doubt about what it meant to Jews living in Judaea at that time. The founder of Zealotism, Judas of Galilee, opposed the Roman tribute when it was first imposed in A.D. 6, on the ground that its payment by a Jew would be an act of apostasy. For it meant taking the resources of the Holy Land of Yahweh, the God of Israel, and giving them to Caesar, a heathen ruler whose subjects venerated him as a god. For the Jews, Judas insisted, there was only one lord, namely, Yahweh, and so they could not thus recognize the Roman Emperor as their lord and the owner of Judaea.

If Jesus, therefore, had ruled in relation to the question of the tribute, "render to Caesar the things that are Caesar's, and to God the things that are God's", there would not have been the slightest doubt in the minds of his Jewish hearers as to what he meant. For to them Judaea belonged to the God of Israel, and not to the Roman Caesar, and Jesus was understood as ruling that the resources of Yahweh's Holy Land could not be given in tribute to Caesar. The answer of Jesus was, indeed, one

The spoils of the Temple, including the Menorah or seven-branch lampstand, being carried in triumph through the streets of Rome (relief on the Arch of Titus, Rome)

that any Zealot might have returned to the same question, and it is significant that, according to the *Gospel of Luke* (xxiii. 2), Jesus was actually accused by the Jewish leaders before Pilate of "forbidding us to give tribute to Caesar".

From this analysis of the Markan tribute passage, it appears therefore that a saying of Jesus' was known among the Christians of Rome which had an embarrassing connection with the Jewish revolt against the Roman tribute. And the fact that this embarrassment was so keenly felt in Rome about A.D. 70 that it caused Mark to re-interpret it in a manner such as to make it appear that Jesus actually endorsed the Jewish obligation, is truly a fact of the greatest significance. For it reveals that the Roman Christians were profoundly affected by the Jewish revolt, and that it was necessary to assure them that Jesus, despite a contrary tradition, had abjured the views of the Jewish rebels.

Evidence of similar import is to be found in the fact that Mark, in giving a list of the twelve apostles of Jesus, names one as "Simon the Cananaean" (iii. 18). Now, this curious designation has a far greater significance than is immediately apparent. Mark wrote in Greek for the Greek-speaking Gentile Christians of Rome. He shows himself to be constantly aware of this fact, in that he is careful to explain Hebrew or Aramaic words and Jewish customs which his readers could not be expected to understand. For example, in the very list of the apostles where "Simon the Cananaean" appears, when he mentions that James and John, the sons of Zebedee, were surnamed "Boanerges", he explains that this epithet meant "sons of thunder" (iii. 16). Only once does he fail to explain a Jewish designation and that is in this instance of "Simon the Cananaean", which would have been quite unintelligible to his Gentile readers and, therefore, requiring interpretation. However, if he had translated the Aramaic title "Cananaean" here into its Greek equivalent, he would have been obliged to write "Zealot", thus revealing that one of the apostles, chosen by Jesus, was a member of the Jewish resistance party against Rome. That Mark thus disguised this fact from his readers, by departing from his practice of explaining Jewish titles, must surely mean that, when he wrote, the name "Zealot" was too opprobrious a term in Rome to be revealed in this connection. The significance of this suppression is immense, and it parallels that of the tribute episode. In other words, the situation of the Christians in Rome about A.D. 70 was such that the Zealot affiliation of one of Jesus' apostles was deemed too dangerous to be admitted.

The evidence of these two passages in the *Gospel of Mark* reveals, therefore, that, contrary to the traditional view, the Christian community in Rome was gravely affected by the Jewish revolt against Rome and the destruction of Jerusalem. Many other passages of the Markan Gospel have a like significance, including pre-eminently the transferring of responsibility for the execution of Jesus from Pontius Pilate to the Jewish leaders and people, which is described in Chapter 16 of this work. Indeed, in the light of our new knowledge, the whole *Gospel of Mark* has to be evaluated as an interpretation of Jesus designed to explain away the embarrassing fact that Jesus was executed for sedition against Rome. And this *apologia* was occasioned by the danger and perplexity that beset the Christians of Rome in consequence of the Jewish revolt against Roman suzerainty in A.D. 66 to 70.

IV

The truth has, in fact, now become very evident that, far from being unconcerned by the events that resulted in the destruction of Jerusalem, the Church's involvement therein was so profound that A.D. 70 marks a definitive turning-point in the evolution of the Christian religion. For the testimony that the Markan Gospel affords is repeated in varying forms in the other Gospels and the *Acts of the Apostles*, when examined more critically in this connection. It can now be seen that the catastrophic end of the Jewish national state closed what might be termed the "Jewish infancy of Christianity", and opened that of Catholic Christianity. Proper explanation of these two phases, and of the profound transformation that the events of A.D. 66 to 70 wrought, is necessarily beyond the limits of this chapter. The subject is very complex, though very fascinating, and it has been dealt with at length elsewhere.[6] It must suffice now, in conclusion, briefly to outline the nature and course of this transformation which changed Christianity from a Jewish Messianic sect into a world religion.

The original disciples of Jesus were Jews who believed that he was the Messiah of Israel. For them his crucifixion by the Romans had shaken their expectations; but they recovered their faith, believing that he would soon return with supernatural power to complete his Messianic role and "restore the kingdom to Israel" (*Acts of the Apostles* i. 6). These Jewish disciples believed it to be their task to convince their fellow Jews that Jesus was the hoped-for Messiah and to prepare them for his coming. They continued to live as zealous orthodox Jews, worshipping in the Temple and observing the ritual Law. They won many converts, including members of the lower orders of the priesthood. Their leader was James, the brother of Jesus, who acquired a great reputation for his austerity and zealous practice of Judaism. As Roman maladministration became more oppressive and popular Jewish resentment increased under Zealot inspiration, the Jewish Christians identified themselves ever more closely with the cause of Israel's freedom. Their link with the lower clergy, who were infected with Zealotism, was probably the cause of James' execution by the high priest Ananus, who was distinguished for his efforts to suppress the growing influence of the revolutionary elements among the people.[7]

One disturbing factor which the Jewish Christians, centred on Jerusalem, had to face was the activity of Paul of Tarsus. Not an original disciple of Jesus, Paul developed his own version of Christianity which he propagated among the Gentiles in various parts of the Graeco-Roman world. Since this version negated the fundamental tenets of Judaism,

---

[6] See the Bibliography to this chapter; various aspects of the subject are also touched upon in Chapters 15, 16, 19 and 21.

[7] Cf. S. G. F. Brandon, "The Death of James the Just: a New Interpretation," in *Studies in Mysticism and Religion* (presented to G. G. Scholem), Jerusalem, 1967.

Coins of the Roman Victory (i) Bronze *sestertius* of Vespasian (A.D. 71). The reverse shows a symbolic palm-tree between the triumphant emperor and the mourning figure of Judaea; (ii) Bronze *sestertius* of Titus (A.D. 80–1). Reverse shows mourning Judaea and a Jewish captive

Paul's activity endangered the reputation for orthodoxy of the Jewish Christians with their fellow-countrymen. Consequently, Paul and his teaching were repudiated, and his arrest by the Romans in *c.* 59 conveniently removed him from the scene and seemingly eliminated his rival version of Christianity.[8]

How this original Jewish Christianity, which was embodied in the Mother Church of Jerusalem, fared when the revolt against Rome finally came in the year 66 is not recorded, except in the writings of Eusebius and Epiphanius which we have found to be valueless in this connection. But the facts speak for themselves. Before A.D. 70, as the Epistles of Paul and the *Acts of the Apostles* show, the Jerusalem Church was the

[8] See Chapter 21.

recognized centre of authority and tradition, from which the Christian movement was controlled. After A.D. 70 nothing more is heard of it, and Christianity now develops new centres of authority and tradition in Gentile cities outside Palestine. In other words, complete oblivion falls upon the Mother Church of the faith at the same time as the city of Jerusalem is utterly destroyed by the Romans. These two facts cannot be unrelated. What had been the reaction of the Jewish Christians in 66 to their country's revolt against the domination of heathen Rome is unrecorded; but whatever evidence is relevant irresistibly points to the conclusion that they identified with their nation's cause and perished in its disastrous overthrow. Some memory may perhaps be preserved of the fate of these Jewish Christians in the minatory words attributed to Jesus in the *Gospel of Matthew* (xxviii. 53): "all who take the sword will perish by the sword."

The destruction of Jerusalem thus ended the control of the Mother Church of Jerusalem, and forcibly broke the bonds that bound the infant Christian faith to its Jewish cradle. Christianity's future henceforth lay among the Gentiles, and after A.D. 70, commencing with the *Gospel of Mark*, Paul's version of the faith was rehabilitated, and what had originally been a Jewish Messianic sect was transformed into a universal salvation religion. Thus, by one of those curious ironies of history, to the Roman destruction of Jerusalem in A.D. 70, are to be traced the origins both of Catholic Christianity and the modern state of Israel.

CHAPTER 19

The Zealots

THE JEWISH RESISTANCE AGAINST ROME A.D. 6–73

Not until three years after the fall of Jerusalem
did Zealot resistance come to a bloody end, when the
garrison of Masada preferred suicide to surrender

I

The long reign of Herod the Great ended in the spring of the year 4 B.C. The Jews rejoiced at his death; they hated him profoundly for his Idumaean ancestry, his pagan tastes and his tyrannical rule.[1] Yet, notwithstanding his many faults, he had preserved them from direct Roman rule. The Empire of Rome now extended on every side of Judaea; but Herod had been a client-prince; so that taxes were paid to him and not to Caesar, and Roman troops did not garrison Jewish towns and fortresses.

Roman rule, despite its ruthless enforcement and its often vicious officials, was not intolerable; and, after the sufferings of the initial period of conquest, most peoples settled down and prospered under the *Pax Romana*. For the Jews, however, Roman rule contained elements that they would inevitably find intolerable whenever they came directly under it. Their religion made them a "peculiar people", both culturally and politically. From his childhood, the Jew was brought up to believe that he was a member of a nation, chosen specially by God, out of all other peoples, for a peculiar destiny. He believed that God, whom he knew

---

[1] Despite his Hellenising policy, Herod was a professed Jew and generally recognised Jewish religious scruples. See Chapter 14.

The Fortress of Masada. One of the Roman camps is visible in the foreground; in the centre of the photograph the ramp built by the Romans to reach the wall can be seen

as Yahweh, had originally revealed His providence in a number of marvellous events. Under the leadership of Moses, He had delivered his ancestors from bondage in Egypt; at Sinai, He had entered into a covenant relation with Israel, as the nation was known; then He had fulfilled His ancient promise to Abraham, the progenitor of the nation, by settling Abraham's descendants in Canaan, which thus became the Holy Land of Israel.

When Herod died, the Jews already had a long chequered history behind them. They had suffered many vicissitudes of fortune, including foreign conquest and exile in Babylonia (586–515 B.C.). Their more recent memories, however, were of the glorious victories of the Maccabees (from 168 B.C.). Under the leadership of various members of the Maccabaean family, they had won freedom from the Seleucid kings of Syria.

But the achievement had not only political significance; subjugation to the Seleucid power had meant subjection to its policy of Hellenization, which had endangered their religion and culture. Revolt against their foreign masters had been an act of faith; for when matched against that of the Seleucid Empire, their military strength was infinitesimal. Yet, after a long struggle and much suffering, they had won. Their success confirmed their conviction in Yahweh's providence for Israel: that they would ever be assured of divine aid, if they risked all for the integrity of their faith. The memory of Maccabaean times also included the ideal of martyrdom for Israel, which found expression in a popular literature of national heroes who had suffered at the hand of the heathen.

The inspiration of such memories and ideals seems gradually to have led many Jews to conceive of Israel as a theocracy, with Yahweh as their true king and with the high priest as his vice-regent on earth.[2] Herod encountered a practical expression of this belief shortly before his death. Probably as a gesture of loyalty to his Roman overlord, he erected a large golden image of an eagle on the main gate of the magnificent Temple, which he had built at Jerusalem for his subjects. Two rabbis incited their students to destroy the image, as being contrary to the divine Law of Israel. Arrested and brought before the King, the rabbis, Judas and Matthias, boldly informed him: "It is not surprising that we considered your decrees less obligatory than the laws which Moses gave us, written at the dictation and instruction of God." They were burned to death.

The Jews saw in the death of Herod an opportunity to regain their freedom; but they were sufficiently realistic to recognize that the Romans were unlikely to allow them to be independent of their control, so they petitioned the Emperor Augustus that Judaea be incorporated into the province of Syria. In the light of subsequent history, it is ironic that they should ever have made such a request. Obviously they could not have reckoned with the realities of direct Roman rule; perhaps they hopefully pictured themselves as a little independent enclave within the Roman Empire, left to govern themselves and pursue their own way of life. Herod had bequeathed his kingdom to his son Archelaus; but the bequest had to have Roman sanction. Augustus compromised by dividing

---

[2] The word "theocracy" was apparently coined by the Jewish historian Josephus (c. A.D. 37–101) in his polemical work entitled *Against Apion*, II, 165. He defined it as "placing all sovereignty and authority in the hands of God."

the realm, making Archelaus the ethnarch of Judaea, with Idumaea and
Samaria, and Herod Antipas, another son, tetrarch of Galilee. The
arrangement survived for ten years. Archelaus proved incapable of efficient
rule; he was deposed and his domain placed under direct Roman rule.
Thus, in the year A.D. 6, the Jews obtained what they had previously
requested in vain: incorporation into the Roman Empire. But the consequences were to prove dire.

To implement the new order, the Roman legate of Syria, P. Sulpicius
Quirinius, was instructed to make a census of the resources and population of Judaea for the purpose of taxation. Coponius, a man of equestrian
rank, was also appointed as procurator, to govern the new territory under
the general supervision of the Syrian legate. The Jews were naturally
accustomed to pay taxes for the upkeep of the government; but until
now that government had been Jewish, even if controlled by the hated
Herodians. To pay taxes, or rather tribute, to Rome was another matter,
and one involving a principle of basic significance for those zealous in
their belief in Israel as a theocracy. To them, Israel belonged to Yahweh,
and to give any part of its products as tribute to Caesar was, in effect,
an act of *lèse-majesté* against its divine owner. But that was not all: such
tribute went to support the government of one who was himself regarded
as a god.[3] In other words, for a Jew the payment of tribute signified
not only acknowledging a foreign overlord, but also blasphemy—that of
accepting as master a man who claimed to be divine.

The high priest Joazar, anticipating trouble, tried to persuade his
people to accept the new situation. But his temporising counsels were
opposed by a rabbi, Judas of Galilee, who was supported by a Pharisee
named Sadduq. According to Josephus, Judas "incited his countrymen
to revolt, upbraiding them as cowards for consenting to pay tribute to
the Romans and tolerating mortal masters, after having God for their
Lord."[4] Judas and Sadduq also maintained that the census would lead
to complete slavery. They called upon the Jews to vindicate their liberty,
and promised that God would bless and assist their act of faith in
opposing the Roman demand.

Josephus, oddly enough, does not tell what resulted, beyond remark-
ing that the people heard the message of Judas with joy and the revolt

[3] The very title of *Augustus*, which Octavian received in 27 B.C., implied divinity.
[4] *Jewish War* II, 118; trans. H. St. John Thackeray in Loeb edn. of *Josephus*, vol. II.

A gate, probably of Byzantine period, on the top of Masada

made considerable progress. The author of the *Acts of the Apostles*, however, represents the famous rabbi Gamaliel as recalling many years later, to his fellow-members of the Sanhedrin, how Judas of Galilee "arose in the days of the census and drew away some of the people after him; he also perished, and all who followed him were scattered." This statement undoubtedly gives a correct report of part of the outcome of Judas's movement. The leaders perished, and the revolt was crushed; but the movement, inaugurated by Judas, did not end there. The survivors took to the hills and the desert areas of the country, whence they maintained a guerrilla warfare against the Romans and those Jews who, too willingly, co-operated with them.

II

The Jewish historian Josephus is, virtually, our sole informant of these events, and of those of the next six decades of Jewish history, which culminated in the fatal revolt against Rome in A.D. 66. This fact is of key importance for our proper understanding of the cause of the revolt that ended the Jewish national state in Palestine until its restoration in 1948; it is a basic factor also for a right appreciation of the origins of Christianity. Consequently, since our information about this period comes almost wholly from what Josephus tells us, it is essential that we should know how far he is a reliable witness. In both his works, *The Antiquities of the Jews* and *The Jewish War*, dealing with these times, Josephus represents the movement started by Judas of Galilee as the main cause of the catastrophe that befell the Jewish nation in A.D. 70. Thus, in the *Antiquities*, he declares: "Since the people joyfully heard their (Judas's and Sadduq's) message, their reckless enterprise made great progress. Every kind of ill stemmed from these men and overwhelmed the nation beyond description: the unceasing violence of war, the loss of friends who might have alleviated our woes, large-scale brigandage, and the murder of our leading men" (XVIII. 6–7). In the *War*, writing with reference to the troubles that marked the census, he says: "in those days the Sicarii clubbed together against those who consented to submit to Rome and in every way treated them as enemies, plundering their property, rounding up their cattle, and setting fire to their habitations; protesting that such persons were no other than aliens, who so ignobly sacrificed the hard-won liberty of the Jews and admitted their preference for the Roman yoke."[5]

Although he thus clearly blames Judas of Galilee and his followers for the ills that afflicted Israel, Josephus betrays, however, an animus against them that obviously does not originate in the objective appraisal of a historian, but was inspired by personal embarrassment. It resulted in distortion and misrepresentation; and this is revealed in a rather curious way. In his accounts of Judas of Galilee, in both the *Antiquities* and the *War*, Josephus states that Judas founded one of the four sects (*haireseis*) of Jewish philosophy.[6] He then proceeds to describe the other three sects, namely, the Pharisees, Sadducees and the Essenes. The first two are, of course, well known from their appearance in the Christian Gospels: the Essenes are now generally identified with the monastic community at Qumrân, whose library has become so famous as the Dead Sea Scrolls. Now, although he groups the sect founded by Judas with these three other sects, Josephus does not give the sect of Judas a name. Clearly, the omission is not due to forgetfulness. Josephus did not wish,

[5] VII, 254–5, trans. Thackeray, Loeb edn. of *Josephus*, vol. III.
[6] He uses this description, since he is writing for a Greek-reading Gentile public.

at this point in his narrative, to divulge to his Gentile readers the name
by which the followers of Judas were known to their fellow Jews—a name,
indeed, that they proudly claimed. This name in its original Hebrew
form was *Qanna'im*, being translated into Greek as *Zēlōtai*, and into
English as "Zealots".

The name had an honourable ancestry in Jewish tradition. It originated from the deed of Phinehas, recorded in *Numbers* xxv. 7–11.
According to the narrative, many Israelites had intermarried with foreign
women; and Yahweh punished the nation by sending a plague. Phinehas,
finding a fellow Israelite with a Midianitish woman, "thrust both of them
through, the man of Israel, and the woman through her belly. So the
plague was stayed from the children of Israel." The narrative continues:
"And Yahweh said to Moses, 'Phinehas, the son of Eleazar, son of Aaron
the priest, has turned back my wrath from the people of Israel, in that
he was zealous with my zeal among them, so that I did not consume
the people of Israel in my zeal.'" Phinehas was thus the scriptural prototype
of the Zealot, providing the classic example of ruthless zeal in the service
of Yahweh, the God of Israel. Subsequent Jewish history afforded other
examples of this zeal: most notably Mattathias, the father of Judas Mac-

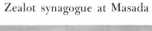

Zealot synagogue at Masada

cabaeus, who slew an officer of Antiochus Epiphanes when he forced Jews to pagan worship, and a Jew who was in the act of conforming (1 *Macc.* ii. 23 ff.). Judas of Galilee, and those who accepted his message, thus followed a godly tradition. Like their revered exemplars, their zeal for the God of Israel impelled them to ruthless action against both the heathen Roman and the conforming Jew. Their policy was fanatical and dangerous; but their willingness to risk all was essentially inspired by their religious faith, which was based on a profound conviction that Yahweh was the only true God, and that Israel was his Chosen People.

That Josephus was not only hostile to the Zealots, but also embarrassed about them, is probably due to two causes. By nature he was cautious and calculating. He had visited Rome; and he had a shrewd appreciation of Roman strength. His attitude towards the folly of challenging Rome's dominion is eloquently expressed in a speech that he represents the Jewish prince Agrippa II making, in an attempt to dissuade the Jews from revolt in A.D. 66: "What sort of army do you rely on? What are the arms you depend on? Where is your fleet, that you may seize the Roman seas, and where are those treasures which may be sufficient for your undertakings? . . . . Will you not carefully reflect upon the Roman empire? Will you not estimate your own weakness?" (*War* II, 361–2). Josephus was not moved by the faith that inspired the Zealots to challenge the might of Caesar in the name of Yahweh. Although a pious Jew, he joined other moderate men in seeking to control the revolutionary movement and to co-operate with the Romans. Forced to take up arms against Rome, he eventually surrendered to the Roman commander Vespasian and served on the staff of his son Titus in the final campaign against Jerusalem. As a client of the Imperial house, he wrote his *Jewish War* to commemorate the Roman victory over his people. A renegade, who prospered in the service of his nation's conquerors, Josephus naturally sought to denigrate those who had led Israel into revolt. But that was not all: Josephus was uncomfortably conscious that the Zealots had sacrificed themselves and their nation, inspired by an uncompromising religious faith that he himself did not possess. In self-justification, therefore, he sought to misrepresent their motives.[7]

His intention finds expression in his use of opprobrious terms for the Zealots. His most frequent name for them is *lēstai*, i.e. "brigands".

[7] See Chapter 20.

They were probably referred to as such by the Romans: and, significantly, the name "brigands" has often been used since that time by other imperialistic powers for the patriots who have resisted them in the lands they have occupied. Josephus' use of the word "brigands" for the Zealots has had serious consequences for the evaluation of Jewish history during this crucial period, and also for that of Christian Origins. Indeed, until the more critical approach of recent years, Josephus' denigratory presentation of the Zealots had generally been accepted as the truth. Consequently, the Jewish resistance movement against Rome has been regarded as one made up largely of criminal characters who aimed at overthrowing orderly government for their own dastardly or misguided ends. This pro-Roman attitude is reflected in the Gospels. It would appear very probable that Barabbas, who lay bound in the Roman prison at the time of the trial of Jesus, was a Zealot; it is also likely that the two *lēstai*, between whom Jesus was crucified (*Mark* xv. 27), were members of the Jewish resistance.

Another name that Josephus uses for the Zealots is "*Sicarii*". This Latin word obviously originated with the Roman forces in Judaea: it was derived from the word *sica* meaning a curved dagger. According to Josephus, this form of the Jewish resistance movement started during the procuratorship of Antonius Felix (A.D. 52–60). It probably represented a new development in resistance tactics. Hitherto the Zealots had operated in the country outside Jerusalem. Now a group moved into the metropolis, to carry out a terrorist campaign of clandestine assassination. Their principal victims were Jews who notably co-operated with the Romans: the Sicarii struck at these in crowded places, with daggers concealed in their clothing.

Josephus does not use the name "Zealot" until he comes to describe the revolutionary events in Jerusalem during the winter of A.D. 66–67. What he then says of them reveals his own attitude. Referring to the Zealots, he comments: "for that was the name they went by, as if they were zealous in good undertakings, and were not rather zealous in the worst actions, and extravagant in them beyond the example of others" (*War* IV, 160–1). In another, even more significant, passage, he denigrates them as "that sort of people that were called Zealots . . . who indeed corresponded to the name; for they imitated every evil work; nor if history suggested any evil thing that had formerly been done, did they avoid zealously to pursue the same; and, although they gave themselves that

Ruins of synagogue at Masada attesting Zealots' devotion to their religion

name from their zeal for what was good, yet was it an ironic description of the evil deeds done by them in their brutal nature, or because they thought the greatest mischiefs to be the greatest good" (*War* VI, 268–270). The name "Zealot" clearly had implications for Josephus which he sought to controvert.

III

If we understand Josephus's attitude to the Zealots, we shall be able to follow the drama of Romano-Jewish relations, until they reached their fatal climax in A.D. 70. Josephus was not, of course, concerned with writing the history of Zealotism; its members only figure in his narrative, particularly in the earlier years of the period, sporadically, and then under the name of "bandits". Moreover, as we shall note, in pursuit of his apologetic theme, Josephus was sometimes intent on presenting some notorious Roman as unjustly afflicting a peaceful Jewish people; in recording such episodes, it was obviously politic to make no mention of "bandit" activity.

Thus after describing the start of the Zealot movement in A.D. 6, Josephus says nothing more about it until the procuratorship of Cuspius

Fadus (A.D. 42–6), except for a passing reference to "banditry" in A.D. 39–40. His silence is the more remarkable, since during the period concerned, Jewish religion was twice threatened with such outrage by the Romans that Zealot reaction should have been immediate and violent. According to Josephus and Philo, the Jewish philosopher of Alexandria, Pontius Pilate, who was procurator[8] from A.D. 26–36, violated the religious scruples of the Jews on several occasions. The Jews were profoundly agitated by these outrages; but nothing is heard of the Zealots. The reason seems plain: in their accounts of the incidents concerned, both Josephus and Philo stress the amazing patience of the Jews under Pilate's callous provocation. From what we otherwise know of the Jews at this time, the picture is unconvincing. The presentation is undoubtedly tendentious. Pilate had, eventually, been recalled to Rome, to answer for his conduct in another affair concerning the Samaritans; so he could be conveniently presented by Jewish apologists as an example of the bad Roman official, who goaded the law-abiding Jews into ultimate revolt. To have mentioned Zealot activity would have spoilt the picture. But certain incidental references in the Christian Gospels indicate that the Zealots were active, and that Pilate had clashed with them.

According to the Markan Gospel (xv. 7), at the time of the trial of Jesus, the Romans had captured Barabbas and others "who had made insurrection with him, and had committed murder in the insurrection". The reference is evidently made from the Roman point of view; for the deaths, doubtless of Romans, caused by the insurgents, are described as "murder" (*phonon*). It was, most probably, two of these rebels who were crucified with Jesus; for they are described, as we have already noted, by the significant term *lēstai* ("bandits"). In the Lukan Gospel (xiii. 1–3), there is an incidental mention of "the Galileans, whose blood Pilate had mingled with their sacrifices". Nothing further is known of the incident; but there is some evidence that the Zealots were sometimes known as "Galileans", probably because their founder, Judas, came from Galilee, as perhaps did also many of his followers. Even more significant is the fact that one of the twelve disciples of Jesus of Nazareth was a Zealot. The author of the Markan Gospel, writing for the Christian community in Rome shortly after A.D. 70, found the fact very embarrassing. Consequently, departing from his usual practice of translating Hebrew and

---

[8] According to a recently discovered inscription, his title was "prafectus." See Chapter 17.

Aramaic terms for his Gentile readers, he merely designated one disciple, Simon, as "the Cananaean" (iii. 18). This was a transliteration into Greek of the singular form of the Hebrew or Aramaic word *Qanna'im,* i.e. Zealots, which we have already noted. Luke, writing later, after the strong feeling aroused by the Jewish War had abated, describes Simon unequivocally as *ho Zēlōtēs,* i.e. "the Zealot "[9].

Zealot activity, ignored during the procuratorship of Pontius Pilate, is again ignored by Josephus and Philo in their accounts of an episode that convulsed Jewish life in A.D. 39–40. This was the attempt of the Emperor Gaius to place a statue of himself, in the form of Zeus, in the Temple at Jerusalem. Although this constituted the most terrible outrage to their religion, the Jews are represented as offering only a passive resistance to the Emperor's mad project. They were providentially spared the ultimate test by his sudden death. Beyond passing reference by Josephus to some "banditry" in connection with the tribute, the Zealots were apparently quiescent while their religion was threatened with the greatest outrage since Antiochus Epiphanes had erected an altar to Zeus in the Temple in 167 B.C. That they would have remained inactive is incredible; for what the Roman Emperor planned to do was tantamount to the dethronement of Yahweh, in his own sanctuary, by a deified man.

Again the silence of the two Jewish writers can be explained by their apologetical interests. Since Gaius was regarded as insane, and his memory was execrated by the Romans, it was politic to represent their countrymen as victims of so infamous an emperor. Some memory of the Zealot attitude may, however, be preserved in the Markan Gospel; for there is reason for thinking that part of the apocalyptic discourse in the thirteenth chapter may incorporate a fragment of a Zealot oracle, concerned with the attempt of Gaius to desecrate the Temple. The passage concerned (verses 14–20) begins: "But when you see the desolating sacrilege set up where it ought not to be . . . then let those who are in Judaea flee to the mountains, . . ." The Zealot strongholds were in the mountainous parts of the country, from which their resistance to Rome was maintained.

The appointment by the Emperor Claudius of a Jewish prince, Agrippa I, to be King of Judaea, relieved the tension caused by Gaius. Although a Herodian, Agrippa manifested a great devotion to Judaism;

[9] See chapter 18.

but unfortunately his reign was brief, and, after his death in A.D. 44, the Jews found themselves again under direct Roman rule. The next procurator, Cupius Fadus, had, Josephus tells us, to clear Judaea of "brigands". More significant is the fact that his successor, Tiberius Alexander (A.D. 46–48), crucified two sons of Judas of Galilee. Josephus gives no other details; but the incident indicates an important fact about Zealotism, attested by later evidence. It is that the leadership of the movement was dynastic. By the Jews the memory of Judas of Galilee was clearly much respected; he had died as a martyr for Israel. His sons succeeded him in organizing resistance to Rome; and they, too, died for their faith. "To take up one's cross and follow" was probably a saying of Zealot origin.

Romano-Jewish relations steadily deteriorated. The narratives of Josephus contain numerous references to "bandit" activity. Particularly interesting is what he records of the procuratorship of Antonius Felix (A.D. 52–60). The whole land is now described as being full of "brigands" and "impostors", who "deceive the people". These impostors (*goètes*) were miracle-workers; and their association with the Zealots is illuminating. They promised "miracles of deliverance". Josephus records various instances: some tried to repeat the miracle of the Exodus by leading their followers out into the desert where Yahweh would deliver them; another assembled a great company on the Mount of Olives, promising, like a second Joshua, that the city's walls would fall at his command, and that he would lead his followers to slaughter the Roman garrison. Roman reaction was always swift and effective. There is much reason for thinking that these "impostors" were Messianic pretenders. Some memory of them is preserved in the Christian Gospels: "Then if any man shall say unto you, Lo, here is the Christ (Messiah), or there; believe it not. For there shall arise false Christs, and false prophets, and shall shew great signs and wonders . . . wherefore, if they say he is in the desert; go not forth: behold, he is in the secret chambers; believe it not (*Matt.* xxiv. 23–6).

Such events reveal the atmosphere of religious fanaticism, the tensions and expectancy, that marked Jewish society as it moved towards its doom during the sixth decade of the first century. The last procurator, Gessius Florus (A.D. 64–66) proved to be the worst; and during his period of maladministration the fatal revolt occurred. It started in a significant way. For some time the lower orders of the priesthood had apparently been infected by Zealot views; and they had become hostile to the sacerdotal aristocracy, which was pro-Roman. In A.D. 66 these lower priests refused to allow the daily sacrifice to be offered in the Temple for the well-being of the Emperor and the Roman people. This symbolic act of defiance was quickly followed by the massacre of the Roman garrisons in Jerusalem and other cities.

These acts of revolt, which committed Israel irrevocably to challenging the Roman dominion, finally achieved what the Zealots had fought and suffered for since A.D. 6. But, ironically, at the very start of the fateful contest, the Zealot movement was robbed of its recognized head— Menahem, the surviving son of Judas of Galilee. He had struck quickly and effectively at the Romans. By a brilliant *coup*, he seized the great fortress of Masada, near the Dead Sea, and possessed himself of its well-stocked armoury. Then, with his Zealots, he moved on to Jerusalem, where he was received as the accepted leader of the revolt. According to Josephus, he arrayed himself as a king and acted in a tyrannous manner. The truth behind this hostile account must be that Menahem was regarded as the Messianic king of Jewish apocalyptic hope. However, he aroused the jealousy of another rebel leader, who caused him to be murdered in the Temple.

The removal of its dynastic, and probably its charismatic, head left Zealotism without a commanding leader. Consequently, Zealot and para-Zealot groups operated in various places under local chiefs. No co-ordinated defence system for the country had been worked out before Roman punitive action was launched in the early autumn of A.D. 66. Brushing aside resistance elsewhere, the Roman army, commanded by Cestius Gallus, the legate of Syria, laid siege to Jerusalem. Then occurred an event that has never been satisfactorily explained. At the very point of breaching the Temple fortifications, Cestius suddenly ordered his troops to withdraw to their camp on Mount Scopus. Next day, the whole army began to retreat northwards before the astonished gaze of the Jews, who had been reduced to extreme despair. Seeing in this strange happening the hand of God, they pursued their retreating foe, and almost annihilated them before they struggled out of Palestine.

A victory so great and unexpected seemed to confirm the promise of Judas of Galilee, that Yahweh would aid those who zealously adventured themselves in his service. A Roman legion, supported by a large force of auxiliaries, had been overthrown as marvellously as had been the army of the Assyrian Sennacherib in 700 B.C. The victory, however,

Zealot coin (bronze), inscribed "Year 2" (i.e. A.D. 67-8). The reverse of
coin, showing vine-leaf, reads "Deliverance of Zion"

was destined to prove fatal to the Jews. In the face of what seemed so
signal a manifestation of divine approval, the nation was swept forward
on a flood tide of faith, believing that the final hour had come of Israel's
freedom and vindication before the nations of the world. This belief finds
eloquent expression in the inscriptions on the new coins struck by the
insurgents. They read variously in Hebrew: "For the Redemption of Zion"
and "Deliverance of Zion".

Unfortunately for the Jewish cause, the lack of an obvious leader
led to an internecine struggle between the various resistance groups. But,
when the renewed Roman attack came, opposition was fierce and devoted.
The towns had been fortified; and it took Vespasian, the Roman commander, three years of arduous campaigning (A.D. 67-9) to clear most
of the country outside Jerusalem. When the siege of the city started in
the spring of A.D. 70 under Vespasian's son, Titus, the insurgent forces
at once presented a united front to the enemy. The Zealots, who included
the priests, having at last found a capable leader in John of Gischala,
held the Temple, which constituted both the focal point of Israel's faith
and the citadel of the city's fortifications. It was defended with a fanatical
courage, and the ultimate breaching of its walls and its subsequent burning
on August 29th that year marked the virtual end of the Jewish state.

The fall of Jerusalem did not end Zealot resistance. The followers
of Menahem, after his death in A.D. 66, had retired to Masada. In A.D.
73 the Romans laid siege to the fortress, and, after a long, bitter struggle,
succeeded in breaching the walls. Seeing that further resistance was

hopeless, the Zealot commander, Eleazar, a descendant of Judas of Galilee, persuaded his followers to commit suicide rather than surrender. The men killed their wives and children; then, drawing lots, they were killed in turn; the last solitary survivor, having seen that all were dead, set fire to the palace, and completed his task by slaying himself. When the Romans broke in, two women and five children crept from a hiding-place, to tell of the fate of the nine hundred and sixty dead, whose corpses testified to the fortitude of Zealot faith.

The last gesture of Zealotism was in Egypt, where a number of the Sicarii had succeeded in escaping from Judaea. Failing to stir the Egyptian Jews to revolt, they were rounded up and executed. According to Josephus, they were previously tortured to make them "acknowledge Caesar as Lord". The renegade historian reluctantly admits that even the children went to their deaths refusing to deny their Zealot faith.

The modern state of Israel has excavated Masada, making it a national monument; for it is the spirit of Zealot fortitude that the modern Israelis seek to emulate. This rehabilitation of Zealotism has its repercussions also for Christianity. The problem has to be faced of the attitude of Jesus to Zealotism, remembering that one of his disciples was a Zealot and two Zealots were probably crucified on either side of him.[10]

[10] See Chapter 18.

CHAPTER 20

Josephus

RENEGADE OR PATRIOT?

*Was Josephus, the famous Jewish historian of the
first century* A.D., *an arch-Quisling of the ancient world?
He "could scarcely have given a worse impression of himself
than that to be derived from the* Jewish War*", whence
he emerges as an unscrupulous opportunist whose conduct
is rendered even more distasteful by a hypocritical
profession of the highest motives.*

I

Probably most people, if asked to name the maiden who danced
for the head of John the Baptist, would promptly reply, "Salome". If
questioned further about the source of their knowledge, many would
answer, "the Bible". Yet in the only account of the celebrated incident—
the *Gospel of Mark,* vi. 14–29—the girl is not named. Her name is known
only by inference from the writings of Josephus. This curious little fact
serves to attest the enormous influence that Josephus has had in unconsciously moulding our common knowledge of the background of New
Testament times. But this knowledge, it must be recognized, is something
we owe to past generations, when the family Bible and Whiston's translation of the works of Josephus represented the chief reading of many
families.

That the writings of Josephus are no longer generally read is unfortunate. Not only have they a great intrinsic interest but they mirror the
mind of a curiously complex personality who played an ambiguous rôle

in one of the great dramas of history. The strange mixture of motives that prompted the conduct of this Jewish historian has usually not·been sympathetically regarded in the past; perhaps today, after the experience of the last three decades, we are better able to appreciate the conflict between loyalty and logic that once confronted Josephus.

Joseph ben Matthias, to give him his Jewish name, or Flavius Josephus as he came to be known when he enjoyed the patronage of the Imperial family of the Flavii, lived at a time that has since been regarded, at least in Western thought, as the unique turning-point of human history. He was born in Judaea in the year A.D. 37–38, about one year after Pontius Pilate had been recalled from his governorship of the country. He was a child when his nation was moved to the very depths of its being by the Emperor Caligula's insane attempt to erect his statue in the Temple of Yahweh at Jerusalem (A.D. 40–41). As as young man he took part, first on the Jewish side and then on the Roman, in the Jewish revolt against Rome, which began in A.D. 66 and ended four years' later in the utter overthrow of the Jewish nation and the signal destruction of its metropolis and national shrine. After witnessing the ruin of his people, he moved to Rome, where he enjoyed the Imperial favour and lived on as a prosperous man-of-letters into the second century A.D. Thus Josephus was not only present at the historic struggle of Israel against the dominion of heathen Rome, but he was a younger contemporary of the Apostle Paul and lived through the vital years of the formation of the Christian Church in the land of its origin.

Presumed portrait of Flavius Josephus: Roman portrait head of the first century, now in the Ny Carlsberg Glyptotek, Copenhagen

As if to exploit the unique distinction of the period and place in which his life was lived, Josephus himself was notably equipped by birth, education and natural ability. The son of a priest and able to claim descent from the ancient Jewish royal house of the Hasmonaeans, he was a precocious child and quickly mastered the rabbinical training that he was given. He claims that he examined personally the teaching of the three leading sects of Judaism, namely, those of the Pharisees, the Sadducees, and the Essenes, before deciding which discipline to adopt as his rule of life. His mention of the Essenes is especially interesting in view of the recent tendency to identify these sectaries with the community at Qumrân, the former owners of the now famous Dead Sea Scrolls. Josephus tells us that for three years he was the disciple of an Essene named Bannus, who lived a life of extreme austerity in the desert. By his nineteenth year, Josephus finally decided to follow the discipline of the Pharisees.

Peculiarly fitted as he was to be an observer and interpreter of the mighty events of his age, Josephus also played an active part in them. But it is in the nature of the part that he played that there resides the basic problem both of his own character and the reliability of much of his testimony.

In the year 66 Josephus returned to Palestine from Rome, where he had successfully negotiated the release of certain Jewish political prisoners. On his arrival in his native land, he found his countrymen on the brink of revolt against Rome. For, since the year 6, when Judaea was finally placed under direct Roman rule, the religious susceptibilities of the Jews had been continuously inflamed by this abiding affront to their cherished ideal of a theocracy; and Roman maladministration had increasingly aggravated their discontent. And so, as the Roman historian Tacitus succinctly puts it: "Jewish patience endured until the procurator-ship of Gessius Florus; under him war broke out" (*Hist*. V. 10). Accordingly, in August 66, within a short while of Josephus' return, by the massacre of various isolated Roman garrisons and the cessation of the daily sacrifice in the Temple for the Emperor, the Jewish patriots proclaimed their repudiation of the sovereignty of heathen Rome.

II

Of his own reactions to these stirring events, Josephus leaves us perplexed by his own conflicting accounts. In his autobiography, which did not appear until some time after A.D. 100, he declares that he at first opposed the revolutionary movement, on the ground that such a challenge to Roman power could only end in disaster for the small Jewish nation. His opposition to the popular mind, so he asserts, brought him into great personal danger, and he had to take refuge within the inner court of the Temple. Nevertheless, after the amazing defeat in November 66 of the Roman punitive expedition led by Cestius Gallus, the legate of Syria, Josephus states, without explaining this unexpected change in his personal situation, that he was appointed, with two other priests, by the leaders (*hoi prōtoi*) in Jerusalem, to organize the defence of Galilee by disarming the revolutionary rabble and equipping what he calls "the most able men of the nation (*tois kratistois tou ethnous*)" with their weapons. This account in the *Life* was written to rebut the accusation, made in a history of the Jewish War by a compatriot, Justus of Tiberias, that Josephus had caused his native city (Tiberias) to revolt against the Romans. In his earlier and most celebrated work, *Concerning the Jewish War*, however, which was published between A.D. 75 and 79 under Imperial patronage, Josephus had written that, after the defeat of Cestius Gallus, he had actually been given the command of Galilee as general (*stratēgos*).

Of his subsequent conduct in Galilee, where the brunt of the next Roman attack was most likely first to fall, the accounts in the *Jewish War* and the *Life* contain so many mutual contradictions that the only sure conclusion that may be drawn from them is that Josephus had found the truth too embarrassing to tell, either from the point of view of his own integrity as a Jewish patriot, or with regard to his later position as a client of the Imperial family in Rome. Nevertheless, there are good reasons for believing that, whatever the depth of his patriotism, Josephus was by nature too much of a realist to assume that the Jewish act of faith, in challenging the might of Rome, would be rewarded by some signal act of divine intervention. As we have already noted, in his *Life* he declared that he had opposed the revolt on the grounds that it was hopeless. This statement is probably a balder, but a franker, admission of his own original conviction, which he had earlier set forth in the *Jewish War* in the form of an elaborate speech, attributed to Agrippa II, the Jewish client-prince and leader of the pro-Roman party among the Jewish sacerdotal aristocracy. Josephus represents Agrippa as making this speech in Jerusalem, on the eve of the revolt, in an effort to prevent the catastrophe. Although undoubtedly a literary composition modelled on the Thucydidean pattern, this speech is a most valuable survey of the strength and resources of

Coin of the Emperor Titus, on
whose staff Josephus served as a
Jewish liaison officer

the Roman Empire—it contains, incidentally, what must be the earliest
extant appreciation of the defensive value of the sea to the people of
Britain (*Jewish War*, II, 378). As evidence of Josephus' own mind, it
surely witnesses to his lively appreciation of Roman strength and of the
futility of revolt on the part of so puny a nation as the Jews.

If this were Josephus' estimate of the situation on the eve of the
revolt in A.D. 66, the unexpected victory over Cestius Gallus may well
have caused him, for a moment, to forget the caution that his intellect
counselled and to make common cause with his people, who had achieved
such spectacular success that their act of faith did indeed seem to receive
divine confirmation. But a more realistic view must soon have prevailed,
and helped to inspire the ambiguous course that he pursued in Galilee as
a leader of the Jewish cause.

In the spring of 67 Vespasian, whom Nero had specially nominated
to deal with what was now a serious threat to the Roman control of the
Near East, advanced with considerable forces into Galilee. The Jewish
army, which Josephus had equipped and trained after the Roman fashion,
proved utterly incapable of withstanding the legionaries in the open field;
and Jewish resistance then took the form of the fanatical defence of fortified cities. Josephus himself sought refuge in Jotapata, where, according
to his own account, for forty-seven days the Roman assault was withstood
by the heroism of the garrison, aided by the ingenious stratagems that
sprang from his own fertile brain. With the fall of Jotapata occurred the
most curious event of Josephus' strange career. According to his own
account, when the town was taken, he succeeded in withdrawing, with
forty other persons, to the safety of a subterranean cavern. Their hiding-

place was betrayed to the Romans; and Vespasian sent a tribune named Nicanor, whom Josephus suspiciously describes as an old friend of his, with the promise that he should not be punished if he surrendered. From this point Josephus' narrative becomes one of the most extraordinary pieces of personal *apologia* that antiquity has preserved for us. He tells us, in the most circumstantial manner possible, that, on hearing Nicanor's proposal, he recalled former dreams, "in which God had foretold to him the impending fate of the Jews and the destinies of the Roman sovereigns". Holding himself to be an interpreter of dreams and "skilled in divining the meaning of ambiguous utterances of the Deity", he accordingly addressed himself in prayer to God, informing Him that "I willingly surrender to the Romans and consent to live; but I take thee to witness that I go, not as a traitor, but as thy minister" (*Jewish War*, III, 354).

Not surprisingly, Josephus found it more difficult to persuade his companions to surrender than to square his own conscience. Despite a long philosophical disquisition from their general on the crime of suicide, these Jewish patriots were resolved on ending their lives together, including Josephus, rather than yield themselves to the Romans. In his dilemma, as Josephus tells us, he put his trust in God's protection and proposed to his fanatical companions that they should draw lots to kill themselves in turn. The proposal pleased them, "for sweeter to them than life was the thought of death with Josephus" (*ibid.*, 390). Then—"should one say by fortune or by the providence of God?" he asks in parentheses—the fall of the lots so happened that all perished except himself and one other, whom he was able to persuade to remain alive. Thus, marvellously

Coin of the Jewish king Agrippa I (A.D. 37–44), with whose son Agrippa II Josephus was closely associated

Mettius Epaphroditus, the Roman
patron to whom Josephus dedicated
his later works (statue in the Villa
Altieri, Rome)

delivered from his predicament, Josephus lost no time in surrendering
himself. Brought before Vespasian, he assumed the rôle of a prophet; and,
when the Roman commander remanded him to be sent to Nero, he
announced that there was no need to send him to the Emperor, for he,
Vespasian, would soon be Emperor, and his son Titus would succeed him
in the office. Josephus himself comments that Vespasian was not impressed
and regarded the declaration as a trick.[1] The course of Roman politics,
however, after the death of Nero in 68, worked wonderfully to confirm
his prophecy; for in 69 Vespasian was proclaimed Emperor at Alexandria
and succeeded in founding an imperial line in which he was followed
in turn by his two sons, Titus and Domitian.

   With Vespasian's elevation, the fortunes of Josephus were established. After his father's departure, Titus assumed the direction of the
Jewish War, which culminated in the siege and destruction of Jerusalem
in the year 70. During these operations Josephus acted as his interpreter

---

[1] The prophecy was made at a private interview at which only Titus and two friends
were present; otherwise it might have had serious repercussions for Vespasian, if it had become
known in Rome at this time. Josephus' prophecy is briefly mentioned by Suetonius, *Vespasian*, V.

and chief intermediary in attempts to negotiate a surrender with rebels. His efforts as a mediator were signally unsuccessful, for the Jews fiercely rejected his overtures, regarding them as the actions of a traitor, and on one occasion nearly succeeded in slaying him. After the fall of the holy city of his people, Josephus accompanied Titus to Rome, where he took part in the spectacular triumph, the sculptured scenes of which still adorn the Arch of Titus in the Forum and show the spoils of the Temple being borne through the streets of Rome by the victorious legionaries.[2] He then settled in the capital, being granted a pension and the right of citizenship by Vespasian, and taking the name of Flavius Josephus in recognition of his dependence on the imperial favour. This patronage was continued by Titus and even by Domitian. In these comfortable circumstances, Josephus continued to live at Rome, occupied in literary work of his own choosing. He enjoyed the patronage of Epaphroditus, the contemporary Maecenas, to whom he dedicated his later writings; and it is even recorded that a statue was raised in Rome in his honour. The exact year of his death is not known; but he survived Agrippa II, who died in A.D. 100.

III

From this *résumé* of his career, it clearly emerges that Josephus had both unique opportunities of knowing the important events that he narrates and powerful reasons for misrepresenting some of those in which he was personally involved. But, allowing for the distortion occasioned by personal considerations, how are we to judge of his general credibility as the historian of the Jewish War against Rome, upon which he is practically our sole source of information? An adequate answer would demand far more space than is available in this chapter; but a few useful indications may be given. In the first place, it must be recognized that his *Jewish War* was a tendentious composition. In the preface to the extant Greek text, Josephus states that this Greek version was a translation of an Aramaic original which he had addressed to "the barbarians in the interior"—that is, to the Jewish Diaspora in Mesopotamia and the inhabitants of Adiabene, whose rulers were converts to Judaism. His purpose in thus writing is undoubtedly summed up in his concluding remark to his description of the power and efficiency of the Roman army—namely, that he was not so much concerned to praise the Romans as "to console

---

[2] See the illustration to Chapter 18, from the Arch of Titus.

View from the top of Masada, looking down on the Roman camps and circumvallation of the fortress, built for the operations against the Zealots in A.D. 73

those whom they have vanquished and to deter others who may be tempted to revolt" (III, 108). This statement of purpose, together with the fact that the work received the *imprimatur* of Titus, who also ordered its publication, invests it with the character of official propaganda. Nevertheless, Josephus understood the craft of a historian, and his account of the Jewish War was constructed from his own careful notes of what he had personally observed in the Roman camp, and the information that he had managed to glean from deserters about the situation in beleaguered Jerusalem. He was also able to use the commentaries (*hypomnēmata*) of Vespasian and Titus; and he maintained a correspondence with Agrippa II during the production of his work. Of the accuracy of his topographical descriptions, some convincing evidence came to light recently during the excavations at Masada, the Dead Sea fortress in which the last remnants of the Zealots held out against the Romans.

Doubts about the truth of Josephus' record of his country's struggle against Rome are concerned rather with matters of interpretation than with the description of events. And, surely, here we see the expression of Josephus' own mind, conditioned as it increasingly was by his own involvement in the interests of the Flavian dynasty. We have noted that his own realistic appraisal of the relative military strength of the Romans and the Jews rendered him proof against the politico-religious fanaticism that moved so many of his people. Consequently, he had no sympathy with the ideals of the Zealots, the extreme nationalist party,[3] and he thoroughly disapproved of their policy of violence—in fact, so deep was his antipathy towards them that he blamed them for the ruin of Israel and found no term too opprobrious with which to condemn them. This failure to appreciate the sincerity of Zealot patriotism is paralleled by his attitude to Messianism. For the age-long belief of the Jews that Yahweh, their god, would ultimately send a mighty champion, his Anointed One (Hebrew: *Mashīah*), to deliver them from their oppressors, had become almost an obsession, as Jewish impatience with their position of subservience to heathen Rome moved towards explosion-point. But this ancient oracle, as he calls it, had a wholly different meaning for Josephus. He did not deny its divine origin; but he maintained that his fellow-countrymen had grievously erred in their interpretation of it; for, according to him, the world-ruler, whose coming it had foretold, was in reality Vespasian, who was proclaimed Emperor on Jewish soil.

IV

Josephus could scarcely have given a worse impression of himself than that which emerges from the *Jewish War;* he reveals himself there as an unscrupulous opportunist, whose obnoxious conduct is rendered even more distasteful by his apparent hypocritical profession of the highest motives. His subsequent literary work, however, proves that he had a real love for his people and was ready, according to his own lights, to labour, and perhaps even endanger himself, on their behalf. Anti-semitism was already current in the ancient world before the atrocities occasioned by the Jewish revolt provided obvious cause for popular hatred of the Jews. Self-interest, therefore, might well have led Josephus to repudiate his native race and faith, as did Tiberius Alexander, an Alexandrian Jew of the same period, who rose high in Roman governmental service. Instead, Josephus undertook the literary defence of his people. He refuted the anti-semitic charges of Apion of Alexandria in a small work known as the *Contra Apionem*—a work that incidentally has an added value for us today because, in seeking to prove the antiquity of the Jewish nation, Josephus quoted extensively from the writings of authors that have not

---

[3] Josephus admits the religious character of Zealotism when he describes the founder of the movement as inciting the Jews to revolt by "upbraiding them for consenting to pay tribute to the Romans and tolerating mortal masters, after having God for their Lord" (*Jewish War*, II, 118.) See Chapter 19.

otherwise survived. But his *magnum opus* in this field is that generally known as the *Jewish Antiquities*. This great work, which Josephus published in his fifty-sixth year, A.D. 93–94, apparently took eighteen years to complete. It comprises a survey of the fortunes of Israel, from the creation of the world to the beginning of the revolt against Rome (A.D. 66). In the preface, Josephus states his belief that the whole Greek-speaking world would find an account of Jewish history and institutions, "translated from the Hebrew records", worthy of attention; and he adds, significantly: "I had indeed ere now, when writing the history of the war, already contemplated describing the origin of the Jews, the fortunes that befell them, the great law-giver under whom they were trained in piety and the exercise of other virtues, and all those wars waged by them through long ages before this last in which they were involuntarily engaged against the Romans."

The aqueduct at Caesarea, built early in the 2nd century by the Xth legion, which had played a prominent part in the Jewish War

By a strange irony of fate, the works of Josephus were treasured by Christians and not by his own countrymen, who continued to execrate his name. To Christians their great worth lay particularly in the record, contained in the latter books of the *Antiquities*, of the affairs of Palestine during the lifetime of Jesus of Nazareth and the beginnings of the Church. So great indeed was their interest that it appears that Christian scribes at an early period tampered with his original text, in order to make Josephus witness more convincingly to the truth of the Christian claim. The problem involved here is a fascinating one, but too complicated to permit an exposition of it in this context. Suffice it to say that, in the extant text of the eighteenth book of the *Antiquities*, an account is given of Jesus of Nazareth, which, if it had been written by Josephus, must surely mean that he was himself a Christian or at least admitted the truth of the Christian case. There is reason for thinking, however, that this account was either a Christian interpolation or an emendation of something unpalatable that Josephus had actually written about Jesus. The fascination of the problem lies in the fact, which we have noted, that Josephus was eminently well placed for knowing the origins of Christianity; and the value of his testimony as an independent witness would be immense, if it could be recovered.[4]

It was perhaps consonant with the irony of fate, expressed in the fact that his works were valued and preserved by members of a faith hostile to Judaism, that Josephus in the book that most discredits him—his autobiography—ends confidently with the words: "Such are the events of my whole life; from them let others judge as they will of my character." A generation that has come to understand the conflict of motives lying behind the terms "resistance" and "quisling" may not be so quick to condemn this ancient Jew for his ambiguous part in his nation's tragedy.

[4] On the problem of the "Slavonic Josephus" see the bibliography to this chapter. See also the author's book *Jesus and the Zealots*, pp. 359–68.

CHAPTER 21

Saint Paul

THE PROBLEM FIGURE OF PRIMITIVE CHRISTIANITY

*St. Paul's letters are full of bitter controversy. His
teachings did not finally prevail against those of
the Mother Church established at Jerusalem until the
Holy City had been overthrown and, in the cataclysm,
that Church had perished.*

I

Whoever turns the pages of that collection of ancient Christian
writings called the New Testament must surely conclude that Paul was
the Apostle *par excellence* of the Early Church. For no less than thirteen
separate items of that collection are entitled "Epistles of Paul", whereas
to no other apostle are more than two letters assigned. And that is not
all: not only do the writings of Paul comprise a quarter of the whole
content of the New Testament; the larger part of the *Acts of the Apostles*,
which sets out to record the early history of the Christian faith, is also
devoted to recounting his career.

But this impression of the primacy of Paul, both as a leader and
a teacher in the early Church, is strangely belied by the internal evidence
of Paul's own writings. When we read many of these documents, we at
once sense an atmosphere of great tension. Paul often appears profoundly
concerned with what he regards as the pernicious influence of certain
opponents who operate among his own converts; he sometimes uses the
fiercest invective against them, but he does so in a curiously oblique way,
never explicitly naming them.

Herein lies one of the fundamental problems that beset our under-

Portrait heads of St. Peter (*left*) and St. Paul (*right*), from a relief now in the Museum of Aquileia

standing of the origins of Christianity. How is it that Paul's own letters are so full of bitter controversy, yet the space given to his letters in the New Testament, as well as the evidence of the *Acts,* so signally attest his pre-eminence as the great leader and exponent of the faith, a position that is also abundantly confirmed in later Christian tradition?

An attempt to answer this question takes us into the intricate study of one of the most crucial episodes in the history of mankind. It is a field, too, where in recent years many new evaluations of traditional views have been taking place. The attempt is worth making; for it will afford an insight into the dramatic clash of two powerful personalities, with whom lay the future of one of the world's greatest religions.

II

It is necessary at the outset to appreciate the nature of our chief sources of information about Paul and his career. His own writings, of course, are of primary importance; but since they mostly comprise letters dealing with specific situations among the Christian communities that he had founded in various places in the Roman Empire, their interpretation is no easy task. Paul rarely outlines the situation with which he is dealing, because it was obviously well known to his readers: consequently, we are obliged to reconstruct the issue from passing references and allusions. Moreover, it must be remembered that the *Epistles* are essentially *ex parte* accounts of the basic conflict; as we shall see, we have no documents giving us the case of Paul's opponents, and our chief information about it must be inferred from Paul's own statements.

The *Acts of the Apostles* constitutes our secondary source. When it was written, some four decades separated it from the events it records; in the interval, the destruction of Jerusalem by the Romans in A.D. 70 had decisively altered the internal situation of the Church. The *Acts*, moreover, is clearly motivated by an apologetic purpose; it is concerned to trace the triumphant spread of Christianity from its beginnings in Jerusalem to its establishment in Rome, the metropolis of the world. Consequently, it gives an idealized picture of the past, passing lightly over the conflicts and representing the leading figures as amicably disposed to each other. However, the evidence of the *Acts* can be of great value when carefully interpreted; and it does supply us with two precious facts about Paul, namely, that he was a Hellenized Jew, being a native of the Cilician city of Tarsus, and that he enjoyed the privilege of Roman citizenship.

Both our sources are clear on one point of basic significance: Paul had never been an original disciple of Jesus, but had joined the Church sometime after the Crucifixion. Another important point on which they agree is that Paul was not converted to the new faith by the original community of disciples living at Jerusalem. His independence of the Jerusalem Christians at this crucial stage in his career was a matter of supreme importance to Paul, and it provides the key to the rôle that he was destined to play in the development of the new faith. Paul gives us his own version of the events that led up to his conversion in a context of great significance. He is writing to his converts in Galatia who are in danger of being won over by his opponents, and he seeks to prove to them the greater authority of his own teaching. The passage must be given in full in view of its fundamental importance: "For I make known to you, brethren, as touching the gospel which was preached by me, that it is not after man. For neither did I receive it from man, nor was I taught it, but *it came to me* through revelation of Jesus Christ. For ye have heard of my manner of life in time past in the Jews' religion, how that beyond measure I persecuted the Church of God, and made havoc of it. And I advanced in the Jews' religion beyond many of mine own age among my countrymen, being more exceedingly zealous for the tradition of my fathers. But when it was the good pleasure of God, who separated me, *even* from my mother's womb, and called me through his grace, to reveal his Son in me, that I might preach him among the Gentiles; immediately I conferred not with flesh and blood. Neither went I up to Jerusalem to them which were apostles before me: but I went away into Arabia; and again I returned unto Damascus. Then after three years I went up to Jerusalem to visit Cephas, and tarried with him fifteen days. But other of the apostles saw I none, save James the Lord's brother. Now touching the things which I write unto you, behold, before God, I lie not." (*Epistle to the Galatians* i. 11–20.)

The witness of this passage is immense. It informs us about three vital aspects of Paul's position. To defend his own teaching to his converts against that of his opponents, Paul asserts that he had not derived it from any human source, and, in particular, that he did not owe it to the original apostles at Jerusalem. This teaching, moreover, so he claimed, had been communicated to him directly by God for the express purpose of revealing "his Son in me, that I might preach him among the Gentiles". In other words, Paul maintains that his teaching was specially designed to be intelligible to those who were not Jews. He, therefore, admits by implication that his teaching differed from the tradition of the original apostles of Jerusalem; and he defends its novelty by claiming for it a direct divine origin.

We begin to perceive, then, the outlines of a truly amazing situation in the Christian Church within some two decades of the Crucifixion.[1] Paul is concerned to assert his independence of the Jerusalem apostles, and to explain that his teaching has been divinely revealed for the Gentiles. Since he had evidently to defend this teaching against certain opponents, it becomes necessary next to attempt to identify these opponents and the cause of their hostility to Paul.

In two separate writings Paul refers to these opponents and their rival teaching in very remarkable terms. In his Galatian letter, in a passage

---

[1] The *Epistle to the Galatians* dates from about A.D. 50.

Paul meets Peter outside the gates of Rome, where according to ancient tradition he suffered martyrdom. Twelfth-century mosaic in the Royal Chapel, Palermo

immediately preceding that quoted above, he writes in admonition to his converts: "I marvel that ye are so quickly removing from him that called you in the grace of Christ unto a different gospel; which is not another gospel: only there are some that trouble you, and would pervert the gospel of Christ. But though we, or an angel from heaven, should preach any gospel other than that we preached unto you, let him be anathema. As we have said before, so say I now again: If any man preacheth unto you any gospel other than that which he received, let him be anathema" (i. 6–9). The extraordinary language here is paralleled in the other passage that occurs in the *Second Epistle to the Corinthians* (xi. 3–6). A situation had apparently developed among his converts in the Greek city of Corinth similar to that with which Paul sought to deal in Galatia. He writes: "But I fear lest by any means, as the serpent beguiled Eve in his craftiness, your minds should be corrupted from the simplicity and the purity that is toward Christ. For if he that cometh preacheth another Jesus, whom we did not preach, or if ye received a different spirit, which ye did not receive, or a different gospel, which ye did not accept, ye do well to bear with *him*. For I reckon that I am not a whit behind the very chiefest apostles. But though *I* be rude in speech, yet *am* I not in knowledge; nay, in everything we have made *it* manifest among all men to you-ward."[2]

Paul's language in both these passages is as amazing as it is significant. Paul does in fact witness to the currency in the Church of two rival interpretations of the faith. For the references to "another Jesus" and "a different gospel" must mean that Paul's opponents were teaching a different version of the meaning of the person and rôle of Jesus from that of Paul.

But, who were these opponents? Obviously they were not some obscure sect of heretics; otherwise Paul would surely have repudiated them with all that vehemence of utterance of which he was so capable. Clearly they were men who could operate so effectively within Paul's own mission-field as to cause him such profound concern. But, most curiously, Paul never explicitly names them or questions their authority. He does, however, give a clue to their identity in the latter of the passages just quoted, when he significantly adds, after referring to this rival teaching, "I reckon that I am not a whit behind the very chiefest apostles".[3]

There can indeed be little doubt, in view of the facts just considered, as well as Paul's concern to assert his independence of the Jerusalem apostles, that those opponents who taught "another Jesus" were either the leaders of the Church in Jerusalem or their emissaries. In his Galatian epistle (ii. 1–10), when describing a later visit to Jerusalem, Paul gives more details of these leaders. They formed a kind of triumvirate of what he calls *stuloi* ("pillars"); their names are James, Cephas and John. The order in which these names are given is significant. James was clearly the leader; he precedes Cephas, i.e. Peter, who had apparently been the leader of the Apostles during the lifetime of Jesus. The fact that James was the brother of Jesus (*Galatians* i. 19) probably accounts, at least in

[2] The whole of this remarkable chapter should be read in the *New English Bible*.
[3] See the previous note.

part, for this pre-eminence. But a mystery seems to surround this James. According to the Gospels, he had not been an original disciple—indeed he had actually been unsympathetic to Jesus.[4] The *Acts* is strangely silent about his antecedents; it represents him suddenly, without explanation, as the head of the Church of Jerusalem. How he ousted Peter from the leadership of the new movement remains a veiled episode in the Christian documents. His blood-relationship to Jesus obviously gave him great prestige; but it is evident that he was also a man of strong character and ability. In his Galatian letter (ii. 11–14) Paul tells of a dispute at Antioch over whether Jewish Christians might eat with Gentile believers: Peter, who had agreed with Paul on the matter, had later withdrawn on the arrival of emissaries from James—surely a significant act of submission.[5]

It was, then, the teaching of the Jerusalem Church, presided over by James, from which Paul differed and against which he tacitly directs his innuendo by describing it as a "different gospel" that taught "another Jesus". But how did this Jerusalem gospel differ so radically from that of Paul? Here, unfortunately, owing to the total loss of the archives of the Jerusalem Church in A.D. 70, we have no direct evidence and can only make inferences from the extant evidence. A reasonable reconstruction, however, can be made that may only be outlined here. Since it is certain that the Jerusalem Christians continued to worship in the Temple at Jerusalem and to practise the ritual customs of Judaism,[6] it is evident that they did not regard their faith in Jesus as inconsistent with Jewish orthodoxy or as separating them from their national religion. To them Jesus was the promised Messiah of Israel. His death by crucifixion was a problem, since there was no expectation that the Messiah should die—rather was he to be the mighty champion who would free Israel from subjugation to a heathen conqueror. But Jesus' death could be explained as a martyr's death for Israel at the hands of the Romans: and it was believed that God had raised him from this death, so that he might soon return with supernatural power to "restore the kingdom to Israel" (*Acts* i. 6). Such, then, was the "gospel" of the Jerusalem Christians; it was

---

[4] James would undoubtedly have been one of those relatives of Jesus who tried to arrest him, believing him to be insane (*Mark* iii. 21).

[5] On the question of James see the present writer's book *The Fall of Jerusalem and the Christian Church*, pp. 27–8, 45–53, 95–100, 110–14; also his article "The Death of James the Just: a New Interpretation," in *Studies in Mysticism and Religion* (presented to G. G. Scholem), Jerusalem, 1967.

[6] See *Acts* ii. 46; iii. 1; v. 12, 42; x. 14; xi. 2, 3; xv. r; xxi. 20–26.

The Street Called Straight, Damascus, the city whither Paul was bound at the time of his conversion

conceived essentially in terms of Jewish thought, and it was calculated to emphasize and maintain that claim to a unique spiritual status and destiny that characterized Judaism. According to the evidence of the *Acts*, a considerable number of priests and Pharisees had, significantly, been won to the new movement (vi. 7; xv. 5).

If such was the "gospel of Jerusalem", what was Paul's version of the new faith? To elucidate this requires much involved exegesis, since Paul nowhere gives a formal statement of his teaching. It may be briefly summarized as follows. It would seem that, before his conversion, Paul was scandalized by the new movement because it taught "a crucified Messiah". On his conversion, whatever be the true nature of that mysterious episode, he became convinced that the crucified Jesus was alive and of divine status. But he had still to explain to himself the apparent scandal of the Crucifixion. It was at this point, so it would seem, that Paul came to differ fundamentally from the Jerusalem Christians and to assert his original independence of them. To him the death of Jesus could not be just a martyr's death for Israel; it must have some more profound and universal meaning. It was in his attempt to interpret this meaning that Paul surely drew, though unconsciously, on his Hellenistic background.

This Hellenistic background teemed with religious cults and esoteric philosophies that promised salvation of various kinds. Consciously Paul would vigorously have rejected them as the service of false gods or "philosophy and vain deceit". But he could not have escaped their influence, since they reflected the aspirations and fears of contemporary Graeco-Roman society and provided the current religious vocabulary. Two ideas of key importance, which these cults and philosophies severally enshrined and propagated, were those of the saviour-god and of the fallen state of man. The classic pattern of the saviour-god was afforded by the ancient Egyptian deity Osiris. The initiates of his mysteries believed that he had once died and rose again to life, and that by ritual assimilation to him they too could win immortal life after death.[7] The various esoteric philosophies that can be described as Gnostic, taught that each human being was compounded of an immortal soul imprisoned in a physical body. This unhappy condition was due to an original fall of the soul from its abode of light and bliss and its involvement in matter. By thus becoming incarnated in this world, the soul had also become subject to the demonic powers that inhabited the planets and controlled the world. From this state of perdition it could be rescued by acquiring a proper knowledge (gnōsis) of its nature; emancipated from its involvement in matter, it would ascend through the celestial spheres to its original home.[8]

Such ideas were foreign to orthodox Judaism. Hence it is significant that Paul, seeking to interpret the meaning of the Crucifixion, does so in terms that presuppose that mankind is enslaved by demonic powers, from whom they are redeemed through the death and resurrection of a divine saviour. Thus he writes: "So we also, when we were children, were held in bondage under the stoicheia of the world. But when the fulness of the time came, God sent forth his Son, born of a woman, born under the law, that he might redeem them which were under the law, that we might receive the adoption of sons" (Galatians iv. 2–5). The word stoicheia, which the Revised Version translates as "rudiments" and the Revised Standard Version as "elemental spirits", means in this context the demonic powers that were identified with the astral phenomena. Consequently, Paul envisages here the human situation as one of subjec-

[7] See Chapter 8.
[8] See Chapter 22.

tion to these demonic powers until redemption is won by the incarnated Son of God. Paul clearly regards the crucifixion of Jesus as achieving this redemption; but of the way in which this was achieved he is not so clear. Sometimes he invokes the concepts of the Jewish sacrificial cultus, thereby implying that the death of Jesus was a sacrifice; but who demanded it and to whom it was made, he is not explicit. A more coherent conception that links up with the thought of the Galatian passage just quoted is found in his *First Epistle to the Corinthians* (ii. 7–8): "But we speak God's wisdom in a mystery, *even* the *wisdom* that hath been hidden, which God foreordained before the *aeons* unto our glory; which none of the *archontes* of this *aeon* knoweth: for had they known it, they would not have crucified the Lord of glory." In this passage Paul professes to explain the Crucifixion as an event, arranged for in a divine plan conceived before the *aeons*, whereby the *archontes* of this *aeon* were led, unwittingly, to crucify a supernatural being called "the Lord of glory". Since "*archontes* of this *aeon*" is in effect an alternative designation for the demonic powers described as the *stoicheia* in the Galatian letter, a further phase of Paul's interpretation of the death of Jesus can be discerned. In other words, the hold which the demonic powers had over mankind was broken when they were deceived into crucifying the "Lord of glory".[9]

By employing ideas and terminology current in the Graeco-Roman world, Paul thus fashioned an interpretation, intelligible to his Gentile converts, of a movement that was in origin and essence Jewish. But that was not all. Whereas the rite of circumcision was the form of initiation into the spiritual privileges of Judaism, baptism was adopted as the means of entry into the Church of Christ. Paul's explanation of it is also significant of the *milieu* of syncretistic faith and practice upon which he drew. He writes to the Christians in Rome: "Or are ye ignorant that all we who were baptized into Christ Jesus were baptized into his death? We were buried therefore with him through baptism into death: that like as Christ was raised from the dead through the glory of the Father, so we also might walk in newness of life. For if we have become united with *him* by the likeness of his death, we shall be also *by the likeness*

---

[9] The (English) Revised Version misleads by translating "*archontes* of this *aion*" as "rulers of this world." The (American) Revised Standard Version is slightly more accurate, but still misleading, with its rendering of "rulers of this age." The *New English Bible* compromises by rendering the words successively as "governing powers of this passing age" and "powers that rule the world." The word *aion* is an essentially esoteric term meaning a period of time; not the physical world.

The Emperor Nero (54–68).
Both Peter and Paul were believed to have been martyred
during the persecutions of his
reign. Bust in the Museum of
the Thermae, Rome

of his resurrection" (*Romans* vi. 3–5). In other words, according to Paul,
in baptism the neophyte was ritually assimilated to Christ in his death
in order to be one with him in his resurrection. When Paul wrote, for
nearly three thousand years in Egypt resurrection from death had been
sought by ritual assimilation with the dying-rising god Osiris.

III

Such, then, was the gospel with which Paul believed that he had
been divinely entrusted for preaching to the Gentiles. In effect it replaced
the presentation of Jesus as the Messiah of Israel by that of Jesus as the
divine saviour of mankind; and it presupposed that all men, whether Jew
or Gentile, were equally in need of the same kind of salvation.

Such a gospel diverged fundamentally from the teaching of the
Jerusalem Christians, and it was obnoxious to them. For, not only did
it equate the Jew with the Gentile, thereby robbing the former of his
cherished sense of spiritual superiority; it made the Messiah of Israel into
the saviour of those hated heathen who had done him to death and daily
oppressed his people.

When the Jerusalem leaders understood the nature and implications of Paul's teaching, they set about opposing it. They were in a strong position to do this: for whereas they could repudiate Paul as a late-comer to the faith, he could not openly challenge their authority as the original disciples and "eyewitnesses" of Jesus. Accordingly, they sent out their emissaries among Paul's converts, asserting that theirs was the original and authentic version of the faith.

As his letters eloquently attest, the activities of these Jerusalem emissaries seriously threatened Paul's position, undermining his authority with his converts and causing them to accept a "different gospel" and "another Jesus". The situation eventually became so serious that Paul resolved to go to Jerusalem in an attempt to negotiate some *modus vivendi* with the authorities there. He sought to strengthen his case by taking with him a delegation of his Gentile converts, and a considerable sum of money which he had collected from his churches for the support of the Mother Church of Jerusalem. Paul seems to have been conscious that a visit to Jerusalem might be dangerous to him, and, according to the narrative of the *Acts*, he received several divine warnings of impending danger (*Acts* xx. 22–3, xxi. 10–14). To have persisted in going against such advice surely attests the urgency of the need that he felt to achieve an understanding with the Jerusalem leaders.

The outcome of the visit is recorded in *Acts* xxi; its testimony must be evaluated in terms of that apologetic purpose, which, as we have already noticed, inspires the work.

Paul was received by James, in the presence of the elders of the Jerusalem Church, and is represented as reporting on the success of his work among the Gentiles. Paul's coming to Jerusalem must clearly have embarrassed the Christians there, and James comes quickly to the point about the matter: "Thou seest, brother, how many thousands there are among the Jews of them that have believed; and they are all zealous for the law: and they have been informed concerning thee, that thou teachest all the Jews which are among the Gentiles to forsake Moses, telling them not to circumcize their children, neither to walk after the customs. What is it therefore? they will certainly hear that thou art come" (xxi. 20–22). The accusation was in fact a calumny; but it represented a plausible deduction from the logic of Paul's teaching. Reference to it by James was an astute move to solve the difficulty that Paul's visit had created. Accordingly, he proposes a test of Paul's Jewish orthodoxy: "Do therefore this that we say to thee: We have four men which have a vow on them; these take, and purify thyself with 'them, and be at charges for them, that they may shave their heads: and all shall know that there is no truth in the things whereof they have been informed concerning thee; but that thou thyself also walkest orderly, keeping the law" (xxi. 23–4). Paul was placed in a dilemma. James had shrewdly detected the weakness of his position, in that, while the logic of his teaching negated the peculiar spiritual claims of Judaism, he still endeavoured himself to remain an orthodox Jew. Now James challenged him to give a public demonstration of his orthodoxy: for the ceremony in which Paul should take part, i.e. the discharge of the so-called Nazarite vow, was performed in the Temple. To refuse the test was tantamount to a declaration of apostasy from his native faith: but, to accept it, was to admit the validity of Judaism on the order of the Jerusalem church.

Paul felt obliged to submit; but the sequel was disastrous to his cause. While performing the rites in the Temple courts, he was set upon by a Jewish mob and only rescued from death by the intervention of the Roman guard from the nearby fortress of the Antonia. To escape subsequent trial and certain condemnation by the Jewish authorities, Paul invoked his right as a Roman citizen to be tried before the imperial tribunal. After recording his survival from shipwreck *en route* for Rome, the narrative of the *Acts* finally leaves Paul a prisoner in the metropolis. What was his ultimate fate is unrecorded. According to ancient tradition he suffered martyrdom in Rome; and there is much reason for thinking that his appeal to Caesar did not prove successful.

The arrest of Paul appears to have taken place about the year 59, and from that date he seems to have been effectively removed from personal contact with his converts. What, then, was the fate of his work?

It would seem reasonable to conjecture that, since Paul had previously felt his position to be gravely threatened by the Jerusalem Christians, after his arrest the defeat of his cause was inevitable. His converts would have been left defenceless to the propaganda of the Jerusalem emissaries. That this did actually happen seems to be confirmed by the prophecy attributed to Paul, when he took farewell of the elders of the Church of Ephesus; it is recorded by the author of *Acts,* who knew what had happened: "I know that after my departure grievous wolves shall enter in among you, not sparing the flock; and from among your own selves shall men arise, speaking perverse things to draw away the disciples after them" (xx. 29–30).

If this situation had continued, without doubt Paul's interpretation

The Trophy of the Cross, from a
sarcophagus of the second half of
the fourth century, now in the
Lateran Museum, Rome

of Christianity would have perished and the faith evoked by Jesus would
have remained but the belief of a small messianic sect within the fold
of Judaism. But this was not to be. In the year 66 the Jewish nationalists
raised the standard of revolt against the Roman rule in Judaea. After four
years of bitter warfare, the Jewish state was finally overthrown, Jerusalem
ruined and its Temple destroyed. In that cataclysm the Christian Church
of Jerusalem disappeared.

In consequence of these tremendous events, the future of Christianity
was completely changed. The hold of the Mother Church of Jerusalem
was broken, and the Gentile Churches left to work out their own destiny.
This signal overthrow of Jewish Christianity led, understandably, to a
rehabilitation of Paul's reputation as the great exponent of the faith. When
the author of *Acts* wrote his story of the beginnings of the Church,
magnifying the part played by Paul, others were searching for Paul's writings
as the inspired teaching of a revered master and saint. Eventually the
Corpus Paulinum was formed, becoming one of the earliest components
of the New Testament, but bearing also within it evidence both of the
eclipse and the rehabilitation of Paul in the mind of the Church. For
the formation of Christian theology this rehabilitation was definitive. From
Paul's teaching has stemmed the foundational doctrine of Christianity,
namely, the incarnation of the Son of God, in the person of Jesus of
Nazareth, to be the saviour of mankind.

CHAPTER 22

The Gnostic Problem
in Early Christianity

Gnosticism was one of those developments of religious thought that, although finally rejected by Christians as heretical, "played a major part in the formation of Christian theology during the first three centuries of the Church's life . . ."

I

When the apostle Paul first came to Athens, he seems clearly to have sensed the drama of his situation. He believed himself to be the apostle divinely appointed to bring the new faith in Jesus, which had originated in Judaea, to the non-Jewish peoples of the Roman Empire. He understood, too, when he came to Athens, that he was at the heart and source of that wonderful Hellenic culture that all races then admired and strove to imitate. When, therefore, he was given the opportunity by certain Stoic and Epicurean philosophers of explaining his new faith at the Areopagus, according to the testimony of the *Acts of the Apostles*, he presented his case with great care and considerable skill.[1] He complimented the Athenians on their piety, evidenced by the superb monuments

---

[1] *Acts* xvii. 16–34. The question of what degree of authenticity is to be attributed to the many and various speeches in the *Acts* has been much debated by scholars. It is generally agreed that, while the author of the *Acts* followed the accepted literary practice of inventing speeches appropriate to specific occasions, he undoubtedly modelled his compositions according to definite traditions. Moreover, Paul's speech to the Athenians is of the greatest significance, even if it were only what the author of *Acts* thought the Apostle would have said on this occasion.

The Acropolis of Athens: the Areopagus, where Paul expounded his new faith, is the rocky eminence to the right of the Acropolis

of their city, and he adroitly quoted from one of their poets. His audience gave him a polite hearing until he came to what was one of the essentials of his message, namely, the resurrection of the dead. At the mention of this idea, he at once lost their sympathy; they began to mock him and, to Paul's evident discomfiture, the meeting broke up.

The episode was one of profound significance, for it revealed a fundamental difference between the Jewish and Greek evaluation of human nature and destiny. The Jew, following the age-long tradition of Semitic thought in this matter, conceived of man as a psycho-physical organism; which meant that belief in a life after death inevitably entailed the idea of the resurrection of the body, since a dis-embodied existence was inconceivable. The Greek, who had been brought up in the tradition of Platonic and Orphic thought, expressed his view of human nature in the saying *sōma sēma*, i.e. "the body, a tomb". In other words, according to this Greek conception of man, the immortal ethereal soul (*psychē*) was imprisoned in the material body (*sōma*); and, at death, the emancipated soul had the opportunity of escaping to that non-material realm to which it rightly belonged. Accordingly, when the Athenians heard Paul speak of the "resurrection of the dead" (*anastasis nekrōn*), to them this meant literally the "standing-up of corpses", and they were revolted by the idea and scandalized.[2]

[2] See Chapter 5.

But Paul seems to have appreciated Greek susceptibilities in this matter; and his subsequent Epistles to his Greek converts at Corinth show him attempting to accommodate his native Jewish conceptions to those of Greek thought. The undertaking was as necessary as it was momentous for the subsequent development of Western culture. For Christianity was not born into the world already equipped with a theology. It began as the personal faith of a small number of Palestinian Jews in the Messianic mission of Jesus of Nazareth. In their minds, this faith was integrated with their general outlook on life, that had been moulded by the distinctive culture of Judaism in which they had been nurtured. But when this faith was taken out of its Jewish *milieu* and preached to men of other races and cultural tradition, it had to be presented in terms of a religion answering to the universal needs of mankind. The difficulty that Paul encountered at Athens was, in fact, part of a greater problem.

To have presented Jesus as the Jewish Messiah to Greeks, Romans, or Syrians would have meant nothing to such people; indeed, it would more likely have offended them, since anti-semitism was strong at this time in the Roman Empire. But to present Jesus as the divine saviour of mankind, as Paul undertook to do, meant that an explanation had to be given of this rôle, which in turn meant explaining how mankind came to be in need of the salvation implied.

Traditional Jewish theology could afford little help here, because in Jewish thought the idea of salvation was closely bound up with the national hope of deliverance from foreign oppression; moreover, in Judaism the Messiah was not thought of as one who would save by his own sacrificial death.[3] In his *Epistle to the Romans*, Paul did indeed make some tentative use of the idea of the Fall of Adam to explain mankind's need of salvation; but his most coherent statement of soteriology is drawn from a very different source.

In his *First Epistle to the Corinthians*, Paul had occasion to contrast his teaching with that of other systems known to his readers; and, in so doing, he was led to give this significant account of his own: "Howbeit we speak wisdom among the perfect: yet a wisdom not of this world, nor of the rulers of this world, which are coming to nought: but we speak God's wisdom in a mystery, *even* the *wisdom* that hath been hidden, which

---

[3] The attempt has been made by some scholars to show that the Jewish community, to whom the now famous Dead Sea Scrolls belonged, believed in a suffering Messiah. The case has not been generally accepted as proved; moreover, if it were, it would only mean that the belief was held by sectaries, and it could not be regarded as representative of the body of contemporary Jewish thought.

God foreordained before the worlds unto our glory: which none of the rulers of this world knoweth: for had they known it, they would not have crucified the Lord of glory" (ii. 6-8). In our official English translations—the quotation here is from the Revised Version—the proper meaning of this passage is obscured at two crucial points. The Greek word translated "world" here, severally in its singular or plural forms, is *aiōn*, which does not mean this physical world or earth, but "time" or "age". Paul's use of *aiōn* here accordingly shows that he was thinking in terms of an esoteric system of "world-ages", that probably derived ultimately from Iranian and Babylonian sources, and that in various forms was much in vogue in current Graeco-Roman thought. Next, the words translated as "rulers of this world" (*archontes tou aionos toutou*) do not refer, as is popularly supposed, to the Roman and Jewish authorities who were responsible for condemning Jesus to death; they denote demonic beings, who were associated with the planets and believed to govern the lives of men on earth. In this passage, then, Paul is found explaining that, before the beginning of a series of world-ages, God determined to send into the world, for the good of mankind, a pre-existent divine being, whom the demonic rulers of the world, not perceiving his real nature, put to death and thereby in some way confounded themselves. This mysterious being, whom he calls "the Lord of glory", he apparently identifies with the historical Jesus, thus implying the operation of some process of incarnation of the divine and spiritual in the human and material.

Such an esoteric doctrine, that was apparently foreign to traditional Jewish thinking, suggests that Paul was using concepts derived from other traditions of religious speculation. But this is not all. Not only was it necessary to describe how the salvation of mankind was achieved; the human situation that required such salvation had also to be explained. The implications of the passage quoted above are confirmed and illustrated by various references and allusions in Paul's Epistles to his converts in Galatia and at Colossae (*Galatians* iv. 3, 8-10; *Colossians* ii. 8-15, 20). In brief, Paul envisaged mankind as enslaved by demonic beings, connected with astral phenomena, whom he describes by a variety of terms such as *archontes tou ainos toutou* and *stoicheia tou kosmou* ("the elemental powers of the universe"). From this mortal slavery mankind had, accordingly, been rescued by the divine being, who, incarnated in the person of Jesus, had been crucified mistakenly by these *archontes* who presumably, by thus unwittingly exceeding their rights, forfeited their control over men.

That Paul was able so adroitly to employ such esoteric ideas is not surprising when the fact of his cosmopolitan background is recalled. Paul, although a Jew by race and upbringing, had been born in Tarsus, a Hellenized city of Cilicia; he had acquired Roman citizenship; and he obviously spoke and wrote Greek with ease. But the fact that such ideas were available for him to use constitutes one of the greatest and most fascinating problems of the origins of Christianity. Its interest has now been greatly increased by an amazing discovery of fresh evidence.

II

That such ideas were current, and that Paul and other Christian missionaries could evoke a sympathetic response from a significant number

Gnostic amulets illustrating religious syncretism.

First row: Osiris, wearing a radiate crown, identifying him with Helios (sun);

Khnoubis or Agathodaemon represented as a lion-headed serpent. The two-horned serpent probably indicates that the amulet belonged to a member of the Ophite sect, who venerated the Serpent (*ophis*) of *Genesis* iii;

Jâo, the Demiurge. The inscription ABRASAX and the stars indicate his connection with Time, and relate him to Zurvān;

Crucifixion of Christ.

Second row: Woman giving birth, with a figure holding the Egyptian *ankh* to her face. Scene possibly represents Isis giving birth to Horus, or Mary to Christ;

Egyptian scarab, symbol of self-created sun-god Rē, with head of Helios;

Harpokrates, as sun-god, rising out of lotus. In the form of Nefertem, the image was an ancient Egyptian conception of the origin of the sun;

Sophia (Wisdom), whom the Gnostics identified with the Holy Spirit and female principle represented as a woman of Aphrodite type.

of men and women in various cities of the Roman Empire, show that, in the world of Graeco-Roman culture, there was a deep-seated concern for spiritual issues. This feeling was concentrated upon certain fundamental topics: the hope of immortality: the conviction that physical matter contaminated the soul: the way by which salvation might be attained.

Such spiritual needs called forth many and varied attempts to meet them. In addition to the ancient Greek mystery cults of Eleusis and of the Orphics, that assured their initiates of some form of immortality, many similar cults of Oriental and Egyptian origin established themselves in the Graeco-Roman world. These cults were usually centred in some divine saviour, of whom Osiris or Mithras are the most notable examples. But of perhaps even greater significance was the development of a body of mystical thought and pseudo-philosophical speculation, concerning human nature and destiny, that found expression in two groups of writings, the one known as *Hermetica* and the other described as Gnostic. Each claimed to mediate a secret knowledge or *gnōsis* that would enable those who comprehended it to understand their own true nature and the means whereby they might emancipate themselves from their present unhappy plight and return to the proper abode of their souls.

The *Hermetica* is so called because its contents purport to be revelations made by Hermes Trismegistos—"the thrice-great Hermes"—the Greek title for the ancient Egyptian god of wisdom, Thoth. The origins of these strange writings are very obscure; and no generally agreed conclusion has yet been reached about them by scholars who have specialized in Hermetic studies. Egyptian, Greek, Chaldean, Iranian, and Jewish influences have all been discerned in them. The problem of their date is equally difficult. Professor A. D. Nock, the latest editor of the *Corpus Hermeticum*, would date it, in its present form, for the period A.D. 100 to 300; but it is evident that some of its documents incorporate much older traditions. Despite all the uncertainty, however, that attends their original form and character, these Hermetic writings are of the highest importance for understanding the thought-world in which Christianity took its rise and formed its fundamental doctrines.

In one of the most notable of these Hermetic writings, entitled the *Poimandres*,[4] there is set forth a strange account of how the composite

---

[4] The meaning of the word "Poimandres" has been much discussed. It has been suggested that it may mean "the Shepherd of Men." In the tractate that bears his name, Poimandres, a semi-divine being, is described as "the Mind of the Sovereignty."

Christ as the Good Shepherd; statue in the Lateran Museum, Rome. The concept of a divine redeemer was held both by the Gnostics and by the early Christian Fathers

character of human nature originated, and how the immortal soul might free itself from its imprisonment in the physical body and return to its proper communion with God. Although this document is full of the most esoteric terms and imagery, its study is important for the insight that it gives into the mentality of many men and women at this period in Graeco-Roman society. The issue with which it is essentially concerned was basic to much religious and philosophical thought at the time: how was it that the ethereal immortal soul of man had come to be bound up in a material mortal body?

The answer given in the *Poimandres* is typical of this Gnostic speculation. It began by assuming the existence of *Anthrōpos,* the archetypal Man, who was the creation of *Nous* ("mind"), the fundamental principle of all reality, whose attributes were also *Zōē* ("Life") and *Phōs* ("Light"). This *Anthrōpos* became desirous of being himself a creator; and so he descended first to the planetary spheres and aligned himself with their seven governors. Not content with his situation here, he plunged lower through the spheres and came to the earth, where he cohabited with *Phusis* ("Nature"). From this union mankind was produced; and this fact explains the duality of human nature. Man is mortal physically through his derivation from *Phusis* ("Nature"); but he contains an immortal element that had descended from *Anthrōpos,* the essential or archetypal Man. Mankind's condition, however, was wretched, being subject to Destiny (*Heimarmenē*) and to those beings who controlled the planets. But the position was not completely hopeless. The individual, who through the divine *gnōsis* understood his own true nature and lived in accordance with that knowledge, would at death be freed from his mortal prison. He would ascend, first through the planetary spheres, where he would resign those qualities that his archetype had taken thence on his fatal descent. Next, he would rise to union with God, which constituted the final goal of those who had the essential *gnōsis.*

It has been well to describe this Hermetic interpretation of human nature and destiny first, because it was clearly a product of pagan thought and, in some of its elements, undoubtedly antedated the rise of Christianity. The similarity between the part played by the planetary powers in this interpretation and Paul's account of the divine scheme of salvation in his first Corinthian Epistle is certainly striking. While it would be unsound to conclude that Paul must have known of this Hermetic doctrine and consciously drew inspiration from it, the existence of such teaching illustrates the mental environment in which he and other early Christian thinkers worked out the theology of their new faith. But the problem that this Gnostic type of thought presents for our understanding of the development of early Christianity is not limited to that of evaluating the significance of the Hermetic tradition. Other forms of speculation of a similar character were closely associated with Christianity, and played a major part in the formation of Christian theology during the first three centuries of the Church's life, although they were finally repudiated as heretical.

Such forms of speculation are known technically as Gnosticism, since they all claimed the authority of some secret *gnōsis* concerning man's nature and destiny. They varied considerably in their terminology, in their cosmological theories and the way of life they inculcated. The early Christian Fathers, who sought to refute it, likened Gnosticism to the fabulous hydra, the monster that grew a new head for each one that was cut off. Despite their many variations, however, these Gnostic systems

shared other common features besides their claim to a secret *gnōsis*. Like the *Hermetica,* they were all essentially concerned to explain the dual nature of man, by means of some theory of the primordial descent of a spiritual entity and its involvement in physical matter. They also agreed in ascribing the creation of the material world to a kind of lower and somewhat evil-intentioned god, called the *Demiourgos.* In this way an attempt was made to separate the supreme god from any responsibility for the existence of physical matter, which was regarded as intrinsically evil. In some Gnostic systems, this *Demiourgos* was identified with the Jewish God of the Old Testament. The third feature that they had in common, and in which, incidentally, they differed from the Hermetic scheme, was the concept of a divine redeemer who descended to the earth to save mankind, the offspring of the fallen divinity which is sometimes called *Sophia.* This redeemer was named either *Sōtēr* ("saviour") or Christus. On his descent to earth, he united himself with the historical Jesus. The act of salvation was not achieved, as the orthodox Christians believed, through the crucifixion of Jesus, but through the secret *gnōsis* that Christ had communicated to a chosen few.

III

In the history of early Christianity, Gnosticism has long been a problem of peculiar difficulty. Despite its esoteric concepts and bizarre imagery, it is evident, from the deep

Mummy case of Artemidorus, *c.* A.D. 200. The top scene shows Anubis embalming the deceased as Osiris; the bottom scene represents his resurrection as Osiris was resurrected. These scenes attest the continuance of the ancient Osirian mortuary ritual into Graeco-Roman Egypt

hostility shown towards it by the Fathers of the Church, that Gnosticism
had constituted a very serious danger to the infant faith. Further, as the
above discussion of Paul's teaching shows, there is much to suggest that
the formative thinking of Christianity was done in an atmosphere greatly
influenced by the type of thought that finds expression in the Hermetic
and Gnostic writings. But hitherto a proper evaluation of Gnosticism
and the part that it played in the early evolution of Christianity has been
gravely hindered by the fact that, except for a few meagre documents,
we knew little of Gnosticism from its own witness. The bulk of our information came from the Christian writers who were concerned to refute
it. Moreover, although these writers did, indeed, know the movement
at first hand, there was reason to suspect that they often misrepresented
it and its exponents. But the situation has now been radically changed
by two discoveries, made during the last two decades, which mark the
beginning of a new phase in the study of this subject, so crucial to the
proper understanding of the development of one of the world's great
religions.

In 1947, the now famous discovery of a number of Hebrew scrolls
in a cave on the shores of the Dead Sea provided a new and wonderfully
rich body of information about Jewish life and thought in the first century
A.D. Although their investigation will take years to complete, several of

The Egyptian god of wisdom, .
Thoth, who, under his Greek title
"Hermes Trismegistos," gave his
name to the Gnostic *Hermetica,* a
collection of writings that purported
to contain revelations made by him.
Statue in the British Museum

these documents have already revealed that in Judaea, during the lifetime
of Jesus, there were communities of Jews whose religious beliefs were
curiously compounded with non-Jewish ideas. In short, we are beginning
to see that in first-century Palestine there was a considerable amount of
religious syncretism that must be thoroughly explored in any study of
the origins of Gnosticism. The discovery of the Dead Sea Scrolls, however,
has tended to divert attention from the significance of another discovery
made some two years earlier in Upper Egypt. In 1945, some natives
digging in the neighbourhood of Nag Hammadi, not far from the site of
the early Christian monastery of Chenoboskion, unearthed a large jar. On
breaking it, they found within thirteen leather-bound codices of papyrus
manuscripts. They sold them for a small sum, and eventually twelve of
the volumes were acquired by the Coptic Museum at Cairo, while the
thirteenth found its way to Zürich, where it was bought for the Jung
Institute and has consequently come to be known as the Jung Codex.
For a variety of reasons, some political, the publication of the contents
of the find has been long delayed; and it is only recently that some of
the manuscripts have been made available for general study.

The find is undoubtedly of the first magnitude in importance. On
examination, it has been found that the thirteen codices contain forty-nine
separate works. They are all written in Coptic, which was the language
of the native Egyptians during the Roman period; but they appear to
be translations into this language of Greek originals. The dates of the
manuscripts are not certain; they are by different hands and were probably
written about A.D. 350 to 400. The original works from which they were
translated are evidently much earlier, and some perhaps date from the
second century A.D. The nature of their contents indicates that these books
formed the library of a Christian Gnostic community.

Space does not permit here of a detailed list of the contents of the
collection, many titles of which would surely appear strange to those
unfamiliar with this field of study. But some representative examples may
be mentioned. There is a *Letter of James*, which purports to be written
by James, the Lord's Brother, giving an account of a revelation that the
Risen Christ is alleged to have made to the Apostles James and Peter
before his Ascension. A document entitled the *Gospel of Truth*, also an
esoteric revelation, is of peculiar interest because it appears to be a work
mentioned by Irenaeus, the celebrated Bishop of Lyons (*c.* 180), and may
perhaps have been composed by Valentinus, a famous Gnostic teacher

Fresco from Herculaneum, showing the worship of Isis, one of the many mystery cults that expressed the "deep-seated concern for spiritual issues" prevalent in the Graeco-Roman world

of the second century. A work attributed to Zoroaster, and four Hermetic tractates, attest the range of the sources upon which these Gnostics drew; and the latter writings also provide significant evidence of a connection between this Christian Gnosticism and the Hermetic tradition of thought.

The work that has so far stirred the greatest interest, which in turn has given it priority of general publication, is the so-called *Gospel according to Thomas*. Its esoteric nature is significantly stated in its preface: "These are the secret sayings which Jesus, the Living One, spoke, and he wrote, even Didymos Judas Thomas." This writing is of the highest importance both to the historian of early Christianity and to the student of the New Testament. For not only is it representative of the Gnostic handling of the Gospel teaching, but it also appears to preserve traditions that derive from some early Jewish Christian source; and it may help to throw light on the enigma of the beginnings of Christianity in Egypt.

The complete publication and thorough study of these Nag Hammadi documents will obviously occupy the attention of specialists for many years. And it is too early yet to attempt to forecast what their conclusions are likely to be. But it is evident that we shall soon be in a position to evaluate Gnosticism from its own witnesses, and not only through the representations of its opponents. For the historian, however, the importance of the issue does not reside primarily in being able to judge how fair to the Gnostics were the defenders of what became the orthodox form of Christianity. It is of far greater moment to understand the way in which the fundamental doctrines of Christianity were evolved in the environment of Graeco-Roman culture where Gnostic speculation flourished and was influential. And that is not all. We need to have a more thorough understanding of those forces within the Christian Church that enabled it to resist certain aspects of Gnostic thought, while formulating a soteriology of a highly speculative character. Christianity has often been distinguished as the historical religion *par excellence;* it was during these vital years of its dependence upon, and resistance to, Gnostic influences that this character was surely formed.

CHAPTER 23

The Devil

IN FAITH AND HISTORY

"The influence of the idea of the Devil in Christian culture has been profound." It has inspired both noble works of art and the most degrading superstitions.

The origin of religion has been explained in terms both of monotheism and polytheism. Mankind, according to the first theory, personified as a single being the creative and controlling power manifest in the universe, locating it in the sky as a "High God". The polytheistic explanation is based on the assumption of a primitive animism, whereby the diverse manifestations of power in the world are assigned to many sources—hence many gods. Which of these interpretations is the sounder, or whether some other theory is more likely, cannot be debated here. But we may remark that, however he has sought to explain the world in which he finds himself, man has to account for the existence within it of both a good, creative and an evil, destructive force. A survey of the many, and often strange, forms in which he has tried to do this is intrinsically interesting, and it repays study for the insight it affords into the mental and emotional bases of the great historic cultures of our race.

I

Such a survey may best begin with a brief examination of the evidence of ancient Egypt; for not only is Egyptian religion the earliest for which we have adequate documentation, but it provides an instructive example of the gradual personification of evil.

337

LE STRYGE.

Le Stryge, the brooding Devil on one of the towers of Notre Dame, Paris (from an etching by Charles Meryon, 1821–68)

Our earliest source, the *Pyramid Texts* (c̠. 2400 B.C.), shows that the Egyptians deified many forms of cosmic phenomena and power; pre-eminent among them was the sun, which, under the title of Atum-Rē, was regarded as the benign creator of the world. Many hostile beings, of supernatural character, are mentioned in these *Texts*, mainly as opposing the dead pharaoh's safe passage to felicity in the next world. They are, however, of minor significance compared with the mysterious figure who plays the criminal rôle in the legend of Osiris. Constant reference is made in the *Texts* to this legend, which provided the explanation of the royal mortuary ritual.[1] Briefly, it related how Osiris, a good king of Egypt long ago, had been murdered by his evil brother named Set. The original nature of Set is obscure: he seems to have been an ancient Egyptian god associated with the desert and with the more violent aspects of nature, such as the tempest, thunder and earthquake. He was identified with various obnoxious animals, and was usually represented with an animal's head,

[1] See Chapter 8.

possibly that of an okapi or an ass. In Egyptian thought, Set progressively
became the personification of all evil: not only was he the murderer of
Osiris, but he was equated with Apophis, the dragon of darkness that
daily threatened the sun-god with extinction. It was probably through
his rôle in the drama of Osiris, however, that he acquired his deepest
emotional significance for the individual Egyptian. Since Osiris became
a type of "Everyman", in that each Egyptian hoped, by the efficacy of
the mortuary ritual, to be one with Osiris in his death and resurrection,
Set came to typify the death that strikes down each individual. As the
personification of evil, Set, in the process of time, had also a strange career
outside the main stream of Egyptian tradition. Thus, in the first century
A.D., we find him identified by the Greek writer Plutarch with the monstrous Typhon of Greek mythology: while among the Gnostics he was
assimilated with Jaldabaôth, the evil being with whom they equated the
god of the Jews, vilified by them as the wicked creator of this lower
material world.

When we turn to the other great civilization of the ancient Near
East, we find a curiously different situation. The peoples of Mesopotamia
never personified evil in the sense of having a god of evil, although they
had a lively belief in maleficent demons, to whom they attributed disease
and other misfortunes. This remarkable omission is undoubtedly due to
their practical and realistic view of the universe, and of man's place in
it. They regarded the universe as divided into four parts: heaven, earth,
the waters under the earth, and the *kur-nu-gi-a*, the "land of no-return",
that is, the abode of the dead. Each of these cosmic divisions had its
own divine ruler. Nergal, who ruled the dead, by virtue of his office
was regarded as a terrible being and was greatly feared. But he was not
seen as the god of evil, who opposed the good order of the other gods;
instead, he was an essential representative of the divine economy. According to the Mesopotamian vision of human destiny, mankind was created
to serve the gods, who had withheld immortality from its members. The
raison d'être of the individual, therefore, was to serve his divine masters
for so long as they chose: if he served well, they would reward him with
prosperity; if badly, they left him exposed to maleficent demons. When
they had no further use for him, he had no destiny here, and he passed
below the earth to the realm of Nergal.[2]

_____

[2] See Chapter 10.

A medieval representation of Christ rescuing a human soul from the Devil
(from a MS in The John Rylands Library, Manchester)

II

From the records of these two earliest civilizations we may now turn
to two kindred traditions, in which the personification of evil or the
destructive factor in life finds most notable expression. These traditions
may be designated Indo-Iranian, because they stem from a common
source, namely, from the culture of those Aryan peoples who invaded
Iran and north-western India during the latter part of the second millennium B.C.

There is reason for thinking that these Aryans once worshipped a
sky-god of ambivalent character who personified both light and darkness,
creation and destruction. Vestiges of such a deity are found in some of

the references of the *Ṛig-Veda* to two closely associated gods, Varuṇa and Mitra; some scholars have discerned similar traits behind the Iranian deities Ahura Mazdāh, Vayu, and Zurvān. Investigation of such origins is still a matter of lively debate among the specialists concerned. More certain is the situation at the later period, both in India and Iran.[3]

We get perhaps our best initial insight into the Indian conception of deity through the great theophany passage in that supreme classic of Hinduism, the *Bhagavad-gita* or "Song of the Lord". This great epic, which probably dates from about the second century B.C., is concerned to set forth the duties of the pious Hindu, who is a devotee of the god Vishnu. The exposition takes the form of a dialogue between the prince Arjuna and his charioteer: the latter proves to be Krishna, one of the *avatars* or incarnations of Vishnu. After Arjuna recognizes the real nature of his companion, the deity reveals his divine power and splendour. But Arjuna feels that he has not seen all; and he implores Vishnu to unveil his true self. The god assents; and the revelation is terrible. Before, Vishnu had shown himself as the beneficent creator and sustainer of the world. Now, he shows the other side of his being—Arjuna is appalled by the vision and cries for succour:

> Thy mighty form with many mouths beholding,
> O mighty-armed, with eyes, arms, thighs, and feet,
> With many bellies, and many dreadful fangs,
> The worlds all tremble, even as I do also.

The affrighted Arjuna sees all forms of being passing swiftly to their destruction in the awful mouths of Vishnu. Then the god speaks in explanation:

> Know I am Time, that makes the worlds to perish,
> When ripe, and come to bring on them destruction.[4]

This ambivalence of deity, whereby the creative and destructive forces of the universe are personified as twin aspects of the same being, takes a curious form in the other great Hindu god, Śiva. Here the two basic aspects of existence are represented in the dual guises of the god. He personifies the dynamic persistence of life, symbolized by the *lingam*,

---

[3] See Chapter 13.
[4] XI. 23, 32, trans. E. J. Thomas, *The Song of the Lord* (Murray, 1948), pp. 85, 86.

the mighty generative organ of the creator. Conversely, he is Bhairava, "the terrible destroyer", who haunts cemeteries and the places of crema- tion, wreathed about by snakes and with a necklace of skulls. But stranger is another development that has especially appealed to the Hindu imagina- tion. The activating energy (*śakti*) of Śiva has been transformed into the goddess Kālī ("Time"): in her image the Indian artist concentrates all the symbolism of destructive evil. The colour of Kālī is black: her red tongue lolls out between her hideous fang-like teeth; she wears a chaplet of severed heads, and her many hands hold symbols of her nature—the exterminating sword, scissors that cut short the thread of life, the lotus of eternal generation. To Western eyes she appears a veritable devil; yet she is not so to the Indian view. For Kālī personifies an essential aspect of reality. Although decay and death be evil to man, in the Hindu evaluation they are necessary factors of temporal existence, and, as such, they must be venerated.

Before turning to consider the ambivalent conception of deity in ancient Iran, we must note another development of Indian demonology. In the later Vedic literature, reference is made to Māra, a personification of death. This Māra becomes an important figure in Buddhism, acquiring the title of *pāpman*, "the evil one". According to Buddhist tradition, at a critical moment of the Buddha's enlightenment, Māra played the rôle of the demonic Tempter. He appeared as the lord of this world and all its sensual delights, to distract the Buddha-to-be from his purpose of learning the cause of suffering and the way of release therefrom, which knowledge he was to pass to mankind. The episode is often depicted in Buddhist art: the meditative hero is shown encompassed by the seductive forms of the daughters of Māra, who typify Desire, Unrest, and Pleasure.

In Iran, the ancient Aryan view of creation and destruction as complementary aspects of divine activity produced an interpretation that differed from the Indian. Our earliest literary evidence is the teaching of Zarathustra as recorded in the *Gathas*.[5] According to the prophet, the universe was the battle-ground of two primordial spirits: the "Bounteous Spirit" (*Spenta Mainyu*), characterized by Truth and Light; the Evil Spirit (*Angra Mainyu*) or the Lie (Druj), the principle of Evil and Darkness. Over them stood Ahura Mazdāh, the "Wise Lord", whose relationship to them was obscure—he was probably their creator, or they were orig-

[5] See Chapter 13.

Et dinibolus q̃ ſeducebat illos miſſus ẽ ī ſtag-
nũ igniſ ꝛ ſulphuriſ ubi ꝛ beſtia, ꝛ pſeudo ꝓ̃he
te cruciabũtur die ac noctè in ſcla ſclõꝝ.

The Mouth of Hell, from a medieval illuminated manuscript in The John
Rylands Library, Manchester

inally aspects of him. In the process of time, this dualism was greatly
elaborated in detail, and to Ahriman (as the *Angra Mainyu* was later
known) was ascribed everything evil. Thus his baleful activity is described
in the *Greater Bundahishn* (ninth century A.D.): "From the material
darkness which is his own essence (the Destructive Spirit) fashioned forth
the body of his creation in the form of coal (?), black and ashen, worthy
of the darkness, damned as the most sinful noxious beast. From material
self-will he fashioned forth concupiscence (*varan*). . . . Next he created
the essence of the demons, evil (disorderly) movement, that spiritual
property from which destruction came to the creatures of Ohrmazd (i.e.
Ahura Mazdāh). For he created a creation by which he made his own
body more evil that (in the end) he might be powerless."[6]

In the religion that stemmed from Zarathustra, the destructive principle, operative in the universe, was thus definitely regarded as evil and
contrary to the will and purpose of the supreme deity. Moreover, its
activity was believed to be of a limited duration. According to later
eschatological speculation, Evil, personified in Ahriman, would wage a
battle of cosmic proportions against Good, personified in Ohrmazd, for

[6] Translated by R. C. Zaehner, *The Dawn and Twilight of Zoroastrianism* (Weidenfeld and Nicolson, 1961), pp. 253-4.

nine thousand years: at the end of this period, after variations of fortune, Ohrmazd would prevail and Ahriman, with the demonic hordes, be overthrown.

The Iranian personification of evil, which thus found expression in Zoroastrianism, also had its place in the cult of Mithra. In this cult, which became so popular in the Roman Empire, it took the form of Time that brings decay and death to all men. It was represented in the *mithraea* as a monstrous being, having a human body and a lion's head. It was winged, signifying the flight of Time; and about its body was entwined a great serpent that symbolized the tortuous passage of the sun through the zodiac. Its hands held the keys of destiny and a long sceptre, denoting authority—for, as "Time the Destroyer", it was identified with Ahriman, the Prince of Darkness, who, for a while, was Lord of this world.[7]

This Iranian dualism profoundly affected the religious thought of the Graeco-Roman world through various channels. We have just seen its importation to the West in Mithraism. Its influence is equally obvious in Gnosticism, where the evil demiurge was closely associated with Time—indeed, Gnosticism provides a most interesting case of syncretism, in that Jaldabaôth, the wicked creator of the world, was identified with both the Egyptian Set and the Persian Ahriman. On Manichaeism also, which so gravely troubled the early Christian Church, the impress of Iranian dualism is clearly evident; Ahriman was the prototype of the principle of darkness, of evil, and of matter, against which Mani urged his disciples to struggle. But the particular importance of this complex of imagery, centred in the personification of evil, is that it provides the setting in which both the Hebrew and Christian conceptions of the Devil received their definitive form.

III

The personification of evil, so that it becomes an independent power hostile to the supreme deity, encountered two mutually opposing currents of thought in Hebrew religion. The exaltation of Yahweh, the god of Israel, as the sole Lord and Creator of the universe, meant that he must also be the author of all things. On the other hand, the prophets proclaimed, with increasing emphasis, that Yahweh loved righteousness and hated iniquity. The inevitable tension between these two doctrines grad-

[7] See illustrations to Chapter 4.

ually made itself felt; and the process is reflected in the evolution of the idea of Satan.

The ancient Hebrews shared, with other neighbouring Semite peoples, in a multifarious demonology. They believed that spirits of various kinds, usually malevolent, invested many places, especially the desert, and were intent on attacking mankind. Although they were greatly feared, none of these demons, however, was regarded as a "god of evil", ruling and directing the forces of evil. On the other hand, since Yahweh was held to be all-powerful, in the earlier stages of their culture down to the Babylonian Exile in 597 B.C., the Hebrews were ready to ascribe evil actions to Yahweh himself or to demons employed by him. Thus, in the account of the final plague of Egypt, which probably dates from about 800 B.C., Yahweh is depicted as passing through Egypt on that fatal night to kill the first-born of both man and beast (*Exodus* xi. 4–8, xii. 29–30). Or, to take another example, in the tragic story of Saul, the first king of Israel, it is related that it was an evil spirit from Yahweh that induced the madness that brought Saul to his disastrous end—it caused him, among other things, to attempt the murder of David: "And an evil spirit from the Lord (i.e. Yahweh) was upon Saul, as he sat in his house with his spear in his hand; and David played with his hand. And Saul sought to smite David even to the wall with the spear . . ." (1 *Sam.* xix. 9–10).

A new concept of evil appears from about the time of the Return from the Exile (538 B.C.), which takes the form of a supernatural being, whose attitude towards men is particularly hostile. This being is called Satan: the name derives from a root meaning "to oppose". The word, used with the article, in the sense of "the Adversary", first occurs in *Zechariah* iii. 1–2, where the prophet recounts a vision: "And he shewed me Joshua, the high priest, standing before the angel of the Lord, and Satan standing at his right hand to be his adversary. And the Lord said unto Satan, the Lord rebuke thee, O Satan: yea, the Lord that hath chosen Jerusalem rebuke thee." In this passage, Satan is represented as a kind of public prosecutor ranged against the high priest on an occasion of deep national dejection. That this Satan, though hostile in character, was not yet regarded as the opponent of Yahweh, is evident from the part he plays in the prose prologue to the *Book of Job*.[8] There he appears, curiously

[8] See Chapter 12.

"The Knight, Death and the Devil"; engraving by Albrecht Dürer (1471–1528). The Devil is here represented in animal form, strangely reminiscent of Set, the Egyptian god of evil

but significantly, as one of the "sons of God": "Now there was a day when the sons of God came to present themselves before the Lord, and Satan came also among them" (*Job* i. 6). He is described as a kind of observer of human conduct. To God's question, "Whence comest thou?", Satan replies: "From going to and fro in the earth, and from walking up and down in it." When Yahweh praises the integrity of Job, Satan scoffs, insinuating that it is motivated only by self-interest. In the subsequent testing of Job, Satan acts with the permission of Yahweh, subject to one proviso—that Job must not be killed (*Job* i–ii. 7).

It will be well to pause here in our survey, and note the significance of a celebrated passage in the pre-Exilic literature. It is the Yahwist account of the Temptation of Adam and Eve (*Genesis* iii. 1–23). Through the suggestion of the serpent, the first human pair are led to disobey their Creator, and so bring upon themselves and their descendants the penalty of death and other evils. Owing to the use of this story in Christian theology, the serpent has been equated with Satan or the Devil; but this equation is not made in the original text.[9] Although it is described as "more subtil than any beast of the field which the Lord God has made," the serpent is essentially an animal and a creature of Yahweh. In the narrative, however, it serves as the agent through whom mankind incurs its fatal destiny. While nothing is said of the serpent's intention towards Adam and Eve, the impression is given that the original responsibility for the Fall lies with the serpent and not ultimately with the divine Creator. In other words, we may perhaps discern here a dawning awareness of the impropriety of attributing the origin of evil to Yahweh.[10]

More certain evidence of this change of attitude is found by comparing two versions of a curious episode in the reign of David. In the earlier account (2 *Sam.* xxiv. 1–15), it is told how "the anger of the Lord was kindled against Israel, and he moved David against them, saying, Go, number Israel and Judah." Having thus caused David to take a census, Yahweh then punishes him for the deed by sending a terrible pestilence on the nation. This account of Yahweh's conduct clearly shocked the later author of the *Books of the Chronicles* (c. 250 B.C.), who attributes the idea of the fatal census to the suggestion of Satan (1 *Chron.* xxi. 1).

The ascription of the origin of evil to Satan becomes the established tradition of Jewish thought during the Hellenistic period. In the apocalyptic writings of the age, a demonology is developed that is virtually dualistic, and was undoubtedly influenced by Iranian ideas. As there was no official direction or definition of theological doctrine in early Judaism, various lines of interpretation were pursued, often containing contradictory elements. This tendency shows itself especially in the demonology. For example, whereas the author of the *Wisdom of Solomon* (first century B.C.) held that death entered the world "by envy of the devil" (ii. 24), the writers of the *Book of Enoch* and *Jubilees* (second to first centuries B.C.)

[9] In Hebrew literature the equation is first made in the *Wisdom of Solomon*, ii. 24; see below.
[10] See Chapter 12.

speculated on the curious fragment of folklore preserved in *Genesis* vi. 1-7, telling of the union of the "sons of God" with the "daughters of men." They interpreted the act as a fall from grace of certain supernatural beings, who, in consequence, became demons, bringing evil into the world. Their leader, named variously Satan, Mastema, Semyaza, Azazel (in other sources, Belial or Beliar), became the supreme adversary of God. His original high estate is remembered in the myth of Lucifer, and is doubtlessly alluded to by Jesus of Nazareth, when he exclaims in a moment of evangelical success: "I beheld Satan fallen as lightning from heaven" (*Luke* x. 18). The idea of a primordial war in heaven was also developed as an alternative explanation for the origin of Satan and his hosts. It appears in the Christian *Book of the Revelations,* being evidently derived from Jewish sources and an ancient myth concerning the dragon of chaos: "And there was war in heaven: Michael and his angels *going forth* to war with the dragon; and the dragon warred and his angels; and they prevailed not, neither was their place found any more in heaven. And the great dragon was cast down, the old serpent, he that is called the Devil and Satan, the deceiver of the whole world; he was cast down to the earth, and his angels were cast down with him" (*Rev.* xii. 7-9).

This gradual evolution of a dualistic view of the world in Hebrew religion could, with some reason, be interpreted as the necessary outcome of the prophetic teaching, that Yahweh was both omnipotent and moral. Israel did not live in a cultural vacuum, however; and it is significant that it is in the post-Exilic period, when Iranian influences began to penetrate the Mediterranean area, that the idea of a supernatural adversary, personifying evil, first emerges. Any doubt that may have existed, that Judaea was immune from such extraneous ideas, ended with the discovery of the Dead Sea Scrolls in 1947. For, in the so-called *Manual of Discipline,* that records the views of this Jewish community at the beginning of the present era, a dualism thoroughly reminiscent of that of Zoroastrianism finds expression: "In the abode of light are the origins of truth, and from the source of darkness are the origins of error. In the hand of the prince of lights is dominion over all sons of righteousness; in the ways of light they walk. And by the angel of darkness is all dominion over the sons of error; and in the ways of darkness they walk. And by the angel of darkness is the straying of all the sons of righteousness, and all their sin and their iniquities and their guilt, and the transgressions of their works in his dominion, according to the mysteries of God, until his time, and

The Last Judgment: bas-relief on the Cathedral of Orvieto. In this Italian Christian picture of the Devil some trace of ancient Etruscan demonology may be discerned

all their afflictions and the appointed times of their distress in the dominion of his enmity."[11]

IV

It was from such a background of belief that Christianity stemmed. The dualism, manifest therein, is even more thorough in the Gospels than in most of the Jewish sources. It is strikingly expressed in the account of the temptation of Jesus. In the Matthaean version (iv. 1–11) the spirit of evil is called, in turn, "the devil" (*diabolos*),[12] "the tempter" (*ho peirazōn*), and Satan. He is represented, without apparent contradiction, as claiming authority over the kingdoms of the world: "And the devil said unto him, To thee will I give all this authority, and the glory of them: for it hath been delivered unto me; and to whomsoever I will I give it " (*Luke* iv. 6). In the Gospels, the Devil is also pictured inflicting disease on people and leading some into evil action; he is described as "the prince of this world," and "the prince of the devils." In other writings, he is described as "fashioning himself into an angel of light," and as having "the power of death."

[11] Trans. M. Burrows, *The Dead Sea Scrolls* (Secker and Warburg, 1956), p. 374.
[12] Our word "devil" is ultimately derived from the Greek *diabolos*, meaning "slanderer," therewith commemorating Satan's original rôle.

In the development of Christian soteriology, the idea of the Devil played a major part. When the death of Jesus began to be interpreted as a sacrifice to redeem mankind, two fundamental questions had to be answered: from what situation had mankind to be redeemed, and to whom was the sacrifice made? We find the first attempts to provide an answer in the writings of St. Paul. This great Apostle, who was mainly responsible for making an originally Jewish movement intelligible to the peoples of the Roman Empire, regarded mankind as subject to demonic powers that ruled the universe (*Galatians* iv. 3). To deliver men from their bondage, Paul taught that God had sent His Son into the world in the form of a human being, i.e. Jesus. The demonic powers, deceived as to his true identity, crucified him, and thereby incurred defeat, losing their hold over men (2 *Corinthians* ii. 6–9 ; *Colossians* ii. 15, 20).[13]

This Pauline interpretation was quickly elaborated by subsequent Christian thinkers into a contest between God and the Devil. It took two main forms. The motif of the deception of the Devil became particularly popular. According to Amphilochius of Iconium (*c.* 340–395) and Gregory of Nazianzus (329–389), the Devil was caught like a greedy fish: for God baited the fish-hook of Christ's divinity with the bait of his humanity. St. Augustine of Hippo (354–430) preferred the simile of a mouse-trap: the Devil was enticed by the Cross, baited with the blood of the incarnated Christ. Sometimes a less mythological imagery was used. The idea of a ransom-price was evoked; Christ's death being the payment made by God to redeem men from the hold that the Devil had justly acquired over them.

Christ's descent into Hades was also another favourite subject of early Christian speculation concerning the Devil. Inspired doubtlessly by the metaphor of entering into the house of the "strong man" and spoiling his goods in *Matthew* xii. 29, the belief grew up that, after dying on the Cross, Christ entered the underworld of Satan to release the souls of the just who had died before his coming. In the so-called *Gospel of Nicodemus* or *Acts of Pilate,* which may date from the fourth century, the defeat of Satan is graphically described: "Then the King of Glory took hold of the head of the chief ruler Satan, and delivered him unto the angels and said: Bind down with irons his hands and feet and his neck and his mouth, and he delivered him unto Hades saying: Take him and keep him safely until my second coming."[14]

[13] See Chapter 21.
[14] Trans. M. R. James, *The Apocryphal New Testament* (Oxford, 1926), p. 136.

It seems to have puzzled the early Christians why, if so signally defeated, Satan was still so evidently active in the world. Hippolytus of Rome actually put the question: "Were the Devil already bound, how could he then still mislead the faithful and persecute and plunder mankind?" The evidence of personal experience to the contrary was indeed too strong; and the Devil remained a disturbing reality to Christians for many generations.

Medieval art and hagiography attest as strongly, and certainly more vividly, the current belief in the Devil that the theologians expounded in treatise and sermon. The diabolical image, brooding over Paris, on the cathedral of Notre Dame, is a superb example of many figures elsewhere that reminded men of their supreme Adversary.[15] In churches, realistic representations of Doomsday also familiarized the faithful with the demonic assistants of Satan who would consign the damned to eternal perdition in Hell. And the legends of the saints told of many dire struggles with the Devil and his minions, the temptation of St. Anthony being the classic example, so strangely and so terribly illustrated by Hieronymus Bosch.

The manner in which the Devil was conceived affords an interesting insight into the human imagination. Various traditions contributed to the image: memories of the pagan gods, regarded as demons by Christians; Etruscan demonology; the promptings of primitive fears; Biblical allusions, especially from the *Book of the Revelations*. This variety of source finds expression in a strange variety of images. The identification of Satan with the primaeval dragon and the "old serpent," in *Revelations,* provided an obvious motif. Its ominous associations caused black to be generally recognized as the fitting hue of the prince of darkness and evil. His shape was usually conceived as anthropomorphic; but it could be completely animal, as in Dürer's famous etching of the "Knight, Death and the Devil." Dante saw him in the lowest circle of the Inferno having three heads, and eternally employed, devouring the three arch-traitors, Judas Iscariot, Brutus and Cassius. The more familiar figure, with horns, tail, and cloven hooves, is clearly reminiscent of the classical god Pan and the satyrs; but it may perhaps preserve some memory of the Celtic god Cernunnos, whose horned image appears on several surviving monuments. As the horned god, the Devil was most notably the object of the witchcult that survived on into the seventeenth century. Indeed, so closely was the

15 The so-called "Le Stryge" was actually set up by Viollet-le-Duc, sometime before 1850; but this and other diabolical monsters replaced those of the Middle Ages on Notre Dame.

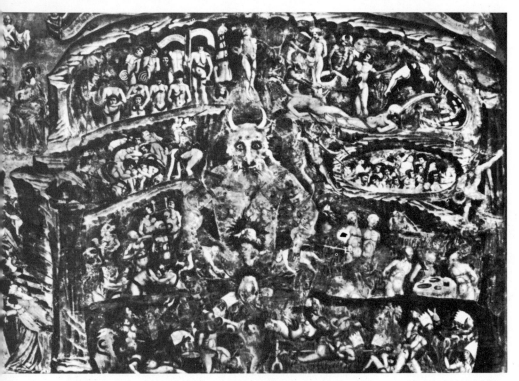

The Devil presiding at the centre of Hell. From the "Last Judgment" of Andrea Orcagna (1308–1368), in the Camposanto, Pisa. Some of the imagery is probably derived from Dante's *Inferno*

Devil associated in the popular mind with witchcraft that, in 1,279, a Northumberland jury actually acquitted a man who had speared to death **an alleged witch, on the ground that he acted "in self-defence, as against** the devil."

The influence of the idea of the Devil in Christian culture has been profound. It inspired some of Milton's noblest verse, and provided the *raison d'être* of the Faustus legend, which has continued to prove so pregnant a theme in European literature. Equally, it has been the source of some of the most degrading superstitions and terrible acts of fanaticism: Satanism, "black masses", the practice of witchcraft and the horrors of its suppression, demoniac possession and its exorcism, culminating in the cruel and scandalous happenings at Loudon in 1634. With the growth of rationalism and the secularization of Western society, belief in a per-sonalized form of evil has inevitably declined. It is difficult to assess how far professed Christians now believe in the Devil. The Churches vary in the degree and nature of their acceptance or rejection, the traditional view remaining stronger in Catholicism. In their liturgical practice, however, most Churches continue to use prayers, litanies, hymns, and credal affirmations that assume the Devil's existence and activity. Indeed, so integral is the personification of evil to the structure of Christian theology that its complete abandonment cannot be foreseen. It is perhaps not without significance that at the entrance of Coventry Cathedral, so widely acclaimed as the latest expression of Christian thought in art, the sculptured figure of the Archangel Michael stands over that of the recumbent and fettered Satan.[16]

Repulsive though its expressions have often been, in the history of human ideas the personification of the destructive factor, operative in the universe, has had an immense cultural influence. Where it has been identified as a necessary aspect of reality, resignation has tended to characterize the attitude taken towards life. Where it has been regarded as evil, and opposed to the purpose of a good Creator, it has produced a dynamic optimism that looks forward to the ultimate triumph of the good. A comparative study of the civilizations concerned will significantly attest the difference.

[16] See the illustration on p. 369.

↘ CHAPTER 24

Angels

THE HISTORY OF AN IDEA

> *The images of angelic ministrants that play so large*
> *a part in Christian symbolism were derived by European*
> *painters and sculptors from the religious conceptions*
> *of the ancient Near East, of Greece and Etruria*

I

Each day, throughout the world, wherever the Christian liturgy is performed, the celebrant addresses God in words long hallowed by centuries of use: "Therefore with Angels and Archangels, and with all the company of heaven, we laud and magnify Thy glorious Name . . ."[1] These solemn words recall the tremendous imagery of the *Revelation of John*, which was in turn inspired by Isaiah's vision of the seraphim (*Isaiah* vi. 1–3). Thus, daily, Christians invoke imagery already ancient when the prophet John wrote towards the end of the first century A.D.—imagery that was in fact current in Israel as far back as the eighth century B.C. This imagery has, moreover, been conceived in a very realistic manner, as the long tradition of Christian art vividly attests.

But what of the nature of the beings who figure in this ancient and revered imagery as "Angels and Archangels?" The name itself provides little information. Our English word transliterates a Greek word *angelos*, which in the Greek version of the Hebrew Bible translates the word *malâk*, meaning "messenger." This term denotes a characteristic function of

---

[1] The words quoted here are from the Anglican *Book of Common Prayer*, which translate corresponding passages in the Latin Mass and the Greek Eucharistic Liturgy.

354

The Winged Victory of Samothrace, now in the Louvre. From "Victories" such as this, Christian artists seem to have adapted the conventional representation of an angel

angels in both Hebrew and Christian thought: namely, the conveying of messages from God to men. Beings who perform such an office are not, however, known only to Hebrew religion and Christianity. Homer tells how "wind-footed, swift Iris," possibly a personification of the rainbow, bore the messages of Zeus from lofty Olympus down to the world of men. Greek mythology, moreover, provides the classic figure of the divine herald in Hermes, complete with his staff and winged sandals. The traditional Christian representation of angels as winged anthropomorphic beings, clad in long flowing robes, also affords little clue to their origin; indeed, it serves rather to suggest that the Christian conception is a fusion of ideas derived from several religious traditions. Thus, for example, in the Etruscan tomb of the Volumni, near Perugia, two winged figures kneeling beside a sarcophagus might well represent Christian angels but for the fact that they were carved more than a century before the birth of Christ. Similarly, at Pompeii, in the celebrated frescoes of the Villa of the Mysteries, a winged figure, reminiscent of an angel, was depicted scourging an initiate to the rites celebrated there before Vesuvius overwhelmed the city by its eruption in A.D. 79.

These examples, selected from among many that could be cited, show that here, as in other aspects of its faith and practice, Christianity probably borrowed from other religious traditions. That it should have done so from Judaism is readily understandable, since Christianity originated in Judaea, and its founder and his first disciples were Jews. But the essential Christian doctrines were thought out in the world of Graeco-Roman culture; and it was natural that ideas current there should also have had some influence. Judaism moreover had not developed in a cultural vacuum: throughout their long history, the Jews had absorbed many ideas from neighbouring peoples. Syncretism in religion is, indeed, a well-known phenomenon of human culture; and it has to be carefully assessed in evaluating the growth of human ideas and institutions; for often syncretism reflects some basic intellectual or emotional need. A historical and comparative study of the idea of angels is accordingly both interesting and instructive.

II

When we get our first insight into the human mind through the written records of Egypt and Mesopotamia, about the middle of the third millennium B.C., we find that religion is already complex in belief and practice. Many supernatural beings are recognized: some form a hierarchy of deities, who rule respectively over various parts of the universe or the lives of men; others appear to be of lesser status, and their attitude towards mankind may be benevolent or hostile. The ancient Mesopotamians conceived of protecting genii called *shêdu* and *lamassu*. The latter were represented as huge winged lions or bulls, human-headed, and images of them stood at the entrances of temples and palaces to ward off evil. These genii were also looked upon as guardian spirits by ordinary persons as the following invocation from a magical text shows: "May the good *Shêdu* walk on my right hand, may the good *Lamassu* walk at my left hand." The people of ancient Egypt also conceived of a supernatural personal guardian; but one that more nearly anticipated the Christian idea of a guardian angel. It took the curious form of the *ka*, a kind of invisible double, or *Doppelgänger*, that was born with every person and accompanied him throughout life, its function being denoted by a hieroglyphic symbol of two protecting arms. Another facet of the primitive mind, relevant to our subject, finds significant expression on an Egyptian votive stele, of the New Kingdom period (1580–1090 B.C.), which was erected

Angelic musicians, as portrayed by the fifteenth-century sculptor, Agostino di Duccio, on the facade of the Oratorio di San Bernardino at Perugia

by a father in honour of Amun-Rē for healing his son. Amun-Rē was the great state god of Egypt; the father, a humble craftsman. Consequently the father thinks no more of addressing the deity directly than he would the King. Instead, he conceives of an "Amun who hears the prayers," sitting before the portal of Amun's great temple at Thebes, as a vizier would receive petitions for transmission to the Pharaoh. In other words, the protocol of the royal court on earth naturally suggested what would be the order of things in heaven, or wherever the deity was thought to dwell.

Another important factor in the evolution of the idea of angels has been the tendency to monotheism in certain religions. The process has rarely been so logically pursued that belief in the existence of other deities has been completely eliminated. The idea of such supernatural beings has usually been too firmly established in tradition; and it was easier to transform than to eradicate. The classic example of such transformation occurs in Zoroastrianism. The prophet Zoroaster (c. 567 B.C.), when he exalted Ahura Mazdāh as the only god of the universe, changed the *daevas*,

who were the deities of his people's ancestral religion, into demons; but
there were certain other divinities designated later as the *Amesha Spentas,*
or "Bounteous Immortals," whom he represented as the personified
attributes or companions of Ahura Mazdāh.[2] These beings, known in later
Mazdeism as the Amshaspands, were conceived as surrounding the throne
of the Supreme Deity, and serving him in governing the universe; they
seem later to have been associated with the planets, and, as such, played
an important rôle in the astralism and Gnostic cults that were so influential
in the world of Graeco-Roman culture—it has been suggested that they
provided the prototypes of the later Jewish idea of seven archangels who
waited immediately upon God.

We find, then, that among the peoples of the ancient Near East,
who were neighbours to the Israelites, supernatural beings were known
who mediated between the gods and men. They were generally conceived
as benevolent and protective: the conception reflected the need of ordinary
people for the assurance of a divine guardian or helper who would be
closer to them than the great gods of the official cults. It is on the
background of such belief that we may now evaluate the Hebrew conception of angels, both in its origin and in its evolution.

III

The earliest forms of Israelite angelology are obviously to be sought
in the pre-Exilic literature (before 597 B.C.). What is found there is
exceedingly strange; and it clearly reflects a very primitive stage in the
development of Hebrew religion. In a number of passages reference is
made to a class of beings called "beni ha-Elohim," or "sons of God."[3]
In *Genesis* vi. 1–2, 4, they figure in a curious episode, the very crudity
of which attests its great antiquity: "When men began to multiply on
the face of the ground, and daughters were born to them, the sons of
God (*beni ha-Elohim*) saw that the daughters of men were fair; and they
took to wife such of them as they chose. . . . The Nephilim were on
the earth in those days, and also afterward, when the sons of God came
in to the daughters of men, and they bore children to them. These were
the mighty men that were of old, the men of renown."[4] Here we surely

---

[2] See Chapter 13.
[3] *Elohim* is plural, meaning "gods." In its plural form it is invariably used for the god
of Israel.
[4] Most Bible quotations here are from the American Revised Standard Version.

have a piece of primitive folklore. *Nephilim* is a rare word meaning "mighty ones," "heroes," or "giants." Accordingly, there appears to be preserved in this passage some recollection of a tradition, similar to that found among other ancient peoples, that once there was a race of mighty men, the offspring of divine fathers and human mothers. The "sons of God," who appear here in a somewhat doubtful guise as progenitors of giants, are represented elsewhere as closely associated with Yahweh, the god of Israel—this is clearly implied in *Psalm* lxxxix.6: "Who among the sons of God is like unto Yahweh?" Even more remarkable perhaps is the picture given of them in the *Book of Job* (i. 6–8): "Now there was a day when the sons of God came to present themselves before the Lord, and Satan also came with them. The Lord said unto Satan "Whence have you come?" Satan answered the Lord, "From going to and fro on the earth, and from walking up and down on it'." In this passage the *beni ha-Elohim* appear as a company of attendants in the court of Yahweh, and Satan is obviously one of them. Whether Satan's activity in patrolling the earth was typical of the others, and for what purpose, is not disclosed.

Another aspect of early Hebrew thought in this connection is found in a number of passages where reference is made both to the "angel (*mâlak*) of Yahweh" and to Yahweh himself, in such a manner that the two appear to be equated. An instance occurs in the famous account of Moses and the Burning Bush in *Exodus* iii. 2–4: "And the angel of the Lord (i.e. Yahweh) appeared to him (Moses) in a flame of fire out of the midst of a bush. . . . And Moses said, 'I will turn aside and see this great sight, why the bush is not burnt.' When the Lord (Yahweh) saw that he turned aside, God called to him out of the bush . . ." From such passages it would seem that no clear distinction was yet drawn between Yahweh and his angel, and that the latter connoted a special localized manifestation of Yahweh. Later, the distinction was made; and we read in *Isaiah* lxiii. 9 of the "angel of his (Yahweh's) presence" as a separate being acting on behalf of Yahweh.

A further development, possibly indicating a transformation of the earlier idea of the *beni ha-Elohim*, is found in *Psalm* ciii. 20–1: "Bless Yahweh, ye angels of his, ye mighty in strength that fulfil his word, hearkening unto the voice of his word. Bless Yahweh, all ye his hosts; ye ministers of his that do his pleasure." Here the angels are conceived not only as members of Yahweh's heavenly court, but also as his agents and emissaries.

Already, in the pre-Exilic period, other supernatural beings were known that were later incorporated into the angelic hierarchy attendant on Yahweh. The prophet Isaiah, in recording a vision that he had in the year of King Uzziah's death (742 B.C.), tells how he saw Yahweh enthroned in the temple, and "above him stood the seraphim; each had six wings: with two he covered his face, and with two he covered his feet, and with two he flew" (*Isaiah* vi. 1 ff.). These seraphim are mysterious beings; they clearly derive from a very primitive stage of Hebrew culture. In this passage they are regarded as anthropomorphic, since they have hands and feet and can speak. But the word "seraphim" means "burning ones"; and it is evident that originally they were supernatural serpents, with a burning bite—indeed, as the curious episode recorded in *Numbers* xxi. 6 indicates, they were once worshipped; for the bronze serpent that was then made was called a *saraph,* and it continued to be a cult-object in Judah down to the reign of Hezekiah (716–687 B.C.). Equally mysterious are the cherubim. According to *Psalm* xviii. 10, they transport Yahweh: "He (Yahweh) rode on the cherub, and flew; he came swiftly upon the wings of the wind." Their association in this passage with storm-clouds appears more clearly in Ezekiel's account of the vision of Yahweh which he had when an exile in Mesopotamia (593 B.C.): "As I looked, behold, a stormy wind came out of the north, and a great cloud, with brightness round about it, and fire flashing forth continually, and in the midst of the fire, as it were gleaming bronze. And from the midst of it came the likeness of four living creatures. . . . And this was their appearance: they had the form of men, but each had four faces, and each had four wings. . . . As for the likeness of their faces, each had the face of a man in front; the four had the face of a lion on the right side, the four had the face of an ox on the left side, and the four had the face of an eagle at the back. Such were their faces. And their wings were spread out above . . ." (*Ezekiel* i. 4–5, 10–11). There is much reason for thinking that Ezekiel's conception of these fantastic beings was coloured by his acquaintance with the images of the *lamassu,* guarding the temples and palaces of Mesopotamia. Ezekiel seems to envisage the cherubim as bearing the chariot of Yahweh; but there were other conceptions. According to *Genesis* iii. 24, Yahweh set the cherubim to guard the Garden of Eden after Adam had been expelled for his disobedience. In the instructions, given in *Exodus* xxv. 18–20, for the construction of the Ark of Yahweh, which was the chief cult-object in the original Temple of Jerusalem, Moses is directed: "you shall make two cherubim of gold; of hammered work shall you make them, on the two ends of the mercy seat. . . . The cherubim shall spread out their wings above, overshadowing the mercy seat with their wings, their faces one to another; toward the mercy seat shall the faces of the cherubim be." Specialist opinion today is inclined to think that the cherubim were similar to the winged sphinxes found in Phoenician art—their images adorning the Ark are also reminiscent of the winged figures of the goddesses Isis and Nephthys that protect the shrine of Tutankhamen.

It would seem, therefore, that, in the pre-Exilic period, as Hebrew religion emerged gradually from its primitive polytheism, many supernatural beings, of diverse origin and status, were recognized alongside Yahweh. The tendency was to regard them as the companions or ministers of Yahweh; and, since at this stage the idea of the Devil had not emerged, these beings were sometimes regarded as emissaries of Yahweh to bring evil as well as good on men; which they did, most notably, on Saul and Ahab.[5]

After the Babylonian Exile (*post* 538 B.C.) Jewish angelology rapidly developed into a complicated structure of belief. With the final triumph of monotheism, the tendency grew increasingly stronger to emphasize the transcendence of Yahweh. Consequently, it became necessary to ascribe all divine activity in this world as due, not to the direct interposition

[5] I *Sam.* xviii. 10–12; I *Kings* xxii. 19–23. Cf. Chapter 23.

Byzantine archangel; panel of an ivory diptych, executed in the sixth century

of Yahweh, but to supernatural agents acting on his behalf. This led to a multiplication of angels to perform the multifarious tasks that human hopes and fears ascribed to divine providence. Hence it was believed that there were angels charged with certain cosmic functions, and others to represent specific nations; angels to execute special missions; angels to record human conduct; while each human being (or each Jew) had his own guardian angel—the last belief finds incidental, but significant, expression in the words of the apostles when, incredulous on hearing of Peter's escape from prison, they exclaim: "It is his angel" (*Acts of the Apostles* xii. 15).

Besides this elaboration of the Angelic office, personal names now begin to be given to certain angels—according to Rabbinic tradition, angel-names were brought back to Palestine by the exiles returning from Babylonia. At the head of the hierarchy were seven archangels. A concise list of them, and of their respective offices, is given in the apocalyptic *Book of Enoch* (xx), which, in the section concerned, probably dates from about 200 B.C.: "And these are the names of the holy angels who watch. Uriel, one of the holy angels, who is over the world and over Tartarus. Raphael, one of the holy angels, who is over the spirits of men. Raguel, one of the holy angels, who takes vengeance on the world of the luminaries. Michael, one of the holy angels, to wit, he is set over the best part of mankind and over chaos. Saraqâêl, one of the holy angels, who is set over the spirits, who sin in the spirit. Gabriel, one of the holy angels, who is over Paradise and the serpents and the Cherubim. Remiel, one of the holy angels, whom God set over those who rise." [6] It is interesting to note that Death now became personified in the form of an angel called Sammael, who is imagined as armed with a sword; sometimes he is regarded as one of the fallen angels, and is equated with the Serpent that brought the penalty of death on mankind.

In the post-Exilic period the angels are also divided into two groups: those who continue faithful in their service of Yahweh, and those who revolt against him and fall from their original high estate. The origin of this idea of fallen, and therefore, evil angels is obscure. One of the most notable explanations is derived from the account of the liaison of the *beni ha-Elohim* with human women, recorded in *Genesis* vi. 1-2, 4, which has already been mentioned. In that account there is no explicit con-

---

[6] Trans. R. H. Charles, *The Book of Enoch* (S.P.C.K., 1921), p. 46.

demnation of the liaison; later, however, it was seen as the cause of these angels' downfall. The *Book of Enoch* is again informative on this development of belief. In the passage concerned (chap. xix), the archangel Uriel is represented as showing Enoch the terrors of Sheol, the Hebrew underworld: "And Uriel said to me: 'Here shall stand the angels who have connected themselves with women, and their spirits, assuming many different forms, are defiling mankind, and shall lead them astray into sacrificing to demons as gods (here shall they stand, till the day of the great judgment in which they shall be judged till they are made an end of'."[7] This belief finds a curious reflection in St. Paul's warning that women should veil their heads at divine service, "because of the angels" (I *Corinthians* xi. 10).

There was much speculation also concerning the angelic nature. Philo of Alexandria (30 B.C.–A.D. 45), the Jewish *savant* who sought to synthesize Hebrew religion and Greek philosophy, identified angels with the Greek *daimones*, spiritual beings who mediated between gods and men. He defined the angels as "the army of God, blessed spirits (*psychai*),

[7] Trans. R. H. Charles.

One of the winged spirits of Etruscan mythology carries off a dead woman; painted plaque of the sixth century B.C., from a tomb at Cerveteri, now in the Louvre

without bodies." It would also seem that, despite the inferences drawn from *Genesis* vi. 1–2, 4, the angels were regarded as sexless. In the celebrated dispute between Jesus of Nazareth and the Sadducees over the resurrection of the dead, recorded in *Mark* xii. 18–27, Jesus declares: "when they arise from the dead, they neither marry nor are given in marriage, but are like the angels in heaven."

Much thought was also given during this period to the organization of the angelic hierarchy and the number of the angels. According to certain rabbis, the heavenly host was mustered in seven divisions, each under the command of an archangel, and each numbering 496,000 angels. Such speculation seems to be reflected in the words attributed to Jesus when he was arrested in Gethsemane: "Do you think that I cannot appeal to my Father, and he will send me more than twelve legions of angels?" (*Matthew* xxvi. 53).[8]

I V

This rich and complex angelology the Christian Church inherited. It invests the Gospel narrative of the life of Jesus from beginning to end. The conception of the future Saviour is announced to Mary, his mother, by the archangel Gabriel; angels proclaim his birth to the shepherds, and minister to him after his temptation in the wilderness. Frequent reference to angels occurs in the recorded teaching of Jesus; he foretells his Second Coming in glory, accompanied by the angels, and he is strengthened by an angel during his agony in Gethsemane. The accounts of the Resurrection and the finding of the Empty Tomb are especially significant for showing how quickly angelic action in this miracle was elaborated in the primitive Christian communities. In the earliest account (*Gospel of Mark* xvi. 1–8), the women find "a young man . . . dressed in a white robe," sitting in the Empty Tomb, who tells them that the crucified Jesus is risen and departed from the Tomb. In the later Lukan Gospel (xxiv. 4) this "young man" (in the original Greek, *neaniskos*, not *angelos*) has become "two men (in Greek, *andres*) . . . in dazzling apparel," whom the women apparently identified as angels (xxiv. 22–3). The record of the Matthaean Gospel, of about the same period but of a different provenance, is more dramatic: "And, behold, there was a great earthquake; for an angel of the Lord descended from heaven and came and rolled

---

[8] A Roman legion mustered 5,000 infantry in the early Principate.

back the stone, and sat upon it. His appearance was like lightning, and his raiment white as snow" (xxviii. 2–3).

In the *Acts of the Apostles*, which traces the progress of Christianity from its beginnings in Jerusalem to its establishment in Rome, the intervention of angels is also mentioned on several crucial occasions. These descriptions of angelic activity in the narrative writings of the New Testament reflect a deeply rooted belief that powerfully influenced the formation of Christian doctrine in the vital period of the first century. St. Paul, that great seminal thinker, who left an indelible impress on Christianity, envisaged the universe as inhabited and, to a large degree, controlled by supernatural forces. He designates these by a variety of names. Some are evidently derived from the angelology of Jewish apocalyptic tradition; for beside angels, he mentions "thrones" (*thronoi*), "dominions" (*kuriotētes*), "principalities" (*archai*), and "authorities" (*exousiai*). His attitude towards them is curiously ambivalent. In his *Epistle to the Colossians*, he associates them closely, in one place (i. 15–17), with Christ. The passage requires quotation: "He (Christ) is the image of the invisible God, the first-born of all creation; for in him all things were created, in heaven and on earth, visible and invisible, whether thrones or dominions or principalities or authorities—all things were created through him and for him. He is before all things, and in him all things hold together." In this passage Paul was evidently feeling his way towards some definition of Christ more transcendental than that of the Jewish Messiah, with its overtones of nationalist politics. The monotheistic tradition, in which he had been nurtured, forbade his identifying Christ absolutely with God. On the other hand, he was profoundly concerned to exalt Christ far above the angelic powers. He claims, accordingly, that these powers were created by Christ, and, therefore, were inferior to him in nature and status. As he develops his thought here, Paul, however, goes on to equate these angelic powers with the "elemental spirits (*stoicheia*) of the universe," and claims that, by his Crucifixion, Christ "disarmed the principalities and powers and made a public example of them, triumphing over them in it (the Cross)" (*Colossians* ii. 8, 15). Behind this strange language and thought lies an esoteric system that modern research is gradually elucidating from the Gnostic and Hermetic writings of the early Roman Empire. Speculation concerning human nature and destiny at this period had drawn upon many sources, pre-eminently on Mesopotamian astralism and Jewish angelology. The misery of man's

Angel with sickle, from
an early fourteenth-century
manuscript of the Apoca-
lypse at Trinity College,
Dublin

existence in this world of space and time was explained as due to the
involvement of man's soul with matter, owing to the fall of his archetype
from his original place with God. The situation meant also that man was
alienated from God, and subject to supernatural powers who ruled the
planetary sphere above the earth. Man's salvation, therefore, meant his
deliverance from these powers—the *stoicheia*, or *archai*, and *exousiai*. This,
according to Paul, Christ had accomplished.[9]

A somewhat later facet of this primitive Christian concern to
differentiate Christ from the angels, and to show his essential superiority
to them, is seen in the *Epistle to the Hebrews*. Thus the author declares:
"When he (Jesus) had made purification for sins, he sat down at the right
hand of the Majesty on high, having become as much superior to angels
as the name he has obtained is more excellent than theirs. For to what
angel did God ever say, 'Thou art my Son, today I have begotten thee'?"

[9] See Chapter 22.

. . . "we see Jesus, who for a little while was made lower than the angels, crowned with glory and honour because of the suffering of death, so that by the grace of God he might taste death for every one " (*Hebrews* i. 3-5, ii. 9).

Since the logic of Christian soteriology demanded the deification of Jesus, this primitive concern to define the status of Jesus *vis-à-vis* the angels soon passed; as did the disposition to worship angels that both Paul and the author of the *Revelation of John* condemned. The Gospel picture of the angels as ministers of Christ prevailed, being powerfully reinforced by the majestic imagery of the *Revelation of John*. In this writing, which dates from the end of the first century, angels are mighty anthropomorphic beings, able to perform the prodigious acts through which the divine plan, in its full cosmic extension, was revealed to the Christian seer. One most notable episode therein provided an abiding stimulus to Christian imagination in subsequent ages. Drawing from diverse traditions concerning a primaeval dragon of chaos and fallen angels, an apocalyptic explanation is given of the evil forces with which Christians found themselves contending in the world: "Now war arose in heaven, Michael and his angels fighting against the dragon; and the dragon and his angels fought, but they were defeated and there was no longer any place for them in heaven . . . he (Satan) was thrown down to the earth, and his angels were thrown down with him" (xii. 7-9). Nothing is told of the origin of this conflict, or of God's part in it. The rôle ascribed to Michael is remarkable; but it had been anticipated in earlier Jewish apocalpytic literature. As the champion of God and leader of the angelic host, Michael became a popular figure in Christian devotion. His prowess against the Devil led to his invocation in times of crisis. At the moment of death his succour was especially sought: already, in a fourth-century Coptic writing, Michael was represented standing by a dying man, and then, together with Gabriel, receiving and caring for his soul when he expired.[10] The cult of this archangel dates from the fourth century; and it was greatly stimulated by his alleged appearance at Monte Gargano, in Apulia, in 492. In the early Middle Ages, many churches were dedicated to him on hill-tops, once sacred to pagan gods; in the calendar of the Western Church, the feast of Michaelmas on September 29th perpetuates his memory.

[10] Cf. *Die Geschichte von Joseph dem Zimmermann*, ed. S. Morenz (Berlin, 1951).

V

The representation of angels in Early Christian art shows a curious change of concept about the end of the fourth century. Before that time, it would seem, from the few surviving examples, that angels were depicted in contemporary male attire, without wings, and sometimes bearded. This, to our eyes, strange form was probably derived from contemporary Jewish iconography—a trousered male figure, representing an angel, was found in the ruins of the synagogue at Dura, dating from before A.D. 256. The conventional winged figure, with long flowing robes, appears to have been borrowed from the winged "Victories" of contemporary Roman art. Why this change occurred is not known: possibly it was inspired by the references to flying angels in the Bible. Although the pagan "Victories" were female, the new winged Christian angels kept their male attire; in process of time, however, the distinction was lost—it is possible that Muhammad's denunciation(Qur'ān, xliv. 18) of those who made angels female relates to some Christian custom in the East. It may be noted here that in Islam, too, angels play an important part; much of the lore concerning them being derived from Jewish and Christian tradition. Four have names: Jabrīl (Gabriel), who bore the messages of Allāh to Muhammad; Mīkā'īl (Michael), who controls the forces of nature; 'Azrā'il, the angel of death; and 'Isrāfil, who will sound the trumpet for the Last Judgment.

Angels figured much in the speculations of the Greek and Latin Fathers of the Early Church. Their speculations were essentially inferences, in terms of Greek metaphysic, from the Bible and Jewish apocalyptic literature. The origin and nature of the angels were matters of particular interest. At the Second Council of Nicaea (A.D. 787), the opinion was expressed that angels were not altogether incorporeal or invisible, but endowed with a thin ethereal or fiery body. The custom of depicting them and venerating their images was approved. The constitution of the angelic hierarchy was also a subject of concern. About A.D. 500, the scheme of the so-called Pseudo-Dionysius was propounded, and it became the basis of all subsequent speculation. Nine orders were defined, being obviously derived from Jewish angelology: Thrones; Cherubim; Seraphim; Dominions (kuriotētes); Authorities (exousiai); Powers (dunameis); Principalities (archai); Archangels; Angels. The angelic nature was authoritatively defined for the Eastern Church by John

Michael the Archangel subduing Satan. A modern conception of the Archangel by Epstein on the new Cathedral of Coventry (by the kind permission of the Provost and Chaplain of Coventry Cathedral and Rev. Richard Sadler)

of Damascus (*c.* 675–749): "An angel, then, is an intellectual substance, always mobile, endowed with free will, incorporeal, serving God, having received, according to grace, immortality in its nature, the form and character of whose substance God alone, who created it, knows."

The theologians of medieval Christendom continued to occupy themselves in speculations about the angels: that supreme exponent of Scholasticism, Thomas Aquinas (*c.* 1225–74), devoted a tractate to the subject in his great *Summa Theologica*, which remains the basis of Roman Catholic theology. The interest of the scholars was equalled by the devotion of ordinary Christians. The comforting assurance of a guardian angel had its inevitable appeal; and the idea was soon incorporated into

Christian belief. Already in the second century A.D., Hermas had taught that each man has two angels, one which prompts him to righteous acts, the other to works of evil. So strong was the belief, and such was the gratitude for angelic succour, that Pope Paul V (d. 1621) decreed a festival of the Guardian Angels, to be kept on each October 2nd.

Christian art, both during the Middle Ages and the Renaissance, vividly attests the reality of contemporary belief in angels. The belief survived the Reformation, although it has perhaps been less emphasized in Protestantism than in Catholicism. It is, however, doubtful how far, or in what manner, liberal Christian thinkers today accept the existence of such beings. But, be that as it may, Epstein's bronze figures of Michael and Satan, and the engraved windows of John Hutton, that adorn the new Coventry Cathedral, witness to the continuing vigour of the traditional image of the angels. And so, alike in literature and art, in hymns and liturgy, this esoteric belief, rooted far back in religions of the ancient Near East, is perpetuated in our twentieth-century world.

CHAPTER 25

B.C. and A.D.:
The Christian Philosophy of History

*After the sack of Rome by the Goths in the year 410,
the Roman world experienced some of the unease
that afflicts Western civilization today; it found
assuagement in the writings of Saint Augustine*

I

In the year 410 the Gothic leader Alaric made a sudden attack on the city of Rome: seizing it with amazing ease, he pillaged it. The shock to the civilized world was tremendous. Although barbarian peoples had long violated the provinces of the Roman Empire, and had even invaded Italy, to all men Rome was still the "Eternal City." Now the proud imperial metropolis was overthrown and ravaged. Faced with a catastrophe so great, many sought its cause, not in the military unpreparedness of the capital, but in something more sinister and disturbing. Rome had achieved world mastery when she had served Jupiter Capitolinus and her other ancient gods; but under the Emperor Constantine (312–337) an alien religion, Christianity, had received imperial recognition. Under his successors this favour was progressively extended: in 356 Constantius prohibited all pagan sacrifices and closed the temples, and in 382 Gratian ordered the final removal of the altar that stood before the statue of Victory in the Senate House. This last act was taken by those still loyal to the old religion as a fatal affront to both the faith and traditions of their ancestors.

The sack of Rome, that so soon followed, was hailed by the pagans

A fourth-century Christian
family (gold glass from
the Museo Civico, Brescia)

as a signal act of retribution: the ancient gods had withdrawn their
protection, and the new Christian god had been powerless to save the
city from barbarian destruction. That the logic of the situation gravely
disturbed the Christians, triumphant in their recent victory over paganism,
is evident. An answer was sorely needed to the pagans' case: it was
provided in a work that became the classic exposition of the Christian
philosophy of history.

The occasion had found its man in Augustine, bishop of the city
of Hippo Regius in the Roman province of North Africa. A man of wide
culture and powerful intellect, whose *Confessions* vividly describe his
spiritual pilgrimage to Christianity, Augustine was already a leader of
Christian thought. In a later work, the *Retractationes,* he tells how he
came to meet the challenge that now confronted the Church: "At this
time Rome was invaded by the Goths, under their king Alaric, and
succumbed to the shock of an immense disaster. The mob of devotees
of the false gods—the 'pagans' as they are commonly called—set themselves
to blame Christianity for this catastrophe, blaspheming the true God with
unprecedented violence and bitterness. And so, afire with zeal for the
house of God, I formed the project of writing the books of *The City of
God* to refute their blasphemies and their errors."

The City of God, or, to give it its Latin title, the *De Civitate Dei,*
is an immense work. In it Augustine drew upon his vast learning to show

that it was the purpose of God that the Church,[1] the *Civitas Dei*, should supersede the *civitas terrena,* the earthly state or organization of society. Utilizing what he knew of Egyptian, Assyrian, Greek and Roman history, he described the inevitable decline and ruin of the *civitas terrena,* of which the fall of Rome had just provided so signal an example.

That Augustine should have sought to meet this crisis by an appeal to history, or what he took to be history, is significant. It was the instinctive response of a Christian thinker, and it testifies to the essentially historical character of Christian thought. How this attitude originated and developed, and how powerful has been its influence in Western culture and civilization, is a subject of great intrinsic interest: it also has a considerable bearing upon the present confusion of outlook and purpose in Western society.

II

Christianity, by virtue of its Jewish origins, inherited the peculiar Jewish view of the past. According to this view, which is graphically set forth in the Hebrew scriptures, Yahweh, the God of Israel, had guided the whole course of history, from the Creation, for the benefit of his chosen people. This amazing claim, and the form in which it was originally presented, seems to have arisen from the need, felt about the tenth century B.C., to explain Israel's conquest of Canaan as due to the providence of Yahweh.[2] The subsequent vicissitudes of fortune that Israel suffered, however, after its settlement in Canaan, gradually caused a reorientation of outlook. As Israel's political position worsened, and the nation was in turn subjugated by Babylonians, Greeks and Romans, the memory of the Exodus inspired, ever more fervently, belief in an ultimate act of divine deliverance. Prophets foretold that, as he had once freed Israel from bondage in Egypt, so would Yahweh marvellously deliver them from their present oppressors. This hope of redemption gradually focussed on the figure of the Messiah, God's Anointed One, specially charged to fulfil the divine promise and vindicate Israel before the nations of the world. In contemporary Jewish apocalyptic literature, the nature of the Messiah and the means by which he would accomplish his mission are never defined clearly. However, whether he were thought to be human or

---

[1] Although he never precisely defines or identifies his *Civitas Dei*, it is clearly the Church, integrated into a Christian state, that he has in mind.
[2] See Chapter 11.

superhuman, it was generally believed that he would be endowed with
supernatural powers, and that his coming would coincide with the nadir
of Israel's fortunes and mark the end of the existing world-order.

The original Jewish disciples of Jesus identified him with the
Messiah, and believed that he "would restore the kingdom to Israel" (*Acts
of the Apostles* i. 6). How far, if at all, Jesus became implicated in a Messianic revolt against the Roman government in Judaea remains a problem
for further historical research. What is certain is that he was executed by
the Romans as a revolutionary. His death inevitably cut short the Messianic expectations of his followers; that it did not utterly destroy their
hopes can only be explained by their subsequent conviction that God
had raised him to life again. Believing still that this risen Jesus was the
Messiah, they looked forward to his eminent return, this time with
supernatural power and glory, to bring the existing world-order to an
end.

The first generation of Christians, accordingly, did not contemplate
an extended future for the Church in a world that was soon to perish.
For them the purpose of God would be completed by the return of their
Lord and the Final Judgment which he would deliver on mankind. These
eschatological expectations seem to have been greatly stimulated by the
sequence of events that marked the end of the reign of Nero and the
elevation of Vespasian to the imperial power, and led to the destruction
of Jerusalem in A.D. 70. The apocalyptic passage in the Markan Gospel
(xiii. 1–37) appears to reflect the excitement of Christian thought at this
time. Christians are warned: "when you hear of wars and rumours of wars,
do not be alarmed; this must take place, but the end is not yet. For nation
will rise against nation, and kingdom against kingdom; there will be
earthquakes in various places, there will be famines; this is but the
beginning of the sufferings" (xiii. 7–8).[3] Then comes a reference to the
destruction of the Temple at Jerusalem, which the Roman troops had
desecrated by sacrificing there to their standards: "when you see the
desolating sacrilege set up where it ought not to be (let the reader
understand) . . ." (xiii. 14). This signal catastrophe that befell the Jewish
nation had thus profoundly stirred the infant Church that had originated
in Jerusalem: it was seen as presaging the return of Christ and the end
of the world. As the following verses show, excitement was intense, and

[3] For an identification of these references see Brandon, *The Fall of Jerusalem and
the Christian Church* (S.P.C.K,, 1968), p. 203, and in *New Testament Studies*, vol. 7
(1960–1), pp. 136–8.

warning has to be given: "then if any one says to you, 'Look, here is the Christ!' or 'Look, there he is!' do not believe it. False Christs and false prophets will arise and show signs and wonders, to lead astray, if possible, the elect" (xiii. 21-3). The writer of the Gospel, however, is convinced that all these events pointed to the imminence of the end: "when you see these things taking place, you know that He (Christ) is near, at the very gates" (xiii. 29). And he represents Christ as assuring his faithful: "Truly, I say to you, this generation will not pass away before all these things take place. Heaven and earth will pass away, but my words will not pass away" (xiii. 30-1).

But that generation did pass away, and the next; yet still Christ did not return. Gradually Christians had to adjust themselves to living in a world that unexpectedly continued to exist. They did not abandon their eschatological hopes; but they became steadily less occupied with them, postponing their fulfilment to an indefinite future. This readjustment of outlook in turn necessitated a re-interpretation of the purpose of God. Hitherto they had accepted the Jewish view of that purpose: that it culminated in the coming of the Messiah. But, if Jesus were the Messiah, he had already come; yet the world still continued, and its continuance had to be regarded as part of the divine plan. Accordingly, the purpose of God, as revealed in history, came to be seen as having two parts or phases. The first extended from the Creation and Fall of Man to the birth of Jesus, the Messiah. This first phase was documented by the Hebrew scriptures; and its theme was seen as the preparation of Israel for the coming of Christ. The Apostle Paul had already referred to the sacred writings of his people as the "old covenant" or "testament" (*palaia diathēkē*); and he spoke of Jesus instituting a "new covenant" (*kainē diathēkē*) in his blood. Such language was derived from Jewish sacrificial ideas, and Paul used it theologically; but it provided powerful suggestion and sanction for what was to be the specifically Christian interpretation of History.

The birth of Jesus came thus to be regarded as dividing the stream of time into two parts, marking the completion of the first phase of the divine purpose and the beginning of the second. Paul had already defined the chronological significance of the incarnation of Christ as "when the fulness of the time came, God sent forth His Son, born of a woman, born under the (Jewish) Law" (*Gal.* iv. 4). And the author of the *Gospel of Luke,* writing towards the end of the first century, was evidently so

Under the Emperor Constantine
(312–337), "an alien religion received imperial recognition"

concerned with this time-factor that, in recording the birth of Jesus and
the beginning of his ministry, he makes an elaborate synchronization of
these events with secular history. "In those days a decree went out from
Caesar Augustus that all the world should be enrolled. This was the first
enrolment, when Quirinius was governor of Syria" (ii. 1–2); "In the
fifteenth year of the reign of Tiberius Caesar, Pontius Pilate being governor
of Judaea, and Herod being tetrarch of Galilee, and his brother Philip
tetrarch of the region of Ituraea and Trachonitis, and Lysanias tetrarch
of Abilene, in the high-priesthood of Annas and Caiaphas, the word of
God came to John the son of Zechariah in the wilderness" (iii. 1–3).[4]

Paul's ascription of a unique temporal significance to the birth of
Jesus derived from his soteriology. For he saw in the historical Jesus of
Nazareth not only the Messiah of Israel, but also the incarnated Son of
God. His crucifixion he interpreted as part of the divine plan to save
mankind from their enslavement to the demonic forces that ruled the
world.[5] This evaluation of Jesus as the Saviour of the world, rather than
his being the Messiah of Israel, predominated in the Church's new
assessment of its rôle. The Church now saw itself as having a twofold

[4] Each of these synchronizations contains difficulties. According to the first, Jesus would
have been born in A.D. 6, whereas *Matthew* ii. 1 places his birth in the region of Herod the
Great, who died in 4 B.C. John (the Baptist) was, of course, regarded as the forerunner of Christ.
[5] See Chapter 21.

mission. It had to win men and women from paganism to acceptance of Christ as Saviour, and, when converted, to guide and strengthen their spiritual life by its ministrations.

Since Christianity had emerged in the Roman Empire, that Empire constituted its world, within which it lived out the formative years of its life. Consequently, it was the society of that Empire that it sought to win to the Gospel of Christ; and it was under Roman law and government that it had to live and conduct its affairs. This situation faced the Church with a struggle on two fronts. Loyalty to the Roman government meant acceptance of the divinity of the Emperor and recognition of the state gods. The inability of Christians to conform to those requirements caused the faith to be suspect, and a policy of suppression was officially adopted. Although this policy was not consistently enforced, the Church did suffer periods of severe persecution. Such experience naturally heightened the sense of drama with which the Church regarded its mission. When, therefore, with the accession of Constantine to supreme power (312), persecution was replaced by imperial favour, the sense of triumph through tribulation was immense. The Church's confidence in its divine destiny was greatly strengthened—truly, as Tertullian (*c.* 160–200) had declared in his *Apology*, addressed to the Roman magistrates: "The blood of Christians is like seed; the faster you mow us down, the thicker we spring up."

Although the constancy of its martyrs thus won converts for the Church, Christian leaders also felt the need to prove the superiority of Christianity over the pagan religions. Most of these religions were immensely old: the cult of Isis and Osiris was already flourishing in Egypt in the third millennium B.C. In the face of such venerable antiquity, which was greatly prized in Graeco-Roman society, Christians felt embarrassed by the newness of their own faith. The Roman historian Tacitus (*c.* 55–116) had caustically remarked that Christianity was a new superstition, its founder having been executed during the reign of the Emperor Tiberius. Christian thinkers, accordingly, felt obliged to prove that Christianity was not just a novel cult, thrown up by the underworld of the Levant, but that it was older than any other faith. Tertullian undertakes to prove this in a significant way. He argues that Christianity "rests on the very ancient books of the Jews," and that these are far older than any book, city, cult or race of the pagan world (*Apology*, XIX. i–XXI. i).

This assumption of the ancient Hebrew scriptures as the heritage

of the Church, with the implied assumption of a legitimate continuity
between Hebrew religion and Christianity, had been prepared for by Paul.
Faced with the fact that only a tiny minority of the Jews had accepted
Jesus, Paul had identified these with the "true Israel," to which he added
the Gentile converts, declaring that they were the true inheritors of God's
promises to Israel. Having at first no sacred books of their own, Christians
had used the Hebrew scriptures, regarding them, as we have seen, as
the "Old Testament." When, by the third century, a canon of Christian
scripture had been formed, it was known as the "New Testament," thus
giving concrete expression to the emerging philosophy of history, namely,
that the divine purpose for mankind had two epochs or phases.

Believing, then, that Christianity was the expression of the age-old
purpose of God, Christian writers soon began to formulate their belief
into elaborate chronological systems. According to Julius Africanus
(c. 160–240), the world was to last for six thousand years from its creation.
By dating the birth of Christ for the year 5500 from the Creation, he
could look forward to a future of about three hundred years for the
accomplishment of the Church's mission. Eusebius, Bishop of Caesarea,
who has the distinction of being the first to write an ecclesiastical history—
that is, a narrative record of the past of the Church—prepared for this
task by compiling a chronicle of world history. Tabulating what he knew
of the history of the Assyrians, Egyptians, Greeks and Romans, he related
this record to the history of the Chosen People, beginning with Abraham,
whose birth he dates for the year 2017 B.C. Eusebius wrote in the reign
of Constantine, when the Church had just emerged triumphantly from
its long and painful struggle with the pagan government of Rome. Although now confident of its future, Eusebius still felt the relative newness
of Christianity to be a problem. To meet this, he began by showing that
it had been necessary for God to prepare in earlier ages for the incarnation
of Christ. Thus, he hopes that "the real antiquity and divine character
of Christianity will be equally demonstrated to those who suppose that
it is recent and foreign, appearing no earlier than yesterday."[6] Accordingly, after describing this divine preparation, he declares that the right
moment came in world history for the birth of Christ or the divine Logos:
it was when the Emperor Augustus established the *Pax Romana*, after
the miseries and disorder of the civil war that marked the end of the

---

[6] *Eccl. hist.*, I, ii. i; trans. Kirsopp Lake, Loeb Classical Library edn. of Eusebius.

Christ in Majesty, accompanied by the symbols of the Four Evangelists (from the Royal Porch of Chartres Cathedral, one of the finest monuments of medieval Christianity)

Republic. "Then, at last, when all men, even the heathen were now fitted for the benefits prepared for them beforehand, for the reception of knowledge of the Father, then again that same divine and heavenly Logos of God, the teacher of virtues, the minister of the Father in all good things, appeared at the beginning of the Roman Empire through man."[7]

Thus was the historical pattern of Christian thought established. Whereas other religions current in the Graeco-Roman world referred only to events that had occurred in a vague and remote past, a mythical "age of the gods," Christians saw their faith as expressing the purpose of God in History. The only other religion that made a comparable appeal to history was Judaism, from which Christianity had stemmed. But Christian thinkers had reinterpreted the Jewish view, which was essentially concerned with the fortunes of Israel. They gave to Hebrew history a universal significance by seeing it as the *praeparatio evangelica*—the divine preparation for the Gospel of Christ.

It is understandable, therefore, that, when he undertook to explain

[7] *Eccl. hist.*, I, ii. 23; trans. Kirsopp Lake, Loeb Classical Library edn.

the fall of Rome, Augustine's *apologia* took the form of a philosophy of history. Shocking though the ruin of the Eternal City was to his contemporaries, the event had to be seen in the context of the mighty purpose of God as it unfolded in world history.

Closely connected with Augustine's *City of God* is the work of his disciple Orosius entitled *Adversum Paganos*. Augustine suggested the undertaking, feeling that the theme of Book III of his *City of God*, concerning the evils suffered by Rome when still pagan, needed elaboration. What Orosius sought to do was, in effect, to write a history of the world in terms of all the ills suffered by mankind, thus demonstrating to his pagan contemporaries that their misfortunes were neither new nor worse. For Orosius this catalogue of ills attested the working of divine providence throughout history, whereby mankind was educated by "most kindly chastisements." Banal as was the theme, the number of surviving manuscripts of the work proves that it enjoyed a reputation in the Middle Ages almost equal to that of Augustine's *City of God*.

III

When we seek to evaluate this Christian philosophy of history in relation to Graeco-Roman thought, what is at once most striking is the teleological character of the Christian view. The ancient world generally regarded time as moving in cycles. According to the Stoic idea of the "Great Year," the present world was the existent example of a series of worlds that had been and that would be, each repeating the same pattern of events. Their beginning and end were determined by the movement of the stars. Through each revolution of the cycle the same order of events would occur: "The stars again move in their orbits, each performing its revolution of the former period, without variation. Socrates and Plato and each individual man will live again, with the same friends and fellow-citizens. They will go through the same experiences and the same activities." [8]

In contrast to this ever recurring cycle of existence, which rendered history meaningless, Christians saw time as the linear process of the purpose of God. Initiated by a divine act of creation, it moved towards a definite *telos* or end, which would mark the achievement of the divine purpose. Consequently, for Christians history was teleology, the record

---

[8] J. von Arnim, *Stoicorum Veterum Fragmenta*, II, frag. 625 (Nemesius), trans. E. Bevan.

The earliest portrait of
St. Augustine of Hippo, dating
about A.D. 600 (from a fresco in
the Papal Library of the Lateran)

of the unfolding of God's purpose. Deriving this teleological conception from Judaism, Christianity extended its scope to cover all mankind, dividing it by the Incarnation into two eras, the one consequent on the other. Thus the birth of Christ became the focal point of history. The purpose of God was seen as moving towards it from the Creation: from the moment of its occurrence that purpose took on a new character—it became concerned, through the sacrificial life and death of Christ, with the salvation of each human being. A formal definition of these two eras actually came rather late into general usage. In 525 a Roman abbot, Dionysius Exiguus, introduced the system of reckoning time as *anni Domini* ("years of the Lord") from the birth of Christ; but it was not until the eighteenth century that it became customary to designate the preceding era "before Christ" (B.C.). The comparative lateness of this nomenclature, is, however, incidental: for, as we have seen, Paul had already invested the birth of Christ with a unique temporal distinction.

The Church survived the break-up of the Roman Empire in the West; and it gradually converted the barbarian invaders who were to form the nations of Europe. This process of conversion meant that the Christian philosophy of history came to form the accepted world view of medieval

"The End of the World" (the "Last Judgment" of Hubert van Eyck, d. 1426). Christ appears as Judge, accompanied by saints. The dead rise from their graves in the earth or sea, while the damned fall through Death into the torments of Hell (The Metropolitan Museum of Art, Fletcher Fund, 1933)

Christendom. It found expression in literature and art, and in religious drama. Encyclopedic surveys of history were compiled, such as the *Speculum historiale* of Vincent of Beauvais (*c.* 1190–1264), which inspired the decoration of cathedrals and churches. From them artists learned to depict in sculpture, in mural paintings or coloured glass, a traditional series of events, illustrating or typifying the divine plan of man's salvation, ranging from the Old Testament, through the New, on to the Acts of the Saints. The calendar of the Church's liturgical year also kept the faithful constantly aware of the sacred history. And the passage of time came to be invested with a significance unknown in the world before: across the fields and through the streets of cities in medieval Europe the sound of bells informed the Christian of the liturgical hours, while the doleful notes of the passing bell reminded him of the inevitability of death.

The medieval world view was an ingeniously contrived synthesis, which integrated the destiny of the individual Christian with the purpose of God manifest in history. He was taught to believe that Christ had died centuries before to redeem his soul. At death, he would go to purgatory to expiate his venial sins and wait until God completed the number of His Elect. Then Christ would return to earth, the world come to an end, and the Final Judgment be enacted on all mankind. If he were among those counted righteous, then he would pass to the eternal enjoyment of the Beatific Vision of God.[9] And so would he complete his part in that mighty drama that had begun to unfold with the creation of the universe.

IV

The Renaissance did not change the Western world view in this respect. The authority of the Christian philosophy of history continued supreme; and it is significant that Augustine's *City of God* was among the first works to be printed. But new knowledge, of various kinds, began to emerge that was destined to render that traditional view obsolete and untenable. The opening up of the world by maritime exploration acquainted Europeans with other peoples and civilizations, some of great antiquity and achievement, hitherto unknown. The Christian churches seized the opportunity, thus presented, of spreading the Gospel: but this

[9] See Chapter 7.

wider horizon caused the more reflective to see that the Christian interpretation of history was based upon a very limited knowledge of the past
of mankind—in fact, upon that of only a few peoples in the ancient Near
East. The development of the science of geology also began to provide
doubts; for it became apparent that the earth must have existed long before
the year 4004 B.C., the date assigned for it in the seventeenth century
by Archbishop Ussher according to Biblical evidence. Then, Darwin's
Origin of Species (1859) and T. H. Huxley's *Man's Place in Nature* (1863)
demanded a new conception of the origin of mankind. But, even before
scientific research had thus questioned the Christian view of the past,
the authority of the Bible was being doubted on literary grounds. Already,
in 1670, the Jewish philosopher Spinoza, and in 1678 a French priest
Richard Simon, had pointed out certain discrepancies, proving that Moses
could not have written all the books of the Pentateuch. Gradually the
critical investigation of the Bible, extended in time to the New Testament,
undermined the basis upon which the Christian interpretation of history
had been built. Nor was this all: palaeontology, anthropology and archaeology steadily pushed back the beginnings of human culture to an age
hitherto unsuspected: it became known that the emergence of *homo sapiens*
had been preceded by hominids such as Neanderthal Man. Such evidence
obviously contradicted the Biblical view that mankind had fallen from
an original state of perfection, and that the beginning of life had been
a Golden Age.

Except for the conflict in Victorian England between divines and
scientists over evolution, and the Fundamentalist controversy in America,
the abandonment of the Christian philosophy of history has been a gradual
and almost imperceptible process. The change of outlook was undoubtedly
eased by the adoption of a kind of secularist version of the Christian view
that there is purpose in history. The belief in progress that characterized
the nineteenth century, inspiring an optimistic attitude towards the future,
was fundamentally teleological. History was interpreted as the progress
of mankind from the ignorance of barbarism and superstition to a rational
ordering of life. Improvement of the material conditions of life through
scientific knowledge would go together, it was believed, with improvement
of social conduct: mankind was seen as moving towards a Golden Age.

The experience of two world wars has shattered such belief. We have
grown afraid of the products of our science and of our ability to use them
well. Moreover, the outlook sanctioned by our scientific knowledge is that

of a universe in which mighty impersonal forces operate in ways beyond our comprehension. Similarly, our immensely increased knowledge of the past of the human race allows us to perceive no purpose other than the biological—that our species has been wonderfully successful in the struggle for existence. In the rise and fall of peoples and their civilizations, however, no law or pattern can be demonstrated, despite the efforts of Oswald Spengler[10] and Arnold Toynbee.[11]

The *malaise* that seems to afflict Western culture today may reasonably be traced to an awareness that we can find no inspiring purpose in history. Yet our thought and outlook are and remain instinctively teleological; for they stem ultimately from centuries of Christian tradition, and a deep grounding in the doctrine of progress. And so it would seem that, despite all disappointment, the question will be continually asked: what does the history of mankind mean?

[10] Spengler's great work *Der Untergang des Abendlandes*, first published in 1918, was translated into English as *The Decline of the West*.

[11] To Toynbee's great corpus *A Study of History* should be added in this connection his Gifford Lectures entitled *An Historian's Approach to Religion* (1956).

ANNOTATED BIBLIOGRAPHY

Note: E.T. means English Translation.

1 *The Origin of Religion*

(a) There is no recent account of the history of the comparative study of religion. The following works are valuable so far as they go in date: L. H. Jordan, *Comparative Religion: its genesis and growth* (London, 1908); E. Pinard de la Boullaye, *L'étude comparée des religions,* tome I (Paris, 1922). Useful material will be found in these recent studies: P. H. Ashby, "The History of Religions," in *Religion,* ed. P. Ramsey (The Princeton Studies: Humanistic Scholarship in America. 1965); A. de Waal Malefijt, *Religion and Culture* (Collier-Mac., 1968); S. G. F. Brandon, "Ideas of the Origin of Religion," in *Dictionary of the History of Ideas* (forthcoming publication from Charles Scribner's Sons, New York). Reference should also be made to the following journals: *Numen* (Leiden, from 1954); *History of Religions* (Chicago Univ. Press, from 1961); *International Bibliography of the History of Religions* (issued by the International Association for the Study of the History of Religions, from 1954).

(b) For the second part of the article see: H. Breuil, *Four Hundred Centuries of Cave Art* (Montignac, France, 1952); J. Maringer, *The Gods of Prehistoric Man* (E. T., Weidenfeld and N., 1960); S. Giedion, *The Eternal Present: The Beginnings of Art* (Oxford, 1962–4); S. G. F. Brandon, *Man and his Destiny in the Great Religions* (Manchester, 1962); G. Clark, *The Stone Age Hunters* (Thames & H., 1967); P. J. Ucko and A. Rosenfeld, *Palaeolithic Cave Art* (Weidenfeld & N., 1967); A. Leroi-Gourhan, *The Art of Prehistoric Man in Western Europe* (E. T., Thames & H., 1968); A. Laming-Emperaire, *La signification de l'art rupestre paléolithique* (Paris, 1962).

2 *"In the Beginning"*

The most recent and detailed study in English of the subject is the author's *Creation Legends of the Ancient Near East* (Hodder, 1963), in which full documentation of the sources and extensive bibliographies are given. The book deals with the cosmogonies of ancient Egypt, Mesopotamia, Israel, Greece and Iran.

3 *The Personification of Death in Some Ancient Religions*

The footnotes give references to the relevant literature, to which the following works should be added: J. Harrison, *Prolegomena to the Study of Greek Religion* (reprint New York, 1955), pp. 174–8 (on the *kéres*); *Oxford Classical Dictionary,* p. 475

('Keres'); G. Dennis, *The Cities and Cemeteries of Etruria* (Everyman edn., 1907), vol. ii, frontispiece and pp. 183–6; A. Grenier, *Les religions étrusque et romaine* (Paris, 1948), pp. 59–68; A. Hermann in *Reallexikon für Antike und Christentum*, I, under "Charon"; S. G. F. Brandon, *History, Time and Deity* (Manchester, 1965). It is interesting to note that G. E. Lessing wrote an article entitled "Wie die Alten den Tod gebildet," which dealt with Greek and Roman tradition on the subject; it was published in 1769.

4   Time as God and Devil

The religious significance of Time has been dealt with at length by the author in his book *History, Time and Deity* (Manchester University Press, 1965), which contains a full bibliography and documentation, to which may be added his essay entitled, "Time and the Destiny of Man," in *Voices of Time*, ed. J. T. Fraser (A. Lane, 1968).

5   The Idea of the Soul Part I: in the West

The author's books *Man and his Destiny in the Great Religions* (Manchester University Press, 1962) and *Creation Legends of the Ancient Near East* (Hodder, 1963) deal at length with the subject under the various religions concerned, and contain extensive documentation and bibliographies. Various aspects of the subject are studied in the following works: H. Bonnet, *Reallexikon der ägyptischen Religionsgeschichte* (Berlin, 1952), under "Ba" and "Ka"; *The Intellectual Adventure of Ancient Man*, ed. H. and H. A. Frankfort (Chicago University Press, 1946); A. R. Johnson, *The Vitality of the Individual in the Thought of Ancient Israel* (University of Wales Press, 1949); E. Rohde, *Psyche: the Cult of Souls and Belief in Immortality among the Greeks*, 2 vols (reprint New York, 1968); R. B. Onians, *The Origins of European Thought* (Cambridge, 1951); S. Cave, *The Christian Estimate of Man* (Duckworth, 1944); H. W. Robinson, "Soul (Christian)," in *Encyclopaedia of Religion and Ethics*, ed. J. Hastings, vol. XI (1920); S. G. F. Brandon, *The Judgment of the Dead* (Weidenfeld & N., 1967); *Anthropologie religieuse*, ed. C. J. Bleeker (Leiden, 1955).

6   The Idea of the Soul Part II: in the East

The subject is dealt with according to the religions concerned by the author in his book *Man and his Destiny in the Great Religions* (Manchester University Press, 1962), and in *Anthropologie religieuse*, ed. C. J. Bleeker (Leiden, 1955). On the Hindu view see: S. Dasgupta, *A History of Indian Philosophy*, vols. I and II (Cambridge, 1922, 1932); P. Deussen, *The Philosophy of the Upanishads* (E. T., Edinburgh, 1906); P. T. Raju, "The Concept of Man in Indian Thought," in *The Concept of Man: a Study in Comparative Philosophy*, ed. S. Radhakrishnan and P. T. Raju (London, 1960); R. C. Zaehner, *Hinduism* (Oxford, 1962); *Hindu Scriptures* (New York, 1966). On the Buddhist view: E. Conze, *Buddhism: its Essence and Development* (Cassirer, Oxford, 1957); H. Günther, *Das Seelenproblem im älteren Buddhismus* (Konstanz, 1949); Th. Stcherbatsky, *The Central Conception of Buddhism and the Meaning of the Word "Dharma"* (London, 1923); E. J. Thomas, *The Life of Buddha* (Routledge, 1949) and *The History of Buddhist Thought*

(Routledge, 1951); P. V. Bapat (ed.), *2,500 years of Buddhism* (Publications Department, Government of India, 1959); C. A. F. Rhys Davids, *Buddhist Psychology* (London, 1914). On the Zoroastrian view: L. C. Casartelli, "Soul (Iranian)," in *Encyclopaedia of Religion and Ethics*, ed. J. Hastings, vol. XI (1920); M. N. Dhalla, *Zoroastrian Theology* (New York, 1914); M. Molé, "Daēnā, le pont Cinvat et l'initiation dans le Mazdéisme," in *Revue de l'histoire des religions*, t.CLVII (Paris, 1960); J. H. Moulton, *Early Zoroastrianism* (London, 1913); J. D. C. Pavry, *The Zoroastrian Doctrine of a Future Life* (New York, 1929); Geo Widengren, "Stand und Aufgaben der iranischen Religionsgeschichte," in *Numen*, vols. I and II (Leiden, 1954, 1955); R. C. Zaehner, *The Dawn and Twilight of Zoroastrianism* (Weidenfeld & N., 1961). On the Chinese view: W. T. Chan, "The Concept of Man in Chinese Thought", in *The Concept of Man: a Study in Comparative Philosophy*, ed. S. Radhakrishnan and P. T. Raju (London, 1960); Fung Yu-Lan, *A History of Chinese Philosophy*, vol. I (Oxford, 1969); M. Granet, *La pensée chinoise* (Paris, 1950); D. H. Smith, "Chinese Concepts of the Soul," in *Numen*, vol. V (Leiden, 1958); *Chinese Religions* (Weidenfeld & N., 1968). On the Islamic view: Tor Andrae, *Mahomet: sa vie et sa doctrine* (Paris, 1945); R. Eklund, *Life between Death and Resurrection according to Islam* (Uppsala, 1941); S. Lane-Poole, "Death and Disposal of the Dead (Muhammadan)," in *Encyclopaedia of Religion and Ethics*, ed. J. Hastings, vol. IV (1911); J. W. Sweetman, *Islam and Christian Theology*, 3 vols. (London, 1945–55).

7   *The Judgment of the Dead*

The author's book entitled *The Judgment of the Dead* (Charles Scribner's Sons, New York, 1969) is the only comprehensive study of the subject in English. It deals in turn with the idea of a *post-mortem* judgment in Egypt, Mesopotamia, Israel, Graeco-Roman society, Christianity, Islam, Iran, Hinduism and Buddhism, China, and Japan. The volume has extensive documentation and bibliographies, to which the following works may be added: D. Milošević, *The Last Judgment* (E. T., Verlag Bongers: Tandem, 1967)—it is vol. 3 of the "Pictorial Library of Eastern Church Art"; Beat Brenk, *Tradition und Neuerung in der christlichen Kunst des ersten Jahrtausends: Studien zur Geschichte des Weltgerichtsbildes* (Wiener Byzantinische Studien, Band III, Vienna, 1966). The fourth volume in the French series *Sources Orientales*, sub-titled *le jugement des morts* (Paris, 1961), is a valuable survey of the theme in many Near, Middle and Far Eastern, and South-East Asian religions; it omits Graeco-Roman and Christian conceptions of *post-mortem* judgment.

8   *Osiris*

The *Pyramid Texts* are translated and edited by S. A. B. Mercer, *The Pyramid Texts*, 4 vols. (New York, 1952); see also *The Pyramid of Unas*, translated with commentary by A. Piankoff (Princeton University Press, 1968). There is, unfortunately, no English translation of the *Coffin Texts*; but a magisterial edition of the original texts is provided by A. de Buck, *The Egyptian Coffin Texts*, 6 vols. (Chicago University Press, 1935–56). There are many translations of the *Book of the Dead*: see especially E. A. W. Budge, *The Book of the Dead: the Papyrus of Ani*, 2 vols. (Routledge, 1960); T. G. Allen, *The Egyptian Book of the Dead* (University of Chicago Press, 1960); P. Barguet, *Le Livre des Morts des Anciens Egyptiens* (Paris, 1967). A convenient translation of Plutarch's *De Iside et Osiride* is provided in Plutarch's *Moralia*, vol. iv, in the Loeb Classical Library. The following books contain important studies of Osiris: L. Gwyn Griffiths, *The Origins of Osiris* (Müncher ägyptologische Studien, 9; Berlin, 1966); E. A. W. Budge, *Osiris and the Egyptian Resurrection*, 2 vols. (London, 1911); K. Sethe, *Urgeschichte und älteste Religion der Aegypter* (Leipzig, 1930); A. Erman, *Die Religion der Aegypter* (Berlin, 1934); H. Frankfort, *Kingship and the Gods* (Chicago University Press, 1948); J. Vandier, *La religion égyptienne* (Paris, 1948); H. Bonnet, *Reallexikon der ägyptischen Religionsgeschichte* (Berlin, 1952); J. Spiegel, *Die Idee vom Totengericht in der ägyptischen Religion* (Gluckstadt, 1935); H. Kees, *Totenglauben und Jenseitsvorstellungen der alten Aegypter* (Berlin, 1956); S. G. F. Brandon, "The Ritual Technique of Salvation in the Ancient Near East," in *The Saviour God*, ed. S. G. F. Brandon (Manchester University Press, 1963); E. Otto, *Egyptian Art and the Cults of Osiris and Amon* (E. T., Thames & H., 1968).

9   *Akhenaten*

The latest and most valuable study of Akhenaten is by C. Aldred, entitled *Akhenaten: Pharaoh of Egypt—a new study* (Thames & H., 1968). In view of the fragmentary and enigmatic nature of the extant evidence, it is unlikely that a definitive interpretation of Akhenaten and his times will ever be achieved. The following works should also be consulted for alternative views: K. Lange, *König Echnaton und die Amarna Zeit* (Munich, 1951); J. A. Wilson, *The Culture of Ancient Egypt* (University of Chicago Press, 1960); H. Bonnet, *Reallexikon der ägyptischen Religionsgeschichte* (Berlin, 1952), art. "Aton"; A. H. Gardiner, *Egypt of the Pharaohs* (Oxford, 1961); A. Erman, *Die Religion der Aegypter* (Berlin/Leipzig, 1934); J. H. Breasted, *The Dawn of Conscience* (New York, 1933); W. H. Fairman, "Once again the so-called Coffin of Akhenaten," in *Journal of Egyptian Archaeology*, vol. 47 (1961); S. Morenz, *Aegyptische Religion* (Stuttgart, 1960); G. Roeder, *Der Ausklang der ägyptischen Religion mit Reformation, Zauberei und Jenseitsglauben* (Zürich/Stuttgart, 1961). It is still interesting to look at A. Weigall's *The Life and Times of Akhnaton* (London, 1922).

10   *The Epic of Gilgamesh*

For modern annotated translations see E. A. Speiser in *Ancient Near Eastern Texts relating to the Old Testament*, ed. J. B. Pritchard (Princeton University Press, 1955); A. Heidel, *The Gilgamesh Epic and Old Testament Parallels* (Chicago University Press, 1949); see also W. G. Lambert, *Babylonian Wisdom Literature* (Oxford, 1960). On Mesopotamian civilization and religion see: S. N. Kramer, *Sumerian Mythology* (Philadelphia, 1944) and *From the Tablets of Sumer* (Colorado, 1956); P. Jensen, *Das Gilgamesch-Epos in der Welt-Literatur*, Band I (Strassburg, 1906); B. Meissner, *Babylonien und Assyrien*, Band II (Heidelberg, 1925); E. Ebeling, *Tod und Leben nach den Vorstellungen der Babylonier*, I (Berlin/Leipzig, 1931); M. David, *Les dieux et le destin en Babylonie* (Paris, 1949); E. Dhorme, *Les religions de Babylonie et d'Assyrie* (Paris, 1945); *The Intellectual Adventure of Ancient Man*, ed. H. and H. A. Frankfort (Chicago University Press, 1946); F. M. Th. de Liagre Bohl, "Das Menschenbild in babylonischer Schau," in *Anthropologie religieuse*, ed. C. J. Bleeker (Leiden, 1955); F. R. Kraus, "Altmesopotamische Lebensgefühl," in *Journal of Near Eastern Studies*, vol. XIX (Chicago, 1960); H. W. F. Saggs, *The Greatness that was Babylon* (Sidgwick & Jackson, 1962); S. G. F. Brandon, *Man and his Destiny in the*

Great Religions (Manchester, 1962) and *The Judgment of the Dead* (Weidenfeld & N., 1967).

11   *The Jewish Philosophy of History*

Various aspects of the subject are treated in the following works: G. von Rad, *Das formgeschichtliche Problem des Hexateuchs* (Stuttgart, 1938); M. Noth, *Das System der Zwölf Stämme Israels* (Stuttgart, 1930) and *The History of Israel* (E. T., Black, 1960); R. H. Pfeiffer, *Introduction to the Old Testament* (New York, 1948); W. F. Albright, *From the Stone Age to Christianity* (Baltimore, 1946) and *Yahweh and the Gods of Canaan* (Athlone Press, 1968); A. Alt, *Der Gott der Väter* (Stuttgart, 1929); *The Old Testament and Modern Study*, ed. H. H. Rowley (Oxford, 1951); H. H. Rowley, *From Joseph to Joshua* (London, 1950); A. Lods, *Israël: des origines au milieu du viiie siècle* (Paris, 1932), and *Les prophètes d'Israël et les débuts du Judaisme* (Paris, 1935); H. Wildberger, *Jahwes Eigentumsvolk* (Zürich, 1960); M. Burrows, Essay in *The Idea of History in the Ancient Near East*, ed. R. C. Denton (Yale University Press, 1955); S. G. F. Brandon, *History, Time and Deity* (Manchester, 1965), chapter V.

12   *The Book of Job*

The many literary problems of the *Book of Job* are dealt with in S. R. Driver and C. B. Gray, *Job* (International Critical Commentary, Edinburgh, 1921); R. H. Pfeiffer, *Introduction to the Old Testament* (New York, 1948). For the interpretation of various aspects of *Job* see W. O. E. Oesterley and T. H. Robinson, *Hebrew Religion* (S.P.C.K., 1937); H. H. Rowley, *The Faith of Israel* (S.C.M. Press, 1961) and "The Book of Job and its Meaning," in *The Bulletin of the John Ryland's Library*, vol. 41 (Manchester, 1958); *Religion in Geschichte und Gegenwart*, III (1958), 355–60; J. Pedersen, *Israel: its Life and Culture*, vol. I–II (London, 1926); *Wisdom in Israel and in the Ancient Near East*, ed. M. Noth and D. Winton Thomas (Leiden, 1955), contributions by G. R. Driver, P. Humbert, S. N. Kramer, G. Von Rad; S. G. F. Brandon, *Man and his Destiny in the Great Religions* (Manchester, 1962). On the "Babylonian Job" see W. G. Lambert, *Babylonian Wisdom Literature* (Oxford, 1960).

13   *Zarathustra and the Dualism of Iran*

The following works deal with the subject and its various disputed aspects: W. B. Henning, *Zoroaster: Politician or Witch-Doctor?* (Oxford, 1951); R. C. Zaehner, *The Dawn and Twilight of Zoroastrianism* (Weidenfeld & N., 1961) and *Zurvān: a Zoroastrian Dilemma* (Oxford, 1955); H. S. Nyberg, *Die Religionen des alten Iran* (Leipzig, 1928); G. Widengren, *Hochgottglauben im alten Iran* (Lund, 1938) and "Stand und Aufgaben der iranischen Religionsgeschichte," in *Numen*, vol. I and II (Leiden, 1954, 1955); J. Duchesne-Guillemin, *Zoroastre* (Paris, 1948); *Ormazd et Ahriman* (*l'aventure dualiste dans l'antiquité*) (Paris, 1953) and *The Western Response to Zoroaster* (Oxford, 1958); I. Gershevitch, "Zoroaster's Own Contribution," in *Journal of Near Eastern Studies*, vol. XXIII (Chicago, 1964) and *The Avestan Hymn to Mithra* (Cambridge, 1959); M. Molé, "Une histoire du mazdéisme est-elle possible? Notes et remarques en marge d'un ouvrage récent," in *Revue de l'histoire des religions*, t. 162 (Paris, 1962). See also J. H. Moulton, *Early Zoroastrianism* (London, 1913); J. Bidez and Fr. Cumont, *Les mages hellénisés*, 2 vols. (Paris, 1938); R. Ghirsham, *Iran* (Harmondsworth, 1954); R. N. Frye, *The Heritage of Persia* (Weidenfeld & N., 1963); W. Culican, *The Medes and Persians* (London,

1965); M. A. R. Colledge, *The Parthians* (Thames & H., 1967); S. G. F. Brandon, *Man and his Destiny in the Great Religions* (Manchester, 1962), chapter VIII.

14 Herod the Great

The chief original source is Josephus, *Jewish Antiquities*, Books xiv–xv, and *The Jewish War*, Book i. The most convenient edition of the text and translation is the Loeb Classical Library edition of Josephus, vols. ii, vii and viii. Important material will be found also in the remains of the universal history written by Herod's minister Nicolaus of Damascus in *Fragmenta Historicorum Graecorum*, ed. Müller, vol. 3, and Julius Africanus, *Chronica*, who incorporates relevant fragments that may come from the lost history of Justus of Tiberias (in *Reliquiae Sacrae*, ed. Routh, vol. ii). For modern studies see E. Schürer, *Geschichte des jüdischen Volkes im Zeitalter Jesu Christi*, Band I (3rd and 4th eds., Leipzig, 1901), English trans. *The Jewish People in the Time of Jesus Christ* (Edinburgh, 1890); W. Otto, art. in *Real-Encyl. d. class, Altertumswissenschaft* (Pauly-Wissowa-Kroll), Suppl. Band I; A. Momigliano, *Cambridge Ancient History*, vol. X (1934), chap. XI; F. J. Hollis, *The Archaeology of Herod's Temple* (London, 1934); A. H. M. Jones, *The Herods of Judaea* (Oxford, 1938); S. Perowne, *The Life and Times of Herod the Great* (Hodder, 1956); A. Reifenberg, *Israel History in Coins* (London, 1953); Y. Yadin, *Masada: Herod's Fortress and the Zealots' Last Stand* (Weidenfeld & N., 1966); K. Kenyon, *Jerusalem: Excavating 3,000 Years of History* (Thames & H., 1968).

15 The Jesus of History

The literature on this subject is immense. Attempts to reconstruct the life of Jesus up to 1901, and including his own famous interpretation, are described by A. Schweitzer in his epoch-making book *The Quest of the Historical Jesus* (E. T., London, 1910). The following are significant studies since that date: B. H. Streeter, *The Four Gospels* (Macmillan, 1924) and "The Rise of Christianity," in the *Cambridge Ancient History*, vol. XI (1936); J. Klausner, *Jesus of Nazareth* (E. T., Collier-Mac., 1943); M. Goguel, *The Life of Jesus* (E. T., London, 1933) and *The Birth of Christianity* (E. T., Allen & Unwin, 1953); Ch. Guignebert, *Jesus* (E. T., London, 1935) and *Le Christ* (Paris, 1943); A. T. Olmstead, *Jesus, in the Light of History* (New York, 1942); R. Bultmann, *Die Geschichte der synoptischen Tradition* (3rd ed., Göttingen, 1957) and *Ergänzungsheft* (1958); G. Bornkamm, *Jesus von Nazareth* (Stuttgart, 1958); J. M. Robinson, *A New Quest for the Historical Jesus* (S.C.M. Press, 1959); E. Stauffer, *Jesus and his Story* (E. T., London, 1960); H. Conzelmann, "Jesus Christ," in *Religion in Geschichte und Gegenwart*, III (Tübingen, 1959); M. S. Enslin, *The Prophet from Nazareth* (New York, 1961); M. Simon and A. Benoit, *Le Judaïsme et le Christianisme antique* (Paris, 1968); S. G. F. Brandon, *Jesus and the Zealots* (Manchester, 1967–8). See bibliography to Chapter 16: "The Trial of Jesus."

16 The Trial of Jesus

The interpretation set forth in this chapter is more fully presented by the author in his book *The Trial of Jesus of Nazareth* (Batsford, 1968), where full documentation is given and other interpretations discussed; an extensive bibliography is also appended. This book is closely related to the author's *Jesus and the Zealots* (Manchester, 1967–8). The following important studies should also be consulted: P. Winter, *On the Trial of Jesus* (Berlin, 1961), "Zum Prozess Jesu," in *Das Altertum*, 9 (1963) and "The Marcan Account of Jesus' Trial by the Sanhedrin," in *Journal of Theological Studies*, vol. XIV (Oxford, 1963); J. Blinzler, *The Trial of Jesus* (E.T., Cork, 1959); T. A. Burkill, "The Trial of Jesus," in *Vigiliae Christianae*, vol. XII (Amsterdam, 1958); H. Leitzmann, "Der Prozess Jesu," in *Kleine Schriften*, II (Berlin, 1958, originally published in Berlin, 1934); R. W. Husband, *The Prosecution of Jesus* (Princeton University Press, 1916); W. Koch (ed.), *Zum Prozess Jesu* (Weiden, 1967); A. N. Sherwin-White, *Roman Society and Roman Law in the New Testament* (Oxford, 1963) and "The Trial of Christ," in *Historicity and Chronology in the New Testament* (S.P.C.K., 1965); S. Zeitlin, *Who Crucified Jesus?* (New York, 1942); C. H. Dodd, "The Historical Problem of the Death of Jesus," in *More New Testament Studies* (Manchester University Press, 1968).

17 *Pontius Pilate in History and Legend*

The best edition of Philo's account of Pilate is by E. M. Smallwood, which also contains an English translation; it is entitled *Philonis Alexandrini Legatio ad Gaium* (Leiden, 1961). The relevant sections of Josephus' *Jewish Wars* and *Jewish Antiquities* are conveniently presented in Greek text and English translation in the Loeb Classical Library edition of *Josephus*, vols. ii and ix. There is no book especially devoted to Pontius Pilate. The fullest accounts will be found in the author's *Jesus and the Zealots* (Manchester, 1967–8) and *The Trial of Jesus of Nazareth* (Batsford, 1968), both of which give extensive documentation and bibliographies. For the so-called *Acts of Pilate* see M. R. James, *The Apocryphal New Testament* (Oxford, 1926), and for Coptic and Ethiopic legends about Pilate see M.-A. Van den Oudenrijn, *Gamaliel: äthiopische Texte zur Pilatusliteratur* (Freiburg, 1959). The following works should also be consulted: E. Schürer, *Geschichte des jüdischen Volkes im Zeitalter Jesu Christi*, Band I (Leipzig, 1901); E. M. Smallwood, "High Priests and Politics in Roman Palestine," in *Journal of Theological Studies*, vol. XIII (Oxford, 1962); J. Spencer Kennard, *Politique et religion chez les Juifs au temps de Jésus et dans l'Eglise primitive* (Paris, 1927); C. H. Kraeling, "The Episode of the Roman Standards at Jerusalem," in the *Harvard Theological Review*, vol. xxxv (1942); J. Blinzler, "Die Niedermetzelung von Galiläern durch Pilatus," in *Novum Testamentum*, vol. II (Leiden, 1958); A. D. Doyle, "Pilate's Career and the Date of the Crucifixion," in the *Journal of Theological Studies*, vol. XLII (Oxford, 1941); P. L. Maier, "Sejanus, Pilate, and the Date of the Crucifixion," in *Church History* (U.S.A.), vol. xxxvii (1968). Professor Maier has recently produced a biographical novel entitled *Pontius Pilate* (New York, 1968).

18 *The Fall of Jerusalem*, A.D. 70.

This new evaluation of the consequences of the Fall of Jerusalem for Christianity is presented, with full documentation and bibliographies, by the author in the following books: *The Fall of Jerusalem and the Christian Church* (2nd ed., S.P.C.K., 1957, reprinted 1968): *Jesus and the Zealots* (Manchester, 1967–8); *The Trial of Jesus of Nazareth* (Batsford, 1968).

19 The Zealots

The most comprehensive work on the subject is M. Hengel, *Die Zeloten* (Leiden, 1961). The following works should also be consulted: W. R. Farmer, *Maccabees, Zelotes and Josephus* (New York, 1956); C. Roth, *The Historical Background of the Dead Sea Scrolls* (Blackwell, Oxford, 1958), "The Zealots—a Jewish Religious Sect," in *Judaism*, vol. viii (New York, 1959), "The Zealots in the War of 66–73," in *Journal of Semitic Studies*, vol. iv (Manchester, 1959); G. R. Driver, *The Judaean Scrolls* (Blackwell, Oxford, 1965); Y. Yadin, *Masada: Herod's Fortress and the Zealots' Last Stand* (Weidenfeld & N., 1966); S. G. F. Brandon, *Jesus and the Zealots* (Manchester, 1967–8), articles on "Sicarii" and "Zealots" in the forthcoming *Encyclopaedia Judaica*.

20 Josephus

The best English edition of the text and translation of the works of Josephus is in the Loeb Classical Library, comprising nine volumes (1925–65), which are the work respectively of H. St. John Thackeray, R. Marcus, A. Wikgren, and L. H. Feldmann. The introductions, notes and appendices of these volumes are invaluable. For studies of Josephus and his writings see: H. St. John Thackeray, *Josephus: the Man and the Historian* (New York, 1929); B. Niese, article on Josephus in the *Encyclopaedia of Religion and Ethics*, ed. J. Hastings, vol. VII (1914); R. Eisler, *The Messiah Jesus and John the Baptist* (London, 1931), which is an abbreviated English version of his large two-volume German work entitled ΙΗΣΟΥΣ ΒΑΣΙΛΕΥΣ ΟΥ ΒΑΣΙΛΕΥΣΑΣ (Heidelberg, 1929–30); G. Ricciotti, *Flavio Giuseppe, lo Storico guideo-romano* (Turin, 1937); F. J. Foakes-Jackson, *Josephus and the Jews* (London, 1939); W. R. Farmer, *Maccabees, Zealots and Josephus* (Columbia University Press, 1957); R. J. H. Shutt, *Studies in Josephus* (S.P.C.K., 1961); G. A. Williamson, *The World of Josephus* (London, 1964); S. G. F. Brandon, *The Fall of Jerusalem and the Christian Church* (2nd ed., S.P.C.K., 1957, reprinted 1968); *Jesus and the Zealots* (Manchester, 1967–8). On the problem of the "Slavonic Josephus," particularly of the passages purporting to deal with Christian Origins, see the original Slavonic text and French translation in the work entitled *La Prise de Jérusalem de Josèphe le Juif*, by V. Istrin, A. Vaillant and P. Pascal: 2 vols., Paris, Institut d'Etudes slaves (1934, 1938). English translations of the relevant passages are printed in vol. iii of the Loeb edition of Josephus. For studies of the problem see the works of Eisler cited above; the volumes by Brandon and Riciotti; J. W. Jack, *The Historic Christ* (London, 1933); J. M. Creed, "The Slavonic Version of Josephus' History of the Jewish War," in the *Harvard Theological Review*, vol. xxv (1932); A. Rubinstein, "Observations on the Old Russian Version of Josephus," in *Journal of Semitic Studies*, vol. ii (Manchester, 1957).

21 Saint Paul

There is an enormous literature on St. Paul. The present writer has presented the interpretation of Paul set out here in greater detail, with relevant documentation and bibliographies, in his books *The Fall of Jerusalem and the Christian Church* (2nd ed., S.P.C.K., 1957, reprinted 1968); *Jesus and the Zealots* (Manchester, 1967–

68). To the list of relevant books listed there the following recent addition should be made: M. Simon and A. Benoit, *Le Judaïsme et le Christianisme antique* (Paris, 1968).

22   The Gnostic Problem in Early Christianity

On the Hermetic literature and its background see: *Corpus Hermeticum*, ed. A. D. Nock and A.-J. Festugière, 4 vols. (Paris, 1945–54); A.-J. Festugière, *La Révélation d'Hermès Trismégiste*, 4 vols. (Paris, 1943–54); Ph. Derchain, "L'authenticité de l'inspiration égyptienne dans le 'Corpus Hermeticum'," in *Revue de l'histoire des religions*, t.161 (Paris, 1962). On Hermeticism and Gnosticism generally see: A.-J. Festugière, "Hermétisme et Gnose païenne," in *Histoire générale des religions* (ed. M. Gorce and R. Mortier), t.III (Paris, 1947); C. H. Dodd, *The Bible and the Greeks* (Hodder, 1954); R. Mc.L. Wilson, *The Gnostic Problem* (London, 1958); J. Doresse, *The Secret Books of the Egyptian Gnostics* (E. T., London, 1959); R. M. Grant, *Gnosticism and Early Christianity* (London, 1959) and *Gnosticism: an Anthology* (London, 1961); C. Quispel, *Gnosis als Weltreligion* (Zürich, 1951); *The Jung Codex*, ed. F. L. Cross (London, 1955); W. C. van Unnik, *Evangelien aus dem Nilsand* (Frankfurt-am-Main, 1960); R. Bultmann, *Gnosis* (E. T., 1952) and *Primitive Christianity in Its Contemporary Setting* (E. T., Fontana, 1960); S. G. F. Brandon, *Man and his Destiny in the Great Religions* (Manchester, 1962) and *History, Time and Deity* (Manchester, 1965); *Kleine Pauly*, II (Stuttgart, 1967), 830–39; U. Bianchi (ed.), *The Origins of Gnosticism* (Leiden, 1967).

23   The Devil

See generally the articles on "Demons and Spirits" in the *Encyclopaedia of Religion and Ethics*, ed. J. Hastings, vol. IV (1911); the article under "Teufel" in *Die Religion in Geschichte und Gegenwart*, Band VI (1962–3). On particular aspects of the subject dealt with in Chapter XXII see H. Bonnet, *Reallexikon der ägyptischen Religionsgeschichte* (Berlin, 1952), art. on "Seth"; R. C. Thompson, *Devils and Evil Spirits of Babylonia*, 2 vols. (London, 1903); W. Q. E. Oesterley, *Immortality and the Unseen World* (London, 1930); J. Doresse, *The Secret Books of the Egyptian Gnostics* (E. T., London, 1960); G. Dumézil, *Mitra-Varuna* (Paris, 1948); H. Zimmer, *Myths and Symbols in Indian Art and Civilization* (Washington, D.C., 1946); T. Ling, *Buddhism and the Mythology of Evil* (Allen & Unwin, 1962); R. C. Zaehner, *The Dawn and Twilight of Zoroastrianism* (Weidenfeld & N., 1961); J. Duchesne-Guillemin and H. Dörrie, art. on "Dualismus," in *Reallexikon für Antike und Christentum*, Band IV (1959); G. Widengren, *Mani and Manichaeism* (E. T., Weidenfeld & N., 1965); E. R. Dodds, *The Greeks and the Irrational* (University of California Press, 1951): H. W. Hupperbauer, *Der Mensch zwischen zwei Welten* (Zürich, 1959); *Satan*, ed. Pere Bruno de Jesus-Marie, O.C.D. (London, 1951); J. A. MacCulloch, *Mediaeval Faith and Fable* (London, 1932); M. Summers, *History of Witchcraft and Demonology* (Routledge, 1965), S. G. F. Brandon, *Man and his Destiny in the Great Religions* (Manchester, 1962) and *The Judgment of the Dead* (New York, 1969).

24   Angels

The most thorough and recent treatment of the subject (to A.D. 600) is the series of articles by J. Michl under "Engel" in the *Reallexikon für Antike und Christentum* (ed. T. Klauser), Band V (Stuttgart, 1962), 53–332. Michl does not treat the earlier Egyptian, Mesopotamian or Iranian material. Useful information is to be found in the articles on "Demons and Spirits" by various writers in the *Encyclopaedia of Religion and Ethics* (ed. J. Hastings), vol. IV (Edinburgh, 1911). Various aspects of the subject are dealt with in A. Erman, *Die Religion der Aegypter* (Berlin, 1934); E. Dhorme, *Les religions de Babylonie et d'Assyrie* (Paris, 1945); W. O. E. Oesterley, *Immortality and the Unseen World* (London, 1930); G. Dumézil, *Naissance d'Archanges* (Paris, 1945); R. C. Zaehner, *The Dawn and Twilight of Zoroastrianism* (Weidenfeld & N., 1961); Y. Yadin, *The Scroll of the War of the Sons of Light against the Sons of Darkness* (Oxford, 1962), 9 "The Angelology of the Scroll"; M. Werner, *The Formation of Christian Dogma* (E. T., Black, 1957); *Dictionary of Comparative Religion*, ed. S. G. F. Brandon (New York, 1970), articles under "Angel."

25   B.C. and A.D.: *the Christian Philosophy of History*

The author has dealt at length with this theme in his book: *History, Time and Deity* (Manchester, 1965), where full documentation and bibliographies are given; see also his essay "Time and the Destiny of Man," in *The Voices of Time*, ed. J. T. Fraser (A. Lane, 1968), and *The Judgment of the Dead* (Weidenfeld & N., 1967). For various aspects of the subject, in addition to the bibliography to Chapter XI, see: J. Baillie, *The Belief in Progress* (Oxford, 1950); E. H. Carr, *What is History?* (Harmondsworth, 1964); S. J. Case, *The Christian Philosophy of History* (University of Chicago Press, 1943); R. G. Collingwood, *The Idea of History* (Oxford, 1946); O. Cullmann, *Christ and Time* (S.C.M. Press, 1962); E. Dinkler, "Earliest Christianity," in *The Idea of History in the Ancient Near East,* ed. R. C. Dentan (Yale University Press, 1955); F. J. Foakes-Jackson, *A History of Church History* (Cambridge, 1939); V. Goldschmidt, *Le système stoicien et l'idée de temps* (Paris, 1953); H. S. Hughes, *Oswald Spengler: a Critical Estimate* (New York, 1952); P. de Labriolle, *History and Literature of Latin Christianity* (E. T., London, 1924); K. Löwith, "Christentum und Geschichte," in *Numen*, vol. II (Leiden, 1955); R. L. P. Milburn, *Early Christian Interpretations of History* (Black, 1965); A. Momigliano (ed.), *The Conflict between Paganism and Christianity* (Oxford, 1963); *Philosophy and History*, ed. R. Klibansky and H. J. Paton (Oxford, 1936); G. Quispel, "Time and History in Patristic Christianity," in *Man and Time* (*Papers from the Eranos Yearbooks*), ed. J. Campbell (Routledge, 1958); H.-J. Puech, "Temps, histoire et mythe dans le Christianisme des premiers siècles," in *Proceedings of the Congress for the History of Religions* (Amsterdam, 1951); W. H. Walsh, *An Introduction to the Philosophy of History* (Hutchinson, 1967); C. A. Patrides, *The Phoenix and the Ladder: the rise and decline of the Christian View of History* (University of California Press, 1964).

INDEX OF NAMES AND SUBJECTS

ILLUSTRATION ACKNOWLEDGMENTS

Archives Photographiques: p. 163

Archivio Fotografico Vaticano: pp. 335, 381

Art Reference Bureau:

    Alinari: pp. 26, 61, 68, 235, 239, 241, 277, 304, 311, 323, 330, 349, 355, 357, 372

    Anderson: pp. 19, 79, 224, 226, 229, 314, 320

    Bruckmann: p. 264

    Foto Marburg: pp. 134, 141

The Bettmann Archive Inc.: pp. 166, 174

Bibliothèque Nationale: p. 100 (Supplément turc 190)

Bodleian Library, Oxford: p. 207

Photographs by Mrs. I. A. Brandon: pp. 215, 218, 227, 231, 232, 245, 248, 250, 257, 260, 261, 266, 269, 274, 286, 288, 306, 308, 325

Photograph by S. G. F. Brandon: p. 110 top

British Museum, London: pp. 41, 155, 159, 176, 178, 202, 210, 212, 328, 332, 333, 346, 361

    Papyrus of Ani: pp. 103, 106

E. A. W. Budge, editor, *Book of the Dead, The Papyrus of Ani*, London, 1913 (Oriental Division, The New York Public Library): pp. 71, 122

————, *Osiris and the Egyptian Resurrection*, London, 1911 (Oriental Division, The New York Public Library): p. 123

Photographie BULLOZ: pp. 110 bottom, 253

Photograph by John Champion Ltd., Salisbury: p. 117

Cincinnati Art Museum: p. 198

By the kind permission of the Provost and Chaplain of Coventry Cathedral. Photograph by Richard Sadler AIBP, Coventry: p. 369

G. Dennis, *Cities and Cemeteries of Etruria*, vol. 2, London, 3rd edition, 1883: p. 42

Directorate General of Antiquities, Baghdad, Iraq: p. 153

École Biblique et Archéologique Française, Jerusalem: p. 188

Edinburgh University Library: p. 205

Éditions Charentaises d'Art A. Gilbert, Jarnac: p. 12

Les Éditions d'Art et Histoire: p. 13

Éditions "TEL": p. 150

Reproduced by permission of the Syndics of the Fitzwilliam Museum, Cambridge: p. 126

Photograph by Foto Rossi, Turin: p. 173

Henri Frankfort, *Cylinder Seals*, Macmillan and Co. Ltd., London, 1939: p. 22

Gabinetto Fotografico Nazionale, Rome: p. 236

J. E. Harrison O. U. P., *Prolegomena to the Study of Greek Religion*, Cambridge, 1903: p. 78

Hirmer Fotoarchiv, Munich : pp. 4, 120, 128, 132

India Museum, London: p. 55

Reproduced by courtesy of the Israel Department of Antiquities and Museums: p. 255

Israel Information Services: pp. 283, 291

Reproduced from defunct *Journal of the Asiatic Society of Bengal,* 1893, vol. XI, pt. 1: p. 86

Photograph by Kurt Lange: p. 169

Drawings by Miss E. A. Lowcock: pp. 15, 20, 21, 50, 65, 113

Courtesy, Manchester Museum: pp. 5, 262, 271, 280, 296, 302, 303

The Mansell Collection: pp. 317, 379

The Metropolitan Museum of Art: Bequest of Mary Clark Thompson, 1926, p. 376; Fletcher Fund, 1933: p. 382

Musée Guimet, Paris: p. 97

National Gallery, London: p. 221

J. Needham, *Science and Civilization in China,* vol. 2, Cambridge University Press, 1954–59: p. 94

The New York Public Library (Prints Division): p. 338

Ny Carlsberg Glyptotek, Copenhagen : pp. 34, 299

Paul Popper Ltd.: pp. 194, 244

Rijksmuseum van Oudheden, Leiden: p. 171

By courtesy of the Governors of the John Rylands Library, Manchester: pp. 81, 340, 343

Service de Documentation Photographique de la Réunion des Musées Nationaux: pp. 161, 363 (both Louvre)

Staatliche Museen, Berlin : pp. 46 (*Forsuchungen und Berichte,* Academie-Verlag, I Band, S. Morenz, *Das Werden zu Osiris,* Abt. I), 143, 147, 186

The Tate Gallery, London: p. 184

Permission of the Librarian of Trinity College, Dublin: p. 366

Türk-Islam Eserlerei Museum, Istanbul: p. 191

Reproduced by permission of the Victoria and Albert Museum, London: p. 48

T. Tindall Wildridge, *The Dance of Death,* George Redway, London, 1887: p. 67

Zionist Archives and Library: p. 219